RECOMMENDED COUNTRY INNS®
NEW ENGLAND

NINETEENTH EDITION

Connecticut / Maine / Massachusetts
New Hampshire / Rhode Island / Vermont

ELIZABETH SQUIER

Revised and updated by Eleanor Berman

Illustrated by Olive Metcalf

INSIDERS' GUIDE®

GUILFORD, CONNECTICUT
AN IMPRINT OF THE GLOBE PEQUOT PRESS

INSIDERS' GUIDE®

The prices and rates listed in this guidebook were confirmed at press time. We recommend, however, that you call establishments before traveling to obtain current information.

Contents

How to Use This Inn Guide

This inn guide contains descriptions of country inns in the six New England states. You'll find them in alphabetical order by state—Connecticut, Maine, Massachusetts, New Hampshire, Rhode Island, and Vermont—and alphabetically by town within each state. Preceding each state listing are a map and a numbered legend of the towns with inns in that state. The map is marked with corresponding numbers to show where the towns are located.

I or one of my trusted associates have personally visited every inn in this book. There is no charge of any kind for an inn to be included in this or any other Globe Pequot country inn guide.

Indexes: At the back of the book are various special-category indexes to help you find inns on a lake, inns that serve Sunday brunch, inns that have cross-country skiing on the property, and much more. There is also an alphabetical index of all the inns in the book.

Rates: All prices listed are for two people, unless otherwise specified. With prices fluctuating so widely in today's economy, I quote an inn's current low and high rates only. This will give you a good, though not exact, indication of the price ranges you can expect. Please realize that rates are subject to change. I have not included the tax rate, service charge, or tipping suggestions for any of the inns. Be sure to inquire about these additional charges when you make your reservations. The following abbreviations are used throughout the book to let you know exactly what, if any, meals are included in the room price.

Abbreviations:

EP: European Plan. Room without meals.

BP: Room with full breakfast.

CP: Room with continental breakfast.

MAP: Modified American Plan. Room with breakfast and dinner.

Credit cards: MasterCard and Visa are accepted unless the description says "No credit cards." Many inns also accept additional cards.

Personal checks: Inns usually accept personal checks unless the description says "No personal checks."

Reservations and deposits: At most of the inns, be prepared to pay a deposit when you make your reservation. Be sure to inquire about refund policies.

Meals: Meals included in the cost of the room are indicated with the rates; other meals available at the inn will be in the "Facilities and activities" section of an inn's description. I list some of my favorite foods served at an inn to give you a general idea of the type of meals you can expect, but please realize that menus are likely to change.

Children: Many inns are ideal for children, but you know your child best; an inn's description will help you decide if it's a place where your child will be happy.

Pets: Pets are not permitted at the inns unless otherwise stated in the description. If you need to find a place to leave your pet, call the inn before you go. They may be able to make arrangements for you.

Wheelchair accessibility: Some inns have wheelchair accessibility to rooms or dining rooms, and some have at least one room specially equipped for the physically disabled. Check the index in the back of the book for inns with wheelchair-accessible rooms. You might also want to call to check for updated information.

Air-conditioning: The description will indicate if an inn has rooms with air-conditioning. Keep in mind that there are areas of New England where air-conditioning is usually unnecessary.

Alcoholic beverages: Some inns permit their guests to bring their own bottle (BYOB), especially if there is no bar service. If this fact is of interest to you, look in the inn's description for a mention of a bar, liquor license, or BYOB.

Smoking: Most inns today do not allow smoking indoors, although a few may have designated smoking areas. Call an inn directly to find out about its exact smoking policies.

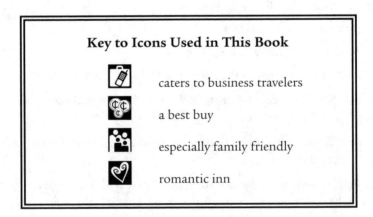

Key to Icons Used in This Book

caters to business travelers

a best buy

especially family friendly

romantic inn

Recommended

COUNTRY INNS®

NEW ENGLAND

Connecticut

Connecticut

Numbers on map refer to towns numbered below.

The Inn and Vineyard at Chester

Chester, Connecticut 06412

INNKEEPER: Edward Safdie

ADDRESS/TELEPHONE: 318 West Main Street; (860) 526–9541; fax (860) 526–1607

WEB SITE: www.innatchester.com

ROOMS: 44 rooms and suites; all with private bath, air-conditioning, flat-screen TV, cordless phone, high-speed Internet access, clock radio with CD player, robes; 2 with fireplace; many suites with terraces.

RATES: Rooms, $135 to $450 CP.

OPEN: All year.

FACILITIES AND ACTIVITIES: Dining room, bar and bistro, twenty acres with fitness trails, tennis, massage and other spa services, wellness programs. Nearby: Canoeing, kayaking, fly fishing, Goodspeed Opera House.

BUSINESS TRAVEL: Located 40 minutes from Hartford or New Haven, 2 hours from Boston or New York; 4 meeting rooms, audiovisual capabilities, board room; event coordinator on staff; entire inn wired for high-speed Internet access; room phones with voice mail and message light.

John D. Parmelee, the original owner of this inn that was built from 1776 to 1778, would not know the place today, but he would probably enjoy it.

The inn reopened in the summer of 2003 under the new ownership of Edward Safdie, who is well known for developing other luxury spa properties,

The Swinging Bridge

Driving into East Haddam on Route 154, you cross the Connecticut River on a metal bridge that pivots to a position parallel to the banks to allow large boats to pass. Some say this is the world's longest swing bridge; it certainly is the longest one in New England. One of just a handful of bridges linking the eastern part of the state to the west, the bridge also links the two sides of East Haddam, the only river town that has land on both sides of the Connecticut. The bridge dates from 1913. During World War I a militia unit was housed in the opera house at Goodspeed Landing to protect the bridge from sabotage by German submarines.

such as the Sonoma Mission Inn and Spa in California, the California Terrace & Spa in the Hotel de Paris in Monte Carlo, Monaco, and the Greenhouse Spa in Dallas, Texas. He has invested millions to bring this comfortable old inn up to his four-star standards. The results can be seen inside as well as out, where the twenty-acre grounds now include a vineyard, a tennis court, and wooded trails.

Designer-decorated rooms might be called "updated New England," featuring pencil-post and canopy beds as well as up-to-the-minute technology such as flat-screen TV, cordless phones, CD players, and high-speed Internet access. The entire inn has been wired for the Internet; you can even access your e-mail while dining on the terrace.

Nice touches include fireplaces in some rooms and French doors to the outdoors in all ground-floor rooms.

The inn's dining room, housed in a former 1800s barn, includes a loft, a giant fireplace, and rough-hewn wood-panel walls. A big bay window overlooks the pond and fountain outdoors. The updated menu includes innovative dishes such as pork chops served with fig salsa, bacon-braised cabbage, and horseradish-lentil salad, or cranberry lacquered diver scallops with a smoked cheddar polenta cake and curried leeks. The bar and bistro has a lighter menu in a more casual setting. In warm weather, you can order from either menu on the shady Maple Terrace. For those who are watching their waistlines, the inn offers a spa menu taken from Edward Safdie's books *Spa Food* and *New Spa Food*.

The inn has some interesting special events from time to time, including culinary classes, wine seminars, and fly-fishing and cross-country-skiing programs. Check for the current offerings.

HOW TO GET THERE: Coming from New York and other points south, take Interstate 95 north to exit 63. Go left onto Route 81 north, continue for 14 miles, and then turn right onto Route 148. The inn is 3²/₁₀ miles farther on the left. Coming from the north, follow I-95 south to exit 69, Route 9 north. Take exit 6 from Route 9 onto Route 148 and proceed 3²/₁₀ miles. The inn will be on the right.

Griswold Inn

Essex, Connecticut 06426

INNKEEPERS: The Paul family; Alan A. Barone, general manager

ADDRESS/TELEPHONE: 36 Main Street; (860) 767-1776; fax (860) 767-0481

WEB SITE: www.griswoldinn.com

ROOMS: 31, including 12 suites; all with private bath and phone; some with fireplace.

RATES: Rooms, $100 to $220 CP; Suites, $160 to $255 CP.

OPEN: All year.

FACILITIES AND ACTIVITIES: Lunch, dinner, Sunday brunch, children's menu, taproom, wine bar.

BUSINESS TRAVEL: Located 15 minutes from railroad station; 1 hour from Hartford's Bradley International Airport. All rooms with phone; fax available; meeting rooms.

*E*ssex is a very special town right on the Connecticut River. Although it was settled long before the Revolution, Essex is still a living, breathing, working place, not a re-created museum of a town. The first warship of the Continental Navy, the *Oliver Cromwell,* was built and commissioned here in 1776.

Located in the heart of the village is The Griswold Inn, one of the oldest continuously operated inns in the country. "The Gris," as the inn is fondly called by everyone, is one of the highlights of anyone's trip to Essex. When you come in from the cold to the welcome of crackling fireplaces, you are doing what others have done before you since 1776.

You can lunch or dine surrounded by maritime art in the Library, the Covered Bridge and Essex Rooms, or in the Gun Room, which features a collection of guns dating from the fifteenth century.

In the spring of 2005, the Gris converted the Steamboat dining room into a stunning wine bar, which has a nautical flavor that fits right in with the rest of the inn. I'm so glad to see that the much loved, 18-foot rocking steamboat mural on the wall remains as a backdrop. The Wine Bar adds a nice selection of small plates to the menu choices, as well as more than fifty wines available by the glass.

There is music every night in the Tap Room—old-time banjos, sea chanteys, Dixieland jazz, or just good piano.

In the bar a great, old-fashioned popcorn machine offers treats for all. It's one of many personal touches that make this nice inn such a special place.

The Hunt Breakfast is the renowned Sunday brunch at the inn. This bountiful fare is worth a trip from anywhere. The selection is extensive, with enough good food to satisfy anyone's palate. Dinner just gets better every time I visit. I've enjoyed maple-basted smoked pork chop and scallops in puff pastry. There's always lots of freshly caught seafood on the menu and New England game in season.

The guest rooms have been nicely upgraded, with an appropriate colonial look and lots of antiques and good reproductions. Some are small and simply furnished, as you would expect in an inn of this age. The most special accommodations are the deluxe suites in separate buildings. The Fenwick and Garden Suites have wood-burning fireplaces, and several other rooms have cozy gas fireplaces.

HOW TO GET THERE: Take Interstate 95 to exit 69, and follow Route 9 north to exit 3. Turn left at the bottom of the ramp to a traffic light, turn right, and follow this street right through town to the river. The inn is on your right, about 100 yards before you get to the river.

The Homestead Inn

Greenwich, Connecticut 06830

INNKEEPERS: Theresa and Thomas Henkelmann

ADDRESS/TELEPHONE: 420 Field Point Road; (203) 869-7500; fax (203) 869-7502

WEB SITE: www.homesteadinn.com

ROOMS: 18 rooms and suites; all with private bath, TV, VCR, clock radio, robes, and phones with modem connections.

RATES: $250 to $495 EP.

OPEN: All year except last week in February and first week in March.

FACILITIES AND ACTIVITIES: Full breakfast, lunch Monday through Friday, dinner 7 days a week. Bar.

BUSINESS TRAVEL: Located 45 minutes from New York City. Phone and desk in room; small conference center; audiovisual equipment, fax, computer available.

There are very good reasons why this lovely 1799 inn has been chosen as one of the best country inns in the country. One of them is that the entire staff makes you feel like royalty. I think we all need this kind of treatment once in a while.

The inn's rooms are beautifully refurbished and redecorated with designer furniture, Frette linens, and original artwork. I stayed in Room 26, where William Inge wrote *Picnic* while staying at the inn in the 1950s. Room 32 has delicate stencils on the walls; the stencils were found under six layers of wallpaper dating from 1860. Room 23 has a king-size, four-poster bed and a marvelous eighteenth-century highboy.

The Inn-Between is the newest building on this lovely property. There are eight glorious rooms out here. The bathrooms are large and have tub, shower, and bidet. All the rooms have porches, and the furnishings are wonderful. The cottage has a newly renovated boardroom and plenty of function spaces.

The inn's superb contemporary French restaurant, Thomas Henkelmann, is named for its enormously talented owner/chef. The food is more than fabulous—a few years ago this establishment was named one of the top restaurants in America by *Esquire* magazine. The restaurant is elegant in a rustic fashion—hand-hewn chestnut beams, brick walls, fireplaces, skylights, and well-spaced tables with comfortable chairs.

The presentation of the food is so picture perfect, with exquisite china and stemware. The presentation plates are objets d'art themselves, commissioned from an artist in France. The restaurant is known for its spectacular flower arrangements.

Besides the extensive menus, there are many specials. One that I had was Dover sole, poached and filled with saffron mousse, the best I have ever eaten, and rack of veal is a dinner favorite. The restaurant is noted for its fresh fish and splendid, tender veal prepared in many interesting ways. One of the luncheon dishes is grilled tenderloin of veal, served with fettuccine and

a tomato fondue. The desserts, needless to say, are spectacular. You must try the warm chocolate soufflé with a liquid chocolate center and housemade vanilla bean ice cream—wow!

HOW TO GET THERE: From New York take Interstate 95 north to exit 3. Turn left at the bottom of the ramp, then left again at the second light onto Horseneck Lane. Turn left at the end of the lane onto Field Point Road. The inn is ¼ mile on the right.

From Boston take I–95 south to exit 3. Turn right at the bottom of the ramp. Turn left at the first light onto Horseneck Lane and proceed as described above.

Copper Beech Inn
Ivoryton, Town of Essex, Connecticut 06442

INNKEEPERS: Ian and Barbara Phillips

ADDRESS/TELEPHONE: 46 Main Street; (860) 767-0330 or (888) 809-2056

WEB SITE: www.copperbeechinn.com

ROOMS: 4 in inn, 9 in carriage house; all with private bath and telephone; carriage house rooms with whirlpool tub, deck, and TV.

RATES: $135 to $350 CP.

OPEN: All year.

FACILITIES AND ACTIVITIES: Restaurant closed on Monday; Tuesday in winter; Christmas Day. Dinner, full license. Victorian-style conservatory.

One of the most beautiful copper beech trees in Connecticut shades the lawn of this lovely old inn and is the reason for the inn's name.

This gracious 1800s Victorian inn is better than ever, with new sophistication under owners Ian and Barbara Phillips, experienced innkeepers formerly of the Bradley Inn in Maine, who took over in April 2002. All of the guest rooms in the main house have been restored and redecorated with period antiques, Oriental rugs, and rich fabrics. Rooms in the Carriage House, a converted turn-of-the-twentieth-century carriage barn, have been furnished in Queen Anne and Chippendale style, and several have four-poster or canopy beds. The upstairs rooms have cathedral ceilings and their original beams. All the Carriage House rooms have whirlpools and televisions, and they open to decks overlooking nearby woodlands. Two have their own private decks.

Dinner is served in one of three charming dining rooms or on the Garden Porch, my favorite spot, with just four tables. The former living room in the original home has become the elegant Ivoryton Room, decorated with a soft floral wallpaper and formal Queen Anne chairs. The one-time billiard room is now the Comstock Room, with dark oak paneling, and the original dining room, now known as the Copper Beech Room, overlooks the garden.

The chef has gotten rave reviews from area newspapers for his French country menus using fresh New England ingredients. It's easy to see why when you sample dishes such as his version of coquilles Saint-Jacques of grilled scallops and shrimp with a Pinot Noir sauce, or a classic French cassoulet, grilled goose, house-made duck sausage, pork, and white beans. Grilled veal chop with wild mushroom sauce and rack of lamb are other special dishes.

The wine selection is tremendous—more than 5,000 bottles in this exceptional cellar. And don't miss the crème brûlée for dessert, served with a delicious hint of chocolate.

Ivoryton is close to Essex, the Goodspeed Opera House, and all the attractive Connecticut River towns, so there's lots of strolling nearby to work off your dessert.

HOW TO GET THERE: The inn is located 1¾ miles west of Connecticut Route 9, from exit 3. Follow the signs to Ivoryton; the inn is on Ivoryton's Main Street.

Stonecroft Inn ♥

Ledyard, Connecticut 06335

INNKEEPER: Joan Egy

ADDRESS/TELEPHONE: 515 Pumpkin Hill Road; (860) 572-0771 or (800) 772-0774; fax (860) 572-9161

WEB SITE: www.stonecroft.com

ROOMS: 4 rooms in main house, 3 with fireplaces; 6 rooms in the Grange with double whirlpool tubs, fireplaces, and air-conditioning; all with private bath and robes.

RATES: House, $140 to $190 BP; Grange, $195 to $250 BP.

OPEN: All year.

FACILITIES AND ACTIVITIES: Dinner daily except Tuesday. Patio, lawns, gardens, nature preserve with trails adjacent. Nearby: Mystic Seaport, Mystic Aquarium, casinos.

This creamy yellow 1807 Georgian, listed on the National Register of Historic Places, represents many people's fantasy of the perfect country house. It is surrounded by six and a half acres of lawn, old stone walls, and woodland, with all the character of the old retained and enhanced by stylish decor.

The house has become part of an elegant inn. The post-and-beam barn was converted into the building known as the Grange, adding luxury accommodations with whirlpool baths for two and a restaurant that food critics call one of the best in the area.

The front entry of the house is a charming introduction to what lies ahead, with a cheerful mural featuring hot-air balloons ascending the staircase. The Great Room lives up to its name, with a big, inviting floral sofa placed in front of a 9-foot-wide Rumford fireplace. Like much of the house, the furnishings here are French country in style, and the deep yellow walls make the room seem sunny year-round. The Snuggery, the original borning room of the house, is now a small library, and the Red Room is another quiet spot for reading. Old wooden floors throughout are graced with handsome rugs.

Choosing a favorite guest room in the house is a happy dilemma. Joan's nomination is the Buttery on the main floor, the oldest room at Stonecroft (circa 1740), still with its original beams, doors, and hardware, and with its own terrace. But the Stonecroft Room upstairs is hard to resist, with a working fireplace and a wraparound mural showing the inn and grounds as they might have looked in 1820. Guests are challenged to find the resident ghost—and to spot a bit of artistic license, the Beatles, tucked into the picture. The room is furnished with a beautiful reproduction handmade tiger maple pencil-post bed and a chest-on-frame to match.

The other two bedrooms are also inviting. The Westcroft Room is a world of English country pine, with a handsome crewel pattern rug, its own fireplace, and magical sunsets out the window. The Orchard Room (so named because it overlooks the orchard) offers flowers and ribbons, lacy curtains, a graceful brass and wood headboard, a fireplace, and a soaking tub.

While I'm partial to the house, the Grange allows for more spacious and luxurious quarters and newer amenities like whirlpool baths for two. The two upstairs suites, Shubel and Sarah, are romantic retreats with beamed and vaulted ceilings, charming furnishings, and enormous baths with his and hers sinks, bidets, and walk-in showers. The whirlpool tub can be enclosed with cozy shutters or left open for a view of the fireplace while you soak.

The highly rated restaurant at the Grange offers an eclectic international menu. Appetizers include Thai-style marinated shrimp, lobster and asparagus crepe, Maryland shrimp and crab cakes, or spicy chicken satay. For the main course, you might choose pan-seared ahi tuna and spicy shrimp, saltimbocca, grilled premium Hereford beef fillet, or sesame-crusted North Atlantic salmon. In fine weather, the French doors are opened for dining on the stone terrace overlooking a grape vine–shaded pergola and water garden.

The grounds of Stonecroft are exceptional, especially the many old stone walls. The sense of being away from it all is made stronger by the Nature Conservancy land that surrounds the property. An equestrian center down the road offers rides on the Conservancy grounds, a wonderful way to appreciate this very special rural setting.

HOW TO GET THERE: Take I–95 to exit 89, Allyn Street, and proceed north for 3½ miles.

Tollgate Hill Inn
Litchfield, Connecticut 06759

INNKEEPER: Alisha Pecora

ADDRESS/TELEPHONE: 571 Torrington Road (Route 202) (mailing address: P.O. Box 160); (860) 567–1233 or (866) 567–1233; fax (860) 886–9483

WEB SITE: www.tollgatehill.com

ROOMS: 21 rooms and suites in 3 buildings; all with private bath, TV, free Wi-Fi access; suites have fireplace, VCR, refrigerator.

RATES: Rooms, $95 to $170 CP; suites, $160 to $190 CP.

OPEN: All year.

FACILITIES AND ACTIVITIES: Lunch, dinner Wednesday to Saturday, Sunday brunch. Nearby: Historic town, shopping, museums, hiking, swimming, parks, gardens.

In spite of an ideal location in the leafy hills outside the beautiful town of Litchfield, this inn had fallen on hard times and was closed for quite a while. It took courage, determination, and a lot of years for Alisha Pecora to restore and reopen the inn in 2003, but she persevered, and Litchfield once again has an inn that matches its long history.

The centerpiece of the inn is the Captain William Bull Tavern, built in 1745 and listed on the National Register of Historic Places. The original pre-Revolutionary tavern served as a way station for travelers between Hartford and Albany. Now it houses a properly colonial paneled taproom with high-backed wooden booths and a fireplace, and a delightful beamed dining room in period decor with murals of early Litchfield on the walls. The wide plank floors and some of the original iron hardware remain.

The six spacious rooms upstairs have wooden floors and the definite aura of age; some have canopy beds and their original fireplaces.

The William Bull House, added to the property in 1992, offers colonial decor with more modern amenities such as TV and Internet access, and many rooms have outdoor decks. The suites are prime, with canopies, wood-burning

fireplaces, VCRs, and guest refrigerators. Four more rooms are in the School-house, an old schoolhouse circa 1789, moved here from Berlin, Connecticut. Some of the rooms connect, making them good choices for families.

The decor may be colonial, but there is nothing old-fashioned about the menu, which features entrees such as jerk-roasted breast of chicken stuffed with pumpkin, pan-seared red snapper, corn-fed veal chop with a garlic potato gratin, New York strip steak with goat cheese fondue, and a barbecued double-cut pork chop. Chocolate mousse with a raspberry drizzle and pump-kin cognac cheesecake are among several desserts too good to miss.

The Sunday brunch is also highly recommended. Begin with a Mimosa or Bloody Mary, followed by a starter plate of fruits, cheese, and smoked salmon with a variety of muffins and breads. Then you can choose a breakfastlike entree, perhaps a ham and goat cheese omelet, or lunch dishes such as crab cakes, burgers, salads, or a pasta of the day. Either way, you'll be well fortified for a day of exploring the beautiful Litchfield Hills. Litchfield itself is on almost every list of "most beautiful colonial towns." It boasts dozens of lovely colonial homes and one of New England's most photographed white-spired churches. Interesting shops surround the long colonial green.

The town is also home to two unique nurseries with lavish display gardens open to the public spring through fall: White Flower Farm, internationally known for its perennial plantings and bulbs, shown off on ten acres of display gardens, and the Litchfield Horticultural Center, with twenty theme gardens on thirty-two acres. Neither should be missed.

HOW TO GET THERE: From Litchfield center, turn right onto Route 202 and proceed 2¼ miles to the Inn. It will be on your left.

Madison Beach Hotel
Madison, Connecticut 06443

INNKEEPERS: Carolyn Smith, manager; Betty and Henry Cooney Sr., Kathleen and Roben Bagdasarian

ADDRESS/TELEPHONE: 94 West Wharf Road (mailing address: P.O. Box 546); (203) 245–1404; fax (203) 245–0410

WEB SITE: www.madisonbeachhotel.com

ROOMS: 31, plus 4 suites; all with private bath, air-conditioning, cable TV, and phone.

RATES: In-season, $135 to $160; suites, $175 to $275 CP; off-season, $80 to $90; suites, $125 to $175; EP.

OPEN: March through November.

Shopping the Shoreline

If sunbathing isn't your cup of tea, you might want to explore the charming shops of Madison and Clinton. Madison is well known for its independent boutiques, its Front Parlour Tea Room—yum—at the British Shoppe (203-245-4521), its coffee shops, and its outstanding bookstore, R. J. Julia Booksellers (203-245-3959), one of the best independent bookstores in the nation. Located just east of Madison, the town of Clinton is famed for its many antiques shops. Just drive or walk down Route 1 from shop to shop—you'll find plenty of treasures. Also in Clinton is a premium outlet mall of seventy top designers and manufacturers. Called Clinton Crossing (860-664-0700), it has bargains on Ralph Lauren, Liz Claiborne, Tommy Hilfiger, Jones New York, Anne Klein, Waterford/Wedgwood, Le Creuset, Coach, Dooney and Bourke, and many others. You'll find it off I-95, exit 63.

FACILITIES AND ACTIVITIES: Lunch, dinner. Bar, lounge; private beach on Long Island Sound.

BUSINESS TRAVEL: Located 20 minutes from New Haven. Phone and modem in room; conference room with overhead projector; fax available; corporate rates.

*L*ocation, location, location. It is a rare location—directly on a beach along a curve of the Connecticut coastline where Long Island Sound is its widest—that makes this old-fashioned, breezy Victorian a special haven to many visitors. The history dates from the 1800s, when the building was a boardinghouse for shipbuilders during the great whaling days. The Cooneys arrived in 1968 and in various renovations over the years cut the original fifty-three rooms to thirty-one chambers, each with a balcony with a water view. Rooms are furnished with oak dressers and lots of wicker and rattan, nothing fancy, just what you might expect in a relaxed beach place. Four additional suites on the fourth floor have kitchens.

There is a distinct nautical flavor to the Wharf dining room and the lovely Crow's Nest dining room on the upper level. As you might expect, seafood gets the emphasis here. Appetizers include fried calamari, steamers, and Prince Edward Island mussels. Boston baked scrod and a classic Maine lobster dinner are favorite entrees, and the Wharf seafood casserole is delicious, a

combination of lobster, shrimp, scallops, crabmeat, and white fish with mushrooms, baked in a sherry cream sauce. Lobster rolls are a house specialty, served cold for lunch and hot for dinner. Landlubbers aren't forgotten, however. Barbecue baby-back ribs, char-grilled Delmonico steak, and several pastas are also on the menu. Among the desserts, black-bottom pie caught my eye, and the crème brûlee was excellent; of course, there are more. And on Friday and Saturday nights, there is live music on the upper level.

The staff, starting with Carolyn at the desk to the guys and gals who wait on you, are very nice.

The beach is private, 75 feet of it. The water is clear with no undertow, so children are safe, and there is good fishing off the inn's pier. Or sit on the porch in one of the many wicker rockers and just enjoy the view. Few inns can match it.

HOW TO GET THERE: From Interstate 95 turn right onto Route 79 if coming from New York and left if coming from Rhode Island. Go right at the third traffic light onto Route 1. Turn left at the Madison Country Club. The inn is at the end of the road, on the water.

The Inn at Mystic 💜
Mystic, Connecticut 06335

INNKEEPER: Jody Dyer

ADDRESS/TELEPHONE: Routes 1 and 27; (860) 536–9604; restaurant, (860) 536–8140 or (800) 237–2415; fax (860) 572–1635

WEB SITE: www.innatmystic.com

ROOMS: 5 in the inn with whirlpools; 4 in gatehouse with whirlpools and fireplaces; 12 in east wing, with fireplaces, some with whirlpools.

RATES: $165 to $195 Sunday through Thursday, $195 to $315 weekends and holidays, EP, includes afternoon tea. MAP available.

OPEN: All year.

FACILITIES AND ACTIVITIES: Breakfast, lunch, Sunday brunch, dinner every night except Christmas Eve. Bar, lounge, room service, swimming pool, tennis, canoes, sailboats, walking trails. Nearby: Mystic Seaport Museum, Mystic Marinelife Aquarium, charter boats and tours, miniature golf and driving range; Foxwoods Casino is about a half hour north in Ledyard.

Every time I think about this beautiful spot, I want to go back. The views from the inn extend from Mystic Harbor all the way to Fishers Island; they are absolutely breathtaking.

The inn section, comprised of an elegant 1904 mansion and gatehouse, sits amid pear, nut, and peach trees and English flower gardens, at the top of

Mystic Attractions

You might never want to leave the Inn at Mystic, but lots of attractions are in this popular tourist area. In the summer months, there's even a shuttle that will pick you up at the inn and take you from place to place to help you avoid the traffic and enjoy the sights.

Mystic Seaport Museum (888-9SEAPORT; www.mysticseaport .com) is one of the nation's leading maritime museums. See an entire nineteenth-century village re-creation, tall ships, and much more. The Mystic Marinelife Aquarium (860-572-5955; www.mysticaquarium .org) is recently expanded and totally redone with lots of exhibits about the ocean and its creatures. See a 750,000-gallon beluga whale pool, an amazing coral reef display, and much more.

You might also enjoy the Denison Pequotsepos Nature Center (860-536-1216; www.dpnc.org), with 7 miles of hiking and cross-country skiing trails, a trail-side museum, a gift shop and bookstore, and lots of guided walks and talks for visitors of all ages. In nearby Groton, across the Thames River, you can visit the Historic Ship *Nautilus* and the Submarine Force Museum (800-343-0079; www.ussnautilus.org).

a fifteen-acre hillside complex that also includes a large, upscale motor inn with many facilities, such as a pool and tennis court, that are shared by inn guests. From the Victorian veranda—furnished, of course, with beautiful old wicker—the view of the natural rock formations and ponds (I watched birds have their baths) and beyond to the harbor is worth a trip from anywhere.

The large living room has walls covered with magnificent pin pine imported from England and contains lovely antiques and comfortable places to sit. The rooms in both the inn and the gatehouse are beautifully done, some with canopy beds. Each room has an interesting bath with hair dryer and whirlpool soaking tub or Thermacuzzi spa. One has a view across the room to the harbor. Now that's a nice way to relax. Look south out the windows and you'll see Mason's Island; on a clear day you can see Long Island and Montauk.

The mansion is listed on the National Register of Historic Places. It adds to the romantic mystique to know that Humphrey Bogart and Lauren Bacall spent part of their honeymoon here in the 1940s.

The modern motor inn also offers well-decorated rooms and some with views of the water. The east wing closest to the inn duplicates the inn's room decor, offers fireplaces, and, in many cases, whirlpools and balconies with water views.

The Flood Tide restaurant has long been one of the finest in the Mystic area, with a French and continental menu that is consistently first-rate. The luncheon buffet is lavish, and the Sunday brunch is a bountiful affair. Afterward you can retreat up the hill to your mansion and enjoy the view for dessert.

The lounge is pleasant for lighter fare and is right at the swimming pool. A piano player provides music on a parlor grand piano every night and during Sunday brunch. A wedding up here would be ambrosia.

HOW TO GET THERE: Take exit 90 from Interstate 95. Go 2 miles south through Mystic on Route 27 to Route 1. The inn is here. Drive up past the motor inn to the inn at the top of the driveway.

Roger Sherman Inn
New Canaan, Connecticut 06840

INNKEEPER: Thomas Weilenmann; Didier Moesch, restaurant manager

ADDRESS/TELEPHONE: 195 Oenoke Ridge; (203) 966-4541; fax (203) 966-0503

WEB SITE: www.RogerShermanInn.com

ROOMS: 17, all with private bath, air-conditioning, TV, minibar, and phone.

RATES: $140 to $350 CP.

OPEN: All year except Christmas Day, Fourth of July, Memorial Day, Labor Day.

FACILITIES AND ACTIVITIES: Lunch, dinner, Sunday brunch, piano bar. Nearby: Golf, tennis, nature center.

*S*et amid gardens and towering maple trees, this local landmark, built in 1740, has been nicely restored and remodeled without losing its historic charm. Spacious guest rooms in the renovated main house and the carriage house provide comfortable colonial-style accommodations with nice features like cozy wing chairs for reading and desks with ample work space. The inn is within easy walking distance of New Canaan's town center.

The dining room, with its columns and paintings of historic events, is a properly elegant setting for a continental menu, which features many Swiss specialties. The soufflés are legendary. After dinner, folks gather around the sociable piano bar in the library lounge.

The restaurant is a year-round favorite. In warm weather, you can dine outdoors on the porch. On Sunday from November to March, the chef offers a Swiss cheese raclette and fondue, perfect dishes for a cold winter's night.

Six function rooms of varying size and decor make the inn a popular choice for private events and weddings.

HOW TO GET THERE: The inn is located on Route 124 north in New Canaan.

Lighthouse Inn
New London, Connecticut 06320

INNKEEPER: Maureen Clark; owners, Jim and Marylis McGrath

ADDRESS/TELEPHONE: 6 Guthrie Place; (860) 439-6812 or (888) 443-8411; fax (860) 443-5729

WEB SITE: www.lighthouseinn-ct.com

ROOMS: 27 in main house, 24 in carriage house, all with air-conditioning, private bath, phone, dataport, high-speed Internet service, iron, room service; many with microwave and refrigerator.

RATES: Inn rooms, $135 to $379 EP, carriage house, $99 to $229 EP.

OPEN: All year.

FACILITIES AND ACTIVITIES: Breakfast, lunch, dinner, Sunday brunch; tavern with live entertainment nightly; outdoor pool, tennis court, private beach, bicycles for guests, salon, spa. Nearby: Privileges at New London Country Club golf course, Ocean Beach Workout World fitness club; Long Island Sound beaches, outlet shopping, theater, museums, casinos.

olive Metcalf

I love inns with a rich history, especially when they have a happy ending, and the Lighthouse Inn, a National Historic Landmark, definitely qualifies.

The original building went up in 1902 in Spanish colonial style, built as a lavish summer home for Charles Guthrie, a Pittsburgh steel tycoon, with grounds by the famous Olmsted company. Sold by his widow, it became an inn in 1927, a playground for the wealthy and for stars appearing at the nearby Ivoryton Playhouse, including Bette Davis and Joan Crawford. In the early 1950s, pianist Roger Williams, who was playing in the inn lounge, wrote his classic "Autumn Leaves" in his upstairs quarters.

Changes in ownership and a fire in 1979 changed the inn's fortunes for a while, but there was a lot to celebrate by the time the inn celebrated its seventy-fifth anniversary in 2002. Jim and Marylis McGrath had bought the property the year before, and a wonderful renovation was under way. New London chef Timothy Grills decided that year to move his very popular restaurant to the inn.

Now much of the charm of the original home has been restored, including the fine woodwork and paneling and the grand stairway to the second floor. All the wall coverings, carpets, and curtains have been replaced and the baths redone in black and white mosaic tiles. Among the twenty-seven rooms in the main building, those on the second floor are the largest. I loved my room done all in soft blue and white, with a four-poster bed and seating in front of the fireplace (nonworking but attractive anyway). Two corner waterfront suites with canopy beds are the choicest accommodations, popular as honeymoon suites. In all, eleven rooms offer water views.

Third-floor rooms are smaller, but equally pleasant. I liked Room 26, with a balcony and a canopy bed.

The Carriage House, located across the lawn from the main house, was rebuilt after a 1944 fire. The twenty-four rooms are smaller and more modern, decorated in country French style.

Timothy's Restaurant and the 1902 Tavern are popular not only with guests but with residents of the area, and it is easy to see why. The restaurant is a Victorian beauty with beams, paneling, and arched doorways. The windows look out to Long Island Sound, just a block or so away. The food is among the best in the area, and the menu has more than a dozen classic choices, from baked shrimp and pork loin medallions to Long Island duckling and Atlantic salmon, all expertly prepared. Friday and Saturday, the house specials are prime rib and lobster. You won't be able to resist the desserts, which include crème brûlée, chocolate pyramid, apple strudel with caramel sauce, and New York cheesecake. Timothy's monthly wine dinners are very popular, as are the lobster bakes held on the lawn in summer.

The 1902 Tavern is warm and inviting, with ship-pattern wallpaper and photos and clippings of New London history on the walls. The long, sociable L-shaped bar is always busy, especially on weekends when a live jazz group plays. The tavern menu offers light fare such as burgers, salads, wings, fish and chips, chili, and, for hearty appetites, a pasta dish and a Delmonico steak.

Days fly by in summer, with an outdoor pool, tennis court, and private beach on the sound to keep you busy. Whenever you come, New London has some special attractions, including the Coast Guard Academy, and the excellent Lyman Allyn Art Museum at Connecticut College.

Near the waterfront, you'll see a statue of the town's best known resident, Eugene O'Neill, as a young boy. You can still have a drink at the Dutch Tavern, where the adult O'Neill was a frequent patron, and visit his boyhood home, Monte Cristo Cottage. His famous play *Long Day's Journey Into Night* was set here. If you visit in summer, be sure to check the previews of work by promising new playwrights at the Eugene O'Neill Theater Center in neighboring Waterford.

HOW TO GET THERE: From Interstate 95 north take exit 83 and follow signs for downtown New London. Continue straight onto Huntington Street, which becomes Tilley Street. At the sixth traffic light, take a right onto Bank Street. At the next light, go left on Howard Street, continue to the first traffic circle, and take the first exit to Pequot Avenue. Continue about 1½ miles to Guthrie Place, go right, and the inn is at the end of the street. From I–95 south take exit 84S, and keep left at the fork in the ramp to Route 32, which becomes Eugene O'Neill Drive. Continue to the end, and at the intersection to left, turn right at the next light onto Bank Street, and continue as above.

Boulders Inn
New Preston, Connecticut 06777

INNKEEPER: Greer Bernstein

ADDRESS/TELEPHONE: Route 45; (860) 868–0541 or (800) 455–1565; fax (860) 868–1925

WEB SITE: www.bouldersinn.com

ROOMS: 20 rooms and suites in main lodge, carriage house, and hillside cottages; all with private bath; many with fireplace and double whirlpool; 1 specially equipped for the physically disabled.

RATES: $350 to $595 BP with afternoon tea.

OPEN: All year.

FACILITIES AND ACTIVITIES: Swimming, boating, bicycling, hiking, cross-country skiing, fitness room and spa, library, Victorian bar.

The name is apt, since the inn is built of rustic stone boulders. The setting is spectacular. Take a hike up Pinnacle Mountain behind the inn. From the top of the mountain, you'll be rewarded with a

panorama that includes Lake Waramaug, New York State to the west, and Massachusetts to the north.

If you're not a hiker, you can partake of the marvelous countryside right from the inn. There is an outside terrace where, in summer, you may enjoy cocktails, dinner, and spectacular sunsets over the lake. The spacious living room has large windows, and its comfortable chairs and couches make it a nice place for tea or cocktails. The dining room is octagonal and provides a wonderful lake view. Some very good food is served here. Appetizers include the Boulder's own lobster bisque, Thai crab cakes, and a delicious caramelized four onion and Gruyère tart. Wok-roasted Peking duck, maple-roasted poussin, applewood-grilled center pork chop, and wild Alaskan king salmon are among the tasty main dishes.

An added reason to go to the inn: It has received *Wine Spectator*'s Award of Excellence and has some 400 wines on its list.

The guest rooms as well as the public rooms were completely refurbished in 2003, and everything is fresh and in good taste. Instead of colonial, the mood is now more in keeping with an elegant country lodge, with leather and dark wicker seating in the living room and a clean, chic look in the guest lodgings. The renovations included a spa suite and a fitness room, adding new options for guests.

All the rooms have a view of either the lake or the woods. The hillside guest houses with double whirlpool tubs and fireplaces offer extra privacy and are just the right choice when romance is on the menu.

HOW TO GET THERE: From New York take Interstate 84 to Route 7 in Danbury; follow it north to New Milford. Take a right onto Route 202 to New Preston. Take a left onto Route 45, and you will find the inn as you round onto the lake.

The Hopkins Inn
on Lake Waramaug 🪙
New Preston, Connecticut 06777

INNKEEPERS: Franz and Beth Schober and son Toby

ADDRESS/TELEPHONE: 22 Hopkins Road; (860) 868–7295

ROOMS: 11, plus 2 apartments; 8 with private bath.

RATES: $100 to $110 EP.

OPEN: All year.

FACILITIES AND ACTIVITIES: Breakfast, lunch, dinner (breakfast only meal served January–late March). Bar, lounge; private beach on lake. Nearby: Golf, tennis, horseback riding, biking, and hiking.

*S*urrounded by majestic trees on particularly beautiful grounds, this inn has glorious views of lovely Lake Waramaug. In season there is dining under the magnificent maple and horse chestnut trees. The inn has a trout pond where you can pick the fish you fancy. The trout meunière is delicious; fresher fish would be hard to find.

Franz is the owner/chef, and Austrian dishes are among his specialties. Lunch choices include lamb curry, veal piccata or milanaise, and beef bourguignonne. For dinner how about bay scallops in garlic butter, and Wiener schnitzel? On Sunday, instead of brunch, Sunday dinner is served all day with wonderful lamb and pork roasts. Strawberries Romanoff, meringue glacé, coupe aux marrons, and homemade cheesecake are on the dessert menu. Need I say more?

The dining rooms are cheerful. The fireplace has ceramic square tiles across the mantel, and the decorations are wine racks full of wines from all over the world. Naturally, the wine list is quite impressive and pleasantly, fairly priced.

There is a private beach across the road at the lake for use by inn guests. Bicycling, hiking, horseback riding, golf, and tennis are available nearby.

The air-conditioned rooms are clean, neat, and country-inn comfortable. Best of all, almost all have a view of the lake.

HOW TO GET THERE: Take Interstate 84 to Route 202 east to Route 45 in New Preston. Turn left on Route 45 and follow it 2 miles past the lake. Take your first left after the lake, then take the second right onto Hopkins Road.

Silvermine Tavern
Norwalk, Connecticut 06850

INNKEEPER: Francis C. Whitman Jr.

ADDRESS/TELEPHONE: 194 Perry Avenue; (203) 847–4558 or (888) 693–9967; fax (203) 847–9171

WEB SITE: www.silverminetavern.com

ROOMS: 10, all with private bath; Mill Pond Suite in cottage beside the pond.

RATES: $130 to $170; suite, $210; CP.

OPEN: All year.

FACILITIES AND ACTIVITIES: Lunch, dinner, Sunday brunch. Live jazz Thursday through Saturday evenings. Restaurant closed Tuesday. Bar; TV in parlor.

Although the colonial crossroads village known as Silvermine has been swallowed up by the surrounding Fairfield County towns of Norwalk, Wilton, and New Canaan, the Silvermine Tavern still lies at the heart of a community of great old-world beauty. It has a remarkable way of sweeping you back in time.

This is one of the most popular dining places in the area, known for its contemporary American menu that also includes many traditional New England favorites. Thursday night is set aside for a fantastic buffet supper featuring steaks, fried chicken, and many salads, all of which you top off with a great array of desserts. Sunday buffet brunch features twenty different dishes. Some of the inn specialties are grilled rack lamb chops with charred tomato,

scallion, and mint salsa, and old-fashioned New England chicken potpie. The food can be savored in one of the six dining rooms or on the riverside deck, which is open from June through September. On the old millpond below, the ducks and swans wait, hoping for some leftovers. Live jazz adds to the fun after 9:00 P.M. on Thursday, Friday, and Saturday.

Silvermine Tavern is furnished with old Oriental rugs, antiques, old portraits, and great comfortable chairs and sofas surrounding the six huge fireplaces. The main dining room is decorated with more than 1,000 antiques, primarily old farm tools and household artifacts. One of the fun antiques is an 1887 Regina music box. The drop of a coin will turn a huge disk, and the music will begin. In the front parlor you can end your day by enjoying sherry and petit fours in front of a cheery fire.

The guest rooms are comfortably furnished, many of them with old-fashioned tester beds. The Mill Pond Suite has its own deck overlooking the lovely millpond.

If you wish, you can stroll by the waterfall and feed the ducks and swans on the millpond. Across the road from the tavern you will find the Country Store, run by Frank's wife. Do take a leisurely drive around the back roads near the inn, too. They are a delight. And don't miss the exhibits at the well-known Silvermine Guild of Artists.

HOW TO GET THERE: From the Merritt Parkway take exit 40A onto Main Avenue South. Go south to the third traffic light and turn right onto Perry Avenue. Follow it to the second stop sign and turn left. The inn is on the right.

The Norwich Inn and Spa
Norwich, Connecticut 06360

INNKEEPER: John G. O'Shaughnessy
ADDRESS/TELEPHONE: 607 West Thames Street; (860) 425-3506 or (800) 275-4772; fax (860) 886-9483
WEB SITE: www.thespaatnorwichinn.com/ourinn
ROOMS: 50 in hotel, 50 in villas; all with private bath, TV, clock radio, CD player, robes, turndown service; villas have wood-burning fireplaces, balconies.
RATES: Inn rooms and suites, $225 to $325 EP; villa rooms, $300 to $350 EP; villa suites, $450 to $900 EP.
OPEN: All year.
FACILITIES AND ACTIVITIES: Breakfast, lunch, dinner; outdoor pool; full-service spa with indoor pool, sauna, steam, whirlpool, fitness room; 2 tennis courts; salon; boutique. Nearby: Golf, casinos.

This stately redbrick Georgian inn, circa 1930, is located on forty-two beautifully landscaped acres overlooking a golf course. It is best known for its lavish spa, a real bonus for guests, offering an indoor pool, classes, and many treatments and amenities. The grounds are beautifully landscaped, with gardens, ponds, and a reflecting pool, nice for walking or just for gazing from a chaise on the deck.

The inn is listed on the National Trust's Historic Hotels of America, and there is indeed an interesting history here. The building is located at the seventeenth tee of what is now the Norwich Public Golf Course. In its early years, guests including the likes of George Bernard Shaw, Frank Sinatra, and the Prince of Wales came to relax and play golf. After changing hands several times, the inn began to decline. The golf course was sold to the city of Norwich in the mid-1970s to help pay the tax bill, and eventually the inn itself went to the city in lieu of taxes. Things sank so low, the building became a boardinghouse, and part of the basement was used by the town police department for overflow prisoners.

All that changed in 1983 when Edward Safdie, known for his posh Sonoma Mission Inn and Spa in California, bought the property and supervised a complete renovation as well as the construction of a stylish separate spa building and the development of condominium villas on the property.

For a while the inn was attracting a slew of new celebrities, including names such as Barbra Streisand, Michael Douglas, and Cheryl Tiegs. Then Mr. Safdie moved on (his latest venture is the Inn at Chester) and things were going downhill once again until 1994, when the Mashantucket Pequot Tribal Nation used some $14 million of their profits from the nearby Foxwoods Resort to purchase and renovate the property.

While this may seem an unlikely group to run an inn, they seem to be doing a first-class job. With the funds to run things property, the Norwich Inn is once again spiffy, has doubled in space, and the elegant spa is now connected to the main building. The official name is now the Spa at Norwich Inn, emphasizing the main selling point. Not surprisingly, transportation to Foxwoods is offered on weekends.

The spacious lobby is impressive, with a grand piano and three chandeliers, and two seating areas done in beige and soft reds and tans. Rooms in the inn are modern in feel, with pencil-post beds, coordinated bedspreads, and swag-top window curtains, and lots of amenities, from robes and slippers to a daily newspaper at the door. Among the four suites, the Terrace Suite is prime, with a private deck in the treetops and a whirlpool for two.

The villa compound separate from the inn is called the Club. If you don't mind being away from the main building, these are attractive quarters, many with decks and kitchens and pull-out couches. The Club area has its own two outdoor pools.

A walk through the tree-lined Palm Court, where afternoon tea is served, leads to Kensington's Restaurant, a cozy paneled room with floral decor and a fireplace. Some tempting lunch choices include chicken bruschetta and a lobster tail BLT. At dinner, a wide variety of entrees might include bourbon sautéed scallops, seafood scampi over linguine, Kobe tenderloin of beef, a honey-miso marinated ahi tuna, or some appealing vegetarian dishes such as a pistachio and spinach phyllo. Every dish on the menu lists a calorie, fat, protein, and carbohydrate count, so if you are serious about your spa stay, you can watch your diet.

A big outdoor deck overlooking the pool and grounds is a lovely place to dine when the weather is agreeable.

Follow the corridor to the spa, and you are in a serene world apart. Relaxing is easy here, in the two-story sitting room with a fireplace, the beautiful indoor pool, the whirlpool tub beneath a skylight, or the "official" meditation and relaxation room. The spa offers a roster of classes, from pool aerobics to belly dancing, plus state-of-the-art fitness equipment, and many kinds of treatments. Fitness packages include classes and treatments, or you can choose them a la carte. Inn guests also share some nice complimentary activities, such as morning walks and meditations and the indoor pool.

HOW TO GET THERE: From Interstate 90 (the Massachusetts Turnpike) or Interstate 95, take Interstate 395 to Route 2A east to exit 1, less than ½ mile. Use the left ramp lane to the traffic light. Take a left onto Route 32 north. The inn is 1½ miles on the left, behind a high privacy hedge.

Bee and Thistle Inn
Old Lyme, Connecticut 06371

INNKEEPERS: Marie and Philip Abraham

ADDRESS/TELEPHONE: 100 Lyme Street; (860) 434–1667 or (800) 622–4946; fax (860) 434–3402

WEB SITE: www.beeandthistleinn.com

ROOMS: 11, plus 1 cottage; all with private bath and phone.

RATES: $89 to $189; $295, cottage; EP.

OPEN: All year except Christmas Eve, Christmas Day, New Year's Day, and three weeks in January.

FACILITIES AND ACTIVITIES: Breakfast. Lunch Wednesday to Saturday and dinner every day except Monday and Tuesday. Sunday brunch. Bar, lounge, library.

BUSINESS TRAVEL: Located 20 minutes from New London, 45 minutes from New Haven. All rooms with phone; fax available; meeting space for small groups; corporate rates.

Getting an Impression of Old Lyme and Lyme

At the turn of the twentieth century, Miss Florence Griswold of Old Lyme welcomed a group of artists to summer at her pretty yellow mansion on the Lieutenant River. Soon a colony was established there, as now-famed painters such as Childe Hassam, William Chadwick, and many others studied the light and shadows of the woods and shoreline. The Lyme Art Colony was responsible for a new style of painting known as American Impressionism. Now Miss Florence's house is a growing museum devoted to American art and the history of the colony and the region. Open year-round, the Florence Griswold Museum (860-434-5542; www.flogris.org) is just steps away from both the Bee and Thistle Inn and the Old Lyme Inn.

If you'd prefer to get your own impression of the area, explore the Old Lyme Historic District on foot, then explore Route 156 by bicycle or car. North on this roadway is the beautiful hamlet of Hamburg Cove on the Eight-Mile River. You might even see an artist with an easel painting at the riverside—a frequent sight here. Devil's Hopyard State Park, Selden Neck State Park, and the Nehantic State Forest are all nearby. Ask your innkeepers for tips on visiting these areas.

This lovely old inn, built in 1756, sits on five and a half acres bordering the Lieutenant River in historic Old Lyme, Connecticut. During summer the abundant flower gardens keep the inn filled to overflowing with color.

The guest rooms are all air-conditioned and tastefully decorated. Your bed may be a four-poster or canopy; many are covered with a lovely old quilt. The bath towels are big and thirsty—how I love them! The cottage has a sitting room with a fireplace, a glass-enclosed sun room, a bedroom with queen-size bed, a kitchen, and a bath. A deck goes around the outside. There is a private dock on the river.

The inn boasts six fireplaces. The one in the parlor is most inviting—a nice place for a cocktail or just good conversation. On weekends there may be live music.

Breakfast features muffins and pastries made fresh each day, eggs Benedict, pancakes, omelets, and much more. Sunday brunch is really gourmet. Shrimp acorn hash served in a popover, crab cakes, or breakfast favorites like waffles, French toast, or a smoked trout fritatta—I could eat the menu. And, of course, dinners here are magnificent, with candlelit dining rooms, a good selection of appetizers and soups, and entrees such as venison, salmon, and rack of lamb. Grilled choices include lamb chops, tournedos of beef, shrimp and scallops, and tuna steak. Desserts are wonderful. The menu changes seasonally, each time bringing new delights.

The inn just keeps winning awards. In the past, *Connecticut* magazine readers have voted it Best Overall Restaurant, Best Service, and Most Romantic Place to Dine in the state.

This is a fine inn in a most interesting part of New England. You are in the heart of art, antiques, gourmet restaurants, and endless activities. Plan to spend a few days when you come.

HOW TO GET THERE: Traveling north on Interstate 95, take exit 70 immediately on the east side of the Baldwin Bridge. At the bottom of the ramp, turn left. Take the first right at the traffic light, and turn left at the end of the road. The inn is the third house on your left. Traveling south on I-95, take exit 70; turn right at the bottom of the ramp. The inn is the third house on your left.

Old Lyme Inn
Old Lyme, Connecticut 06371

INNKEEPERS: Keith and Candy Green

ADDRESS/TELEPHONE: 85 Lyme Street (mailing address: P.O. Box 787); (860) 434-2600 or (800) 434-5352; fax (860) 434-5352

WEB SITE: www.oldlymeinn.com

ROOMS: 13, plus 4 in a nearby bed-and-breakfast; all with private bath, air-conditioning, phone, clock radio, and TV.

RATES: $135 to $185 CP.

OPEN: All year.

FACILITIES AND ACTIVITIES: Lunch, dinner, Sunday brunch. Bar and dining room.

BUSINESS TRAVEL: Located 45 minutes from Hartford. Phone in every room. Meeting rooms; fax available; dataport for computers.

*E*ven a fine inn can sometimes benefit from the energy and taste of new owners, and that is certainly the case with this 1850s mansion, long a mainstay in town. Local residents Keith and Candy Green bought the inn in 2001 and have upgraded both rooms and the restaurant, which was already well regarded.

The guest rooms are a mix of Empire and Victorian furnishings, with canopy and four-poster beds and comfortable seating areas. Eight rooms in the newer north wing area are larger than the five rooms in the original house. The Four Poster Room has a fireplace and a big bay window. The most luxurious rooms actually are down the street in Rooster Hall, the Green's own home, where four bedrooms were converted into a bed-and-breakfast in 2002.

The main floor of the inn is devoted to dining. The front taproom, parlor, and lower-level library space are now known as the Grill. The Winslow dining room, down one level, is a more elegant space used for dining on Friday and Saturday nights, accompanied by live piano music. Both rooms share the same excellent menu. Among the continental specialties are roasted duck, braised veal osso buco, rack of lamb, tandoori swordfish, roasted duck, and some classics such as beef Wellington and prime rib. One of the favorites at the inn is the Prime Steak Menu, offering several kinds of grilled steaks and chops with three sauces: béarnaise, horseradish whip, and the inn's special "chef's heartbreak."

The inn is ideally located for Old Lyme sightseeing, right across the road from the Florence Griswold Museum.

HOW TO GET THERE: Traveling north on Interstate 95, take exit 70 immediately on the east side of the Baldwin Bridge. At the bottom of the ramp, turn left. Take the first right at the traffic light, and turn left at the dead end. The inn is on the right. Traveling south on I-95, take exit 70. At the bottom of the ramp, turn right. The inn is on the right.

Saybrook Point Inn and Spa 📱
Old Saybrook, Connecticut 06475

INNKEEPER: Stephen Tagliatela; Karin Nelson, restaurant manager; Andrew Abels, general manager

ADDRESS/TELEPHONE: 2 Bridge Street; (860) 395–2000 or (800) 243–0212; fax (860) 388–1504

WEB SITE: www.saybrook.com

ROOMS: 81, including 16 suites and 1 lighthouse suite; all with private bath, phone, TV, air-conditioning, high-speed Internet access, and refrigerator; 55 with working fireplace. Some smoke-free rooms and suites.

RATES: $179 to $469 EP. Package plans available.

OPEN: All year.

FACILITIES AND ACTIVITIES: Breakfast, lunch, dinner, Sunday brunch. Banquet and meeting facilities; health club with whirlpool, sauna, and steam; spa; indoor and outdoor pools; marina with 120 slips and floating docks. Nearby: Charter boats, theater.

BUSINESS TRAVEL: Located 10 minutes from railroad station. All rooms with 2 phones, high-speed Internet, refrigerators; suites with fax achines; meeting rooms; secretarial services available.

"Experience the magic at Saybrook Point Inn." These are the inn's words, and they're so true. The panoramic views of the Connecticut River and Long Island Sound are magnificent. From the moment you walk into the lobby, the Italian marble floors, beautiful furniture, and glorious fabrics let you know this is a special inn. Even the carpet is hand-loomed.

Most of the guest rooms and suites have a water view and a balcony. They are lavishly decorated with eighteenth-century–style furniture, and Italian marble is used in the bathroom with whirlpool bath. Also in the rooms are a miniature wet bar and refrigerator; double-, queen-, or king-size bed; and hair dryer. The suites feature fax machines. DVD players are also available, as is an exercise room with life bikes.

There is a full spa, with indoor and outdoor pools, steam room, sauna, and whirlpool. The licensed staff will pamper you with a therapeutic massage, European facial, manicure, pedicure, or even a quality makeup application.

Planning a wedding or business conference? No problem. The inn has banquet facilities for all occasions. The ballroom seats 240 people. Smaller meetings would be ideal in the library, which holds up to sixteen people, or in the executive suites.

Breakfast, lunch, and dinner are served in an exquisite room that overlooks the inn's marina, the river, and Long Island Sound. There was a full moon the evening I dined here. What a beautiful sight to enhance the memorable food! Appetizers such as pancetta-wrapped grilled shrimp, poached Prince Edward Island mussels, and sesame and ginger seared "rare" tuna get dinner off to an elegant start. Veal osso buco and grilled swordfish steak with saffron and baby shrimp risotto are among a dozen dinner choices. My rack of lamb was one of the best I've tasted.

Sunday brunch is also a winner. Too much to list, but believe me, you will not go away hungry. I was here for Easter, and the food was glorious.

HOW TO GET THERE: From Interstate 95 northbound take exit 67 (southbound, take exit 68) and follow Route 154 and signs to Saybrook Point.

The Elms Inn
Ridgefield, Connecticut 06877

INNKEEPERS: The Scala family; restaurant proprietors, Cris and Brendan Walsh

ADDRESS/TELEPHONE: 500 Main Street; (203) 483–2541; fax (203) 438–2541; restaurant (203) 438–9206

WEB SITE: www.elmsinn.com

ROOMS: 18 rooms and suites; all with private bath, phone, TV, air-conditioning, wireless Internet access.

RATES: $155 to $425 CP.

OPEN: All year.

FACILITIES AND ACTIVITIES: Nearby: Museums, shops, antiquing.

*T*his colonial home has been on Ridgefield's leafy Main Street since 1750 and has been accommodating guests since 1799. The Scalas have been in charge for more than fifty years, supplying the warmth that can only be found in a family-run inn.

The complex has three buildings. Most rooms are in the guest house, decorated with floral prints, fishnet canopy beds, brass lamps, and armoires to hide the TV set. Rooms on the third floor have cozy eaves. A continental breakfast will be delivered to your door, with breads, pastries, yogurt, juice, and tea or coffee.

The Seymour House, built by a master colonial cabinetmaker, was renovated recently to add three luxurious suites with kitchens and oversize baths. One has a walk-in double shower, another has a skylight in the bath.

The restaurant is an independent operation under the auspices of Brendan Walsh, a CIA graduate who has garnered raves for his creative American menus. "Cutting edge in the country," said one review.

This venerable building has four working fireplaces and a choice of moods. The Grill, with low ceilings and beams, features main courses such as wood-grilled salmon and spice-rubbed hanger steak along with daily blackboard specials that might be chicken potpie or potted brisket of beef. The main dining room offers a more formal colonial setting, and here is where you can sample the best of Walsh's talents. Start with Louisiana crawfish bisque or pulled wild boar barbecue on johnnycake. For a main course, what about filet mignon, thyme roasted pheasant, or Connecticut seafood stew? Irresistible desserts such as apple pan dowdy or chocolate velvet terrine are a sweet end to a delightful dinner. When the weather is fine, you can dine on the patio.

Ridgefield's Main Street offers two quite different attractions, within walking distance of the inn. Keeler Tavern, circa 1772, has been meticulously restored with authentic furnishings and accessories and with a cannonball still embedded in the shingles as a memento of a British attack during the Revolutionary War. And down the street in a 1783 white house is the Aldrich Museum, with a modern gallery filled with the latest in avant-garde art and with an abstract sculpture garden in back, quite a surprise in this tradition-oriented town.

HOW TO GET THERE: From Interstate 95 or the Merritt Parkway, take Route 7 headed north, turn left on Route 102, and follow for 4 miles to the end. Take a right on Route 35 to the center of Ridgefield and go through three lights. The inn is just past the third light on the right. From Interstate 684 headed north, take exit 6, Katonah, Route 35. Go right off the ramp and follow Route 35 for 12 miles to the center of Ridgefield, then continue as above. From Interstate 84 eastbound, take exit 3, Route 7, and turn right onto Route 35 south. Follow for 4 miles, through four lights. The inn is ½ mile past the fourth light, on the left.

Stonehenge
Ridgefield, Connecticut 06877

INNKEEPER: Douglas Seville

ADDRESS/TELEPHONE: P.O. Box 667; (203) 438–6511

WEB SITE: www.stonehengeinn-ct.com

ROOMS: 14, plus 2 suites; all with private bath, color TV, phone, Internet access.

RATES: Rooms $120 to $160; suites $200 CP. Winter rates available.

OPEN: All year except New Year's Day.

FACILITIES AND ACTIVITIES: Breakfast, dinner, service bar, lounge.

The setting for Stonehenge is serenely beautiful. Outside is a lovely pond, bedecked with swans and aflutter with Canada geese and ducks stopping in on their migratory journeys. When I visited here in the spring, the red and yellow tulips were at their best.

Whether you're in the guest house, cottage, or inn, the accommodations are elegant, color coordinated, and comfortable. Most of the rooms have a queen- or king-size bed. All overlook the pond and wooded hillside.

A lovely continental breakfast is brought to you in your room, along with a copy of the morning newspaper. The breakfast consists of freshly squeezed juice, delicious muffin or Danish pastry, and coffee.

The common room has a fireplace flanked by bookcases. Picture windows in the large dining room overlook the pond and terraces. Stonehenge is justifiably famous for its gourmet dinners. The original Stonehenge shrimp in crisp beer batter with a pungent sauce is glorious. Some of the appetizers are a crepe of wild mushrooms with Gruyère cheese, and fresh hearts of palm wrapped in prosciutto. A choice of salads is followed by entrees like crisply roasted duckling with wild rice and black currant sauce, or breast of chicken filled with fresh spinach and Gruyère cheese, wrapped in puff pastry and served with a champagne sauce. You can even have roast baby suckling pig (five days' notice for this one). The desserts are stupendous, and decaffeinated espresso definitely gets my vote.

This is a beautiful place for a wedding or any other special function. The Terrace Room is available for corporate meetings.

HOW TO GET THERE: From the Merritt Parkway take exit 40. Go north on Route 7. The inn's sign is in 13 miles, on the left. From Interstate 84 go south on Route 7. The inn's sign is 4½ miles on the right.

West Lane Inn and Bernard's
Ridgefield, Connecticut 06877

INNKEEPERS: M. M. Mayer and Deborah Prieger

ADDRESS/TELEPHONE: 22 West Lane; (203) 438–7323; (203) 438–8282

WEB SITE: www.westlaneinn.com

ROOMS: 16, all with private bath, air-conditioning, phone, wireless Internet, and TV; some with fireplace and kitchen.

RATES: $145 to $190 BP.

OPEN: All year.

FACILITIES AND ACTIVITIES: Lunch, dinner, Sunday brunch; bar, lounge.

We have a first here: two separate inns next door to each other. West Lane Inn has the rooms and serves breakfast and a light menu from the pantry. Bernard's serves delicious lunch and dinner.

Rich oak paneling and lush carpeting, along with a crackling fire, greet you as you enter West Lane. The bedrooms are comfortable, with individual climate control, color television, radio, and telephone with voice mail and modem jacks. Each room has either one or two queen-size beds. Some have a working fireplace, delightful on a chilly night.

The breakfast room is bright and cheerful, and the orange juice is fresh squeezed. A West Lane breakfast special is yogurt with bananas, honey, and nuts. Cold cereals in the summer, hot cereals in the winter; Danish, muffins, or toast; or a poached egg is offered. Pantry selections available from noon until late in the evening include tuna fish salad plates and several sandwiches such as grilled cheese and peanut butter and jelly.

At lunch or dinner time, step across the lawn to Bernard's and be ready for a treat. Bernard Bouissou and his wife, Sarah, who met while working at Le Cirque in New York, have brought fine French cuisine to Ridgefield. Wait until you taste dishes like his pan-seared portobello-crusted halibut fillet, served with asparagus, wild mushroom risotto, and a balsamic mushroom reduction, or the Beef Duo, braised short ribs and roasted sirloin in a red wine sauce. Sunday brunch is not to be missed, whether you choose something simple like eggs Benedict, or a frittata with smoked ham, cheddar cheese, and caramelized onions, or opt for a more substantial meal such as roast lamb top sirloin or braised breast of veal stuffed with mushrooms in a truffle sauce.

Both inns are just around the corner from the famous Cannon Ball House, which was struck by a British fieldpiece during the Revolution. There are quite a few stores to browse in, as well as antiques stores. The Aldrich Museum is in town, and you are close to several fine summer theaters. Ridgefield is such a pretty town to visit.

HOW TO GET THERE: Coming north from New York on Interstate 684, or the Saw Mill Parkway, Route 7 from the Merritt Parkway, get off on Route 35 and follow it to Ridgefield. The inns are on Route 35 at the south end of town.

Old Riverton Inn
Riverton, Connecticut 06065

INNKEEPERS: Pauline and Mark Telford

ADDRESS/TELEPHONE: 436 East River Road (mailing address: P.O. Box 6); (860) 379-8678 or (800) 378-1796; fax (860) 379-1006

WEB SITE: www.rivertoninn.com

ROOMS: 12, all with private bath.

RATES: $90 to $200 BP.

OPEN: All year except the first week of January and the first two weeks of March.

FACILITIES AND ACTIVITIES: Dinner Friday through Sunday, seasonally. Dining room has wheelchair accessibility. Bar.

This delightful old inn listed on the National Register of Historic Places dates from 1796, when it was a stagecoach stop known as Ives Tavern, along the Hartford to Albany route. The Telfords, who

A Riverton Ramble

Antiques, galleries, the delightfully old-fashioned Riverton General Store, the Village Sweet Shop, and the Catnip Mouse Tea Room are all on the lovely stretch of Route 20 that is Riverton's main street. All are well within walking distance of the Old Riverton Inn, and most are open year-round or at least from April through December.

have been in charge for more than twenty years, have nicely maintained the charm of the past while adding modern comforts.

Riverton's main claim to fame was the factory that makes Hitchcock furniture; in fact, it was once known as Hitchcocksville. So it is no surprise to find that the inn features Hitchcock furnishings The guest rooms are simply and pleasantly decorated. Room 2 and the suite have canopy beds and a fireplace. A comfortable lounge and library on the second floor offers lots of games and books.

The colonial dining room has, of course, Hitchcock chairs and a lovely bow window chock-full of plants. Among the many tempting dinner appetizers, I recommend the homemade soups. I had the onion soup, and it was delicious. There are several seafood entrees, each one looking better than the last. The menu changes seasonally to take the advantage of fresh locally grown produce, but you can always count on some of the inn's traditional specialties, such as roast turkey and baked stuffed shrimp.

The bar boasts a stained-glass window and a fishing motif inspired by the scenic west branch of the Farmington River nearby.

One of my favorite spots here is the enclosed Grindstone Terrace for its history. According to the records, the grindstones that pave the floor were quarried in Nova Scotia and traveled by ship across Long Island Sound and up the Connecticut River and transported finally by oxcart to be used in the making of axes and machetes. They are serving a more peaceful purpose now.

All of quaint Riverton is chock-full of history, and it is also nicely situated for outdoor fun. Overlooking the Wild and Scenic west branch of the Farmington River and less than a mile from the People's State Forest, Riverton is a perfect home base whether your pleasure is trout fishing, canoeing, tubing, hiking, biking, cross-country skiing—or just finding a scenic spot for a picnic.

HOW TO GET THERE: The inn is 3½ miles from Winsted. Take Route 8 or Route 44 to Winsted. Turn east on Route 20, and it is approximately 1½ miles to the inn.

The White Hart
Salisbury, Connecticut 06068

INNKEEPER: Kendra Tobin

ADDRESS/TELEPHONE: Box 545; (860) 435-0030 or (800) 832-0041; fax (860) 435-0040

WEB SITE: www.whitehartinn.com

ROOMS: 23, plus 3 suites; all with private bath, cable TV, phone, Internet access, and air-conditioning; 1 specially equipped for the physically disabled.

RATES: $120 to $300 EP.

OPEN: All year.

FACILITIES AND ACTIVITIES: Breakfast, lunch, dinner. Taproom, garden room, private function and meeting rooms. Nearby: Swimming, boating, skiing, horseback riding; Tanglewood and Jacob's Pillow.

*T*his is the kind of place people imagine when they think of a New England inn, a venerable, rambling, gabled 1806 white building on the village green, listed on the National Register of Historic Places, with a wraparound porch where everyone seems to gather for a drink and a chance to catch up on the local news. It has been an inn since it was expanded in 1867. The series of owners has included Edsel Ford, who wanted to be assured of a pleasant and convenient place to stay when he visited his son, who was enrolled in the nearby Hotchkiss School. One of the rooms is named for him.

olive Metcalf

The mood of the inn is unpretentious and informal. The lobby is done with comfortable wing chairs and sofas. To the left is the Hunt Room, used for receptions, but it has a chess table that guests can enjoy when the room is not in use. All three meals are served in both the cozy Tap Room and the bright and sunny Garden Room on the ground floor.

The imaginative menu offers such dishes as grilled marinated lamb tenderloin with green olive and caper couscous, chicken breast with calvados cream sauce and vegetable quinoa pilaf, and duckling with dried cherries and Grand Marnier, served with wild rice. Lunch offerings include salads, pizzas, and sandwiches; dishes like wild mushroom ravioli; and a quiche of the day.

Rooms upstairs are decorated traditionally with flowery Waverly wallpapers and fabrics and furnished usually with colonial-style Thomasville mahogany, though a few rooms are done in country pine. Most have two double beds or one queen bed.

The White Hart is welcoming year-round, but it really comes into its own when the weather turns warm. On a pleasant day, there is no nicer pastime than watching the world go by from a wicker chair on the front porch of this classic inn.

HOW TO GET THERE: Go north from the Merritt Parkway (Route 15) to Route 7. The inn is on the green in Salisbury, at the intersection of Routes 44 and 41.

Simsbury 1820 House 🖤 📱
Simsbury, Connecticut 06070

INNKEEPER: Jan Losee, general manager

ADDRESS/TELEPHONE: 731 Hopmeadow Street; (860) 658–7658 or (800) 879–1820; fax (860) 651–0724

WEB SITE: www.simsbury1820house.com

ROOMS: 34 rooms and suites, 22 in main house, 12 in carriage house; all with private bath, phone, TV with VCR, wireless Internet, complimentary movie rental; 2 with wheelchair accessibility.

RATES: $119 to $225 CP.

OPEN: All year.

FACILITIES AND ACTIVITIES: Dinner Monday through Thursday; cafe. Nearby: Shopping, antiquing.

BUSINESS TRAVEL: Located 25 minutes from Hartford. All rooms with phone, high-speed wireless Internet; conference rooms; fax, computer, and overhead projector available; corporate rates.

uilt in 1820 and listed on the National Register of Historic Places, Simsbury House stood vacant for twenty-four years. Vandals, time, and weather took their toll, but you would never know it today. After a lot of hard work, frustration, and expense, it has been beautifully transformed into a fine inn and restaurant.

Relatives of the former owners provided old photographs of the house that were a good reference as it was restored. Two local craftswomen made leaded-glass windows to match the originals. The furniture consists of antiques and fine handmade reproductions from England. For example, the four-poster mahogany beds were carved by English cabinetmakers, and they are beauties. Some of them are king size and oh, so comfortable.

Twelve hundred rolls of wallpaper and 5,000 yards of fabric were used in restoring the inn and carriage house. The color schemes—blue, beige, and gold—recur among the rooms. Rooms have down feather beds, pillows, and comforters and Belgian linen sheets. The suites in the carriage house are sumptuous. One has a whirlpool tub. All the rooms are different, and some have an outside terrace. There are two wheelchair-accessible rooms.

The inn's cafe serves dinner Monday through Thursday from 5:00 to 8:00 P.M. The dining room is reserved for private parties on Friday and Saturday evenings.

Grilled salmon with a spiced orange cabernet reduction, medallions of pork with bourboned apple butter, and shrimp and sea scallops served on a crispy noodle cake with a Thai-inspired broth are among the choices on the appealing menu. Save room for dessert; you won't want to miss it.

Not far from the Simsbury 1820 House, on Simsbury's main Route 10, also known as Hopmeadow Street, the International Ice Skating Center of Connecticut (860–651–5400) draws crowds of skaters and spectators who would like to share the ice with or simply watch in awe such champion figure skaters as Ekaterina Gordeeva, Viktor Petrenko, Oksana Baiul, and Scott Davis. This world-class twin-rink facility is their home base. Visitors can skate, take lessons, and see both figure skating and hockey events and practices. A cafe, a restaurant, and coffee shop are all here. It's open year-round from 6:00 A.M. to midnight; call for public skating sessions. Rent some skates and have fun.

HOW TO GET THERE: From Interstate 84 take exit 39 onto Route 10 and go to Simsbury. The inn is on the left.

The Mayflower Inn 📱
Washington, Connecticut 06793

INNKEEPER: John Trevenen; Adriana and Robert Mnuchin, owners

ADDRESS/TELEPHONE: 118 Woodbury Road (mailing address: P.O. Box 1288); (860) 868–9466; fax (860) 868–1497

WEB SITE: www.mayflowerinn.com

ROOMS: 18, plus 7 suites; all with private bath, TV, two-line phones, Wi-Fi, dataports, and air-conditioning; many with balcony and fireplace. 30 rooms in new spa building with private bath, soaking tubs, steam showers, fireplaces, robes, Wi-Fi, TV.

RATES: Rooms $400 to $600; suites $650 to $1,300 EP. Spa weekends, two nights, $1,850 per person; 5-day program, $2,310 per person.

OPEN: All year.

FACILITIES AND ACTIVITIES: Breakfast, lunch, dinner. Bar and lounge, gift shop, outdoor pool, tennis, 58 acres of lawns and gardens, fitness club, full-service spa with indoor pool, treatments, and classes. Nearby: hiking.

BUSINESS TRAVEL: Phones in rooms; conference area. The teahouse is fully equipped for meetings or conferences.

The Mayflower Inn is one of New England's jewels, a gracious, tasteful retreat modeled after the finest European country house hotels and surrounded by acres of lawn and gardens. The traditional gray shingle architecture of the original inn and several recently added buildings is called American Shingle and reflects New England, but the furnishings would be at home in old England.

The elegant sitting room could be a page from *House Beautiful*, filled with English and French antiques, Persian rugs, and works of art, many of them collected by the Mnuchins during their travels over the years. The cherry-paneled library with cashmere throws over the back of the chairs tempts you to take one of the books off the shelves and settle in for the afternoon.

The twenty-five guest rooms are spread over three buildings: the main house, the Standish, and the Speedwell. No two are alike. They are decorated in fine prints with coordinated stripes and solids and lovely antiques in color schemes from soft blue to deep red, green to peach. Some have sleigh beds, some canopies, some wrought-iron headboards, and many have a fireplace. Even Room 18 in the main building, the smallest of the rooms, is appealing, with a half-canopy bed and a bay-window view that makes you feel you are in a tree house. All the rooms have a small library of books and exquisite accessories from hand-painted soap dishes to alarm clocks of English leather.

Though the food is elegant, the dining room is warm and unpretentious, and when weather permits, everything moves to the terrace, where you have wonderful views of the garden and grounds. The menu changes often to take advantage of local produce. The pastas and breads are homemade, and the salmon is smoked in-house. I had a wonderful grilled veal chop with sundried tomato risotto, but I was also sorely tempted by the braised monkfish with lobster ravioli in a basil saffron broth. And who can resist desserts like a warm chocolate pudding cake or a chestnut honey-glazed peach tart with white peach ice cream? When you are in the mood for something less formal, the convivial piano bar will oblige.

If you want to work off your calories, head for the tennis court or the pool. The grounds are a walker's paradise, planted with specimen trees and gardens. In fact, there's little that isn't wonderful at this special inn.

In April 2006 the Mayflower opened its newest facility, a totally luxurious full-service destination spa with thirty guest rooms. The 20,000-square-foot spa building includes a heated indoor pool and domed whirlpool, steam rooms, yoga and Pilates studios, exercise rooms, and a fully equipped fitness studio. The program for spa guests (only from Monday to Friday) includes indoor classes and outdoor activities such as guided hikes, biking and tennis, a full spectrum of treatments, and a low-calorie menu. On weekends, the facilities and classes are open to all guests.

The Mayflower management requires a minimum two-night stay, but that's hardly a problem since once you come, you won't want to leave. **HOW TO GET THERE:** From Hartford take Interstate–84 west to exit 15, Southbury. Follow Route 6 north through Southbury to Woodbury. It is exactly 5 miles from I–84 to "Canfield Corners" (an 1890s building on your right). Go left here on Route 47 to Washington. It is $8^{2}/_{10}$ miles to the inn.

Water's Edge Resort and Spa
Westbrook, Connecticut 06498

INNKEEPER: Tina Dattilo, general manager

ADDRESS/TELEPHONE: 1525 Boston Post Road; (860) 399–5901 or (800) 222–5901 (outside Connecticut)

WEB SITE: www.watersedge-resort.com

ROOMS: 94 rooms, 68 villas; all with private bath, cable TV, and phone; villas have kitchen, fireplace, deck, VCR.

RATES: $185 to $240 weekdays, $285 to $340 weekends; EP.

OPEN: All year.

FACILITIES AND ACTIVITIES: Breakfast, lunch, dinner, Sunday brunch. Bar, lounge; room service; entertainment on holidays and special occasions; full-service spa; indoor and outdoor pools; banquet rooms; tennis; private beach on Long Island Sound.

BUSINESS TRAVEL: Located 30 minutes from New Haven, 45 minutes from Hartford. All rooms with phone; 6 conference rooms, 12 meeting rooms.

There is a song that says, "This one's for me." Well, here it is, and what a gem! Sitting up high, overlooking Long Island Sound, the inn is like a turn-of-the-twentieth-century resort. With its own sparkling private beach, it offers swimming, plus boating on the inn's fleet of catamarans, sailfish, and paddleboats.

The dining room is decorated in soft shades of peach, rose, and gray. The food is magnificent. The seafood and lobster bisque with crab is excellent. There is a choice of several salads. I had the scrod entree one night and duckling another. Both were very good. I love the way the food is arranged so prettily on the plates.

Sunday brunch is a delight. It is so popular that reservations are a must. Chefs make Belgian waffles to order, as well as omelets with a choice of ingredients inside. Roast beef, roast turkey, fish, fruit, and vegetables are also offered. The pastries are delicious!

There's an outdoor patio for cocktails and dining in summer, called Le Grille. It is just fabulous, with its view of the Sound. The lounge is warm in feeling and has a nice fireplace, besides. The bar sports comfortable chairs and has the style of a pub.

The rooms and suites are sumptuous. Most of them have a king- or a queen-size bed, and all have comfortable chairs. Some have a balcony, and there is a wet bar in the suites.

The health club has the latest equipment, day and night tennis courts, indoor and outdoor swimming, sauna, and a full menu of massages and spa services. There are banquet and conference rooms for 10 to 350 persons. The inn's grounds are very nice for a walk. And there is much to do in this lovely area—marinas, state parks, the lovely town of Essex nearby, and much more.

HOW TO GET THERE: From Interstate 95 take exit 65 at Westbrook. Go south to Route 1, then go east approximately ¼ mile and look for the inn's sign.

The Inn at Woodstock Hill
Woodstock, Connecticut 06281

INNKEEPER: Richard Naumann

ADDRESS/TELEPHONE: 94 Plaine Hill Road; (860) 928-0528; fax (860) 928-3236

WEB SITE: www.woodstockhill.com

ROOMS: 18 in main house, 3 in guest cottage; all with private bath, TV, phone, radio, free Internet access, air-conditioning; 8 with working fireplaces.

RATES: $130 to $195 CP.

OPEN: All year.

FACILITIES AND ACTIVITIES: Lunch Tuesday through Saturday, dinner daily, Sunday brunch. Nearby: Hiking, state parks, Roseland Cottage (house museum), New England Center for Contemporary Art; Old Sturbridge Village is less than 30 minutes away.

*N*o, this isn't the famous Woodstock, but a country cousin, a hamlet of stone walls and historic houses that date from 1686. In the center of things on the crest of a long ridge is Woodstock Hill, where huge old trees shade handsome country houses spanning a couple of centuries of architecture. And at the top of the hill is the inn, built in 1816 for William Bowen, a descendant of one of the town's original settlers. It remained in the Bowen family until 1981, with reconstructions and additions over the years, and a caretaker's cottage added in 1927 with three bedrooms. In 1985 the property was sold to a consortium of investors who converted the main house and barn into an inn and restaurant. Most of the many acres of farmland surrounding the inn still belong to the Bowen family, as they have for three centuries.

There is still the look of yesterday when you drive up to the large white clapboard building with a steeply pitched hip roof and dormers. There's a cozy, cluttered look to the several sitting rooms, with flowery wall and window treatments, Oriental rugs, fireplaces, and lots of books and plants. Upstairs, the rooms are attractively done in colonial style with white walls, and Waverly print fabrics in soft shades of peach and blue. Six of the rooms have four-poster beds, eight have fireplaces (six are wood-burning), and one room has an atmospheric beamed cathedral ceiling. The decor is old-fashioned, but the amenities are not; every room offers a TV and free high-speed Internet access.

There are two dining rooms, a small charmer in the Carriage House with a fireplace, and a more formal long, narrow dining room with floral wallpaper, blue wood trim, and windows looking into the surrounding open fields and woods. Dinner is by candlelight, served on fine china and crystal and with soft music in the background. The menu is varied enough to please every taste. Recent fish choices ranged from pecan-crusted red snapper to blackened tuna with a slightly spicy Creole sauce. On the meat menu were filet mignon, and veal medallions topped with morels and mushrooms a la crème. My favorite dish was the duck breast served on a wild mushroom couscous and drizzled with ginger-cognac bordelaise sauce. The continental breakfast offers fresh fruit, cereals, and freshly baked muffins and bread.

The Inn at Woodstock Hill is located on Route 169, an officially designated scenic highway, and a drive takes you through a series of some of the delightful unspoiled towns that make up the northeastern "Quiet Corner" of Connecticut. This beautiful section is still relatively unknown, and it is an area well worth discovering.

HOW TO GET THERE: The Inn at Woodstock Hill is on Route 169 in the center of Woodstock. From the south take Interstate 395 north to exit 95, Kennedy

Drive. Turn right at the bottom of the ramp to the second light, then left onto Route 171 west. Travel for 5 miles and the road will turn into Route 169 north. The inn is past the Woodstock fire station and town hall, at the top of the hill on the left. Coming from the north, take I-395 exit 97, Putnam, and turn onto Route 44 west. At the second light turn right to Route 171 west and continue as above.

Select List of Other Connecticut Inns

Bishopsgate Inn

7 Norwich Road
P.O. Box 290
East Haddam, CT 06423
(860) 873-1677
Fax (860) 873-3898
Web site: www.bishopsgate.com
5 rooms, 1 suite with sauna; all rooms with private bath; 4 with fireplace; 1818 colonial within walking distance of Goodspeed Opera House and Connecticut River.

Wake Robin Inn

106 Sharon Road (Route 41)
Lakeville, CT 06039
(860) 435-2515
Fax (860) 435-2000
Web site: www.wakerobininn.com
23 rooms in 1896 main inn, all with private bath; 15 rooms in summer building/ motel.

Whaler's Inn

20 East Main Street
Mystic, CT 06355
(860) 536-1506 or (800) 243-2588
Web site: www.whalersinnmystic.com
49 rooms, all with private bath; historic inn near Mystic River.

Three Chimneys Inn

1201 Chapel Street
New Haven, CT 06511
(203) 789-1201 or (800) 443-1554
Fax (203) 776-7363
Web site: www.threechimneysinn.com

10 rooms, all with private bath; 3 with nonfunctional fireplaces; all with air-conditioning, TV, phone, dataport for computer; on-site parking; within walking distance of Yale University.

Randall's Ordinary

Route 2
P.O. Box 243
North Stonington, CT 06359
(860) 599–4540 or (877) 599–4540 (toll free)
Web site: www.randallsordinary.com
18 rooms in 300-year-old colonial house and renovated 1819 barn; suite in silo has fireplace and a winding staircase up to a Jacuzzi. Authentic seventeenth-century open-hearth cooking in restaurant.

The Inn at Longshore

260 Compo Road South
Westport, CT 06880
(203) 226–3316
Web site: www.innatlongshore.com
12 rooms, including 3 suites; all with private bath; 1890s seaside inn with extensive outdoor sports facilities and views of Long Island Sound.

The Inn at National Hall

2 Post Road West
Westport, CT 06880
(203) 221–1351 or (800) 628–4255
Fax (203) 221–0276
Web site: www.innatnationalhall.com
16 rooms, including 8 suites; all with private bath; luxurious 1873 National Register of Historic Places Italianate building overlooking Saugatuck River.

Maine

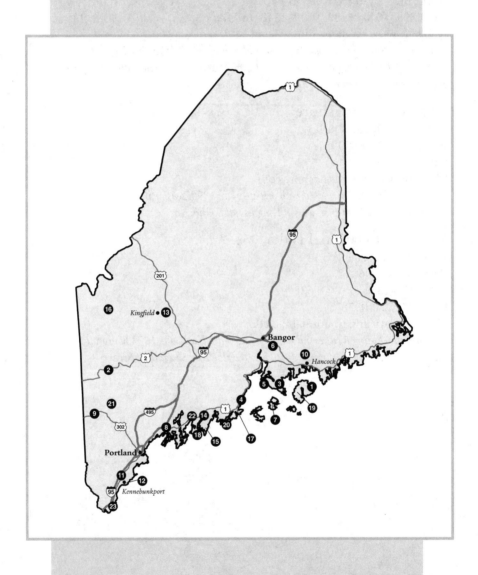

Maine

Numbers on map refer to towns numbered below.

Bar Harbor Hotel–Bluenose Inn
Bar Harbor, Maine 04609

INNKEEPER: David J. Witham

ADDRESS/TELEPHONE: 90 Eden Street; (207) 288-3348 or (800) 445-4077

WEB SITE: www.barharborhotel.com

ROOMS: 97 rooms and suites, all with private bath; 41 with gas fireplace, phone, cable TV, air-conditioning, minifridge.

RATES: $75 to $405 EP. Ask about the many packages.

OPEN: Late April to late October.

FACILITIES AND ACTIVITIES: Breakfast and dinner, bar, lounge. Indoor and outdoor heated pools. Fitness center, spa. Nearby: Boating, parks, and beauty.

hy it's taken me so long to get back to Bar Harbor I may never know, but I'm here now, and the view is breathtaking—especially from this perfectly located resort. The name "inn" is misleading, as this is really a hotel resort, not the usual inn you expect to find in this book. But the superb site atop a granite terraced hilltop overlooking the water is just too good to leave out. And while the hotel is large, it is made very comfortable by the owner and his staff.

The Mizzentop, built in 1995, has the registration office, a great room and bar, a function room, fifty-two of the guest rooms, and Raspbeary's gift shop. A lot of bears and bunnies, all handmade, live here.

The bar's a beauty of handcrafted cherrywood; the great room has a huge wood fireplace. There are fresh flowers everywhere, handsome chandeliers, and good couches and comfortable chairs.

Stenna Nordica, another lodging, has forty-five rooms, a glass-front elevator, and much comfort. All the rooms have views of Frenchman Bay.

There are thirty-nine suites in all, and I was in one on the fourth floor that had a fireplace, two televisions (one for the sitting area, one for the bed area), and a porch overlooking the bay. Even the standard rooms are beauties, and the suites are fabulous.

A third building houses a lavish indoor pool, the spa and fitness center, and the Rose Garden restaurant, a gourmet haven that has earned a four-diamond rating from AAA. The three-course dinners are truly memorable. The only problem is deciding what to order. For starters, you might choose petite crab cakes, locally smoked salmon with golden caviar, Maine lobster bisque, or chilled mango soup with jumbo shrimp. Entrees include Maine lobster, of course, or grilled North Atlantic salmon, sautéed halibut with saffron risotto, roasted rack of lamb, venison with wild rice, or fillet of beef with portobello–garlic cream potatoes. You won't be surprised to hear that desserts are fantastic. I was torn between the lemon custard Napoleon with fresh berries and the mango mascarpone cheesecake with Grand Marnier white chocolate sauce. But both were forgotten when I saw another choice—dark chocolate silk mousse cake with a trio of sauces. Who could resist that?

Acadia National Park is a short drive away, and the dock for the *Cat* ferry to and from Nova Scotia is 600 yards away. The *Cat* is a high-speed ferry that gets to Nova Scotia in two-and-a-half hours.

There's also the *Margaret Todd*, a four-masted schooner. Listen to the wind in the rigging while you sail Frenchman Bay. Watch for whales and puffins.

This inn is perfect for conferences, weddings, bridal showers, and much more. Dinner meetings in the Rose Garden can seat as many as fifty guests.

In case you are wondering about the name Bluenose Inn, the original inn was constructed in 1884 as a summer estate. All that is left from that palatial "cottage" is the stonework, which is now part of the present Mizzentop building.

HOW TO GET THERE: Northbound travelers follow Interstate 95 over the bridge into Maine and continue on I-95 to exit 45A. Take this exit and follow Route 395 east to Route 1A to Ellsworth. Go straight on Route 3 to Bar Harbor. Pass the *Cat* Ferry Terminal. The Bar Harbor Hotel–Bluenose Inn is 600 yards beyond the ferry terminal on the right, across from the College of the Atlantic.

Southbound travelers take I–95 to exit 45A and follow northbound directions. The hotel sits high on an elevated site overlooking Frenchman Bay.

The Bethel Inn and Country Club
Bethel, Maine 04217

INNKEEPERS: Dick Rasor; Allen Connors, manager

ADDRESS/TELEPHONE: P.O. Box 49; (207) 824–2175 or (800) 654–0125

WEB SITE: www.bethelinn.com

ROOMS: 148 in main inn and surrounding buildings; all with private bath, phone, and cable TV; 60 with fireplace; 2 specially equipped for the physically disabled.

RATES: $89 to $159 per person, MAP. Luxury townhouses, $179 to $279. Package rates available.

OPEN: All year.

FACILITIES AND ACTIVITIES: Dining, bar, lounge. Golf, tennis, swimming pool, lake house with kayaks and canoes, cross-country skiing center, whirlpool, sauna, exercise room, indoor games, golf school, supervised activities and summer day camp for children. Wireless Internet in

common areas. Wheelchair access to lobby, conference center, dining room. Free shuttle to downhill skiing at Sunday River and Mt. Abram.

The Bethel Inn faces the village common of Bethel, Maine, which is a National Historic District complete with beautifully restored churches, public buildings, and private homes. The rear of the inn overlooks its own 200 acres and eighteen-hole championship golf course.

Guest rooms have private baths and direct-dial telephones. They are well done and very comfortable. A number of rooms have been redecorated with country-print wallpaper, thick carpeting, and fresh paint. The Bingham Suite, where I stayed the last time I was at the inn, has a fireplace and a Jacuzzi—glorious!

The huge lobby, the Gibson room, and library are beautifully furnished, and the piano is a Steinway.

Dining is a pleasure, either in the charming main dining room, the Millbrook Tavern and Grille, or on the year-round enclosed dining veranda overlooking the golf course. You'll find such entrees as prime rib, roast duck, and lobster and crabmeat casserole on the extensive menu. Just before sunset, look out over the golf course. You'll see literally hundreds of swallows diving into the chimney of the utility building next to the course.

Downstairs is the MillBrook Tavern. Mill Brook cuts through the golf course and was the site of Twitchell's mill, erected in the early 1700s in Sudbury, Canada, which is now Bethel, Maine.

There is a light supper menu that is nice for the late hiker or skier. In the winter you can have hot cider, hot buttered rum, and glögg. Lunch is nice in the screened-in terrace lounge, but the drinks are even better. They're called the Kool Krazy Bouncy and Hot drinks. I managed to taste three of them—oh boy!

The lake house, 3 miles away on Lake Songo, features clambakes and barbecues and all water sports.

Skiing is super up here, with Sunday River (I love that name) and Mt. Abram right at hand. The inn has special ski packages. And as a special special, the inn has its own Nordic ski and snowshoe center and more than 25 miles of groomed cross-country trails for your pleasure.

The recreation center has a heated, ninety-two-degree outdoor swimming pool for use all year, plus saunas, exercise room, lounge, and game room.

Afternoon teas, punch parties, and lobster bakes are nice to find at an inn. You'll never be at a loss for something to do at the Bethel Inn.

HOW TO GET THERE: Bethel is located at the intersection of U.S. Route 2 and Maine Routes 5 and 26. From the south take exit 11 off the Maine Turnpike at Gray and follow Route 26 to Bethel. The inn is on the town common.

The Sudbury Inn
Bethel, Maine 04217

INNKEEPERS: Bill and Nancy White

ADDRESS/TELEPHONE: Main Street (mailing address: P.O. Box 369); (207) 824–2174 or (800) 395–7837; fax (207) 824–2329

WEB SITE: www.sudburyinn.com

ROOMS: 18, plus 8 suites in 2 buildings; all with private bath, air-conditioning, and cable TV.

RATES: $79 to $199 BP.

OPEN: All year.

FACILITIES AND ACTIVITIES: Dinner, bar, lounge. Nearby: Skiing, ice skating, canoeing, tennis, golf, hiking.

Olive Metcalf

*T*his inn is located in the very pretty village of Bethel in the mountains of western Maine. The town is home to Gould Academy, one of Maine's foremost prep schools, which was founded in 1836. Bethel is truly a town for all seasons. There's easy access to the White Mountain Forest and hiking on the Appalachian Trail, as well as tennis, golf, and canoeing, both flat and white water. In fall the foliage is breathtakingly beautiful, and in winter, ice skating, miles of maintained cross-country ski trails, and top-notch downhill skiing are nearby.

The front of the inn was built in 1873, and the rear was added in the early 1900s. The inn recently has been upgraded, as the Whites, who purchased the property in June 2000, have installed modern amenities like air-conditioning and cable TV in every guest room. The furnishings remain simple, homey, and comfortable, and the comfy rockers remain on the front porch.

The warmth and comfort of the main dining room and its enormous fireplace also remain. Appetizers include treats such as potato and wild mushroom lasagna, and a fabulous lobster and artichoke dip served with grilled focaccia bread points.

One of the inn's specialties is cioppino, a fish stew featuring Maine lobster, rock crab claws, jumbo shrimp, and fresh mussels served in a spicy seafood bouillon with fresh vegetables and tomato. Divine! Other entrees include beef tournedos, rack of lamb, and roast duckling topped with Maine maple syrup and wild blueberry glaze. Some favorite homemade desserts are classic crème brûlée or Chocolate Perfection, a flourless chocolate torte with a touch of rum, served in an oatmeal crust. A cup of espresso completes a great meal.

How can I think of breakfast? Well, how can you resist Belgian waffles? Or eggs any way you like them, fresh yogurt with fruit, and French toast seasoned with nutmeg?

Subs Pub, on the lower level, was created when the old granite-walled basement was dug out and expanded. A lighter menu is served down here, along with thirty draft beers, featuring Maine microbrews. The pub, a longtime favorite with the après-ski crowd, offers live entertainment Friday and Saturday nights during ski season. Thursday night year-round is "Hoot Nite," when locals show off their musical talent in an open-mike format. It's unpredictable, but always fun.

HOW TO GET THERE: Take exit 11 off the Maine Turnpike and follow Route 26 to Bethel. The inn is on lower Main Street.

Blue Hill Inn
Blue Hill, Maine 04614

INNKEEPERS: Don and Mary Hartley

ADDRESS/TELEPHONE: Route 177; (207) 374–2844 or (800) 826–7415

WEB SITE: www.bluehillinn.com

ROOMS: 11, all with private bath; 3 with fireplace; 1 luxury suite.

RATES: Inn rooms, $148 to $195 BP; Cape House, $165 to $295 BP. Special packages available.

OPEN: Inn open mid-May through October 31; Cape House cottage suite available all year.

FACILITIES AND ACTIVITIES: Breakfast and hors d'oeuvres daily. Wine dinners offered in May and October. Wheelchair access to dining room, parlor. Full license. Nearby: Acadia National Park, hiking, boating, concerts.

Built in 1830 as a private home, Blue Hill has been an inn since 1840, with an unbeatable location at the top of the hill from the head of the bay. The property is lovely, shaded with tall beautiful elms and with a garden that is a heavenly setting for cocktails in summer.

There are two common rooms to relax in. You can feel free to curl up in a chair and read—the fireplaces are so cozy, especially if there is a chill in the air.

There is an 1850 pump melodeon to play if you are so inclined. All the rooms are comfortable, and all have their own private bath, but each is different. You'll find some with queen- and king-size beds and some fireplaces. The furnishings are nineteenth-century antiques and reproductions.

A variety of packages are offered each season, featuring sailing or cruising, concerts, hiking, or antiquing. Packages including wine dinners are a special treat. The dinners are multicourse affairs served by candlelight, with each course accompanied by a wine carefully chosen to complement the foods.

Blue Hill Mountain, an exhilarating hike, rewards with views of Camden, Deer Isle, and the bay. Every evening before guests depart for dinner, they are invited to the innkeepers' reception, where hors d'oeuvres are served and cocktails are available. The inn guests enjoy meeting one another and making new friends.

Breakfasts are hearty and filling, with freshly made bread, omelets, Maine blueberry pancakes, and more.

The Cape House cottage suite, which is available for guests even when the main house is closed for the winter, comes with a kitchen, king-size bedroom and bath, living room with a raised hearth fireplace, cable TV, phone, air-conditioning and heat, and a private deck. It is ideal for families.

HOW TO GET THERE: From Belfast follow Route 3 east through Searsport to Bucksport. Bear right after crossing the Bucksport Bridge. After a few miles, turn right onto Route 15 south to Blue Hill. Turn right on Main Street, then bear right again onto Route 177 west. The inn is the first building on your left at the top of the hill.

Blue Harbor House
Camden, Maine 04843

INNKEEPERS: Terry and Annette Hazzard

ADDRESS/TELEPHONE: 67 Elm Street; (207) 236–3196 or (800) 248–3196; fax (207) 236–6523

WEB SITE: www.blueharborhouse.com

ROOMS: 11, including suites; all with private bath, phone, TV, wireless Internet, and air-conditioning.

RATES: $95 to $205 BP. Special packages available.

OPEN: All year.

FACILITIES AND ACTIVITIES: Afternoon refreshments, dinner ($40) by reservation. Nearby: Tennis, golf, boating, hiking.

Camden, Maine, is called the jewel of the Maine coast with very good reason: It is situated at a beautiful spot where the mountains meet the sea, making for one of New England's most picturesque harbors. And Blue Harbor House, a restored 1810 Cape Cod home, is a cozy spot to enjoy this special town.

The guest rooms have king or queen beds, some of which are canopied. You're sure to like the quilts on the beds. All the rooms have telephones and televisions, and air-conditioning. In the front rooms, where there might be noise from Route 1, the innkeepers have installed a white-noise generator and added soundproofed windows. The carriage house suites have a sitting room, king-size bed, gas fireplace, and whirlpool tub and shower or oversize soak tub.

Breakfast is a joy and just a bit different. Terry and Annette, who hail from Scotland, have Apple Bakers, and a baked apple never tasted so good. It's filled with vanilla ice cream, of course. You could also start your day with fat-free stuffed French toast. Or blueberry pancakes with blueberry butter—the way to go!

Dinner offerings include a Downeast Lobster Feast, stuffed rack of lamb, and other regional specialties.

I love the glass-walled sun porch here, a perfect place to relax with books or catch up on TV in the evening. And it's just a short walk to the picture-perfect waterfront, with its shops and great boats. Take your car, and Terry will direct you to Route 52; it's a really beautiful drive. Or go to the top of Mt. Battie and take a look at Camden Harbour from 900 feet up.

HOW TO GET THERE: Coming from the south, take exit 6A from the Maine Turnpike to Interstate 295, which joins Interstate 95 just north of Portland. A few miles north of Freeport, take exit 22 (Coastal Route 1, Brunswick). Continue north on Route 1 through Waldoboro. Six miles past Waldoboro, turn left onto Route 90 and follow it for 10 miles until it rejoins Route 1. Turn left onto Route 1 and continue for 2 miles toward Camden. Blue Harbor House is on your left as you come into town.

Camden Harbour Inn
Camden, Maine 04843

INNKEEPERS: Sal Vella and Patti Babij

ADDRESS/TELEPHONE: 83 Bay View Street; (207) 236–4200 or (800) 236–4266; fax (207) 236–7063

WEB SITE: www.camdenharbourinn.com

ROOMS: 22, all with private bath, TV, phone, dataport; 8 with fireplace; 8 with balcony or deck.

RATES: $155 to $275 BP.

OPEN: May to mid-October.

FACILITIES AND ACTIVITIES: Breakfast only. Wheelchair access to dining room. Meetings, conferences, and special events. Nearby: Golf, skiing, sailing, hiking.

Camden Harbour is one of the best-known ports in Maine, and it's one of the prettiest, too. In the late nineteenth century, when Camden was bustling with cargo and fishing schooners, the inn was built to accommodate passengers who traveled from Boston to Bangor by steamship. Today, boats of yesteryear, both sail and power, as well as beautiful modern-day yachts, moor here by the rolling mountains that come right down to the rocky shores. The inn sits up high above all this and provides a panoramic view. The porch is terrific, and guests enjoy it from early morning coffee to evening nightcaps.

Mt. Battie and Camden Hills State Park

A 25-mile hiking trail system and a 1⁶/10-mile auto road in Camden Hills State Park (207–236–3109) have helped to open this beautiful area to the thousands of visitors who come here yearly to see the glorious views of Penobscot Bay. A stone mountain tower at the peak marks the location of the former Summit House, built as a hotel in 1887 by Camden resident Columbus Bushwell. Such notables as Theodore Roosevelt and poet Edna St. Vincent Millay climbed to the top of the mountain on an old carriage road that is now a part of the trail system. Visitors today can hike that same footpath year-round or drive up on the auto road from May 1 through November 1. Hikers agree that the view is worth every step. In winter the park offers snowshoeing, cross-country skiing, and downhill skiing at the Camden Snow Bowl.

In addition to Mt. Battie, the 6,500-acre park includes Mt. Megunticook. The highest point on the Camden Hills as well as one of the highest elevations on the whole Eastern Seaboard, Megunticook is also a popular destination for hikers and picnickers. A small admission fee is charged at the park entrance on Route 1.

All the guest rooms are different in character. They are furnished with period antiques, Victorian pieces, canopy and brass beds, and wicker. Many overlook the harbor and bay and have outside decks. There is a suite with a foyer, a wet bar, a sitting room adjacent to a large deck, and a comfortably furnished bedroom with a working fireplace. Another room has a large sitting area and a brick patio that overlooks the outer harbor. Other rooms have a fireplace, and some have a private outside entrance with reserved parking. Rooms 22 and 28 have ruffled canopy beds, and several rooms have clawfoot tubs.

The inn has stopped serving dinner since I last visited, but it remains a favorite. The views are terrific, and this is a wonderful town to muddle about in for days. There is hardly a spot in this whole lovely Maine town that is not worth a visit. I was here for two wonderful days, and I had such a nice time—wonderful innkeepers and help.

HOW TO GET THERE: From Route 1, which runs through the center of town, turn up Bay View Street to number 83.

Whitehall Inn
Camden, Maine 04843

INNKEEPERS: Greg and Sue Marquise

ADDRESS/TELEPHONE: 52 High Street (mailing address: P.O. Box 558); (207) 236–3391 or (800) 789–6565; fax (207) 236–4467

WEB SITE: www.whitehall-inn.com

ROOMS: 44, 38 with private bath; 1 three-bedroom suite.

RATES: $89 to $199 BP with private bath; $89 to $119 BP with shared bath.

OPEN: Late May to mid-October.

FACILITIES AND ACTIVITIES: Restaurant, shuffleboard. Nearby: Boating, biking, swimming, golf, hiking, windjammers.

"All I could see from where I stood / Was three long mountains and a wood; / I turned and looked another way, / and saw three islands in a bay."

These are the words of Edna St. Vincent Millay, describing the view above Camden, a town where the mountains meet the sea. She was a young unknown in 1912 when she read these first lines from her celebrated poem "Renascence" for the first time at the Whitehall Inn. Guests were delighted to discover such a promising new talent, and the inn shared in her fame.

olive Metcalf

This 1834 sea captain's home became an inn more than a century ago when the captain's widow began taking in guests to make ends meet. Greatly expanded over the years, the classic white-columned building with rockers on the wide porches is now on the National Register of Historic Places.

This is a deliberately old-fashioned inn because guests like it that way. There is no television, but a chess board is by the fire, a jigsaw puzzle is always in progress in the library, and there are plenty of books to borrow. Rooms are simply furnished with antiques, and sheer white ruffled curtains are at the windows.

The pleasant dining room has window walls to bring in the sunshine. For breakfast, Maine blueberries are almost always on the menu, and dinner is by candlelight with classical music in the background. Entrees feature fresh local seafood, including Maine shrimp and scallops, crabmeat, haddock, salmon, and halibut. Steamed lobster is always an option. Those who prefer meat or chicken will find them, as well. Before dinner, the Spirits Room offers libations at tables made from old pedal sewing machines or on the veranda surrounded by flower beds.

Camden is a town with many attractions. At the scenic harbor, you can get out on the water in a variety of ways, from windjammers to canoes. Camden Hills State Park, just north of town, offers a drive or a hike to the top of Mt. Battie. The view of mountains and sea is just as spectacular as when it inspired Edna St. Vincent Millay.

HOW TO GET THERE: The inn is on Route 1, up the hill just north of Camden, on the left.

The Castine Inn
Castine, Maine 04421

INNKEEPERS: Tom and Amy Gutow

ADDRESS/TELEPHONE: P.O. Box 41; (207) 326–4365; fax (207) 326–4570

WEB SITE: www.castineinn.com

ROOMS: 19, all with private bath.

RATES: $90 to $295 EP.

OPEN: Late April through early October.

FACILITIES AND ACTIVITIES: Full breakfast daily, dinner daily in season. Pub, sauna, perennial gardens. Nearby: Harbor.

Castine is a beautiful town on Penobscot Bay, and this inn is a lovely focal point on a hill overlooking the harbor. Gardens add to the charm of the setting, and the porches have chairs set out for savoring the view. The house was built in 1898, and guests are as warmly received now as in the past when they came by boat (which some people still do). You enter a large front hall and a parlor with a wood-burning fireplace that is routinely lit in the evening to ward off the chill of coastal Maine. Books and games await if you want diversions.

The dining room has a lovely hand-painted mural of Castine covering the walls. There are three ways to dine here. The cozy pub offers an informal menu of dishes such as fish and chips, pasta salad with smoked chicken, or the inn's special crabmeat cake with mustard sauce. On weekends in season, a reasonably priced three-course prix fixe menu of traditional Maine fare might start with a saffron scallop and mussel stew, followed by chicken potpie, and ending with strawberry shortcake. Or you can opt for the gourmet dinner, a six-course tasting menu, with the option of pairing each course with a wine from the inn's cellar. Breakfast ideas? How about pancakes with blueberries, apple bread French toast, or corned beef hash.

Guest rooms are cheerful. Many have harbor views, and several have been elegantly redecorated recently.

Castine itself is picturesque. The Maine Maritime Academy is the town's only "industry." The International Guild of Miniatures Artisans holds a conference here each June. The harbor is dotted with sailing ships, yachts, and windjammers.

HOW TO GET THERE: Take Interstate 95 to Augusta and Route 3 east to the coast. Connect with Route 1 at Belfast, and follow Route 1 north to Bucksport. In 2 miles turn right onto Route 175. Follow it to Route 166, which takes you into Castine.

The Pentagöet Inn
Castine, Maine 04421

INNKEEPERS: Jack Burke and Julie Van de Graaf

ADDRESS/TELEPHONE: P.O. Box 4; (207) 326–8616 or (800) 845–1701; fax (207) 326–9382

WEB SITE: www.pentagoet.com

ROOMS: 15, plus 1 suite; all with private bath; suite with fireplace. No-smoking inn.

RATES: $95 to $215 BP.

OPEN: May 1 to November 1.

FACILITIES AND ACTIVITIES: Dinner, pub. Nearby: Fishing, sailing, golf, tennis, kayaking, nature trails.

*T*he Pentagöet is an 1894 Victorian charmer on the shore of beautiful Penobscot Bay, complete with turret, gables, and a wraparound porch with wicker chairs and a swing. The window boxes overflow with flowers. Fresh flowers are also for sale, but typical of the warmth here, you buy on the honor system, depositing your money in a box on the porch.

As you come in the door of the main inn, there is a sitting room to the left with a wood-burning stove and a window in the turret looking down on the

harbor. To the right is a pub with a small, cozy oak bar; wingback chairs; and Empire-style sofas. The walls are filled with an eclectic floor-to-ceiling mix of vintage photos, paintings, and memorabilia from the innkeepers' travels abroad.

The guest rooms are lovely. Some have little alcoves with views of the town and harbor. Some are small and have odd shapes, but this goes well with a country inn. Seven rooms have king-size beds.

The building next door, Ten Perkins Street, is also part of the inn and is more than 200 years old. I stayed in the suite here, and it's a gem with a working fireplace. Wood is supplied so that you can light yourself a fire if there's a chill in the air.

The breakfast is hearty, often with Maine blueberries picked fresh at a local farm that morning. All the baking is done by the owner, Julie, who had an acclaimed pastry shop in Philadelphia for twenty years. Coffee is set outside your door in the morning, a very nice way to start the day.

Good food is served in an intimate dining room, in the pub, or on the porch. The inn offers nightly suppers featuring local seafood and New England specialties. The lobster pie and saffron-scented Spanish seafood stew are two favorites.

Castine is the Maine of your imagination. It was founded as a French trading colony in 1613, nine years before the Pilgrims landed at Plymouth. The town square is lined with stately elms and classic New England buildings straight from a Norman Rockwell drawing. Five times a day you can hear the whistle from the steamboat *Laurie Ellen* that serves the town, and the sound of bell buoys lulls you to sleep.

HOW TO GET THERE: Take Interstate 95 to Augusta; take Route 3 east to the coast. Connect with Route 1 at Belfast and follow Route 1 north to Bucksport. Two miles beyond, turn right onto Route 175. Take Route 175 to Route 166, which takes you into Castine.

The Lucerne Inn
Dedham, Maine 04429

INNKEEPERS: Bion and Durain Foster, Maria Bridges

ADDRESS/TELEPHONE: Route 1A (mailing address: RR 3, Box 540, Holden, ME 04429); (207) 843–5123 or (800) 325–5123; fax (207) 843–6138

WEB SITE: www.lucerneinn.com

ROOMS: 23, plus 8 suites; all with private bath, phone, TV, fireplace, and whirlpool tub.

RATES: $59 to $199 CP. Call for packages including meals.

OPEN: All year.

FACILITIES AND ACTIVITIES: Sunday brunch, dinner, full license, bar. Meeting room for up to 150 people; pool; golf.

The regal mountains around the Lucerne Inn make such a beautiful picture that you feel you could be in Switzerland, especially if you catch a special sunset. Situated on ten scenic acres overlooking Phillips Lake, the buildings were originally a farmhouse and stable but have been serving guests as an inn since 1814.

The location is convenient for touring. It's just forty-five minutes from Acadia National Park and Bar Harbor, ninety minutes from Camden, and twenty minutes from Ellsworth and Bangor, where you'll find theaters and shopping.

But why leave? Besides the lake, the inn also has an outdoor swimming pool, and a golf course is right here.

This is quite an inn. There are still reminders of its long history in the guest and common rooms, in the form of "distinguished" antiques. The rooms have everything you could want—fireplaces, telephones, televisions, private baths, heated towel bars, whirlpool tubs, wonderful views, comfortable beds, and nice furniture.

The dining room has a pleasant view of the lake to accompany the delightful food. A few of the appetizers are crab-stuffed mushrooms with lobster sauce, smoked seafood sampler, baked onion soup, and a soup du jour. One of the entrees that's a real beauty is pasta primavera—assorted vegetables simmered in cream and tossed with pasta. Lobster is prepared in a few different ways, salmon comes broiled, and the rack of lamb is stunning.

Dessert anyone? Come on up to see what they have.

HOW TO GET THERE: The inn is on Route 1A between Bangor and Ellsworth. Take Interstate 95 to exit 45A, just south of Bangor. Take Interstate 395 to Route 1A east. In about ten minutes you will see the inn on your right.

The Pilgrim's Inn
Deer Isle, Maine 04627

INNKEEPERS: Tony Lawless and Tina Oddleifson

ADDRESS/TELEPHONE: 20 Main Street; (888) 778–7505 or phone/fax, (207) 348–6615

WEB SITE: www.pilgrimsinn.com

ROOMS: 12 in main building, 3 cottages; all with private bath.

RATES: Rooms, $105 to $235 BP; cottages, $185 to $245 BP.

OPEN: Mid-May through mid-October; cottages available year-round, but no food or housekeeping provided.

FACILITIES AND ACTIVITIES: Bar and restaurant; frontage on millpond with chairs and kayaks. Wheelchair access to dining room. Nearby: Bicy-

cles, sailboats for charter, hiking, guided kayaking, boat to Isle au Haut (part of Acadia National Park). Golf or tennis at the island country club as the inn's guest.

In 1793 Ignatius Haskell built this lovely house, following the specifications of his wife, who demanded the luxuries of city living on their country estate. He had his own sawmill nearby and built the house out of northern pine. His handiwork can still be seen in the well-worn wooden floors and the walls in the common rooms and taprooms, giving the inn the warm ambience of another time.

All the guest rooms have a view of the pond or Northwest Harbor. The third floor has the best views and rooms with exposed beams that add to their charm.

An attached post-and-beam barn now serves as a cozy tavern for both inn guests and the public. Entrees focus on fresh local ingredients, especially the bountiful and delicious shellfish and lobster. There's a good mix of prices to fit a variety of budgets.

A full breakfast is served, including fruit, muffins, homemade granola, and a choice of two hot dishes.

Isle au Haut, part of Acadia National Park, is accessible by mail ferry from the town of Stonington, 6 miles from the inn. A visit there makes an excellent day trip.

Ginny's cottages are two very private separate units in a house on the grounds. Each one has a living and dining room, queen-size bedroom with cable TV, bath, and a deck with a view. Ginny's I has a full-size sleeper sofa, and Ginny's II has a queen-size sleeper plus a gas stove in the living room. These cottages are well suited for families with small children.

Rugosa Rose Cottage, new in 2002, includes a kitchenette, dining and sitting areas on the lower level, bedroom with gas fireplace, and bath on an upper level. French doors open to a private deck. It's a perfect hideaway for a special getaway for two.

HOW TO GET THERE: From Route 1 turn right after Bucksport onto Route 15 south. Follow signs as the road makes some twists and turns as it takes you down the Blue Hill peninsula, over the bridge to Little Deer Isle, and across a causeway. As you come into Deer Isle village, turn right onto Main Street. The inn is on the left.

Harraseeket Inn
Freeport, Maine 04032

INNKEEPERS: Nancy and Paul Gray

ADDRESS/TELEPHONE: 162 Main Street; (207) 865–9377 or (800) 342–6423

WEB SITE: www.stayfreeport.com

ROOMS: 84, all with private bath, TV, phone, free Wi-Fi, Internet access, and wheelchair accessibility; some with Jacuzzi, fireplace, woodstove, or wet bar; 4 specially equipped for the physically disabled; 9 extended-stay town houses.

RATES: $95 to $400, double occupancy; EP. Special packages available.

OPEN: All year.

FACILITIES AND ACTIVITIES: Lunch, high tea, dinner. Elevator; wheelchair access to dining room. Tavern, full liquor license, function rooms. Indoor pool. Nearby: Shopping, nature walks, fishing, boating, skiing.

BUSINESS TRAVEL: Conference rooms. All rooms with phone and wireless access for personal computers.

The inn is named for the Harraseeket River, which runs through the town and into Casco Bay. Built in 1850 in Colonial Revival style, the inn is the picture of elegance.

Freeport has long been known for L. L. Bean and a ton of other famous outlet stores, all of which are just a short walk from the inn. If shopping is not your thing, however, nearby are Casco Bay and South Freeport Harbor, where

you can rent a boat and go sailing or fishing. Nature lovers will be happy at the Audubon Sanctuary and Wolf Neck Woods State Park.

The rooms and suites are grand. There are canopied beds, antiques, telephones, cable television, and free wireless access for personal computers, should you need it. Twenty-four rooms have a Jacuzzi, sixteen have a fireplace, and one has a woodstove. You can also arrange a meeting or business conference at the inn, as there are function rooms overlooking the terrace that accommodate up to 250 people.

Your day begins with a superlative breakfast buffet. Early birds can have coffee at 6:00 A.M. It's nice to find an inn that serves lunch. I had crepes, and my friend had the chicken stir-fry. You can ask for a lunch basket to take along if you're headed out for the afternoon. The dinner menu is extensive, with lots of entrees, including "Tableside Classics" that are prepared and carved at your table. You can have a whole chicken, roast rack of baby lamb, chateaubriand, and various fruits of the sea. There's even two-tailed lobster. The maple-syrup-braised loin of pork is just one of the feasts from the land. Desserts—well, each one is better than the last. The chocolate fondue is an orgy. The Broad Arrow Tavern has its own lighter menu of burgers, pastas, lobster salad, sandwiches, and buckets of steamed clams. The inn also has a grand room-service menu.

This whole inn is just splendid. The innkeepers are native to Maine, and though this is a large inn, it has not lost its charm.

In the living room, where tea is served, is a player piano, seated at which is the largest stuffed polar bear I've ever seen. There's a lovely fireplace in here, too.

Mast Landing Sanctuary
off Bow Street

The Maine Audubon Society maintains this 150-acre preserve with field, forest, and tidal marsh habitats. This area was once logged for its tall pines that were used to make masts for the ships of the British Navy, thus the name. The sanctuary is open year-round from dawn to dusk. Self-guided trails take visitors past old apple orchards and millstreams, through woods and meadows. A 1-mile loop trail is a nice walk for brief visits. Enjoy the picnic area if you can stay a while. No fee is charged for parking. The sanctuary is on Upper Mast Landing Road, off Bow Street.

Or, if you want another kind of warmth, there's an indoor pool kept at a toasty eighty-five degrees.

HOW TO GET THERE: Take Interstate 295 north to exit 22 to Freeport. The inn is on Main Street.

The Oxford House Inn
Fryeburg, Maine 04037

INNKEEPERS: John and Phyllis Morris

ADDRESS/TELEPHONE: 548 Main Street (Route 302); (207) 935–3442 or (800) 261–7206

WEB SITE: www.oxfordhouseinn.com

ROOMS: 4, all with private bath, wireless Internet, and cable TV.

RATES: $110 to $175 BP.

OPEN: All year.

FACILITIES AND ACTIVITIES: Dinner. Lounge with a full license. Nearby: Canoeing, swimming, fishing, antiquing, hiking, biking, skiing, snow-shoeing, scenic drives, outlet shopping.

This stately Mission-style building was designed as a private country home in 1913 by a famous Maine architect, John Calvin Stevens. The Morrises converted it into an inn in 1983, keeping all the original period charm.

The rooms are charming and very restful. The names of rooms come from the original blueprints. Perhaps you'll sleep in the Sewing Room or the old-fashioned heated Porch Room. All have antiques and king- or queen-size bed, and three rooms offer views of the White Mountains.

At dinnertime you'll delight as I did in the outstanding and creative dishes offered on the menu. House pâté of the day may be how you'd like to begin your meal, or maybe Maine crab chowder will catch your eye. Turkey Waldorf is an entree you'll not find in many places. It is medallions of turkey breast sautéed with apples and walnuts, then splashed with applejack and cream. Scallops l'orange, served in puff pastry, is another treat. Or how about veal Oxford? Very nice indeed. It's good and different. Needless to say, the desserts are all homemade.

On those cold Maine nights, the tavern, known as the Granite Room Lounge, is very inviting. It has a television, books, and a woodstove.

In warm weather the front porch is used for dining. I really like porches, and this one is a beauty. There is also a glassed-in heated porch at the back of the house with gorgeous views. You can sit here and look out at the beautiful surrounding mountains or the lovely gardens. Peace and quiet are at hand.

HOW TO GET THERE: The inn is on Route 302 in Fryeburg, 8 miles east of North Conway, New Hampshire, and 45 miles west of Portland.

Le Domaine

Hancock, Maine 04640

INNKEEPER: Beth Clark

ADDRESS/TELEPHONE: 1513 Route 1 (mailing address: P.O. Box 519);
(207) 422-3395, (207) 422-3916, or (800) 554-8498; fax (207) 422-3252

WEB SITE: www.ledomaine.com

ROOMS: 3 rooms, 3 suites; all with private bath; 2 suites with balcony.

RATES: Rooms, $200 BP; suites, $295 BP; MAP available.

OPEN: June to end of October.

FACILITIES AND ACTIVITIES: Bar, lounge. Badminton, walking trails.
Nearby: Boating, swimming, tennis, golf, fishing, hiking, Acadia National
Park.

Hidden behind the hedges on busy Route 1 is a lovely surprise, an authentic bit of France in Downeast Maine. The inn is best known for its restaurant, but upstairs are charming rooms named after towns in Provence—Sault, Arles, Les Baux, Mausanne, and St. Remy—and decorated in the style of each village, with Provençale furnishings, antiques, and art. Egyptian cotton bedding and goose-down pillows make for a luxurious feel, and guests are pampered with breakfast in bed, on their private balcony overlooking the gardens, or seated in the garden. Freshly baked croissants, French butter, and homemade honey, jam, and jellies are a special treat in any setting.

The menu changes with the seasons. Pâté de foie maison and *saumon fumé d'Ecosse* may be among the appetizers. Move on to dishes such as coquilles St. Jacques Provençale or steak bordelaise. I can't say enough about this food; it

is divine. The country French cuisine has been lauded in many publications. The inn also has an award-winning wine cellar.

There are many things to do in the area, including exploring Acadia National Park. But you may be content roaming the inn's many acres, where a wooded trail leads from the lawn to a secluded pond, or maybe just settling into a wicker chair in the lovely garden. It's hard to imagine a nicer oasis.

HOW TO GET THERE: The inn is about 9 miles above Ellsworth on Route 1.

The Kennebunk Inn
Kennebunk, Maine 04043

INNKEEPERS: Shanna Katherine Horner O'Hea and Brian O'Hea

ADDRESS/TELEPHONE: 45 Main Street; (207) 985–3351; fax (207) 985–8865

WEB SITE: www.thekennebunkinn.com

ROOMS: 19, plus 3 suites with kitchens; all with private bath, cable TV, free wireless Internet, phone, and air-conditioning.

RATES: $85 to $120 CP; MAP available.

OPEN: All year.

FACILITIES AND ACTIVITIES: Dinner in Tavern daily, lunch and dinner in dining room Wednesday through Saturday, Sunday brunch. Nearby: Beaches, museums, shopping, performing arts, cross-country skiing.

This venerable clapboard inn located in the very heart of town began its life in 1799 as a private residence, which it remained until the original house and barn were connected in 1920 and it began a new life as an inn. A brand new chapter in this long history began in 2003 when Brian and Shanna O'Hea took over the reins. The couple, who met when both were students at the Culinary Institute of America, were married in 2001 after each had honed professional skills through assignments from Boston to London. Happily for guests, their goal as innkeepers is to share their passion for good food, both in the elegant dining room and the more casual pub-style Tavern. Their American bistro fare draws on the freshest local ingredients and features fresh twists on old favorites.

In the main dining room, Academe, you can sample such dishes as black truffle and potato ravioli, roasted game hen with duck sausage and apple stuffing, or seared sea scallops over saffron risotto. Desserts are always my weakness, and these were irresistible, from the praline crème brûlée to Shanna's great 3-D Peanut Butter Chocolate Volcano, a chocolate molten cake

with peanut butter three ways—truffle, ice cream, and brittle. The Tavern menu includes salads, burgers, wraps, quesadillas, pizza, and other lighter fare. In summer, dining on the brick patio is delightful.

Rooms in the inn are country fresh, with beams, four-posters, wing chairs, and cozy quilts. Many of the bathrooms feature antique claw-foot tubs.

When you want to be sociable, the sitting room is waiting with a TV, VCR, and games. And when you want to wander, tempting beaches and the many shops of Kennebunkport are just a short drive away.

HOW TO GET THERE: Take exit 3 from Interstate 95 (the Maine Turnpike) to Kennebunk. The inn is right on the town's Main Street.

The Captain Fairfield Inn
Kennebunkport, Maine 04046

INNKEEPERS: Leigh and Bob Blood

ADDRESS/TELEPHONE: 8 Pleasant Street (mailing address: P.O. Box 3089); (207) 967-4454 or (800) 322-1928

WEB SITE: www.captainfairfield.com

ROOMS: 9, all with private bath, telephone, clock/CD player, TV/DVD, wireless Internet, hair dryer, and air-conditioning; many with fireplace.

RATES: $110 to $325, BP and afternoon refreshments, beach passes, and towels.

OPEN: All year.

FACILITIES AND ACTIVITIES: Breakfast only full meal served. Guest refrigerator, off-street parking. Dataport and fax available. Nearby: Ocean, shopping, restaurants, fishing, art galleries.

This inn—an 1813 Federal mansion—was given as a wedding present to James Fairfield and his bride from his father-in-law. They knew how to do things right in those days! Today the inn is listed on the National Register of Historic Places. The gardens are striking, and so are the towering trees. There are numerous other lovely captains' houses in the neighborhood, and you are within walking distance of town, the water, shops, and restaurants.

There's an inviting living room with a wood-burning fireplace and tons of comfort. The captain's portrait hangs over the mantle. The guest rooms are furnished with antiques and period furniture, including four-poster and canopy queen- and king-size beds. All rooms have private bathrooms, and most have fireplaces. All the amenities are there—plush mattresses, down comforters, generous towels, special soaps, bottled spring water, flat-screen TV, hair dryers, and garden flowers.

Breakfast, which is the only meal served here, is generous. Leigh and Bob bake all their own breads and pastries. Maine blueberry crepes, skillet frittatas with harvest vegetables, or eggs Benedict with their own special hollandaise

Christmas Prelude

Kennebunkport and its neighbors are delightful places to be at Christmastime. A ten-day holiday festival called Christmas Prelude (www.christmasprelude.com) is launched in the Kennebunks on the first weekend in December. If you are not in the spirit when you arrive, you will soon be caught up in the magic. A Christmas tree in Kennebunkport's historic Dock Square is decorated with the buoys of local lobstermen, and a community caroling event is held on the first Friday evening. Shopkeepers offer holiday refreshments, Santa arrives by lobsterboat, and the restaurants prepare special Prelude menus. Sleigh rides or hayrides carry revelers through the streets, pageants and concerts are offered at a variety of locations, and twinkling lights are draped on doorways, trees, and shop windows. Before the last two weeks of the Christmas rush begin, Kennebunkport reminds visitors of the true meaning of the holiday.

sauce are among the scrumptious choices. Breakfast is served at tables for two in a sunny dining room where antique carpets grace the beautiful hardwood floors and original art is on the wall.

This area offers many things to do—whale watching, coastline excursions, fishing, golf, shopping, art galleries, and beautiful sandy beaches. Go and enjoy.

HOW TO GET THERE: Take exit 25 off Interstate 95. Turn left onto Route 35 south, and follow it through Kennebunk to the intersection with Route 9. Go left onto Route 9, over the river and into Dock Square. Turn right onto Ocean Avenue. In 5 blocks go left just past the village green onto the one-way street. The inn is 1 block ahead on your right.

Captain Lord Mansion
Kennebunkport, Maine 04046

INNKEEPERS: Bev Davis and husband Rick Lichfield

ADDRESS/TELEPHONE: Ocean Avenue (mailing address: P.O. Box 800); (207) 967-3141 or (800) 522-3141; fax (207) 967-3172

WEB SITE: www.captainlord.com

ROOMS: 16 luxury rooms, all with private bath, phone, gas fireplace, CD player, antique four-poster bed; 7 with whirlpool tub; 5 with massage shower.

RATES: $149 to $499 BP.

OPEN: All year.

FACILITIES AND ACTIVITIES: Breakfast only full meal served. Afternoon tea. BYOB. Gift shop. Nearby: Perkins Cove and Rachel Carson Wildlife Refuge.

BUSINESS TRAVEL: Conference room. All rooms with phone, Wi-Fi.

Kennebunkport abounds with mansions built by wealthy sea captains, but none to match this three-story beauty with a cupola, built in 1812 by Nathaniel Lord, the owner of the ships many of those captains sailed. Grand in scale and lavishly furnished, the inn celebrated its twenty-fifth birthday in 2003 under gracious owners Rick and Bev, who have made it the epitome of luxury, especially with more than a million dollars' worth of improvements in the last few years. Every room has a gas fireplace and antique four-poster beds, and lavish new furnishings have made each worthy of a page in *House Beautiful*. Additions include antique pedestal vanities, double whirlpool tubs, massage showers, heated bathroom floors, CD players, and, for deluxe rooms, a small refrigerator stocked with soft drinks and juices.

There is a decor for every taste. Hesper is one of my favorites, with a colonial feel, a fishnet canopy bed piled high with pillows, loveseat and wing chair in attractive prints, lots of folk art touches, and a charming wallpaper border of an old New England village. Mary Lord, a striking room with a filmy canopy over the bed, has a sophisticated beige and black color scheme and leopard accents; Excelsior is formal, furnished in Queen Anne and Chippendale; and Cactus has more of a country French feel with a pastel color scheme, floral prints on the bed, and pink pouf shades at the windows.

Some of the original Lord furniture is in the house. For example, the handsome dining-room table with carved feet and chairs belonged to Nathaniel Lord's grandson, Charles Clark, and is dated 1880.

A three-story suspended elliptical staircase, a gold vault, and double Indian shutters are more wonderful things to be found in the inn. There are fireplaces, Oriental rugs, old pine wide-board floors, and claw-footed tables. It's almost a comfortable museum and thus is not well suited to children under twelve. Rick knows the history of the house and loves to tell it.

Breakfast is the only meal served in the inn, but what a meal and what a setting! Two long tables in the kitchen are set with Wedgwood blue. There are two stoves in here side by side, a new one and a coal one about a hundred years old. The breakfast bell is a hundred-year-old chime. The menu, served family style, starts with fresh fruits, yogurt, muesli cereal, and baked goodies, followed by the entree of the day, which might be an asparagus soufflé, Maine blueberry pancakes, or Belgian waffles, all served with sausage or bacon.

Want more? Gourmet coffees, Swiss water decaf, chocolate cappuccino— or how about Snickerdoodle? Have fun.

This is a bring-your-own-bottle inn, and from the scenic cupola on its top to the parlors on the first floor, you will find many great places to enjoy a drink.

HOW TO GET THERE: Go through the toll booth onto Maine Turnpike Interstate 95 to exit 3, Kennebunk/Kennebunkport. Turn left onto Route 35 south and follow it about $1^{2}/_{10}$ miles to a set of lights, cross over Route 1, and bear right to continue on 35S/9A for another $3^{1}/_{2}$ miles into Lower Kennebunk Village. At the next set of lights, turn left onto Route 9 east and proceed over the drawbridge into Kennebunkport. At the monument, turn right onto Ocean Avenue (approximately $^{2}/_{10}$ mile), and then turn left onto Green Street. The mansion is on the left. Park behind the building and take the brick walk to the office.

The Kennebunkport Inn
Kennebunkport, Maine 04046

INNKEEPER: Debbie Lennon

ADDRESS/TELEPHONE: One Dock Square (mailing address: P.O. Box 111); (207) 967–2621 or (800) 248–2621

WEB SITE: www.kennebunkportinn.com

ROOMS: 50, all with private bath, TV, air-conditioning, and phone.

RATES: $109 to $339 EP; many packages offered.

OPEN: All year.

FACILITIES AND ACTIVITIES: Breakfast and dinner served daily May through October. Tavern with entertainment in season; pool. Nearby: Beaches, boating, fishing, tennis, golf, shopping.

Right in the middle of everything in Kennebunkport is this charmer, built in the 1890s by a wealthy coffee merchant, one Burleigh S. Thompson. An inn since 1926, it is filled with warmth and charm.

The elegant Mansion Rooms are the most spacious, done in colonial style with floral and flame-stitch fabrics, four-poster beds, and gas fireplaces. Federal Rooms are also pleasant, decorated in deep jewel colors, with florals and lots of antiques and good reproductions. Rooms in the River House, a 1930s annex, are smaller but still have a cozy feel.

The inn's restaurant, the Port Tavern Steakhouse, specializes in grilled steaks and seafood. In summer you can have your dinner on the lovely outside terrace, and in cooler weather each of the two dining rooms has a fireplace for chilly evenings. The lively Port Tavern offers live entertainment in summer and live piano music from late June to October.

Breakfasts at the inn are among the most popular in town, featuring good things like waffles, fluffy omelets, and fresh baked breads.

Born to shop? Well, all the fine shops of Kennebunkport are steps away, offering antiques, arts and crafts, clothing, and lots more. Maybe you'll find a special treasure for your home, like the cut lampshades I bought here a few years ago and still treasure.

HOW TO GET THERE: Take the Maine Turnpike to exit 2, Wells. Go left at the light after the toll booth and follow to the Route 1 intersection. Turn left, north, onto Route 1 and continue for 2 miles to Route 9. Make a right and drive for 6 miles, over the bridge into Kennebunkport and Dock Square. The inn is straight ahead on the left about a block farther. Make a left into the driveway.

Old Fort Inn
Kennebunkport, Maine 04046

INNKEEPERS: David and Sheila Aldrich; Tom and Shania Hennessey

ADDRESS/TELEPHONE: P.O. Box M; (207) 967–5353 or (800) 828–3678; fax (207) 967–4547

WEB SITE: www.oldfortinn.com

ROOMS: 16, all with private bath, air-conditioning, TV, phone, and enclosed wet bar; 6 with Jacuzzi, 6 with gas fireplaces.

RATES: $175 to $395 BP.

OPEN: Mid-April to mid-December.

FACILITIES AND ACTIVITIES: Breakfast only meal served. BYOB. Swimming pool, tennis, antiques shop, 1 block from the ocean.

Here's a charming hideaway on fifteen treed acres, with its own pool and tennis court. When you enter, you are in an excellent antiques shop. Next you are in a huge living room with a covered

porch that overlooks the heated swimming pool. This is a comfortable living room with a fireplace, a super spot to curl up and read a book.

The rooms are charming, furnished with antiques and canopy or four-poster beds. When you arrive, you find fresh baked cookies and Belgian chocolates in your room, a lovely welcome.

The breakfast buffet is superb. You can pick and choose from all types of teas and juices, fresh fruit, baked breads, croissants, sticky buns, and hot entrees. The hot dishes, such as quiche or waffles, change daily.

In the afternoon, refreshments are served in the enclosed porch.

The inn provides a laundry. Until you have been on the road a week or so, you do not know how convenient such a facility is.

The Carriage House has very interesting shadow boxes displaying nineteenth-century clothing. The living room over here is so comfortable and quiet. On the other hand, in the main house's living room you must meet Walter, who "plays" the piano.

HOW TO GET THERE: Take Interstate 95, the Maine Turnpike, to Kennebunkport, exit 25. Turn left on Route 35 for 5½ miles. Go left at the Route 9 intersection, into Dock Square; take the first right along Ocean Avenue for ⁹⁄₁₀ mile. Take a left in front of the Colony Hotel, then go right at the T junction. Follow signs for ³⁄₁₀ mile to the inn.

The Tides Inn by the Sea
Kennebunkport, Maine 04046

INNKEEPERS: Marie Henriksen and Kristin Blomberg

ADDRESS/TELEPHONE: 252 Goose Rocks Beach; (207) 967–3757

WEB SITE: www.tidesinnbythesea.com

ROOMS: 22, plus 3 suites; all with private bath.

RATES: $195 to $325 CP. Family rooms, $325 CP.

OPEN: Mid-May to Columbus Day weekend.

FACILITIES AND ACTIVITIES: Continental breakfast, dinner, and drinks at the inn's Belvidere Club overlooking the ocean. Nearby: Ocean, fishing, boating, harbor cruises.

*L*ocation, location, location. This inn certainly is in a beautiful one. A Victorian inn across the street from the white sands of Goose Rocks Beach, it looks over the sea. Since its beginning at the turn of the twentieth century, it has hosted many ocean lovers, including Teddy Roosevelt and Sir Arthur Conan Doyle, the creator of Sherlock Holmes.

The inn's brochure describes it well: "Wake to the plaintive cries of sea-gulls; stroll miles of sandy beaches, and search for shells; doze to the sounds of the surf. You won't find televisions or telephones in the rooms (both are found in the front parlor) and you won't find rooms that look like any other."

The rooms for the most part are small; so what? In this area, who wants to stay inside? Almost all have a view of the Atlantic Ocean. The inn also has very spacious oceanfront suites with kitchens that rent by the week.

When you enter the inn, the reception desk is on the left, and on the right is a really lived-in living room with a television, magazines, and comfort. The

Seashore Trolley Museum

Take a trip back in time at the Seashore Trolley Museum (207–967-2800), which houses a collection of more than forty fully restored trolleys, streetcars, buses, and subway cars. Board an open-air car for a ride on the old Atlantic Shore interurban trolley line that linked Kennebunkport to Kittery and Biddeford. Visit the restoration shop and watch artisans and mechanics work on the vehicles stored in the car barns. Enjoy a treat at the snack bar or buy a souvenir at the gift shop. Children will especially enjoy the chance to sound the motorman's whistle or even operate the car itself. Special events are held on weekends and holidays throughout the season, from early May through early October. Admission is charged, but you can ride all day if you want to. The museum is on Log Cabin Road, about 3 miles from Dock Square.

food is very good at the inn's highly rated Belvidere Club. Regional appetizer specialties include pan-sautéed crab cakes, homemade she-crab soup, and steamed mussels simmered in white wine and garlic. The entrees vary from homemade meat loaf to rack of lamb to a shellfish cioppino with shrimp, scallops, mussels, and clams in a homemade red sauce, with a nest of pasta. Sip a cocktail on the veranda and enjoy the intoxicating views of Goose Rocks Beach.

Kristin and Marie, a mother-daughter team, have been innkeeping for more than thirty years, and they've gotten it down to perfection.

The inn is a short ride from the center of Kennebunkport, where there are sailboat charters, harbor cruises, fishing, tennis, and more. Timber Island, just off-shore, is for exploring. You can see harbor seals basking on the rocks at Goose Rocks. Do bring your camera.

HOW TO GET THERE: From the Maine Turnpike take exit 3. Follow Route 35 to Route 9 through Dock Square. Follow Route 9 east for 3 miles, to Cape Porpoise. Turn left on Route 9, continue 2½ miles, and turn right at "Clockfarm" onto Dyke Road to its end. Turn left to the inn.

White Barn Inn 📱
Kennebunkport, Maine 04046

INNKEEPER: Roderick Anderson; Laurie J. Bongiorno, owner

ADDRESS/TELEPHONE: 37 Beach Avenue (mailing address: P.O. Box 560-C); (207) 967-2321; fax (207) 967-1100

WEB SITE: www.whitebarninn.com

ROOMS: 16, plus 9 suites and 3 cottages; all with private bath, phone, robes, flat-screen TV, DVD player; some with CD player, VCR, Jacuzzi, and fireplace.

RATES: $325 to $850 CP, afternoon tea. Packages available.

OPEN: All year.

FACILITIES AND ACTIVITIES: Dinner, full license. Outdoor heated pool, boat trips on 44-foot Hinckley power boat, spa, meeting room, bicycles. Nearby: Beach, shops, galleries, golf, tennis.

BUSINESS TRAVEL: Located 25 minutes from Portland. Writing desk and phone in room; conference room; fax and audiovisual equipment available.

A pre–Civil War farmhouse and its signature white barn have been transformed into this lovely inn. It is just a short walk from the beach and the charming village of Kennebunkport, with its colorful shops, galleries, and boutiques. When you consider the inn's

exquisite food and its warmth and graciousness, it comes as no surprise that it is the only Maine member inn of *Relais et Châteaux,* the exclusive worldwide association of luxury inns.

Hospitality is evident throughout the inn. When you enter your room, you find a basket of fruit, flowers, luxurious toiletries, and a comfortable robe. Talk about thoughtful, when your bed is turned down at night, amenities include a little portable book light so that you can read without disturbing a partner.

Twelve rooms in the main inn have hand-painted furniture, New England period furnishings, and coordinated bed and wall coverings. One junior suite offers a whirlpool bath and a steam shower. The carriage house is more luxurious, home to six junior suites with king-size beds, working fireplaces, rain-style showers, and Jacuzzi tubs. Even more spacious are the suites in Mays Cottage, featuring separate living rooms with a double-sided fireplace and marble bathrooms with whirlpool baths for two and separate steam showers.

If money is no object, the waterfront cottages offer private entrances, river views, and waterfront patios. Since they are located about ⁷⁄₁₀ mile from the inn, guests receive a breakfast basket delivered to the door.

The breakfast room is large and cheerfully decorated with flower arrangements. The main dining room is in the barn, along with a lovely lounge and piano bar. Candlelight, linen, and soft music are nice touches.

When I think about the food, I want to go back for more. The restaurant has received five diamonds from AAA and five stars from the Mobil guide; it's one of only fourteen restaurants in the country earning Mobil's highest rating. The menu changes weekly in order to offer the freshest and finest of ingredients. I know the greens are fresh—I watched them being picked. Soups are amazing: A light cream soup of potato, leek, and watercress is scented with thyme; lobster minestrone comes with black beans, roasted tomatoes, olive oil croutons, and a bacon pistou.

The appetizer of homemade ravioli is glorious. Dinner choices the week I was here included pan-seared striped bass with sautéed eggplant, Niçoise olives, and basil oil in a roasted tomato broth. The veal rib chop came grilled with glazed baby turnips, Swiss chard, garlic-roasted Parisienne potatoes, and an herb sauce. You can guess there are more seafood offerings from this Maine inn—lobster, halibut, and salmon were also on the menu.

No matter what size your party—two or eight—when your dinner is ready, that number of waiters arrives to stand behind each diner's chair and on cue serves everyone simultaneously. What a sight.

After dinner, you can relax in the living room with a glass of port or brandy, a book from the inn's well-filled bookshelves, or one of the many current magazines. Or you could be ambitious and go for a ride along the beach on one of the inn's bicycles. I took one and sure did enjoy it.

The pool area is beautifully appointed, and it is wonderful to be able to order lunch right at poolside. But if you really want to feel pampered, order a poolside massage. It will make your day.

HOW TO GET THERE: From the Maine Turnpike take exit 3 to Kennebunk. Follow Route 35 south 7 miles to Kennebunkport, then continue through the traffic light onto Beach Avenue. The inn is in ¼ mile, on the right.

The Inn on Winter's Hill
Kingfield, Maine 04947

INNKEEPERS: Richard and Diane Winnick and Carolyn Rainaud

ADDRESS/TELEPHONE: 33 Winter Hill Street; (207) 265-5421 or (800) 233-9687; fax (207) 265-5424

WEB SITE: www.wintershill.com

ROOMS: 20, in 2 buildings; all with private bath, phone, coffee machines, and cable TV; 1 specially equipped for the physically disabled.

RATES: $85 to $150 EP. Golf, skiing, and fly-fishing packages available.

OPEN: All year.

FACILITIES AND ACTIVITIES: Dinner for public by reservation. Wheelchair access to dining room. Bar, lounge, meeting and banquet facilities. Hot tub, indoor and outdoor swimming pools, tennis, cross-country skiing. Nearby: Downhill skiing, ice skating, hunting, fishing, hiking, golf, canoeing, Stanley Steamer Museum, dogsled rides.

The Inn on Winter's Hill, located in the midst of western Maine's Bigelow, Sugarloaf, and Saddleback Mountains, sits on top of a six-acre hill on the edge of town. This Neo-Georgian manor house was designed by the Stanley (steam car) brothers and built at the turn of the twentieth century for Amos Greene Winter as a present for his wife, Julia. It is listed on the National Register of Historic Places. Today it is owned by a brother and sister who are doing a great job as innkeepers, following a longtime tradition of casual elegance and warm hospitality.

Accommodations are varied and range from the turn-of-the-twentieth-century luxury rooms in the inn to the modern rooms in the restored barn. Every one is very comfortable, with nice bathrooms, wonderful views, cable television, and telephone.

Open during the busy ski season, Julia's Restaurant is elegant, and the food served here is excellent. The night I was here, for appetizers I had crackers and garlic cheese spread and pineapple wrapped in bacon. My garden salad with house dressing was followed by a light sorbet and then Sole Baskets, which were superb. Salmon in phyllo, Atlantic salmon fillet baked in phyllo with a Parmesan-cheese cream sauce, is a special dish. Desserts are grand.

In the lounge area is an old piano that once came by oxcart from Boston for Julia Winter. It took two and a half months to arrive.

Whatever the season, there is much to do up here. Winter brings cross-country skiing from the door, and downhill skiing at Sugarloaf is minutes

away. Hunting, fishing, canoeing, and hiking along the Appalachian Trail welcome outdoors people in the other seasons. If those do not appeal to you, try the pool table or turn on the TV in the bar area. All is watched over by Ming Lee and Kismet, the Shih Tzu inn dogs.

HOW TO GET THERE: Kingfield is halfway between Boston and Quebec City, and the Great Lakes area and the Maritimes. Take the Maine Turnpike to the Belgrade Lakes exit in Augusta. Follow Highway 27 through Farmington to Kingfield. The inn is on a small hill near the center of town.

The Newcastle Inn
Newcastle, Maine 04553

INNKEEPERS: Peter and Laura Barclay

ADDRESS/TELEPHONE: 60 River Road; (207) 563-5685 or (800) 832-8669; fax (207) 563-6877

WEB SITE: www.newcastleinn.com

ROOMS: 15, including 4 suites; all with private bath; some with Jacuzzi or soaking tub, fireplace and/or deck with river views. Inn suitable for older children.

RATES: $125 to $295 BP. Packages available.

OPEN: All year.

FACILITIES AND ACTIVITIES: Dinner served daily (except Monday) from May through October and on Friday and Saturday from November through April. Pub. Nearby: Walking trails, beaches, bicycling, whale-watching, boating.

The Newcastle Inn is in the lovely Boothbay region, only 12 miles from Boothbay Harbor and 16 miles to Pemaquid, with its famous lighthouse, said to be the most photographed lighthouse in Maine, as well as historic Fort William Henry, and a sandy beach.

The beautiful flower known as the lupine is the signature of the inn. A native to this part of Maine, it blooms in early summer, filling the garden with color. Be sure to see the watercolor painting of lupines on the wall in the pub; it was specially commissioned by the innkeepers. The inn's 40-foot terrace overlooks the gardens and the Damariscotta River, a wonderful view. Or you can settle into a chair in the backyard and watch the boats come and go from the harbor.

A delicious prix fixe five-course dinner is served from Tuesday through Saturday in Lupines, the inn restaurant. Every night feels like a party when the

evening begins at 6:00 P.M. with everyone gathering in the common rooms for cocktails and complimentary hors d'oeuvres.

The menu changes daily depending on what is in season. Many of the ingredients come from local farmers, fishermen, and cheesemakers. You might start with famous Damariscotta River oysters or heirloom tomato gazpacho in summer; pumpkin soup with crispy lobster cake in the fall. Entrees always include a meat, fish, and fowl choice, and there is almost always Maine lobster. For dessert, the house specials are the warm chocolate torte and a seasonal fruit turnover served with homemade ice cream. The pub is open nightly and has a good selection of wines from around the world.

The inn also serves a multicourse breakfast. When the weather is cooperative, both breakfast and cocktails are twice as nice served on the terrace.

Each of the inn's rooms is special. All are named after the lighthouses on the coast of Maine. Many have a canopied four-poster bed, and some have a fireplace. The newest suite offers a king-size bed, a soaking tub for two, and a fireplace in the sitting room. Every night (in season) guests are left a gift of Godiva chocolates as part of the inn's turndown service.

The inn's motto: "Come as our guests and leave as our friends."

HOW TO GET THERE: About 7 miles north of Wiscasset, on Route 1, turn onto River Road in Newcastle. The inn is ½ mile down, on the right.

The Bradley Inn
at Pemaquid Point 📱
New Harbor, Maine 04554

INNKEEPERS: Beth and Warren Busteed

ADDRESS/TELEPHONE: 3063 Bristol Road; (207) 677–2105 or (800) 942–5560; fax (207) 677–3367

WEB SITE: www.bradleyinn.com

ROOMS: 12, plus 1 cottage, 3 rooms and 1 suite in carriage house; all with private bath. Rooms with phone and TV; some with gas fireplace.

RATES: $155 to $295 BP. Special packages available.

OPEN: All year except Christmas Eve and Christmas Day.

FACILITIES AND ACTIVITIES: Dinner. Bicycles and helmets. Wedding facilities. Nearby: Ocean, tennis, golf.

BUSINESS TRAVEL: Phone with private line in room; conference facilities.

*P*emaquid, a Native American word meaning "long finger," is an appropriate name for the point of land that extends farther into the Atlantic Ocean than any other on the rugged Maine coast. What a wonderful ride it is out here! And once you arrive, the terrain is breath-

taking. You're just a short walk from the Pemaquid Lighthouse or the beach with its lovely white sand. In the nearby seaside village of New Harbor, you can watch the working boats. Fort William Henry is close by. I drove around the point, parked my car, and watched the surf beating on the rocks below. Then I scrambled down to the water's edge and back up. It was a bit scary but well worth it.

The inn is more than one hundred years old. There's an attractive living room with a fireplace and a baby grand piano. On Friday and Saturday there is live piano music. A folk singer also sometimes performs on Friday nights. The taproom has a long, custom-made bar of Portland granite with a mahogany rail.

The Bradley Inn Restaurant puts you in a nautical mood with ship models and a huge ship's wheel. Some of the appetizers are chilled Spiney Creek oysters and smoked salmon terrine. Entrees may be filet mignon, Maine lobster, and sea scallops. The menu changes monthly. The wine list is impressive, and the dessert that won my vote was Chocolate Decadence cake.

The rooms are charming and very comfortable. Rooms in the inn have four-poster cherry beds and New-England–style furnishings. You can choose your view, bay or garden. The cottage has heat and a wood-burning fireplace, a bedroom and bath, living room, screened-in porch, and a TV.

The carriage house, in the converted barn, has three first-floor rooms with gas fireplaces. On the second floor is a large suite with a kitchen, bedroom, bath, and a cathedral ceiling—a great place for children.

HOW TO GET THERE: Take the Maine Turnpike (Interstate 95) to the Falmouth–Route 1 interchange, exit 9. Take I-95 for 21 miles to Brunswick. Continue on Route 1 for 27 miles to Damariscotta, and from there follow Route 130 for 14 miles to the inn.

The Rangeley Inn
Rangeley, Maine 04970

INNKEEPERS: Dominique and Charles Goude

ADDRESS/TELEPHONE: P.O. Box 160; (207) 864–3341 or (800) 666–3687; fax (207) 864–3634

WEB SITE: www.rangeleyinn.com

ROOMS: 35 rooms in main inn, 15 in lakeside motel unit; all with private bath, TV; some with whirlpool; 4 units in motel with whirlpool and woodstove fireplace.

RATES: $84 to $109 EP; whirlpool/woodstove rooms, $129 EP.

OPEN: All year.

FACILITIES AND ACTIVITIES: Breakfast on weekends, dinner served Friday and Saturday; pub open Tuesday to Saturday. Wheelchair access to dining room, lounge, and public restroom. Many guided tours, including canoeing, moose safaris, fall foliage tours. Nearby: Fishing, boating, swimming, hiking, tennis, golf, hunting, skiing, snowmobiling.

What a wonderful trip it is just to get up here in this beautiful country. The first thing you see when you arrive at the inn is its welcoming long veranda that gives a nice old-fashioned feel of a long-ago summer hotel. The surroundings and the setting on the shore of Haley Pond have been pleasing vacationers since 1907.

The mood is informal and comfortable. The Tavern is a favorite gathering spot for its crackling fire and big-screen TV. You can enjoy a glass of wine, a Maine microbrew, or a cup of espresso. Dinner is served here beside the fireplace five nights a week, including a light menu of soups, salads, and sandwiches and a selection of entrees such as lasagna, steak, chicken dishes, and pasta.

On weekends, more formal fare is served in the lovely turn-of-the-twentieth-century dining room with a tin ceiling and glittering chandeliers. Menus might start with New England clam chowder or a crabmeat fondue. Chicken in a creamy champagne sauce, filet mignon, and a grilled lobster salad are among the favorite main courses. The wine menu boasts some seventy vintages.

Almost all of the rooms are carpeted, and all are very clean. Some of the baths have wonderful claw-footed tubs. A bath in an old tub is heavenly. You can be up to your neck in water. Try this in a modern one—no can do! Some rooms have only showers, and some have double whirlpool tubs.

The inn conducts all kinds of tours—a moose safari, gold panning, fall foliage tours, and a sunrise canoe trip that starts at 5:00 A.M. I'm told the sunrise is so beautiful it takes your breath away.

Spring brings superb fishing for brook trout and landlocked salmon. Some brooks are open only to fly fishing. Wildflowers and migrating birds are plentiful, so bring a camera and binoculars. Summer is ideal for boating, swimming, hiking, tennis, and golf. Fall brings spectacular foliage and hunting. Winter, of course, brings snow activities. Saddleback Mountain is nearby for downhill skiing, and cross-country skiing and snowmobiling are everywhere.

In any season of the year, Angel Falls, 20 miles away, is impressive and worth a visit. It is a 50- to 60-foot fall. Beautiful!

HOW TO GET THERE: From the Maine Turnpike take exit 12 at Auburn. Pick up Route 4 and follow it to Rangeley.

Capt. Lindsey House Inn 💚 📱
Rockland, Maine 04841

INNKEEPER: Drew Schultz; Capts. Ken and Ellen Barnes, owners

ADDRESS/TELEPHONE: 5 Lindsey Street; (207) 596-7950 or (800) 523-2145; fax (207) 596-2758

WEB SITE: www.lindseyhouse.com

ROOMS: 9 rooms, all with private bath, cable television, high-speed Internet access, telephone, dataports, air-conditioning, and hair dryer; 1 room specially equipped for the physically disabled. No-smoking inn.

RATES: $99 to $190 BP, afternoon tea. Packages available.

OPEN: All year.

FACILITIES AND ACTIVITIES: Available for small conferences and retreats. Nearby: Shopping districts of Rockland and Camden; the Farnsworth Museum; cross-country skiing; golfing at the Samoset golf course; six-day Windjammer cruises aboard the historic schooner *Stephen Taber* (22 passengers; no children under 14. For reservations call 800-999-7352).

BUSINESS TRAVEL: Access to fax machine and copying services; computer port in all rooms.

The Capt. Lindsey House Inn is located in Rockland's harbor district. Built in 1832, it was the town's first inn and remains one of its best. There is a story behind the inn's simple brick facade. You see, the bricks were hand-burned on site by the original owner. Imagine that! The inside is simply grand. The decor here is all in deep greens, wines, and

creams, with polished oak floors and rich Oriental rugs throughout. It is all tastefully decorated with fine antiques and family heirlooms.

The living room is quite inviting. It has a cozy fireplace and comfortable couches. There is also a library with a good selection of books. You're invited to take one home if you're still reading it when you're ready to leave.

Accommodations are bright and homey. Each bedroom has wide beds, warm down comforters, tapestry bedspreads, and good pillows. My room had two comfortable reading chairs and original hardwood floors. The large sea trunk at the foot of my bed has been in the Lindsey family since anyone can remember.

In the morning there is a gourmet breakfast buffet with homemade granola, muffins and croissants, fresh fruit, juices, and a variety of hot entrees. What a nice way to start the day. It is served in the cheerful oak-paneled breakfast room.

Afternoon tea is an especially nice feature of the inn. In the summer there is a lovely selection of iced tea, lemonade, tea cookies, and sweet breads. In the winter you'll find tea, hot chocolate, and an assortment of cookies.

I had a wonderful dinner with Ken and Ellen Barnes next door at the WaterWorks Pub and Restaurant. It is no longer owned by the Barnes family, but it remains a convenient choice for dinner.

Rockland is a picturesque area. Take a stroll around the lovely harbor, the home of most of Maine's windjammer fleet, and you'll see the schooner *Stephen Taber*. It was built in 1871 and is the oldest merchant sailing vessel in continuous service. Ken and Ellen serve as captain and cook on six-day sails from Windjammer Wharf. Ken tells wonderful sea stories. Ellen cooks all of the schooner's gourmet meals on a vintage woodstove in the galley. Maine blueberry pancakes with warm maple syrup is a popular breakfast choice. If you sign up for a sail, you'll even feast on steamed lobsters with all the fixings on a midweek stop on a deserted island. You can find Ellen's recipes in her book, *A Taste of the Taber*. The trips are very popular, so you must reserve early.

HOW TO GET THERE: From the south take the Maine Turnpike (Interstate 95) to exit 22, coastal Route 1, into Rockland. From the north take coastal Route 1 through Camden to Rockland. Call the inn for directions once you reach Rockland.

The Lawnmere Inn
Southport, Maine 04576

INNKEEPERS: Scott and Corinne Larson

ADDRESS/TELEPHONE: 65 Hendricks Hill Road (Route 27) (mailing address: P.O. Box 29); (207) 633–2544 or (800) 633–7645

WEB SITE: www.lawnmereinn.com

ROOMS: 32, all with private bath and phone; some with sundeck or air-conditioning; most with water view; 2 cottages, 1 guest house.

RATES: $89 to $189 BP; cottages and guest house weekly in season, $1,500 to $3,600.

OPEN: Mid-May to mid-October.

FACILITIES AND ACTIVITIES: Full breakfast, dinner, Sunday brunch. Bar, lounge, boat dock, free use of inn bicycles and kayaks. Nearby: Boothbay Harbor activities, boat tours, aquarium, theater, sport fishing, kayaking, hiking.

The inn is nicely located on the island of Southport, across a bridge from Boothbay Harbor. As you sit on its porch or relax in the Adirondack chairs on the lawn, you are watching the masts of the moored sailboats sway with the winds and tides.

A Victorian with sunny yellow shutters, this has been a summer hotel since 1898, the oldest operating inn in the Boothbay area. Since Scott and Corinne Larson took over in 2003, things are looking great, with the lobby and dining

room renovated and four guest rooms converted to two deluxe suites. All the common rooms and guest rooms have been refurbished.

Guest rooms are in the main inn and the adjacent east and west annex buildings. They are simply decorated in breezy country style. The one-bedroom Hideaway Cottage on the grounds is for romantics, with a wraparound porch overlooking the lawn and the water. Heartledge Cottage, located near the Southport Bridge, has spectacular views and nicely accommodates families with three bedrooms, a TV, and a washer-dryer. The Pine View Guest House can accommodate twelve, an ideal spot if you are planning a family get-together. Most of the rooms have water views, but note that the annex buildings are not air-conditioned, a consideration in midsummer.

Days begin with a big breakfast, usually featuring wild Maine blueberry pancakes or the inn's famous corned beef hash. The dinner menu offers lots of seafood choices, including the inn's lobster strudel and Zarzuela, a classic Spanish fish stew. If seafood isn't your favorite, you'll find plenty of choices, including pork tenderloin, duckling, steak, and a vegetarian dish such as wild mushroom ravioli.

The inn will loan you bicycles for exploring the countryside or a peddle into town, and kayaks if you want to get out on the water. But once you see the view, you may just decide to settle into an Adirondack chair on the lawn and watch the boats go by.

The nostalgic tall-masted sailing ships known as windjammers arrive in late June every year for the annual Windjammer Days, and I was lucky enough to be here then. What a treat!

HOW TO GET THERE: Take exit 22 from Interstate 95 onto Route 1. Just north of Wiscasset turn on Route 27 south. Go through Boothbay Harbor onto the island of Southport. The inn is on Route 27, 3/10 mile from the Southport Bridge.

The Claremont

Southwest Harbor, Maine 04679

INNKEEPER: John W. Madeira Jr.

ADDRESS/TELEPHONE: P.O. Box 137; (207) 244–5036 or (800) 244–5036; fax (207) 244–3512

WEB SITE: www.theclaremonthotel.com

ROOMS: 24 in the inn, 6 in Phillips House, 14 cottages; all with private bath, fireplace.

RATES: In season: $224 to $250 MAP, $183 to $196 BP; cottages $195 to $265 EP. No credit cards.

OPEN: Early June to mid-October. Cottages from mid-May to mid-October.

FACILITIES AND ACTIVITIES: Lunch in-season, dinner, full license. Tennis court, dock and moorings, croquet courts, badminton, bicycles, rowboats, library. Nearby: 3 golf courses, sailing, freshwater swimming, summer theater, Acadia National Park.

The Claremont has been a landmark on the shores of Somes Sound, the famous fjord of beautiful Mount Desert Island, since 1884. It was entered on the National Register of Historic Places in 1978. I saw an ad that describes the inn well: "For over 100 summers, upholding the traditions of hospitality and leisure on the Maine coast."

The inn offers lots of places to sit and relax. Both the comfortable living room and the library–game room have fireplaces, mighty welcome early or late in the season. If you look hard, you can find a television, but why bother, with all of this beauty around you?

Most activities center on the boathouse and waterfront, where a dock, float, and deep-water moorings are available for guests. The boathouse is open June 25 through August and is nice for lunch and predinner cocktails. What a view you get from here!

The guest rooms in the inn are comfortable and decorated simply. There are also two guest houses. The Phillips House has six large rooms, including a suite, a large living room with a fireplace, and a veranda with views. The Clark House has an additional suite. There are also fourteen housekeeping cottages, each of which has a Franklin stove or a stone fireplace. Most of these have views of the Sound.

The dining room is lovely, with candlelight, linens, fresh flowers, and attentive service. Gentlemen are asked to wear jackets. The food is excellent. Char-grilled steak, seafood paella, rack of lamb, and Maine crab cakes are among the choices, and, of course, Maine lobster. The sky-lit bar is a great place for a drink before or after dinner. An extensive breakfast buffet is put out daily, and afternoon tea is served in July and August.

The hotel hosts a popular lecture and musical recital series in summer, and the first week of August brings the annual Claremont Croquet Classic, a colorful competition of nine-wicker croquet. You can watch the action from a cozy chair at the bay window upstairs. Bring your binoculars, and you can also see all the way to Northeast Harbor, and a procession of lobster boats, sailboats, and yachts sailing by.

HOW TO GET THERE: Take the Maine Turnpike to Augusta, exit 15. Follow Route 3 east through Ellsworth to the Trenton Bridge and Mount Desert Island. Once over the bridge, take Route 102 to Southwest Harbor and follow signs to the Claremont.

The East Wind Inn
Tenants Harbor, Maine 04860

INNKEEPER: Tim Watts

ADDRESS/TELEPHONE: 149 Mechanic Street (mailing address: P.O. Box 149); (207) 372–6366 or (800) 241–VIEW

WEB SITE: www.eastwindinn.com

ROOMS: 26, including 3 suites and 4 apartments, in 3 buildings; 19 with private bath, all with phone and water views.

RATES: $89 to $139 BP; suites $149 to $189 BP; apartments and cottages $169 to $299.

OPEN: All year. From December 1 to April 1, the inn is available only to groups.

FACILITIES AND ACTIVITIES: Breakfast, Sunday brunch, dinner. Wheelchair access to dining room and meeting room. Lounge with full liquor license, meeting room, deep-water anchorage for boats, sailboat charter. Nearby: Golf, tennis, swimming, cross-country skiing.

The inn, built in 1890, stood vacant for twenty years. Tim, a native of the town, watched the old house deteriorate and dreamed of restoring it so others could share the charm of "the country of the pointed firs." He's been able to do just that.

Today you can sit on the wraparound porch of the inn and enjoy a view of Tenants Harbor worthy of a postcard. The inn is within walking distance of the village, where you will find a library, shops, post office, and churches.

The guest rooms are clean and simple, decorated in country style. Some have oak bureaus and Victorian side chairs, while others have brass beds. All the rooms have water views. The Ginny Wheeler cottage has three apartment accommodations, and there is another apartment in the Meeting House, all ideal for families. The Meeting House is nice for a relaxed conference or seminar.

The view and the food compete for your attention here. The dining room has a harbor view and is decorated with sailing ships, and the menu has marvelous specialties from the sea—fresh daily, as you'd expect. The Chadlery, on the inn's wharf, is a great place for fried clams or a lobster roll in a seaside setting.

HOW TO GET THERE: From Route 1, just east of Thomaston, take Route 131 south for 9½ miles to Tenants Harbor. Turn left at the post office and continue straight to the inn.

The Waterford Inne
Waterford, Maine 04088

INNKEEPERS: Barbara and Rosalie Vanderzanden

ADDRESS/TELEPHONE: 258 Chad Bourne Road (mailing address: P.O. Box 149); phone/fax (207) 583–4037

WEB SITE: www.waterfordinne.com

ROOMS: 8; 6 with private bath; some with fireplace.

RATES: $90 to $150 BP.

OPEN: All year.

FACILITIES AND ACTIVITIES: Breakfast, dinner. BYOB. Nearby: Hiking, hunting, fishing, swimming, bird-watching, golf, skiing.

This is a beautiful part of the world. It is secluded, quiet, and restful. The inn is a nineteenth-century farmhouse on a country lane with almost twenty-five acres of woods and fields. There is a fireplace in the parlor and a library full of books and good music for your relaxation. And when the weather is warm, you can while away your days in the rockers on the porch.

The mother and daughter who are the innkeepers bought the inn in 1978 and have done a masterful job of restoring and renovating it. There are antiques in all the rooms, nice wallpapers, and some stenciling. For your comfort there are electric blankets in the winter, and for your visual pleasure there are fresh flowers in the summer. The Appleyard room, the latest addition, is decorated in fresh aqua tones and has a cozy sitting alcove.

Rosalie, the mother, does the cooking. The dinner is a fixed price with one entree served each evening. She is a very good and creative chef. Some sample entrees: pork a la Normande with apples and Calvados or shrimp Pernod over angel-hair pasta. All baking is done right here, and all the vegetables are grown in the inn's garden. Barbara does the serving, and you may be seated at a table for four in the attractive dining room with a fireplace or in a secluded corner just for two.

The picture-perfect village of Waterford is tranquil, but if you want activity, you'll find plenty to do in the area. The western foothills of Maine offer hiking, fishing, swimming, and plenty of scenic drives, and in the winter downhill and cross-country skiing are nearby. If antiquing is your favorite sport, just ask the innkeepers. They can guide you to treasures in all directions.

HOW TO GET THERE: From Norway, Maine, take Route 118 west for 8 miles to Route 37. Turn left and go ½ mile to Chad Bourne Road. Turn right up the hill. The inn is in about ½ mile.

The Squire Tarbox Inn
Wiscasset, Maine 04578

INNKEEPERS: Roni and Mario DePietro

ADDRESS/TELEPHONE: 1181 Main Road, Westport Island; (207) 882–7693 or (800) 818–0626; fax (207) 882–7107

WEB SITE: www.squiretarboxinn.com

ROOMS: 11, all with private bath; 4 with fireplace.

RATES: $99 to $195 BP.

OPEN: April through December.

FACILITIES AND ACTIVITIES: Full license. Bicycles, rowboat, walking trail. Nearby: Beaches, harbors, museums, antiques shops.

This lovely old inn dates from 1763 and is listed on the National Register of Historic Places. Many of the original boards and timbers remain today, along with eight fireplaces.

The squire of the inn's name was Samuel Tarbox, a great-grandson of the first Tarbox who came to America from England in 1639. An enterprising entrepreneur with a thriving fishing and shipping business in the early 1800s, he was given the honorary title because of his wealth and influence in the community.

Accommodations in the Main House, where the squire lived, are formal with high ceilings, decorative moldings, and wood-burning fireplaces. Rooms in the attached 1820s barn are more casual, with exposed beams and a cozy country feel.

Breakfast is served each morning in the 1763 dining room. The choices include freshly baked croissants, homemade bread, yogurt, fresh fruits, cereals, and a hot dish freshly prepared by the chef. Mario, the innkeeper/chef, was born in Switzerland and brings a continental touch to the dinner menu. Among his tempting dishes are sliced veal Swiss style, pork fillet piccata Milanese style with saffron risotto, and Maine sea scallops with garlic and herbs. Forget about calories; there's no turning down desserts like frozen Grand Marnier soufflé or the Pavlova, a house specialty, a meringue-based dessert topped with fresh fruit and whipped cream.

The inn is surrounded by fields, stone walls and woods, and a barn and offers a walking path. You can relax on the screened deck, or a peaceful saltwater marsh with rowboat and dock beckons beyond the pasture. Mountain bikes are available for further adventuring, and you'll definitely want to schedule some time in Wiscasset, a town known for its antiquing. Boothbay Harbor and Bath are a short drive away.

HOW TO GET THERE: From Route 1 between Bath and Wiscasset, turn right onto Route 144 and follow it 8½ miles to the inn, which is on Westport Island.

York Harbor Inn 📱
York Harbor, Maine 03911

INNKEEPER: Gary Dominguez

ADDRESS/TELEPHONE: P.O. Box 573; (207) 363–5119 or (800) 343–3869; fax (207) 363–7151

WEB SITE: www.yorkharborinn.com

ROOMS: 54 guest rooms and suites in 5 buildings; all with private bath, air-conditioning, phone, TV, dataport, iron and ironing board; some with fireplace, Jacuzzi, private deck.

RATES: $99 to $329 CP. Many packages available.

OPEN: All year.

FACILITIES AND ACTIVITIES: Lunch, dinner, Sunday brunch, bar, full license. Nearby: Public beach, fishing, boating, golf, tennis.

BUSINESS TRAVEL: The inn offers more than 5,000 square feet of meeting space and has an inventory of state-of-the-art audiovisual equipment, including a computer video data projector.

Nubble Light

The town of York's most visited—and most photographed—site is the Nubble Light at Cape Neddick, the rocky promontory that stretches nearly a mile into the Atlantic Ocean. On its own little island at the tip—or "nubble"—of the peninsula, the 1879 lighthouse is at the end of Nubble Road off Route 1A at York Beach. English navigator Capt. Bartholomew Gosnold landed at this site in 1602; Capt. John Smith came to chart the area in 1614. It is he who coined the term "knubble." Now automated and maintained by the U.S. Coast Guard, the white iron-sheathed brick tower had a keeper until 1987. Its black-capped light is 88 feet above the high-water mark, still protecting seafarers off Maine's rugged coast.

ow! Three dining rooms with a view of the Atlantic. This is a cozy and comfortable inn, with good food and good grog. Sitting there looking over the Atlantic should be enough, but when you add the excellent food, it is heaven.

The appetizers, such as seafood chowder and Maine crab cakes (I had these on my last trip, and they're delicious), are glorious. Entrees include baked stuffed haddock, Yorkshire lobster supreme, roast rack of lamb, beef tenderloin, and, of course, steamed Maine lobster.

The Ship's Cellar Pub, which once was a livery stable, serves lunch and light pub fare dinners. The bar is a beauty, made of unstained cherrywood joined with holly and ebony woods. The carpenter even put an inlaid tulip in a corner—out of tulip wood, of course. Happy hour is just that, featuring good food and conversation with a lot of local people. There is entertainment Wednesday and Friday through Sunday evenings.

An inn for more than one hundred years, this is one of Maine's loveliest seaside escapes. The cabin room, which was moved here, is more than 300 years old. Originally a fisherman's house, the cabin's sturdy ceiling beams were not for holding up the roof but for hanging up wet sails to dry before the large fireplace.

Rooms have traditional colonial decor and are spread out in several buildings. The main house has both modest choices with double beds and luxury lairs with fireplaces, spa tubs, and ocean view decks. I'm especially partial to Room 14, with a tall four-poster, painted woodwork, and a working fireplace as well as a water view. The Yorkshire Building includes one of the largest accommodations, the three-room "bridal suite."

The Harbor Hill building, completed in 2001, is really elegant. All the rooms have king beds, full or partial ocean views, gas fireplaces, heated bathroom tiles, whirlpool tubs, and dataports for Internet access.

Harbor Cliffs, adjacent to the York Harbor Inn and also owned by the Dominguez family, operates as a separate bed-and-breakfast facility. It was a private residence for many years until purchased in 1997 and converted to an inn. All the rooms have king-size beds and fireplaces, one has a wheelchair-accessible bathroom, and the rest have spa tubs. Many have outstanding ocean views.

The newest property, the 1730 Harbor Crest Inn, opened in 2004, adds seven more luxurious guest rooms with king-size beds, whirlpool tubs, and fireplaces. Located about ½ mile from the main inn, Harbor Crest is a short walk to the shops in town and the Harbor Basin.

When you come to the York Harbor Inn, bring along your camera. The views are guaranteed to keep you busy.

HOW TO GET THERE: Going south on Interstate 95, take the Yorks/Berwicks exit; going north on I-95, take the Yorks/Ogunquit exit. Turn right at the blinking light, left at the first traffic light (Route 1A), and go through the village about 3 miles. The inn is on the left.

Select List of
Other Maine Inns

Mira Monte Inn & Suites
69 Mount Desert Street
Bar Harbor, ME 04609
(207) 288-4263 or (800) 553-5109; fax (207) 288-3115
Web site: www.miramonte.com
13 rooms in 1864 main building, 11 with fireplace, all with private bath; 3 suites in other buildings, all with private bath, fireplace, balcony.

Spruce Point Inn
Atlantic Avenue
Boothbay Harbor, ME 04538
(207) 633-4152 or (800) 553-0289; fax (207) 633-7138
Web site: www.sprucepointinn.com
75 rooms, all with private bath; main inn has restaurant and lounge.

Maine Stay

22 High Street
Camden, ME 04843
(207) 236–9636; fax (207) 236–0621
Web site: www.mainestay.com
8 rooms, all with private bath; 200-year-old farm complex.

English Meadows Inn B&B

Port Road
Kennebunk, ME 04043
Web site: www.englishmeadowsinn.com
(207) 967–5766 or (800) 272–0698
8 rooms, 3 suites, all with private bath; Victorian farmhouse.

Old Granite Inn

546 Main Street
Rockland, ME 04841
(207) 594–9036 or (800) 386–9036
Web site: www.oldgraniteinn.com
12 rooms, 9 with private bath; federal colonial bed-and-breakfast.

The Surry Inn

Route 172
Surry, ME 04684
(207) 667–5091 or (800) 742–3414
Web site: www.surryinn.com
8 rooms, 6 with private bath. A lovely 1834 inn on Contention Cove, chef-owned with dinner served seven days. Wonderful sunsets.

Edwards Harborside Inn

Box 866, Stage Neck Road
York Harbor, ME 03911
Web site: www.edwardsharborside.com
(207) 363–3037 or (800) 273–2686; fax (207) 363–1544
10 rooms and suites, 8 with private bath; Victorian waterfront estate.

Stage Neck Inn

22 Stage Neck Road
York Harbor, ME 03911
(207) 363–3850 or (800) 340–1130; fax (207) 363–2221
Web site: www.stageneck.com
58 rooms, all with private bath; 2 dining rooms; indoor pool; Jacuzzi; fitness room.

Massachusetts

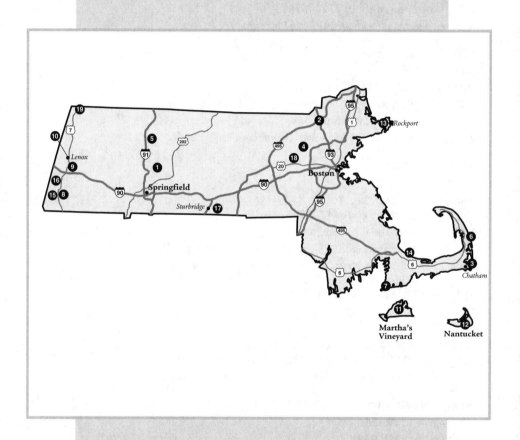

Massachusetts

Numbers on map refer to towns numbered below.

The Lord Jeffery Inn
Amherst, Massachusetts 01002

INNKEEPER: Rick Trahan

ADDRESS/TELEPHONE: 30 Boltwood Avenue; (413) 253–2576 or (800) 742–0358; fax (413) 256–6152

WEB SITE: www.lordjefferyinn.com

ROOMS: 40 rooms, 8 suites; all with private bath, TV, and phone.

RATES: $79 to $239 EP.

OPEN: All year.

FACILITIES AND ACTIVITIES: Breakfast, lunch, dinner, Sunday brunch, tavern, room service for all meals. Elevator. Nearby: Skiing, golf, tennis, antiquing, Emily Dickinson house.

This gracious inn of white brick on Amherst's historic common was named for Lord Jeffery Amherst, a hero of the French and Indian War. The common rooms are spacious and inviting, with bouquets of fresh flowers, cozy couches and chairs, and lots of fireplaces. Guest rooms vary in size, but all have colonial decor and conveniences such as TV and phones with dataports. Some rooms overlook the common, while others face the inn's lovely colonial gardens. Several of these garden rooms have porches.

Breakfast here is a great way to start the day—excellent baked goods, omelets, eggs, sausage, bacon, and lots more. Lunch is hearty. When I last vis-

ited I had a delicious thick tomato and spinach soup and a salad so generous I could not finish it. The dinner menu in the Windowed Hearth varies with the season but often features duck, lobster, rack of lamb, and chateaubriand, a yummy favorite of mine.

If you are in the mood for something lighter, pub fare is available in the Elijah Boltwood Tavern.

The inn, especially the Grand Ballroom, is a popular place for weddings and other special events. Six function rooms in all can accommodate up to 225 guests.

There's plenty to do in this area. Amherst is home to three colleges, Amherst, Hampshire, and the University of Massachusetts, each with a fine campus and many activities. Smith College in Northampton, a few miles away, has outstanding gardens and an impressive art museum, and the town of Northampton is a crafts center, with many galleries on Main Street. If you are looking for golf, tennis, or skiing, you'll find it nearby, as well.

HOW TO GET THERE: Take Interstate 91 to the Amherst exit (exit 19), then go east 8 miles on Route 9 to Amherst.

Andover Inn
Andover, Massachusetts 01810

INNKEEPER: Winthrop Pennock

ADDRESS/TELEPHONE: 4 Chapel Avenue; (978) 475-5903; fax (978) 475-1053

WEB SITE: www.andoverinn.com

ROOMS: 17, plus 6 suites; all with private bath, air-conditioning, TV, phone, CD player, alarm clock, room service, wheelchair accessibility; some with DVD player.

RATES: $125 to $250 EP.

OPEN: All year.

FACILITIES AND ACTIVITIES: Breakfast, lunch, dinner, Sunday brunch. Bar, elevator, salon.

BUSINESS TRAVEL: Located 30 minutes from Boston. Free wireless Internet connections; desk in some rooms; conference room; fax available.

Though it is privately owned, the Andover Inn is located on the campus of Phillips Academy, one of the nation's oldest prep schools. As you would expect in this ivy-clad atmosphere, the decor is traditional, but changes are afoot. New management took over in 2006, and every-

thing is being freshened and upgraded, particularly the guest rooms. The new slogan is "celebrating the arts, culture, and history of Andover."

Some changes are already in place. The public rooms are hung with original artwork from a local gallery, and the inn has been equipped with wireless Internet.

An attractive, welcoming bar just off the lobby has a light bistro menu. The choices range from salads and sandwiches to entrees such as grilled lamb tenderloin and beer-battered cod.

While the dining room is more formal, coat and ties are not required. The new dining room menu changes regularly to take advantage of local ingredients whenever possible. Dinner choices include pan roasted duck breast, braised lamb shank, grilled shrimp and scallops with a wild mushroom risotto, pan roasted halibut, and roasted Maine lobster. The dessert menu offers temptations such as apple tart garnished with calvados and maple ice cream, crème brûlée, and a positively decadent chocolate torte served with champagne poached pears and a vanilla custard sauce. The inn has a popular wine dinner series and schedules a monthly ethnic night in the restaurant.

While the rooms will be redecorated, it is safe to assume that they will retain a traditional look. After all, the inn has been successfully serving the academy and the community for more than seventy years, so no major changes seem necessary.

HOW TO GET THERE: The inn is about 25 miles north of Boston on Route 28. From Boston take Interstate 93 north to exit 41 (Route 125/Andover/North Andover). Follow Route 125 north for 2½ miles. When approaching Route 28 north and south, take Route 28 north and go 3¼ miles. Approaching the Phillips Academy on the right side of Route 28, look for the Andover Inn sign. Turn right onto Chapel Avenue. The inn is located next to the chapel. Coming from Interstate 495 north, take exit 41A onto Route 28 south and proceed 2⁹⁄₁₀ miles. The inn will be on the left, next to the chapel.

The Queen Anne Inn
Chatham, Massachusetts 02633

INNKEEPERS: Guenther and Dana Weinkopf

ADDRESS/TELEPHONE: 70 Queen Anne Road; (508) 945-0394 or (800) 545-4667; fax (508) 945-4884

WEB SITE: www.queenanneinn.com

ROOMS: 31, all with private bath, phone, and TV; many with working fireplace, balcony, Jacuzzi or hot tub.

RATES: $129 to $395 CP.

OPEN: All year except January to February 14.

FACILITIES AND ACTIVITIES: Dinner. Spa, swimming pool. Nearby: Boating, fishing tours can be arranged.

This lovely old inn has a long history. It was built in 1840 as a wedding present for the daughter of a famous sea captain, and since her husband was a minister, it became the first parish house of the First Congregational Church. New owners turned it into an inn back in 1874, and the building acquired added wings as others took over.

Despite this auspicious start, the inn had fallen victim to neglect until the 1970s, when Guenther Weinkopf arrived to restore the original Victorian style and ambience, which he has done in grand style. This is one of the few inns that can claim to have all rooms decorated with original furniture and antiques from the Cape and Nantucket. In fact, much of the antique furniture has been here since 1874.

Murals by artist James Parker were added in various rooms, including a grand mural of Native Americans in the pleasant lounge and a wonderful sea scene with mermaids and fish around the hot tub in the spa, where massages and an assortment of nice treatments are available.

This is an ideal spot for a romantic getaway with many pampering amenities. Garden-view rooms are choice, with private balconies. Some have fireplaces, and Jacuzzis or hot tubs on the balcony. Spacious studios also offer working fireplaces and two-person Jacuzzis, and the Sunset Studio comes with a huge four-poster bed and a four-person-size hot tub on a private veranda. Even the smaller, cozy rooms on the third floor of the inn have working fireplaces.

The Eldredge Room Restaurant is intimate, with sponge-painted walls in deep green and harvest gold. The menu features lots of fresh local seafood as well as standards such as rack of lamb or tenderloin of beef. The inventive chef always has some unusual offerings on the changing menu, perhaps a mushroom gnocchi or Chatham monkfish wrapped in Smithfield ham.

Between the spa and the inn's outdoor swimming pool, there's a lot to keep you busy. And should you decide to wander, Chatham boasts scores of tempting shops, as well as beaches and the chance for seal- and whale-watching excursions.

HOW TO GET THERE: From Route 6 (Mid-Cape Highway), take exit 11, go south on Route 137 to its end, and take a left on Route 28 to Chatham Center. At your first traffic light, in about 3 miles, go right on Queen Anne Road. The inn is on your right.

Wequassett Inn
Chatham, Massachusetts 02633

INNKEEPER: Mark Novata

ADDRESS/TELEPHONE: Route 28, Pleasant Bay, Cape Cod; (508) 432–5400 or (800) 225–7125; fax (508) 432–5032

WEB SITE: www.wequasset.com

ROOMS: 104 rooms and suites; all with private deck, patio, or balcony, TV, phone, hair dryer, coffeemaker, iron, minibar; many with water view; some with fireplace.

RATES: $160 to $1,300 EP.

OPEN: April through November.

FACILITIES AND ACTIVITIES: Breakfast, lunch, dinner; 3 restaurants, bar; swimming pool and beach, tennis, boating, fitness center, croquet court; conference center; 18-hole golf course available to guests at Cape Cod National Golf Club.

*T*his is a handsome resort, an oceanside complex of twenty buildings in Cape Cod style on twenty-two landscaped acres. The name comes from the Native American word meaning "Crescent on the Water."

Guest accommodations are in cottages or villa-style buildings, many have water views, while others look out on the garden. They range from simple to truly grand. Rooms have been recently renovated and are handsome, with country-style furnishings, lots of pine, traditional fabrics, and light colors that complement the seaside setting.

A nineteenth-century sea captain's home houses the inn's highly rated main restaurant, known as 28 Atlantic. The New American cuisine is fine, and it comes with a spectacular view of Pleasant Bay and the Atlantic Ocean beyond. As you might have guessed, the bounty from that sea is the house specialty. A typical meal may start with Chatham "day boat" scallops or a Cape lobster and roasted corn bisque, followed by well-prepared sea bass, local blue fish, or the inn's "petit clambake": butter-poached lobster, potatoes, corn pudding, and asparagus.

All three meals are served here during spring and fall. In summer, lunch is moved to the more informal Outer Bar and Grille or at poolside if you like. Thoreau's is a clubby bar that also offers dining in the evening.

There's so much to do, the only question is where to go first—beach or pool or the tennis court. At the waterfront, you can rent a sailboat or a kayak, and lessons are available for both. Golfers have privileges at the Cape Cod National, one of the region's best eighteen-hole golf courses.

Or, of course, you could just sit back and enjoy the view. It would be hard to beat the serenity of sitting on the porch overlooking the bay at any time of the day, but oh, the early-morning calm! If the summer rates seem steep, think about a visit off-season, when you can enjoy the Cape at its tranquil best.

HOW TO GET THERE: Wequassett Inn is on Pleasant Bay, midway between Chatham and Orleans on Route 28. If you are driving from the north, take Route 6 east to exit 11. Turn left at end of exit ramp; go 25 yards to Pleasant Bay Road (your first left). Go straight through the first stop sign, and when you reach the second stop sign, you have arrived at Wequassett Inn.

Concord's Colonial Inn
Concord, Massachusetts 01742

INNKEEPERS: Jurgen and Rebecca Demisch

ADDRESS/TELEPHONE: 48 Monument Square; (978) 369-9200 or (800) 370-9200; fax (978) 371-1533

WEB SITE: www.concordscolonialinn.com

ROOMS: 45, plus 11 suites; all with private bath, air-conditioning, phone, TV, and free high-speed Internet access.

RATES: $135 to $425 EP.

OPEN: All year.

FACILITIES AND ACTIVITIES: Breakfast, lunch, dinner, Sunday brunch, afternoon tea. Tavern, lounge; gift shop; live jazz or folk music daily.

BUSINESS TRAVEL: Located 18 miles from Boston, 20 miles from Logan Airport. Phone, high-speed Internet access in room; 6 conference rooms; corporate rates.

The history of Concord's Colonial Inn (1716) is tied to the history of young America in famous Concord, Massachusetts. Here was fired the "shot heard 'round the world." Here lived some of the nation's literary greats—Henry David Thoreau, Ralph Waldo Emerson, Louisa May Alcott, Nathaniel Hawthorne. They are all laid to rest on Author's Ridge in Sleepy Hollow Cemetery, a short walk from the inn. There is so much history in Concord, it would take days to see it all.

The Merchant's Row dining room is lovely, with a beamed ceiling and windows full of plants. The seasonal menu changes often. Extensive lunch choices include homemade soups, fresh salads, lobster rolls, burgers, chicken potpies, and crab cakes. Prime rib, crispy potato-crusted cod, Maine lobster, and stuffed sole are among the dinner favorites.

The Liberty Room is a more casual setting for lunch and dinner and has a popular Tap Room for libations. The Rustic Village Forge Tavern serves up lively entertainment at night.

Instead of (or in addition to!) lunch or dinner, you can enjoy high tea, which means sandwiches of cucumber and radish, cream cheese and chives, smoked salmon and watercress, plus crumpets and scones, cream and fresh berries, miniature cakes and fresh fruit tarts. Afternoons here are done right.

Many years ago, I stayed in Room 24 in this inn. Now they tell me it's haunted. Well, the lights came on in the wee hours and woke me. I knew I hadn't turned them on, but I certainly did turn them off—after a while. I wonder who it was?

HOW TO GET THERE: Take Route 2 east to Route 62 east to Concord Center to Monument Square. The inn is at 48 Monument Square.

Deerfield Inn 📱
Deerfield, Massachusetts 01342

INNKEEPERS: Karl and Jane Sabo

ADDRESS/TELEPHONE: 81 Old Main Street; (413) 774–5587 or (800) 926–3865; fax (413) 775-7221

WEB SITE: www.deerfieldinn.com

ROOMS: 23 rooms in 2 buildings, all with private bath, air-conditioning, phone, and color TV.

RATES: $173 to $248 BP.

OPEN: All year except December 24 to 26.

FACILITIES AND ACTIVITIES: Breakfast, dinner Thursday through Monday. Tavern, two living rooms, elevator, color TV in lounge. Nearby: Museums, Deerfield Academy, historic house tours.

BUSINESS TRAVEL: Phone in room; conference rooms; audiovisual equipment and fax available.

This is an inn that has been welcoming travelers since 1884, one of the few structures in New England continuously offering food and lodging. It stands in the center of the beautiful avenue known simply as "The Street," lined with more than sixty fine colonial and Federal homes, many of them open to the public as house museums. Deerfield is such a rare town that the entire village has been declared a National Historic Landmark.

The rocking chairs on the front porch of the inn somehow let you know how lovely things will be inside. The parlors are beautifully furnished, with mostly twentieth-century copies or adaptations of colonial decor. The Beehive Parlor, done in shades of blue, is a restful place for a cocktail or two. The main dining room is spacious, serving the kind of food befitting the setting. The chef prepares a daily special, taking advantage of seasonal and local market offerings. He also does magical things with venison, chicken, and fish. Fresh fish is brought in three times a week.

Historic Deerfield

The Deerfield Inn is smack-dab in the middle of one of the nation's best-preserved historic sites. The village of Deerfield was founded in the 1660s at the edge of the frontier claimed by the British. Attacked several times and nearly destroyed twice by Native American and French raids, the settlement was rebuilt throughout the eighteenth century. Now it stands as a monument to two centuries of colonial and early American life and architecture.

Along the mile-long main street of Old Deerfield are many beautiful private homes and more than a dozen museum homes. Visit the Hall Tavern Information Center at Historic Deerfield: A Museum of New England History and Art (413-774-5581; www.historic-deerfield.org) to see a lovely short film on the history of the village and its restoration, then buy tickets to tour the homes that are open to the public. There are also museums displaying colonial artifacts, textiles, silver and metalware, costumes, and much more. A charming museum store right next to the inn offers beautiful reproductions, needlework, fabrics, books, and other gifts that you can buy as a memento of your visit here.

The menu also offers "casual fare," including moderately priced entrees such as pasta dishes or crab cakes.

The bedrooms are true joys—Beautyrest mattresses, matching bedspreads and drapes, comfortable chairs, and good lights for restful reading or needlework. The baths have been color-coordinated with the rooms they serve. The towels are large and fluffy, and the baths are equipped with hair dryers and magnifying mirrors.

A coffee shop on the lower level leads out to an outdoor garden: a perfect spot for informal meals and a place the children will love.

Take a stroll down the street and around Historic Deerfield. Browse through Memorial Hall Museum, one of the nation's oldest, and through the museum shop. Take time to tour the homes around here—they hold some of the finest collections of Early American furnishings in the country.

HOW TO GET THERE: From Interstate 91 take exit 24 northbound. Go 6 miles north on Route 5. At the sign for Old Deerfield Village, take a left. The inn is on your left, just past Deerfield Academy.

Nauset House

East Orleans, Massachusetts 02643

INNKEEPERS: Diane Johnson, Cindy and John Vessella

ADDRESS/TELEPHONE: 143 Beach Road (mailing address: Box 774); (508) 255–2195 or (800) 771–5508; fax (508) 240–6276

WEB SITE: www.nausethouseinn.com

ROOMS: 13 rooms, plus 1 cottage; 8 with private bath.

RATES: $75 to $170 BP.

OPEN: April 1 to October 31.

FACILITIES AND ACTIVITIES: Full breakfast. Nearby: Ocean.

The best country inns reflect the personality of their owners, and it is the warmth of this family-owned inn that makes Nauset House such a special place. For the past twenty years, Diane Johnson and her daughter and son-in-law, Cindy and John Vessella, have created a welcoming ambience that brings friends back year after year to enjoy their gracious hospitality and one of the most delightful settings on Cape Cod.

The inn combines an 1810 Cape farmhouse with a rarity, a turn-of-the-twentieth-century glass conservatory moved from an estate in Connecticut. Lovely year-round, the conservatory is at its most spectacular in spring when the weeping cherry and camellias bathe the room in pink clouds. It is a wonderful place to sit and relax any time of year, cheerful even on the gloomiest day.

As a bonus, beautiful Nauset Beach is just ½ mile down the road, with 10 miles of peerless dune-backed ocean beach.

Olive Metcalf

The decor of the inn is comfortable country. Guests mingle in the kind of living room you might wish you had at home, with big plant-filled windows and a long sofa and chairs arranged around the fireplace. Shelves are stacked with books, and the coffee table and a side basket are piled high with all kinds of magazines. Almost everyone gathers here late in the day for a sociable hour, enjoying wine or juice and hors d'oeuvres, perusing the stack of local menus, and getting dining tips from the hosts.

Nine guest rooms are in the main inn, and another four larger rooms are in the carriage house, the farm's original barn. Diane is an artist, and even the smallest rooms are filled with charm and individuality that reflect her talents. You can see her touch in the flower sprigs painted to match the name on guest-room doors, the hand-stenciling, trompe l'oeil walls, and the hand-painted furniture pieces.

One very special spot is the Outermost House, a cottage in the apple orchard with barnboard walls, cathedral ceilings, and a bathroom with a faux painted sky.

The day at Nauset House starts with a bountiful breakfast, served in a dining room with brick floors, ceiling beams, and an open hearth. Each day brings a choice of entrees such as banana-blueberry pancakes, scrambled eggs with cheese, or an omelet of the day. Always on the menu are a choice of juices and fresh baked muffins and breads and the inn's homemade granola.

It's just the happy and hearty start you need for a day at the beach, or antiquing or gallery hopping in Orleans and around the Cape. Your hosts can tip you off to all the best places.

HOW TO GET THERE: Take exit 12 (Orleans-Brewster) off Route 6. Turn right at bottom of ramp, then right at first traffic light. Proceed straight, past the next light and across Route 28, Tonset Road. At the next light, turn right onto Main Street. Proceed to the fork and bear left onto Beach Road. The inn is 8/10 mile on the right.

Coonamessett Inn
Falmouth, Massachusetts 02541

INNKEEPERS: Linda and Bill Zammer Jr.; Jim Underdah, general manager

ADDRESS/TELEPHONE: 311 Gifford Street; (508) 548–2300; fax (508) 540–9831

WEB SITE: www.capecodrestaurant.org

ROOMS: 27 suites, plus 1 cottage; all with private bath.

RATES: $89 to $260 EP.

OPEN: All year.

FACILITIES AND ACTIVITIES: Lunch, dinner, bar. Parking.

In 1796, in a rolling field that sloped gently down to a lovely pond, Thomas Jones constructed a house and barn that was to become Coonamessett Inn (a Native American word for "the place of the large fish"). The original residence, barn, caretaker's quarters, and carriage house still stand, on six acres of scenic grounds. The framework of the main house is finished with wooden-peg joints, and much of the interior paneling is original. Many of the bricks in the old fireplaces are thought to be made of ballast brought from Europe in the holds of sailing ships.

The inn is best known for its restaurant, and the food is excellent, offered from a large, varied menu and served by friendly waitresses. Luncheons attract a lot of people, as the inn's food reputation travels far and wide. The famous Coonamessett Onion Rings are glorious. Dinner appetizers are many, including Maine crab cakes and Prince Edward Island mussels. A real winner, and judged to be the best in the East, is the lobster bisque, and I'll second it. And dinner entrees are great, especially the fresh lobster, served steamed or baked and stuffed. There are other seafood dishes, and meat eaters are not forgotten either. There are beef, lamb, and veal entrees, plus the chef's special home-made fresh pasta of the day. (*NOTE:* The innkeepers also own the Flying Bridge Restaurant overlooking Falmouth Harbor.)

The most famous of the three dining areas is the Cahoon Room, named for a renowned local folk artist and featuring eighteen of his paintings, many

of them of the inn itself. This attractive room has high vaulted and beamed ceilings and lighting fixtures in the form of hot-air balloons made of brass and copper. The balloons reflect one of the themes in Cahoon's paintings.

The Cape Cod Room is the newest addition at the inn. Used for private functions, it is large and grand, with windows along one wall overlooking the pond. Outside the Cape Cod Room and the main dining room is a deck large enough for alfresco dining and glorious enough for a wedding ceremony.

The guest suites have a sitting room, bedroom, modern bath, color television, and telephone. They are furnished with country pine and pleasant print and paisley fabrics. These are cottage suites, as there are no guest rooms in the inn itself.

I love the Cape in the off-season, and it's good to know that no matter what day I decide to come, I will receive a cordial welcome here. The inn grounds are beautiful and are kept in mint condition year-round. All around you will see the loveliest array of grass, trees, flowers, shrubs . . . and peace. I wish I lived closer.

HOW TO GET THERE: Take Route 28 at the bridge over the canal, and go into Falmouth. Turn left on Jones Road, and at the intersection of Gifford Street, you will see the inn.

Thornewood Inn
Great Barrington, Massachusetts 01230

INNKEEPERS: Terry and David Thorne

ADDRESS/TELEPHONE: 453 Stockbridge Road; (413) 528–3828 or (800) 854–1008

WEB SITE: www.thornewood.com

ROOMS: 12 rooms, 3 suites with Jacuzzis; all with private bath, telephone, and TV; 3 with fireplace; some with balcony.

RATES: $95 to $295, CP weekdays, BP weekends.

OPEN: All year.

FACILITIES AND ACTIVITIES: Dinner, Sunday brunch at Spencer's Restaurant. Jazz entertainment on special weekends, taproom, swimming pool. Nearby: Skiing, Tanglewood, summer theater, museums, walking trails.

The inn, a Dutch colonial built in 1920, has been restored with care. The rooms have twin, double, queen, or king beds, some of which are four-posters and canopies. All the rooms are comfortable and furnished with antiques and fine reproductions. Three prize rooms offer fireplaces and French doors leading to balconies overlooking the beautiful Berkshire hills.

Spencer's Restaurant, named for the Thornes' grandson, is quite elegant, with tall arched windows to bring in the light. Guests enjoy a continental breakfast weekdays and a full country breakfast on weekends in this lovely setting. At dinner, the seasonal "country continental" entrees include grilled beef tenderloin, pan seared sea scallops, North Atlantic salmon, and New Zealand rack of lamb. Many of the fresh fruits and vegetables are from the inn gardens. The dining room has wonderful views of the Berkshires and the Housatonic River in the distance. On many weekends there is music for dancing.

The inn is minutes away from Tanglewood, summer playhouses, museums, and antiques shops. Winter brings skiing, and summer is ideal for relaxing in the inn's own pool.

HOW TO GET THERE: The inn is at the junction of Routes 7 and 183 in Great Barrington.

Windflower Inn

Great Barrington, Massachusetts 01230

INNKEEPERS: Barbara and Gerald Liebert, Claudia and John Ryan

ADDRESS/TELEPHONE: 684 South Egremont Road; (413) 528–2720 or (800) 992–1993

WEB SITE: www.windflowerinn.com

ROOMS: 13, all with private bath, air-conditioning, and phone; many with a working fireplace.

RATES: $100 to $200 BP.

OPEN: All year.

FACILITIES AND ACTIVITIES: Swimming pool, massage therapist by appointment. BYOB. Nearby: Golf, tennis, downhill and cross-country skiing, music, theater.

Great Barrington was settled in the eighteenth century, and today it is a lovely resort town. The inn was built in the 1850s and is Federal style.

I like the large living room. It has a white brick fireplace, couches, and a huge coffee table covered with magazines. Very conducive to loafing. There is also a reading or game room with a piano and tons of books to read.

The guest rooms are spacious. Most of the beds are queens, and some have canopies. Two rooms have twin beds that can be made into kings. Fireplaces are in some of the rooms. The room on the first floor has its own entrance from the terrace and a large stone fireplace. It's a lovely room.

The dining room features Currier & Ives snow scenes on the walls and works done by local artists. One of them, by Gerald, is of his granddaughter holding a balloon. It's very dear.

A big country breakfast and afternoon tea are served each day. Claudia's homemade breads and pastries, and herbs and raspberries from the garden, are highlights.

The country club across the street is available for golf. The inn's own swimming pool is very relaxing, and in summer you have Tanglewood, Jacob's Pillow, and the Berkshire Theater nearby.

HOW TO GET THERE: The inn is on Route 23, 3 miles west of Great Barrington.

The Morgan House
Lee, Massachusetts 01238

INNKEEPER: Michael Diggin

ADDRESS/TELEPHONE: Main Street; (413) 243-3661; fax (413) 243-3103

WEB SITE: www.morganhouseinn.com

ROOMS: 11; 6 with private bath.

RATES: $50 to $200 BP July through October; CP rest of year.

OPEN: All year.

FACILITIES AND ACTIVITIES: Lunch, dinner, tavern. Nearby: Tanglewood, Jacob's Pillow, golf, tennis, swimming, hiking.

The Morgan House is a great in-town inn. It has a long and interesting history dating from 1817, when it was built as a private home. In 1855 it was converted into a stagecoach inn by Edwin Morgan, and an inn it has remained.

Many illustrious guests enjoyed a stay here during the inn's early years, including Ulysses S. Grant, George Bernard Shaw, and Grover Cleveland. Though nicely renovated, the guest rooms still speak of the past with period furnishings. No two rooms are alike.

You'll also step back to the stagecoach era in the colonial dining room, which has both tables and old-fashioned high-back booths. Lunch offers soups, salads, and grand sandwiches. The dinner menu has something for everyone—pasta, chicken, salmon, filet mignon, and more. Save room for the

dessert, because the chocolate cake is irresistible, as are the tarts, pies, and cobblers.

The tavern serves lighter fare for lunch and dinner, and locally brewed beers. Entertainment keeps things lively on Friday and Saturday nights.

My favorite spot here is the enclosed porch featuring Stickley furniture, where you can settle in with a book or watch the world go by on Main Street.

HOW TO GET THERE: From the Massachusetts Turnpike take exit 2. Follow Route 20 west 1 mile, to the center of Lee. The inn will be on your left.

The Gateways Inn
Lenox, Massachusetts 01240

INNKEEPERS: Rosemary and Fabrizio Chiariello

ADDRESS/TELEPHONE: 51 Walker Street; (413) 637–2532; fax (413) 637–1432

WEB SITE: www.gatewaysinn.com

ROOMS: 11, plus 1 suite; all with private bath, phone with dataport, TV, and air-conditioning; 8 with gas fireplace; some with VCR.

RATES: Rooms, $100 to $295 BP; suite, $230 to $450 BP.

OPEN: All year.

FACILITIES AND ACTIVITIES: Restaurant closed Monday to Wednesday in winter. In summer dinner by reservation preferred. Open for lunch and late light meals daily. Nearby: Berkshires attractions.

The Gateways was built as a summer mansion for Harley Procter. That's Procter of Procter and Gamble, so you can imagine that he had the wherewithal to do something grand. The square building shape with a flat top resembles Mr. Procter's favorite product, Ivory Soap. The oval windows beside the front door and the magnificent stairway alone are worth a visit.

The Chiariellos have done extensive work on the inn, turning it into a luxury property that Mr. Procter no doubt would have approved. Each guest room has its own theme. The Blue Danube is done in blue with prints and paintings of European waterways, rivers, and canals. The Procter Garden Room has floral motifs, and the Berkshire Room is properly colonial, with a four-poster bed, hand-knotted canopy, and Georgian-style dressers and chairs. The Fiedler Suite has its own Jacuzzi. All the bathrooms are stocked with terry robes and plush Egyptian cotton towels.

The dining room is the pride of the inn. The innkeepers and staff work with local farmers and dairies to use their fresh products whenever possible. The menu changes often, but to give you an idea of the possibilities, you might start with seared foie gras with a fig compote or asparagus and scallop ravioli with fresh herb and butter sauce.

Main courses may be boneless Long Island duck breast served with wild rice, sesame-crusted fillet of Atlantic salmon, or rack of lamb. Save room for the apple pie—it's an award winner—unless you'd rather have tiramisu, or a chocolate-chocolate torte in a hazelnut crème sauce. The nightly cheese selection is always tempting, and if you want something lighter, you can choose Italian gelati and sorbets or a cookie and biscotti plate.

A nice addition to the inn is the Terrace Room, with tall French windows all around. The bar has also been enlarged to offer comfortable armchair groupings. Desserts and light meals are served here until midnight.

One thing that needed no improvement is the inn's location in the heart of Lenox, one of the loveliest villages in New England and the home of Tanglewood, where the Boston Symphony spends the summer.

HOW TO GET THERE: Take Route 7 to Route 7A. The inn is on Route 7A, 1 block from the intersection of Routes 183 and 7A.

Wheatleigh 💚

INNKEEPERS: Susan and Linfield Simon; Marc Wilhelm, general manager

ADDRESS/TELEPHONE: Hawthorne Road; (413) 637–0610; fax (413) 637–4507

WEB SITE: www.wheatleigh.com

ROOMS: 19, all with private bath, air-conditioning, TV, DVD, CD player, free high-speed Internet, and phone; 9 with working fireplace.

RATES: $585 to $1,650 EP.

OPEN: All year.

FACILITIES AND ACTIVITIES: Lunch, dinner, Sunday brunch. Lounge. Outdoor heated pool, tennis, cross-country skiing, massage and fitness center, complimentary bicycles.

Wheatleigh is a unique and fabulous property, a summer mansion built in 1893 for a countess and modeled after a sixteenth-century Italian palazzo. The house stands overlooking a lake, amid lawns and gardens, on twenty-two self-contained acres in the heart of the picturesque Berkshires. Patios, pergolas, porticos, and terraces surround the mansion to make the most of the view.

But those who knew Wheatleigh in the past will find dramatic changes. The mansion has recently undergone a multimillion-dollar renovation updating its image.

The furnishings now have a fresh, understated look, and abstract paintings by local artists adorn the walls. The new, more modern palette is a calm-

Jacob's Pillow Dance Festival

This ten-week summer festival celebrates the work of some of the nation's most talented and innovative dance companies. Performing in the rustic country setting of the world-class dance school named Jacob's Pillow, Paul Taylor, Alvin Ailey, Merce Cunningham, Meredith Monk, Twyla Tharp, Margot Fonteyn, and many other dance greats have wowed audiences at both indoor and outdoor theaters. On a hilltop former farm in the town of Becket, just east of Lee, are studios where you can watch rehearsals, a cafe where you can enjoy a light meal, and picnic areas where you can relax while you watch developing dancers practice their art. Call (413) 243–0745 or log on to www.jacobspillow.org for the schedule, prices, and tickets.

ing mix of mustard, wheat, sage, and cypress, planned to blend with the natural beauty just outside the great arched windows. The grand but formal Great Hall has been softened with intimate seating arrangements and warm lighting. Everywhere are lovely small details garnered from around the world—an antique Japanese vase, lacquered boxes from China, light fixtures from Paris.

The architects have also worked their magic on the main dining room, where the outdoor courtyard has been enclosed with glass walls between Palladian columns, extending the room and making the most of the wonderful setting outside. In the main dining room, there is a choice of prix-fixe menus, a three-course dinner, or the lavish chef's tasting menu. These are ultimate dinners, lauded by many critics. The selections change with the seasons. On a recent fall dinner menu, appetizers included a trio of Kumamoto oysters, poached foie gras, and a butternut squash soup. Wild Columbia River sturgeon, heirloom duck, and grass-fed Vermont lamb were among the main dishes, each with appropriate sauces and side dishes, and the dessert menu listed such temptations as chocolate and praline cake, caramel soufflé, and a chocolate and espresso tart with cocoa bean ice cream.

Another major change is the modern look of the Library, which now serves as an intimate, less formal dining room, furnished with velvet sofas and high-back leather chairs. Mahogany cabinets show off owner Susan's handsome collection of blue and white china. A tasty choice of sandwiches, salads, and pastas is available for lunch, and a trendy dinner menu offers choices from braised lamb shank to Scottish salmon.

Those who admire the gourmet cuisine at Wheatleigh will be pleased to know the chef is now offering cooking classes, from two-day Culinary Escapes to half-day and evening classes.

Guest rooms at Wheatleigh are tranquil, with contemporary decor and more intriguing details, such as the bathtubs purchased in a London antiques shop, and handblown sconces to provide the softest of lighting. Many rooms are large, with high ceilings. Some have fireplaces, balconies, and wonderful vistas.

Susan's description of the inn is "elegance without arrogance," and Lin's is "the ultimate urban amenity." Mine is "a perfect country inn." Wish I lived closer!

HOW TO GET THERE: From Stockbridge at the Red Lion Inn where Route 7 turns right, go straight on Prospect Hill Road, bearing left. Travel about 4½ miles, past the Stockbridge Bowl and up a hill to Wheatleigh.

From the Massachusetts Turnpike take exit 2 and follow the signs to Lenox. In the center of Lenox, take Route 183, pass the main gate of Tanglewood, and then take the first left on Hawthorne Road. Go 1 mile to Wheatleigh.

The Charlotte Inn
Martha's Vineyard (Edgartown), Massachusetts 02539

INNKEEPERS: Gery and Paula Conover

ADDRESS/TELEPHONE: 27 South Summer Street; (508) 627–4751

ROOMS: 23, plus 2 suites; all with private bath, air-conditioning, TV, and phone; some with fireplace.

RATES: Rooms, $295 to $650 CP; suites, $550 to $895 CP.

OPEN: All year.

FACILITIES AND ACTIVITIES: In-season, dinner. Off-season, dinner on weekends. Reservations a must. Nearby: Sailing, swimming, fishing, golf, tennis.

This is an island haven of total luxury, an exquisite complex of five buildings amid lush gardens with a restaurant that has long been considered the best in town.

The main house dates from 1864 and gives the feeling of a more elegant era. The foyer is hung with fine nineteenth-century paintings, and guests are greeted at a grand mahogany desk, where they sign an old-fashioned ledger.

Choosing where to stay is a pleasant dilemma. The Carriage House offers private terraces, fireplaces, French doors, and old brick courtyards. The second-floor suite has a fireplace I could live in.

A pathway through the rose garden leads to the Coach House, where a special suite offers glimpses of the harbor through a Palladian window. The veranda of the Summer House is a favorite spot to catch the breeze. Some of the bathrooms in this building are as large as a normal bedroom. The Garden House has an enchanted feel, surrounded by plantings inspired by the traditional English perennial garden, a sign of Paula's talents as a gardener.

Wherever you stay, the rooms are sumptuous. Canopied beds are piled with goose-down pillows and comforters. Most of the furnishings are late-nineteenth-century English, with accents like marble-topped dressers, silk and linen formal draperies, antique trunks, sterling-silver dresser sets, and brass and crystal lamps.

The famous French restaurant here is L'Etoile. On one of my visits, four of us had dinner here, and the food was exquisite. Capon breast stuffed with duxelles, spinach, and sun-dried tomatoes with coriander mayonnaise was the best I have had. I tasted everyone's food—nice occupation I have. Rack of lamb, served rare, with red wine–rosemary sauce and accompanied by potato and yam gratin was excellent. During my last visit I had grilled Angus filet mignon—it was glorious. My friend Audrey had a halibut fillet. They also have a special or two, but then everything is so special, the word does not fit. The menu changes monthly. Desserts the week I was there included blackberry and lemon curd napoleon and rhubarb and raspberry tart. For breakfast I had a strawberry crepe that I can still remember vividly. Freshly squeezed juices and fruit muffins . . . heaven!

Not the least of the pleasures of a vacation here is the forty-five-minute ferry ride to Martha's Vineyard. It's wise to make early reservations for your automobile on the ferry. Or, if you prefer not to take your car, you'll find taxis waiting when the ferry docks.

Gery and Paula are special innkeepers, but they do need the help of Ozzie and Jezebel, a pair of goldens.

HOW TO GET THERE: Reservations are a must if you take your car on the ferry from Woods Hole, Massachusetts. Forty-five minutes later you are in Vineyard Haven. After a fifteen-minute ride, you are in Edgartown, and on South Summer Street is the inn.

Lambert's Cove Inn
Martha's Vineyard (West Tisbury), Massachusetts 02568

INNKEEPERS: Scott T. Jones and I. Kell Hicklin

ADDRESS/TELEPHONE: Lambert's Cove Road (mailing address: RR 1, P.O. Box 422, Vineyard Haven, MA 02568); (508) 693-2298 or (866) 526-2466; fax (508) 693-7890

WEB SITE: www.lambertscoveinn.com

ROOMS: 15, all with private bath, air-conditioning, TV, DVD and CD players, phone, dataport, robes.

RATES: $175 to $325 BP.

OPEN: April through December.

FACILITIES AND ACTIVITIES: Dinner daily. BYOB. Tennis court, swimming pool. Nearby: Private beach.

At the end of a tree-shaded country road, you will find this gem of an inn on seven-and-a-half acres of lawn, gardens, and woodland. The original house was built in 1790. Over the years it was enlarged and a carriage house and barn added.

The decor is English country, and the mood is elegant but still comfortable. When you come in, the dining room is to the left, a romantic room done in warm gold with hardwood floors and a fireplace. To the right is the club room, a little more formal, done in dark green, royal blue, and a bit of gold. Straight ahead and to the right is the comfortable library, a spacious room with a fireplace at one end, a one hundred-year-old grand piano at the other, and French doors opening to a big outdoor deck. The library is done in red with leather furnishings and several cozy sitting areas for reading, relaxing, or

Ferrying to Martha's Vineyard

Sailing from "America," as the islanders call the mainland, to Martha's Vineyard is easily accomplished on one of the ferries that ply the waters between the island and Falmouth, Hyannis, Woods Hole, and New Bedford. All of the ferry services offer parking lots for both day-tripping and overnight travelers.

The **Steamship Authority** (508-477-8600 or 508-693-9130; www.islandferry.com) out of Woods Hole offers the only car-and-passenger service to the island, sailing year-round to Vineyard Haven and from May to September to Oak Bluffs. The crossing takes forty-five minutes, and car reservations are required. In season, service is also available from New Bedford.

The *Island Queen* (508-548-4800; www.islandqueen.com) is a passenger ferry that makes daily trips from Falmouth Harbor on Cape Cod to Oak Bluffs on the Vineyard from late May to mid-October. This crossing takes only thirty-five minutes. This open-air vessel offers a spacious sundeck and a complete snack bar on board as well as secure parking in a private lot not far from the Falmouth dock. Day-trippers and other seasonal visitors can bring bicycles aboard and cycle along the island's shore path and into Oak Bluffs, Vineyard Haven, and Edgartown.

Also in season only, from May through October, **Hy-Line Cruises** (508-778-2600; www.hy-linecruises.com) sails from Hyannis to Oak Bluffs, a one-and-three-quarter-hour trip.

listening to music. At the top of the stairs is a study with a phone and a computer for guests.

Guest rooms are in the main house or the renovated carriage and guest houses, located across the garden. They are decorated lavishly, no two alike. Seaside is prime, the former master bedroom, done with a filmy white canopy bed in front of the working fireplace. Key West is in tropical prints; Chesapeake has sunny yellow walls, beams, and a black and white toile bedspread. All the rooms have comfortable seating, feather beds, 500-thread-count Egyptian cotton linens, and down coverlets and pillows, and all come with comfy robes.

The highly praised inn dining room offers lots of local seafood, including lobster, and farm-fresh produce. You might start with a crab cake or steamed

mussels, and then order sea scallops or striped bass. Or if you are not in the mood for seafood, you'll find nice choices such as duckling, veal, and filet mignon on the menu.

West Tisbury is real country. Walk twenty minutes to the Lambert's Cove beach, or just walk anywhere. It's a beautiful part of the world.

HOW TO GET THERE: Take the ferry to Martha's Vineyard from Cape Cod. After driving off the ferry, take a left, then a right at the next stop-sign intersection. Stay on this road for 1½ miles to Lambert's Cove Road, on your right. Three miles from this point, look for the inn's sign, on the left.

Jared Coffin House 📱
Nantucket, Massachusetts 02554

INNKEEPERS: Philip and Peg Read; Eric Landt, general manager

ADDRESS/TELEPHONE: 29 Broad Street; (508) 228-2400 or (800) 248-2405; fax (508) 228-8549

WEB SITE: www.jaredcoffinhouse.com

ROOMS: 60; 11 in main house, 16 simpler rooms in Eben Allen Wing, 3 rooms in Swain House connected to the Eben Allen Wing, 12 rooms in Daniel Webster House across the patio, 18 rooms in 2 houses across the street.

RATES: $125 to $375 EP.

OPEN: All year.

FACILITIES AND ACTIVITIES: Breakfast, lunch, dinner, taproom. Eben Allen Room for private parties. Nearby: Swimming, tennis.

*I*t is well worth the 30-mile trip by ferry, or the plane trip from Boston or New York, to end up at the Jared Coffin House. Built as a private home in 1845, the three-story brick house with slate roof passed through many hands before it came to the extremely capable ones of Philip and Peg Read.

The public rooms at the inn reflect charm and warmth. The furnishings are Chippendale and Sheraton; showing the results of the worldwide voyaging by the Nantucket whalemen are Chinese and Japanese objets d'art and furniture.

To add to the charm are many fabrics and some furniture that were made right here on the island. In addition to the main house, the inn complex includes several other close-by houses. All are done beautifully for your every comfort. The size and the quantity of the luxurious bath towels in the guest rooms please me greatly. The housekeeping staff does a wonderful job, and the exquisite antiques reflect their loving care.

The taproom, located on the lowest level, is a warm, happy, fun place. Here you meet the local people and spin yarns with all. Old pine walls and hand-hewn beams reflect a cozy atmosphere. Luncheon is served down here, with good burgers and great, hearty soups. During the winter this is a nice spot for informal dinners.

The main dining room, papered with authentic wallpapers, is quiet and elegant. Wedgwood china and pistol-handled silverware make dining a special

Getting to Nantucket

Flying and ferrying are the two preferred methods of traveling to Nantucket, unless you happen to have your own sturdy boat or the means to charter one. Flights are available to Nantucket from Hyannis, Providence, Boston, New York, and Newark. For current airlines flying these routes, contact Nantucket Memorial Airport (508-325-5300; www.nantucketairport.com) or the Nantucket Chamber of Commerce (508-228-1700; www.nantucketchamber.org).

Ferries run year-round from Hyannis only. The Steamship Authority (508-477-8600; www.steamshipauthority.com) offers car-and-passenger, two-and-a-quarter-hour trips and a "fast ferry" high-speed boat that makes the trip in one hour. Hy-Line (508-778-2600; www.hy-linecruises.com) sends its high-speed cat *Grey Lady* on one-hour crossings year-round and its slower MV *Great Point* ferry on two-hour crossings from mid-May to late October. Reservations for cars are a must.

pleasure and reflect the good life demanded by the nineteenth-century owners of the great Nantucket whaling ships.

The inn is located in the heart of Nantucket's Historic District, about ⅛ mile from one public beach and 1 mile from the island's largest public beach and tennis courts. It's a very pleasant 3-mile bicycle ride through the district to superb surf swimming on the South Shore.

HOW TO GET THERE: To get to Nantucket, take a ferry from Hyannis (April through January) or Woods Hole (January through March and summer months). First call (508) 540-2022 for reservations. Or take a plane from Boston, Hyannis, or New York. The inn is located 2 blocks north of Main Street and 2 blocks west of Steamboat Wharf.

The Woodbox Inn
Nantucket, Massachusetts 02554

INNKEEPER: Dexter Tutein

ADDRESS/TELEPHONE: 29 Fair Street; (508) 228-0587; fax (508) 228-7527

WEB SITE: www.woodboxinn.com

ROOMS: 3 queens, plus 6 suites in 2 buildings; all with private bath.

RATES: $180 to $310 EP. No credit cards.

OPEN: Mid-May to Columbus Day. Weekends only from Columbus Day to January 1.

FACILITIES AND ACTIVITIES: Full breakfast, dinner, beer and wine license. Wheelchair access to sunrooms, dining rooms. Nearby: Swimming, boating, biking, tennis.

For a half-century there has been a Tutein running this inn. Built in 1709, it is the oldest inn on Nantucket Island. What a treat to be here!

The suites are unique. In an old building like this, you cannot change the structure to modernize, so the bathrooms have been very inventively fit into corners and odd spaces. Very pretty and comfortable. The suite I was in had a fireplace in the living room; two bedrooms, one with a huge canopy bed; and a lovely little private patio. It was hard to leave.

There are three charming dining rooms in the inn. The setting is romantic—antiques, candlelight, and fine china. I had dinner in what must be one of the oldest public dining rooms in New England. The room has two "king's boards" on the wall of the immense, almost walk-in fireplace.

The inn is famous for its popovers, and I can understand why, having devoured quite a few. The food is truly gourmet. Naturally, the entrees include the catch of the day; I had fresh sea bass that was delicious. My dinner companion had the veal chop, saffron rice, and glazed pear chutney. The house salad dressing is excellent. And for dessert, well, the best crème brûlée I have ever had. The menu changes often, but you can be sure of equally delicious choices. Lately the Woodbox has become known for its wine dinners, featuring winemakers and guest chefs.

The inn's breakfast is a great way to start the day—choose Belgian waffles or pancakes or the eggs Benedict—an inn tradition. The pancakes and waffles come with pure maple syrup, blueberries, strawberries, bananas, or walnuts. Those wonderful popovers come with any egg dish. The chef has cooked several times at the James Beard Foundation in New York City. The inn is also a nine-time winner of *Wine Spectator*'s Award of Excellence.

HOW TO GET THERE: Take the ferry to Nantucket or fly from Hyannis. The inn is at 29 Fair Street. You can walk to it from the ferry.

Yankee Clipper Inn
Rockport, Massachusetts 01966

INNKEEPERS: Randy and Cathy Marks

ADDRESS/TELEPHONE: 127 Granite Street (mailing address: P.O. Box 2399); (978) 546–3407 or (800) 545–3699; fax (978) 549–9730

WEB SITE: www.yankeeclipperinn.com

ROOMS: 16, including 3 suites, in 2 buildings; all with private bath, air-conditioning, cable TV, and phone. Some baths have Jacuzzis.

RATES: $129 to $389 BP.

OPEN: All year.

FACILITIES AND ACTIVITIES: Small function room, heated saltwater pool. Nearby: Fishing, boating, shopping, whale watching.

When you are lucky enough to be here and see a sunset, you will be overwhelmed. It's a golden sea and sky, with the town of Rockport in the distance. No camera could truly capture this scene. Wait a while longer, and the moonlight on the sea is an awesome sight.

The main inn, an oceanfront mansion, has rooms furnished in colonial style. A full breakfast is served here in a cheerful dining gallery with lots of windows.

The Quarterdeck building has large picture windows, providing a panoramic view of the ocean. Upholstered chairs are placed in front of the windows. Sit back and relax; it's almost like being on a ship that does not move. All of the rooms in this building are beautifully furnished, as well.

The special-occasion room is a lovely spot. For any sort of function, from small weddings to executive meetings, it has a wonderful water view, a big-screen TV and VCR, and everything you'd need for your meeting.

You won't be bored in Rockport. The town is filled with galleries and shops, and beaches and whale-watching excursions are within a few minutes' drive. And when you come home to the Yankee Clipper, you can take a dip in the heated saltwater pool, and then have a seat and admire the view from the picture-perfect spot.

HOW TO GET THERE: Take Route 128 north and east to Cape Ann. Route 128 ends at traffic lights. Turn left onto Route 127. Drive 3 miles to where Route 127 turns left into Pigeon Cove. Continue on Route 127 for 1²/₁₀ miles to Yankee Clipper in Pigeon Cove.

The Belfry Inne and Bistro
Sandwich, Massachusetts 02563

INNKEEPER: Chris Wilson

ADDRESS/TELEPHONE: 6–8 Jarves Street (mailing address: P.O. Box 2211); (508) 888–8550 or (800) 844–4552; fax (508) 888–3922

WEB SITE: www.belfryinn.com

ROOMS: 22 rooms and suites in 3 buildings; all but 2 with private bath; many with whirlpools, fireplaces, and/or balconies. The Abbey rooms have air-conditioning and TV as well as whirlpool tubs. The Painted Lady is also air-conditioned.

RATES: $115 to $275 BP.

OPEN: All year.

FACILITIES AND ACTIVITIES: Restaurant. Nearby: Sandwich Glass Museum, Dexter Grist Mill, Heritage Museum and Gardens, beaches, Cape Cod Scenic Railroad.

*T*t isn't often that going to church means visiting a country inn and restaurant, but that's the case at the Belfry Inne and Bistro, where the main house, known as the Abbey, is a former church circa 1900. Owner Chris Wilson is responsible for this unusual transformation, which takes full advantage of the vaulted ceilings and lovely stained-glass windows to create unique spaces and ambience, with skylights added as a modern touch.

Six guest rooms in the Abbey are named for the days of the week, Monday through Saturday, all featuring whirlpool tubs big enough for two. I'm partial to Tuesday, which has a beautiful circular stained-glass window behind the bed, a gas fireplace, and a balcony. Wednesday features a pew headboard and tulip stained-glass sconces, while Friday offers a striking stained-glass window depicting Gabriel the Archangel.

The rooms are located off a balcony looking down at the Bistro dining room, which shares the soaring spaces of the church. Guests enjoy a full buffet breakfast and an interesting dinner menu, which takes full advantage of the Cape's bountiful seafood. The menu changes often, but a typical dinner might start with lobster bisque or prosciutto-wrapped jumbo shrimp. Among main courses you may find rack of lamb, roasted pork tenderloin, sesame marinated chicken breast, black grouper roasted in a banana leaf, or pan seared sea scallops and lobster.

Additional rooms are in the very Victorian Painted Lady next door to the Abbey. It was built in 1882 and was being used as a church rectory until Chris purchased it in 1993. Rooms here have more traditional decor. One of the nicest is Martha Southworth, done in blue and white, with a handsome spool bed and a whirlpool in the bath. Sara Chase, with a soothing mint green and white color scheme, is under the cozy eaves on the third floor. The antique iron-headboard bed faces the gas fireplace, and the bath beckons with a 5-foot soaking tub.

The Painted Lady Cafe has whimsical decor and a less formal menu than the Bistro, offering soups and salads, quesadillas, unusual pizzas, and comfort foods such as chicken potpie, macaroni and cheese, pork chops, or roasted chicken with mashed potatoes. There's a children's menu, as well.

More rooms are available at the more modest Village Inn, on the other side of the Abbey. Built around 1860, it has a wraparound porch with rocking chairs and flower boxes, pretty gardens and old trees, and a carriage house, where painting workshops are held. Rooms have traditional old-fashioned decor, floral wallpapers, lace curtains, and ceiling fans. Two rooms on the third floor share a bath, a good choice for families.

HOW TO GET THERE: From Route 6, the Cape Highway, take exit 2 and go left at the end of the ramp. Follow Route 130 for 1½ miles to a fork. Bear right at the fork (Sandwich Center). Go ²/₁₀ mile to Jarves Street, the first left turn after the Dan'l Webster Inn. The inn is ahead on the right.

The Dan'l Webster Inn
Sandwich, Massachusetts 02563

INNKEEPER: Robert Catania, general manager

ADDRESS/TELEPHONE: 149 Main Street; (508) 888–3622 or (800) 444–3566

WEB SITE: www.danlwebsterinn.com

ROOMS: 53, in 3 buildings; all with private bath, phone, TV, free high-speed Internet connections, and air-conditioning; many with whirlpool tub and fireplace.

RATES: $109 to $399 EP; MAP available.

OPEN: All year except Christmas Day.

FACILITIES AND ACTIVITIES: Breakfast, lunch, dinner, Sunday brunch. Bar, lounge, swimming pool, gift shop, spa. Nearby: Doll museum, glass museum, Heritage Museum and Gardens, beaches, golf.

The original 1692 structure is long gone, but there's still the look of old New England at this classic inn presiding over the center of the oldest village on Cape Cod. It is a favorite for dining as well as for the nicely appointed guest rooms. *Boston Magazine* named it "Best Hotel/Inn" in its 2005 "Best of Boston" issue.

Different dining rooms at the inn give you a choice of moods. The glass-walled Conservatory looks out on the gardens, and there is cozy fireside dining in the Music Room. Both share the same dinner menu, which is classic American, with favorites such as prime rib, filet mignon, and fresh seafood. The more adventurous chef's specials change with the seasons and can range from Cape bay scallops to braised pork shank.

The Tavern, where drinks and lighter fare are served, is an exact replica of the tavern where Daniel Webster himself was once a patron and where patriots came together during the Revolutionary War.

The Conservatory is a cheerful place for breakfast, looking out upon the many bird feeders in the garden. Besides the usual pancakes, eggs, and French toast, the menu offers changing specialties such as an avocado and shrimp omelet or a ham and egg croissant.

Rooms at the inn and in adjacent buildings are nicely appointed with colonial decor, many with canopy and four-poster beds. The most luxurious quarters are in the Jarves Wing, where eight rooms have fireplaces, two-person showers, and oversize step-down whirlpools surrounded with grand columns. Many rooms have private balconies overlooking the gardens.

The Sandwich Glass Museum with glassblowing demonstrations and the working gristmill on the village green are within a short walk, and when you've done with sightseeing, there's a refreshing outdoor pool waiting for you back at the inn.

HOW TO GET THERE: Go over the Bourne Bridge to a rotary; go three-fourths of the way around it, taking the Route 6A exit that parallels the canal. Stay on this road until you come to the third set of lights. This is Jarves Street. Go right, then right again onto Main Street. The inn is on the right, close to the corner.

The Egremont Inn
South Egremont, Massachusetts 01258

INNKEEPERS: Karen and Steve Waller

ADDRESS/TELEPHONE: 10 Old Sheffield Road (mailing address: Box 418); (413) 528-2111 or (800) 859-1780; fax (413) 528-3284

WEB SITE: www.egremontinn.com

ROOMS: 20, including 2 suites; all with private bath, phone, air-conditioning; some with whirlpool.

RATES: $110 to $240, BP weekends, CP weekdays.

OPEN: All year.

FACILITIES AND ACTIVITIES: Dinner Wednesday through Sunday in the dining room and tavern. Live entertainment on Thursday and Saturday. Outdoor pool, 2 tennis courts. Discounted ski tickets.

uilt in 1780, this rambling inn with a wraparound porch is true New England, a wonderful old building with tilty floors and delightful accommodations. When you walk in, you are in a huge living room, called the Pine Room, with a large fireplace, good couches and chairs, and the start of a stuffed-animal collection that you'll find all over the inn. Albert the Duck and Winston A. Bear are there waiting. Yes, Karen has named them all. I relate to this as I've got tons of bears.

To the right of this room is another lovely room with a fireplace, plus a sitting room with yet another fireplace, with a couch right in front of it, and a television. This is where you'll find a lot of board games and a toy chest for children.

The main dining room is warm and attractive. The napery is white, and there are lots of plants and its own fireplace.

The menu is creative American, and the food is grand. Among the appetizers, wild mushroom soup is excellent. The menus change seasonally and feature a variety of fish and meats, and nightly specials.

The comfortable tavern has its own less formal menu. One of the favorites is "Mac" and cheese.

As you might expect in a vintage inn, guest rooms on the second and third floors vary in shape and size. All have pleasant and simple country decor with some antique accents. Many rooms offer cozy quilts on the bed, and all have

a teddy bear or another cuddly creature to keep you company. Couples might opt for the rooms that offer whirlpool tubs, and some rooms are large enough to accommodate families.

Do take the walking tour through town, because there is a lot to see here in a quiet corner of the southern Berkshires. The lovely village and the inn are both on the National Register of Historic Places.

HOW TO GET THERE: From New York go north on Route 22 or the Taconic Parkway to Route 23 east. After the town of South Egremont, turn right at the small island. The inn is 200 yards ahead. From Boston take the Massachusetts Turnpike to exit 2. Follow Route 102 west to Route 7 south. After going through Great Barrington, take Route 23 west to South Egremont. In 3³/₁₀ miles, bear left at the small island. The inn is straight ahead.

The Weathervane Inn
South Egremont, Massachusetts 01258

INNKEEPERS: Jeffrey and Maxine Lome

ADDRESS/TELEPHONE: Main Street (Route 23); (413) 528–9580 or (800) 528–9580; fax (413) 528–1713

WEB SITE: www.weathervane.com

ROOMS: 10, including 1 suite with fireplace; all with private bath, air-conditioning; 2 rooms with wheelchair accessibility.

RATES: $135 to $165 ($245 suite) BP. On weekends, $115 to $150 BP. Minimum of two nights' stay on weekends, three nights on holiday weekends and in the summer. Special seasonal or group packages available, some with dinner.

OPEN: All year except Christmas Day.

FACILITIES AND ACTIVITIES: Breakfast and afternoon tea; optional catered dinner for small groups. Swimming pool, outside games. Nearby: Antiques stores, fishing, hiking, bicycling, golf, tennis, skiing.

BUSINESS TRAVEL: Fully appointed meeting room; audiovisual equipment; copying, faxing, Internet access available.

*T*he Weathervane began its existence as a farmhouse in 1785 and is listed on the National Register of Historic Places. The original fireplace, which was used for both heating and cooking, boasts a beehive bake oven. These are rarely seen today but were a real necessity in early times.

What better way to celebrate the old farmhouse's history than with a hearty country breakfast? Innkeepers Jeff and Maxine Lome offer a homemade French toast with maple syrup from local farmers. It's to die for! Or you can savor fresh baked muffins, like their applesauce strudel muffins, in addition to other hot-off-the-griddle breakfast fare. Don't miss the homemade preserves prepared from fruit grown on the premises. You'll enjoy this feast while looking out over ten beautifully landscaped acres of gardens and trees.

After a day of sightseeing, sports, shopping, or even snoozing (!), don't miss the afternoon tea put out each day. Have a cup of your favorite tea, or try spiced cider or hot chocolate in season. There are always homemade goodies to tempt you, maybe Toll House cookies or fresh banana bread. Dinner is available only by special arrangement, usually for groups of ten or more, although the inn sometimes offers family packages that include a family-style dinner. Ask ahead of time if you're interested.

Guest rooms feature cheerful flowered wallpapers, colorful patchwork quilts, comfortable reading chairs, and queen- or king-size beds, some of them four-poster. The suite has a king-size bed, in-room fireplace, and television with VCR. Luxurious!

All the public rooms are comfortable, and there is so much to do in this area all year that you could stay and stay. Be sure to visit the antiques dealer in the barn. In winter downhill or cross-country skiers will not have far to go. Bicycling or hiking in the area is awesome. Riding horses or fishing the lakes is also a nice thing to do in this beautiful countryside.

HOW TO GET THERE: Follow Route 7 to Route 23 west. You are now 3 miles from South Egremont. The inn will be on your left.

The Red Lion Inn
Stockbridge, Massachusetts 01262

INNKEEPERS: The Fitzpatrick family, owners; Bruce Finn, general manager

ADDRESS/TELEPHONE: Main Street; (413) 298-5545; fax (413) 298-5130

WEB SITE: www.redlioninn.com

ROOMS: 83, plus 25 suites, in inn and adjacent guest houses; 94 with private bath; all with robes; wireless Internet in main inn and some guest houses; some suites with whirlpool; 2 with wheelchair accessibility.

RATES: $89 to $425 EP.

OPEN: All year.

FACILITIES AND ACTIVITIES: Breakfast, lunch, dinner, bar. Heated outdoor swimming pool, fitness room, guest computer work station. Elevator. Red Lion Gift Shop, Country Curtains shop. Nearby: All the museums and performing arts of the Berkshires.

They say if you sit on the porch of the Red Lion Inn long enough, you'll see everyone you know—at least everyone who is visiting the Berkshires. This big clapboard inn with rockers lining the porch is a classic, a fixture in Stockbridge since the 1770s and the center of life in the village. Since 1968 it has been in the capable hands of the Fitzpatrick family, who have kept the feel of the past while continually adding amenities of today. The inn's antiques, china, and colonial pewter collections remain on display throughout the inn, but you'll also find additions like a computer workstation in the library, a fitness room, and a heated swimming pool outside.

Norman Rockwell Museum

Overlooking the Housatonic River in Stockbridge is a museum honoring one of America's most beloved illustrators. Norman Rockwell was a resident of the town for fifty years while he painted magazine covers for *Saturday Evening Post, Look, McCalls,* and *Colliers.* In this beautiful museum, see permanent displays of Rockwell's original artwork, his own studio, and changing exhibitions of other noted illustrators. Stroll the thiry-six-acre grounds to see sculptures by son Peter Rockwell. The museum is open year-round. Call (413) 298-4100 or log on to www.nrm.org for hours and admission.

Dinners in the main dining room are elegant, served by candlelight beneath crystal chandeliers. The menu mixes New England classics including clam chowder and roast turkey with updated dishes such as grilled Moroccan spiced tuna. If you want something less formal, Widow Bingham's Tavern is cozy, with cheerful checked tablecloths, paneled walls, and a menu of soups, salads, and sandwiches. The Lion's Den downstairs offers burgers and pub favorites such as shepherd's pie, and entertainment nightly. Don't miss the Den's bread pudding dessert! In summer, the flower-filled Courtyard is added to the dining choices.

Rooms are in the main inn or one of several neighboring guest houses that have been converted to lodgings. Some of the guest houses have kitchens and porches. All the lodgings are beautifully furnished with canopy and four-poster beds and pretty old-fashioned printed wallpapers.

During one visit I stayed in the 1899 village firehouse, which was once the subject of a Norman Rockwell painting that still hangs inside in what is now a luxury two-story suite. It is furnished with a king-size bed that is part of a lovely wicker set from an old estate. The bathroom has a double whirlpool bath.

If you don't mind being a few minutes' drive from the main inn, you can stay in a very special lodging, Meadowlark. It was once the secluded studio of the famous sculptor Daniel Chester French and is located on the grounds of his estate, Chesterwood.

The Red Lion Inn is a four-season inn. In summer you have the Berkshire Music Festival at Tanglewood and the Jacob's Pillow Dance Festival, both world-renowned. Fall's foliage is perhaps the most spectacular in New England; in winter there is snow on the hills; in spring come the lovely green and flowers. All go together to make this a great spot any time of year.

HOW TO GET THERE: Take exit 2 from the Massachusetts Turnpike and follow Route 102 west to the inn.

Publick House 🏷️ 📱
Sturbridge, Massachusetts 01566

INNKEEPER: Albert Cournoyer

ADDRESS/TELEPHONE: P.O. Box 187; (508) 347–3313 or (800) PUBLICK; fax (508) 347–1246

WEB SITE: www.publickhouse.com

ROOMS: 15, plus 2 suites in main inn; 6 suites in Chamberlain House; 96 rooms in motor lodge (with TV); all with private bath, air-conditioning, phone.

RATES: Rooms, $90 to $135 EP; suites, $125 to $165 EP; motor lodge, $69 to $129 EP. Package rates available.

OPEN: All year.

FACILITIES AND ACTIVITIES: Breakfast, lunch, dinner, bar. Wheelchair access to restaurant. Gift shop, swimming pool, tennis courts, jogging trail, children's play area. Nearby: Old Sturbridge Village, golf, fishing, cross-country skiing.

BUSINESS TRAVEL: Meeting rooms; phone in all rooms; fax available; corporate rates.

*I*t's a real pleasure to me to keep coming back to the Publick House and finding it always the same, always excellent. As a matter of fact, very little has changed here since the inn was built in 1771. The green still stretches along in front of the inn, and the trees still cast their welcome shade. The Publick House is still taking care of the wayfarer, feeding him well, providing a comfortable bed, and supplying robust drink.

The Publick House calendar is fun to read. Throughout the year there are special celebrations for holidays. They do keep the spirit of Christmas alive here. All twelve days of it. The Boar's Head Procession is truly unique, complete with a roast young suckling pig, a roast goose, and plum pudding.

Winter weekends are times for special treats, with chestnuts roasting by an open fire, and sleigh rides through nearby Old Sturbridge Village, a happy step backward in time.

The guest rooms are decorated with period furniture. The wide floorboards and beamed ceilings have been here since Col. Ebenezer Crafts founded the inn. The Chamberlain House adjacent to the inn holds six spacious suites. Families who want the ease of a motel (and the presence of a TV)

might opt for the economical Country Motor Lodge behind the inn, just a short walk away.

The barn, connected to the main house with a ramp, has been transformed into a restaurant. Double doors, topped by a sunburst window, lead into a restaurant that serves hearty Yankee cooking, such as delicious lobster pie. There is a little musician's gallery, still divided into stalls, that overlooks the main dining room. Beneath this is an attractive taproom.

I found my way by following my nose to the Bake Shoppe, where every day fresh sticky buns, deep-dish apple pies, corn bread, and muffins come out of the ovens to tempt me from my diet! Take some along for hunger pangs along the road.

And from home you can order the inn's good jams, mustards, relishes, chowders, and more. They are beautifully packaged and mailed to you wherever you wish.

HOW TO GET THERE: Take the Massachusetts Turnpike to exit 9. The Publick House is located on the Common in Sturbridge, on Route 131. From Hartford take Interstate 84 to exit 2, which brings you right into Sturbridge.

Longfellow's Wayside Inn
Sudbury, Massachusetts 01776

INNKEEPER: Robert Purrington

ADDRESS/TELEPHONE: Wayside Inn Road; (978) 443-1776 or (800) 339-1776

WEB SITE: www.wayside.org/wayside

ROOMS: 10, all with private bath, air-conditioning, and phone.

RATES: $122 to $155 BP.

OPEN: All year except Christmas Day and July 4.

FACILITIES AND ACTIVITIES: Breakfast for house guests only, lunch, dinner, bar. Horses boarded. Gift shop, museum.

BUSINESS TRAVEL: Located 22 miles from Boston. Phone, table, and chairs in room; conference room; fax available.

Generations of travelers have found food and lodging for "man and beast" at the Wayside Inn. Route 20 is the old stagecoach road to Boston, now well off the beaten track. The inn looks much as it did from 1716 to 1861, when it was known as Howe's Tavern, and it still supplies the traveler with hearty food and drink and a comfortable bed.

As with many old buildings, "improvements" were made to the inn in the nineteenth century, but thanks to Henry Ford, a complete restoration in the 1950s afforded the opportunity to put many things back the way they were in the beginning. Now part of the inn serves as a museum with priceless antiques displayed in their original settings.

The inn offers a large dining room and several smaller ones, a bar, a gift shop, and a lovely walled garden. At the end of the garden path is a bust of Henry Wadsworth Longfellow, who was inspired by the inn to link a group of poems known to all schoolchildren as *Tales of a Wayside Inn*.

Henry Ford bought 2,995 acres surrounding the inn in 1923, and since then this historic area has been preserved. A little way up the road stand a lovely chapel, the little red schoolhouse that gained fame in "Mary Had a

Little Lamb," and a stone gristmill that still grinds grain for the rolls and muffins baked at the inn. I bought some of their cornmeal because the muffins I ate at the inn were exquisite. This is a most interesting building to visit, as all of the equipment in the mill is water powered.

As a final touch, the inn boasts what it claims is the oldest mixed drink in America. It is called Coow Woow. You must taste it to discover how well our fore-fathers lived.

HOW TO GET THERE: From Boston take the Massachusetts Turnpike west to Route 128 north. Take exit 26 west onto Route 20. Wayside Inn Road is 11 miles west, just off Route 20. From New York take the Massachusetts Turn-pike to Route 495, and go north to Route 20 east. It is approximately 8 miles to Wayside Inn Road.

Williams Inn
Williamstown, Massachusetts 01267

INNKEEPERS: Carl and Marilyn Faulkner

ADDRESS/TELEPHONE: 1090 Main Street; (413) 458–9371; fax (413) 458-2767

WEB SITE: www.williamsinn.com

ROOMS: 125 rooms and suites, all with private bath, phone, TV, air-conditioning; 6 specially equipped for the physically disabled.

RATES: Rooms, $150 to $290 EP; suites, $375 to $500 EP. Children under 14 free in parents' room.

OPEN: All year.

FACILITIES AND ACTIVITIES: Breakfast, lunch, dinner, Sunday brunch. Indoor pool, hot tub. Nearby: Williams College, Williams College Museum of Art, Clark Art Institute, Massachusetts Museum of Contemporary Art, Mohawk Trail drive, hiking.

This columned inn looks like it has been here a long time, but in fact it was built in 1974, after the original 1912 building was converted to become the first women's dorm at Williams College, now known as Dodd House.

It is now a warm, family-owned lodging with an ideal location, adjoining the Williams campus and just a stroll from the heart of the town that is known as the Village Beautiful.

With an air of the past but amenities of today, the inn offers rooms that are spacious, with traditional New England colonial decor and nice features such as in-room telephones, TV, and air-conditioning. Rooms in a wing added in 2003 come with king-size beds. The main sitting room welcomes with wing chairs around a fireplace; features such as an indoor pool, hot tub, and sauna add to the pleasures of a stay.

The dining room menu combines New England favorites with continental dishes. The offerings change with the seasons. Crisp roast duckling, seafood such as sole and scrod, beef fillet, and lamb dishes are among the favorites, and New England Indian pudding and apple pie are among the traditional desserts. The Sunday brunch buffet is so generous, you probably won't have to eat the rest of the day. Meals are served outdoors on balmy summer days.

The Tavern offers a lighter menu of pizza, sandwiches, salads, and its own Tavern stew. There is live music for dancing here on Saturday nights, a guitarist on Friday, and cabaret entertainment in summer on Sunday and Monday nights.

Two excellent art museums, the handsome Williams College campus, and the glorious scenery of the surrounding Berkshire Mountains make Williamstown a very special destination, and this is just the inn to make the most of it.

HOW TO GET THERE: Take Route 7 from the north or south, or Route 2 from points east to Williamstown. The inn is on the left of the village green at the northerly junction of Routes 7 and 2.

Sterling and Francine Clark Art Institute

Here in the hollows of the Berkshires, far from big-city museums, is one of the finest art collections in the nation. The French Impressionists are among the most notable works—see Monet, Pissarro, Degas, and especially Renoir. American paintings and sculpture by Sargent, Homer, and Remington are here along with European pieces dating from medieval times. The museum itself is grand. Lectures, concerts, poetry readings, and outdoor musical performances in the summer are on the yearlong calendar of special events. A gift shop and seasonal cafe are also here. For information call (413) 458-2303 or log on to www.clarkart.edu.

Select List of Other Massachusetts Inns

The Captain's House Inn
369–371 Old Harbor Road
Chatham, MA 02633
(508) 945-0127 or (800) 315-0728; fax (508) 945-0866
Web site: captainshouseinn.com
16 rooms and suites, all with private bath, fireplace, TV/VCR; many with CD player, whirlpool tub; 1839 Greek Revival bed and breakfast complex on 2 acres, decorated in Williamsburg style.

Walker House
64 Walker Street
Lenox, MA 01240
(413) 637-1271 or (800) 235-3098; fax (413) 637-2387
Web site: www.walkerhouse.com
8 rooms, all with private bath; bed and breakfast in 1804 Federal colonial decorated with antiques; each room named for a composer.

Seven Sea Street Inn

7 Sea Street
Nantucket, MA 02554
(508) 228-3577 or (800) 651-9262; fax (508) 228-3578
Web site: www.sevenseastreetinn.com
15 rooms and suites, all with private bath; serves breakfast; newly constructed inn and period guest houses with authentic Nantucket ambience.

Fernside B&B

162 Mountain Road
P.O. Box 303
Princeton, MA 01541
(978) 464-2741 or (800) 545-2741; fax (978) 464-2065
Web site: www.fernsideinn.com
6 rooms, 2 suites, all with private bath; most with fireplaces; 1835 Federal mansion.

New Hampshire

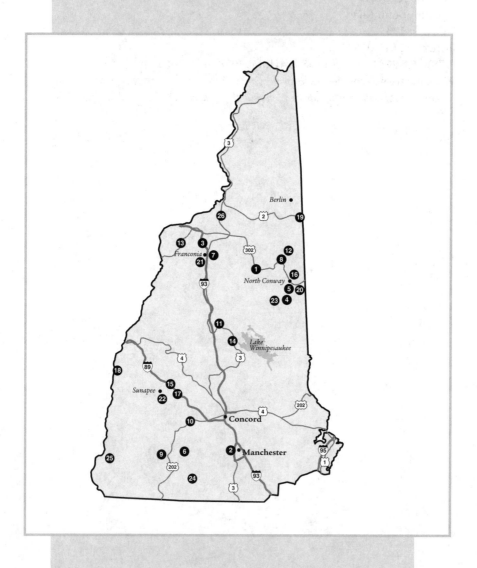

Berlin

Franconia

North Conway

Lake
Winnipesaukee

Sunapee

Concord

Manchester

New Hampshire

Numbers on map refer to towns numbered below.

The Notchland Inn

Bartlett, New Hampshire 03812

INNKEEPERS: Les Schoof and Ed Butler

ADDRESS/TELEPHONE: Route 302; (603) 374–6131 or (800) 866–6131; fax (603) 374–6168

WEB SITE: www.notchland.com

ROOMS: 7, plus 6 suites and 3 cottages; all with private bath and fireplace; 1 cottage specially equipped for the physically disabled; 1 two-and-a-half-bedroom cottage with sauna, whirlpool, kitchen, 2 baths; 1 two-bedroom cottage with kitchenette.

RATES: $265 to $410 MAP. Bed-and-breakfast is available.

OPEN: All year.

FACILITIES AND ACTIVITIES: Full liquor license. Hot tub. Hiking, canoeing, swimming, fishing, bicycling, snowshoeing. Nearby: Downhill and cross-country skiing, sleigh rides, and ice skating. Dinner is not served on Monday or Tuesday.

The inn was built in 1860 by a wealthy Boston dentist, Samuel Bemis, and no expense was spared. He used native granite and timber and made sure that each of the seventeen rooms had a working fireplace. The front parlor was done by none other than Gustav Stickley, a founder of the Arts and Crafts movement. All the rooms have high ceilings and beautiful mountain views. The music room is inviting with its piano and stereo, and the sunroom is full of beautiful plants and a fountain. The dining room dates from 1795, has a raised hearth fireplace, and looks out onto the pond and gazebo.

Of course, there have been a few modern changes over the years, including some additional buildings. An old schoolhouse now holds two suites, one with a deck, a wood-burning fireplace, a whirlpool tub, a queen-size bed, and a comfortable living room. Several of the suites and cottages offer two-person whirlpool baths. Good news for pet owners: With the recent addition of two new cottages, the inn now accepts pets for cottage stays.

Dinner is served five nights a week at 7:00, and patrons are offered a choice of two soups, two appetizers, three entrees, and three desserts. To give you an idea of the varied menu, soup may be lightly curried sweet potato and butternut squash, orange-scented tomato with a fresh herbed yogurt, or Szechuan carrot. Appetizers may be crab cakes or three-tier vegetable pâté with a red pepper coulis. Entrees may be filet mignon with béarnaise sauce, chicken champagne, poached catfish, or poached salmon stuffed with scallops and herbs. And dessert may be very lemon pie, apricot cheesecake, or chocolate walnut tart. Not to worry if you can't decide—seconds are always available! If you can even think about breakfast after such a dinner, you'll delight in the full country breakfast that will start your day right.

Attitash Bear Peak

Outdoor recreation lovers will enjoy the multiseason activities at Bartlett's Attitash Bear Peak (603–374–2368; www.attitash.com) on Route 302. This year-round recreation area and ski mountain has forty-five downhill ski trails, including a vertical drop of 1,750 feet for thrillseekers and a novice trail for beginners. There are complete snow-making capabilities, pay-by-the-run lift tickets, a ski school with classes for ages four to adult, and instruction for snowboarding at the site's snowboarding park and halfpipe.

In the warm months visitors can enjoy the mountain's ³/₄-mile alpine slide with rider-controlled sleds. Water slides and kiddie pools are also part of the fun here. For a breathtaking view of the countryside, you can take the chairlift to the 2,350-foot summit of the mountain, then climb to the top of the White Mountain Observation Tower. In addition, the downhill ski trails are opened to mountain bikers. A 3-mile downhill trail challenges experienced bikers. A less difficult trail traces the banks of the beautiful Saco River and includes interpretive information stops and picnic areas. Bike rentals are available. The base lodge has a cafeteria and restroom facilities. Fees are charged for all the mentioned activities.

There's so much to do in this area that you may have a hard time deciding where to start. The hiking is by far the nicest you'll find almost anywhere. There are beautiful waterfalls and granite cliffs to scale. The Saco River is the place for swimming, fishing, or canoeing, and two swimming holes are on the inn's property. White-water class III and IV are here in the spring, so come on up with your kayak. Or bring your bicycle, as biking is fun here. Skiing of all kinds is very close by (there are 45 miles of ski trails)—or do you want to try snowshoeing? This is the place for it. If more sedentary activities suit your fancy, gliders on the porch and comfy sofas in the living room are ideal for reading and needlework.

The innkeepers love animals as much as I do. Crawford and Abby, their Bernese mountain dogs, are loves and even have cookies to give to guests— boy, are those good! "Abby's Tale" is a feature in the inn's newsletter, and what a wag she is! She reports on all of the animals that visit—ducks, bears, and birds. Keeps her busy.

While you are here, do read the history of the inn; it's a fascinating story. A note to jigsaw-puzzle fans: When you come in the door of the inn, turn left into the living room. A puzzle is in the making at all times; it's always fun to work on it.

HOW TO GET THERE: Follow Route 302 from North Conway to the inn. It is 20 miles north of North Conway.

The Bedford Village Inn 🖤 📱
Bedford, New Hampshire 03102

INNKEEPERS: Andrea and John Carnevale

ADDRESS/TELEPHONE: 2 Olde Bedford Way; (603) 472–2001 or (800) 852–1166; restaurant (603) 472–2001; fax (603) 472–2379

WEB SITE: www.bedfordvillageinn.com

ROOMS: 12 suites, plus 2 apartment-style suites; all with private bath, TV, wireless high-speed Internet, and phone with dataports.

RATES: $210 to $360 BP; MAP available.

OPEN: All year.

FACILITIES AND ACTIVITIES: Breakfast, lunch, dinner, Sunday brunch, taproom. Elevator. Spa opening 2007.

BUSINESS TRAVEL: Located near Manchester. All rooms with well-lighted desk and phone with dataports; conference rooms; fax available; corporate rates.

"Country elegant" is the way to describe this inn. It was a farmhouse built before the American Revolution, and it still retains the original wide fireplaces and wide pine boards.

The former hayloft now holds sumptuous suites, each with a bathroom of Italian marble and a Jacuzzi. The bedrooms are well furnished with Oriental carpets, four-poster beds, and coordinated print coverlets, curtains, and wallpapers. There are nice lamps with three-way switches, a too-often-forgotten detail. Each suite has three telephones: one at the desk, one by the bed, and one in the bathroom. A deck off the luxury suite in the barn's peak overlooks the meadow. One of the apartment-style suites has two bedrooms.

The original milking room has become a common area for inn guests, furnished with couches, lounge chairs, and a nice table for games or whatever.

Breakfast at the inn includes all of the usual items, plus treats such as frittatas with crab, lobster, fresh herbs, and Havarti cheese, and vanilla-bean crepes topped with seasonal fruit sauces. The pastries are beautiful and come straight from the inn's own bakery. The taproom has its own menu.

There are several dining rooms, each one lovely. The oldest dates from around 1700 and has a huge fireplace. Lots of windows make it light and airy. The luncheon and Sunday brunch are ambrosia, and dinner is a delight, earning a AAA four-diamond designation. Traditional New England foods and contemporary specialties are served here, and the menu changes regularly. The inn boasts an 800-bottle wine cellar. Special dinners at the inn include a Christmas feast and wine dinners.

A major addition is under way. The inn is constructing an elegant destination spa with forty-three guest suites, fourteen treatment rooms, and a new restaurant on the premises in a setting that will include walking paths, ponds, gardens, and a fountain. The target date is 2007.

HOW TO GET THERE: The inn is on Route 101, just west of Manchester, about 10 minutes from the Manchester airport.

Adair ♥
Bethlehem, New Hampshire 03574

INNKEEPERS: David and Janet Matteucci

ADDRESS/TELEPHONE: 80 Guider Lane; (603) 444-2600 or (888) 444-2600; fax (603) 444-4823

WEB SITE: www.adairinn.com

ROOMS: 8, plus 1 suite and 1 two-bedroom cottage; all with private bath, air-conditioning in season, CD player, hair dryer, robes.

RATES: $175 to $355 BP.

OPEN: All year. Restaurant closed in April, most of May, and November and on Monday and Tuesday.

FACILITIES AND ACTIVITIES: Dinner (Tim-Bir Alley restaurant). Beer and wine, or BYOB. Tennis, shuffleboard. Nearby: Hiking, skiing, golf, mountain biking.

Adair was built in 1927 as a gift to Dorothy Guider from her wealthy father. She lived in this hilltop mansion until her death in 1991. It is surrounded by 200 acres of sheer beauty in a picture-postcard setting. The house was converted into a glorious inn in 1992.

The landscaping, designed by the Olmsted brothers (sons of Fredrick of Boston Common and Central Park fame), is magnificent. The walking paths offer grand views of the Presidential and Dalton mountain ranges. A very nice patio overlooks the tennis court.

You enter into a formal entry hall. On one side is a large, recently redecorated living room furnished with antiques and original art. There is a wood-burning fireplace and seating areas set apart by area rugs. To the left is a lovely dining room with its own fireplace and garden views.

At 8:30 in the morning, piping-hot popovers are served, followed by good things such as pumpkin pancakes with bacon, ham and cheese frittatas, a variety of juices, and fresh fruit cup and low-fat yogurt for the diet-conscious.

The Tim-Bir Alley restaurant at the inn, under separate management, has long been considered one of the area's best. Menus change often, but you may start with something like a salmon-Brie ravioli with artichoke vinaigrette, or chicken, scallion, and pecan dumplings with honey, soy, and balsamic glaze. Some sample seafood choices are salmon with sunflower-seed crust, sole with wild mushrooms, or sautéed sea scallops on ricotta-herb pancakes. Meats may include pork tenderloin or tournedos of beef with Southwestern spices. Save plenty of room for dessert, such as chocolate glazed espresso cheesecake or a plum-almond tart.

The Granite Taproom is a good spot for relaxing or playing a game of pool. Television and a VCR with a variety of movies are here, too, as is a private telephone. Snacks and soft drinks are complimentary.

The rooms are named for the mountain ranges, and all of them have a view of either mountains or the beautiful grounds. Bathrooms have been recently upgraded, and some now have two-person soaking tubs. Both the second and third floors have shelves of books for guests to share, a nice touch from the hospitable hosts.

HOW TO GET THERE: From Interstate 93 take exit 40, which takes you directly to Adair's driveway. From Route 302 Adair is 3 miles west of the center of Bethlehem village.

The Brass Heart Inn ¢¢¢

Chocorua, New Hampshire 03817

INNKEEPERS: Don and Joanna Harte

ADDRESS/TELEPHONE: 88 Philbrick Neighborhood Road (mailing address: P.O. Box 370); (603) 323–7766 or (800) 833–9509; fax (603) 323–7531

WEB SITE: www.thebrassheartinn.com

ROOMS: 11 in main building, 6 with private bath; 3 cottages, all with bath.

RATES: $130 to $180 BP; cottages $180 to $260 BP.

OPEN: All year. Cottages open spring to fall only.

FACILITIES AND ACTIVITIES: Dinner Thursday through Sunday. Function barn for weddings, parties. Cross-country skiing.

At the end of a quiet country lane, this lovely old gabled farmhouse dating from the 1700s comes with a babbling brook, forests, and views of rolling fields. An inn since the 1890s and known for the past thirty-plus years as Stafford's in the Fields, it has a new name and new owners who promise to keep the tranquillity that has won so many friends.

The Hartes are old hands at innkeeping after years as owners of a small bed-and-breakfast in Coventry, Connecticut. Here they have widened their horizons with a larger property, a dining room, the Boar's Head taproom, and a stunning renovated nineteenth-century barn that is a perfect setting for a country wedding or any other special event. The barn can hold 200 people.

The new, enticing dinner menu offers appetizers such as French onion soup, grilled quail, or sausage wrapped in brioche. Tempting entree choices include rack of lamb, maple-cured pork loin, or pecan-and-lemon-encrusted halibut.

Rooms at the inn are comfortable country, with old-fashioned dressers and mirrors and a mix of iron or wood headboards and several canopy beds. The stencil room in red, white, and blue is especially inviting and offers twin four-poster beds. Third-floor rooms sharing a bath are ideal for families or anyone on a budget. Cottages on the property have private front porches and sitting rooms and can accommodate two to eight guests. Some have cozy fireplaces.

This is a wonderful spot year-round, cool and refreshing in summer, and with on-property cross-country skiing in winter. There's no more warming sight than to turn into the lane some snowy evening and find the glow of the inn to welcome you.

HOW TO GET THERE: Take Route 16 north to Chocorua Village, then turn left onto Route 113 and travel ¾ mile. Take a right on Philbrick Neighborhood Road to the inn. Or, from Interstate 93, take exit 23 and travel east on Route 104 to Route 25, and then to Route 16. Proceed north to Route 16 to Chocorua Village.

Darby Field Inn 🏵️ 💝
Conway, New Hampshire 03818

INNKEEPERS: Marc and Maria Donaldson

ADDRESS/TELEPHONE: Off Route 16 on Bald Hill (mailing address: 185 Chase Hill Road, Albany, NH 03818); (603) 447-2181 or (800) 426-4147 (outside New Hampshire); fax (603) 447-5726

WEB SITE: www.darbyfield.com

ROOMS: 13, all with private bath.

RATES: $140 to $280 BP; MAP and package plans available.

OPEN: All year except April.

FACILITIES AND ACTIVITIES: Restaurant May through March, tavern, gardens. Swimming pool, hiking, 12 miles of cross-country ski trails, sleigh and carriage rides. Massage therapy and other spa treatments, yoga classes; yoga vacations available.

*S*et high atop Bald Hill in New Hampshire's White Mountains with spectacular views of this wonderful country is Darby Field Inn. Located 1,000 feet above Mount Washington Valley and only 3 miles

from Conway Village, the inn delights wanderers adventurous enough to leave the beaten path.

On the grounds are herb, vegetable, and flower gardens; a swimming pool; cross-country ski trails; and stunning mountain views year-round. The bordering White Mountain National Forest offers more opportunities to hike to rivers, waterfalls, and lakes and to cross-country ski and snowshoe in winter. When you come back inside, welcome spa services such as massages ease aching muscles. The inn also offers yoga classes and some special yoga vacations.

Rooms are charming, some with four-poster beds and wall-to-wall rugs. All rooms have private baths. Deluxe accommodations have Jacuzzis, fireplaces, and balconies with a wonderful view.

The inn's huge cobblestone fireplace is the center for warm conversation. The tavern has a wood-burning stove.

Candlelit dinners begin with fine wine and a smashing sunset view up the valley. The food reflects the careful preparation of the chef. You'll always find a chef's special and fresh fish du jour. Whatever you order up here will be excellent. You must try the dessert specialty, Darby cream pie. The Irish Revolution is a libation that will really end your day nicely.

Darby Field, a notorious Irishman, was the first white man to ascend Mount Washington. Had the inn been here in 1642, it is doubtful whether Mr. Field would ever have passed the tavern.

Conway Scenic Railroad

You can't beat the scenery and the sense of adventure when you board the excursion trains at North Conway's grand Victorian railroad depot for a ride on the Conway Scenic Railroad (603–356–5251 or 800–232–5251; www.conwayscenic.com). Choose from a fifty-five-minute ride or a one-and-three-quarter-hour ride on the Valley Train, which stays in the Mount Washington Valley for trips to Conway and Bartlett and back to the depot. You can also take the Notch Train; buy a ticket for this five-hour round-trip, then hop on for the most beautiful ride of your life. This route passes through Crawford Notch on the Frankenstein Trestle, a remarkable structure that carries the train through one of the most awesome landscapes in New England.

Live narration is given on all trips; lunch and dinner runs are available. Coach and first-class seats are available on both trains; fares vary with the age of the passenger, the length of the trip, and the season. The first runs of the Valley trip begin in mid-April and continue into November, with holiday runs in late November and December; the Notch Train runs from mid-June to mid-October, weather permitting. Reservations are highly recommended during September and early October when the foliage is at its peak.

HOW TO GET THERE: Turn on Bald Hill Road, ½ mile south of the Kancamagus Highway, off Route 16, then go 1 mile up the hill and turn right onto Chase Hill Road. The inn is 1 mile beyond.

The Inn at Crotched Mountain
Francestown, New Hampshire 03043

INNKEEPERS: John and Rose Perry

ADDRESS/TELEPHONE: 534 Mountain Road; (603) 588–6840

ROOMS: 13; 8 with private bath; 4 with fireplace.

RATES: $40 to $60 per person BP.

OPEN: All year.

FACILITIES AND ACTIVITIES: Wheelchair access to inn and dining rooms. Bar, tennis, swimming pool, cross-country skiing. Nearby: Golf, fishing, summer theater.

This colonial house, more than 180 years old, is located on the northern side of Crotched Mountain. There is a 40-mile view of the Piscataquog Valley, complete with spacious skies. Both innkeepers went to school to learn their trade, and what a charming house to practice it in. They are both pretty special themselves. Rose is from Singapore, and John is a Yankee.

Come and stay: There are many things to do. There are three golf courses in the nearby valley; the fishing in the numerous streams, ponds, and lakes is great; and there is a wading pool for the young, as well as a 30-by-60-foot swimming pool. Two areas provide skiing—one practically at the front door and another down the road. Two clay tennis courts eliminate that tiresome waiting for a playing area. And come evening there are two summer theaters, one at Peterborough and another in Milford.

Any house that has nine fireplaces needs a wood lot and a man with a chainsaw. Four of the bedrooms here have a fireplace, so remember to request one when you reserve.

Three English cockers live here, Rover, Frances, and Lucy. Come and enjoy this wonderful countryside with the dogs. They would love to have you.

HOW TO GET THERE: Take Route 101A from Nashua to Milford, Route 13 to New Boston, and Route 136 to Francestown. Take Route 47 for 2½ miles, then turn left onto Mountain Road. The inn is 1 mile up the road.

Franconia Inn

Franconia, New Hampshire 03580

INNKEEPERS: Richard and Alec Morris

ADDRESS/TELEPHONE: Route 116 (mailing address: 1300 Easton Road); (603) 823–5542 or (800) 473–5299

WEB SITE: www.franconiainn.com

ROOMS: 29, plus 2 family suites, 1 "inn" suite, and 1 cottage; all with private bath; 2 with Jacuzzi.

RATES: $100 to $305 BP; MAP available.

OPEN: All year except April 1 to Mother's Day.

FACILITIES AND ACTIVITIES: Bar, lounge, game room, airfield, hot tub, swimming pool, 4 tennis courts, cross-country ski center, ice skating, sleigh rides, soaring center, horseback riding, bicycles, croquet, nightly movies. Nearby: Downhill skiing, golf.

This is an inn in the fine tradition of old New England hostelries. The inn is the fourth for the Morris family and run by third-generation innkeepers. Children are welcome, and while they play or watch a movie on the big-screen TV in the movie room, you can relax in the lounge and listen to selected classical and popular music by the glow of the fireplace.

A game room and a library are here for your enjoyment, as are two verandas, one catching the sunrise over Cannon Mountain, the other for watching the sunset over Sugar Hill.

Horseback riding is also available. There are trail rides through Ham Branch stream and around the hay fields.

The living room is paneled with old oak and, with the fireplace, is very warm and cozy. A lovely candlelit dining room, with pink and white napery, serves glorious food. The chef has treated shrimp in an innovative way. They come warmed in pancetta and served over an almond couscous timbale with basil butter. What a superb appetizer! Beer-battered softshell crabs is a winner, and so is seared duck breast with a pear, ginger, and spinach marmalade, served with wild rice.

For winter fun, 30 miles of cross-country trails are right at hand on the inn's 107 acres, and they also have facilities so that you can ski from inn to inn on connecting trails. Downhill skiing is but 10 miles away. Horse-drawn sleigh rides in this beautiful winter wonderland are my idea of heaven. Do come and enjoy.

HOW TO GET THERE: Take Interstate 91 north to the Wells River–Woodsville exit. Go right on Route 302 to Lisbon, New Hampshire. A few miles past Lisbon, go right on Route 117 to Franconia. Crossing the bridge into town, go right at the Exxon station onto Route 116, and you're 2 miles from the inn, which is on the right. Or, if you have a single-engine plane, the inn has its own FAA-listed airfield with a 3,000-foot-long runway.

The Horse and Hound 💲💲

Franconia, New Hampshire 03580

INNKEEPERS: Bill Steele and Jim Cantlon

ADDRESS/TELEPHONE: 205 Wells Road; (603) 823–5501 or (800) 450–5501

WEB SITE: www.horseandhoundnh.com

ROOMS: 6, plus 2 two-bedroom units; all with private bath and phone; Wi-Fi throughout the inn.

RATES: $90 to $145 BP; MAP rates also available.

OPEN: All year except April 1 to Mother's Day, and sometimes November.

FACILITIES AND ACTIVITIES: Dinner. Bar, lounge. Skiing, soaring, biking, hiking. Wheelchair access to bar, lounge, and dining room. Well-behaved pets welcome ($8.50 charge). Nearby: Swimming, boating, fishing, golf, tennis.

The Horse and Hound is located at the base of Cannon Mountain just north of Franconia Notch. Tucker Brook rushes down from the top of the mountain just past the edge of the inn's property. In winter you can set off from the door of the inn on your cross-country skis. In other seasons bicycling is a big thing here, with a 7-mile circuit for you to try. Should be fun up here in these beautiful mountains.

You can also go soaring in a plane or just take an airplane ride. What a way to enjoy the fall foliage. I did it once in a helicopter, and it was sublime.

Back at the inn, three fireplaces are waiting to warm you in the living room and the dining rooms. The library lounge has lots of books, which are well organized in categories such as bike books, children's books, and classics, or you can enjoy checkers and other games. You might enjoy playing with Gus and Max, the inn's cocker spaniels, or Pipper and Fred, the inn's cats.

Comfortable rooms are bright and airy and have lovely views.

The terrace in summer is so lovely for cocktails. The wood-panelled dining room is cozy, and the food is excellent. I liked the baked French onion soup, but there is also a soup du jour. Entrees include filet mignon, duckling, lamb chops, veal, fish, the chef's Vegetarian Fancy, and daily specials. The desserts and pastries all are made here and are delicious!

HOW TO GET THERE: From Boston take Interstate 93 north, exit at Route 18, and turn left. Go 2½ miles to Wells Road, and take a left onto Wells. The inn is on the left. Coming south on Interstate 93, take exit 38 from Franconia, go left on Route 18, travel 2½ miles to Wells Road, and take a right onto Wells.

Lovett's by Lafayette Brook
Franconia, New Hampshire 03580

INNKEEPERS: Jim and Janet Freitas

ADDRESS/TELEPHONE: 1474 Profile Road (Route 18); (603) 823-7761 or (800) 356-3802; fax (802) 823-8802

WEB SITE: www.lovettsinn.com

ROOMS: 21; 3 in main house, 18 in cottages; all with private bath; 14 with fireplace; 4 with Jacuzzi.

RATES: Rooms, $125 to $175 BP; cottages, $135 to $285 BP; MAP available.

OPEN: All year except some weeks in April.

FACILITIES AND ACTIVITIES: Dinner, bar, outdoor pool, 10 acres with 66 kilometers of trails for snowshoeing, cross-country skiing. Nearby: Skiing, tennis, golf, horseback riding, bicycling, fishing, Franconia Notch State Park.

The main building is a classic, dating from 1784 and on the National Register of Historic Places. But it is the dining room that made this inn famous. The legend began more than seventy years ago when Charles Lovett turned the old home into an inn with hospitality and cuisine that brought loyal fans back year after year.

Charlie left more than a decade ago, and things had gone downhill under a series of owners. But since the newest innkeepers, Jim and Janet Freitas, arrived, they have been working hard to regain that top reputation, renovating, refurbishing, stripping old paint off the handsome fireplaces, polishing up the hardwood and heart pine floors, and generally making the inn a

welcoming home base. The popular bar area, featuring a spectacular marble bar, has been almost doubled in size. The sun porch is a comfortable place for watching TV.

With a background as restaurant owners and caterers in Massachusetts, the Freitas were well qualified to take over the kitchen, where Janet is winning new acclaim. Dinners served by candlelight may begin with White Mountain Brie cheese rolled in mixed nuts and baked in phyllo dough, or New England crab cakes, one of the guests' favorites. Main courses include chicken Florentine, stuffed with spinach and goat cheese and served in a herbed cream sauce; pan-seared rainbow trout with lemon caper butter; roast pork tenderloin with a currant glaze; and veal Genovese, a scallopini of veal sautéed in lemon herb sauce. Some of the seasonings come from the herb garden just outside the kitchen. The day begins with a hearty breakfast, always featuring fresh fruit, a choice of a vegetarian or meat omelet, plus special dishes such as pancakes, crepes, or French toast. Guests are also treated to afternoon tea.

The upgrading of rooms has brought many new furnishings, including country antiques. Some of the choicest rooms offer queen beds, Jacuzzis, and mountain views. Most of the rooms in the cottages beside the pool and around the lawn have fireplaces, and the patios are great for gazing at Cannon Mountain. Two-room cottages are ideal for families, and one three-bedroom cottage can be rented as a unit.

In winter, the inn's expansive system of cross-country trails connects with other area inns, so you can ski from inn to inn.

HOW TO GET THERE: Take Interstate 93 north to exit 3, Route 18, and turn left. The inn is on the left, 2 miles down the mountain.

Sugar Hill Inn
Franconia, New Hampshire 03580

INNKEEPERS: Judy and Orlo Coots

ADDRESS/TELEPHONE: Route 117 (mailing address: P.O. Box 954); (603) 823-5621 or (800) 548-4748 for reservations

WEB SITE: www.sugarhillinn.com

ROOMS: 7 rooms in main house, 6 cottage rooms, 2 master suites; all with private bath; suites have fireplaces, decks, and whirlpool baths. Gas fireplaces in all of the cottage guest rooms.

RATES: $155 to $380 BP.

OPEN: All year except April.

FACILITIES AND ACTIVITIES: Dinner, full license; Spa Room. Nearby: Cross-country and downhill skiing, snowshoeing, horseback riding, fishing, canoeing, tennis, golf, hiking, museums, antiques shops, summer theater, hot-air ballooning.

The White Mountains are so beautiful and majestic, it is a joy to find the Sugar Hill Inn tucked into this loveliness. This charming inn was built in 1789 as a farmhouse by one of Sugar Hill's original settlers, and it was converted to an inn in 1929.

The inn has been carefully restored. The innkeepers have made the most of the beautiful old beams and floors and the handsome fireplaces. They have two charming common rooms, each with original fireplaces. Each has comfortable furniture, reading materials, board games, and puzzles. A television is in one of these rooms. Squier's Pub is a cheerful addition.

Guest accommodations in the inn and in the country cottages are lovely and feature handmade quilts, good mattresses, lovely antiques, and stenciled walls. The closets are scented with potpourri.

Orlo prepares all the meals. Big country breakfasts may include gingerbread pancakes or poached eggs with red flannel hash.

Dinner starters may include a smoked chicken and sweet potato pancake, salad, or the soup of the day. Try the pork, grilled swordfish, or roast cornish game hen. Four changing entrees are always offered each evening. Desserts are homemade and delicious; pumpkin pie, apple crisp, or chocolate pâté may be available when you're here.

A tea cart, laden with scones and sweet breads or cool drinks in summer, is in the parlor at 4:00 P.M. every day. And the hot cider on the wood-burning stove for skiers is so nice.

HOW TO GET THERE: Follow Route 18 through Franconia. Turn left on Route 117. The inn is ½ mile up the hill, on the right.

Bernerhof Inn ¢¢¢
Glen, New Hampshire 03838

INNKEEPERS: George and June Phillips

ADDRESS/TELEPHONE: Route 302; (603) 383-9131 or (800) 548-8007 (out of state); fax (603) 383-0809

WEB SITE: www.bernerhofinn.com

ROOMS: 9, all with private bath, TV, phone, free Wi-Fi, and air-conditioning; 6 with Jacuzzi; 1 with fireplace; 1 with sauna.

RATES: $99 to $189 BP.

OPEN: All year.

FACILITIES AND ACTIVITIES: Breakfast, dinner in Rare Bear Bistro, Black Bear Pub; cooking classes. Wheelchair access to dining room. Hiking trail. Nearby: Golf, tennis, canoeing, fishing, cross-country and downhill skiing; discount shopping.

As the brochure says so well, this is "an elegant small hotel in the foothills of the White Mountains." Rooms are light and airy and individually decorated. There are three king-size brass beds and six Jacuzzis. One is in a sensational window alcove. Games and puzzles await in the sitting room.

The inn has maintained its reputation for fine dining under its new owners. The *delices de Gruyère*—a smooth blend of Swiss cheeses, delicately breaded and sautéed and accompanied by a savory tomato blend—is superb. Other Swiss entrees include Wiener schnitzel and, of course, fondues. You might also try the seared duck breast with smoked cheddar risotto or oven-roasted haddock with a brown butter citrus sauce.

You'll want to leave room for dessert, it's so good. One of the house specialties is apple galette, a mini pie served with vanilla ice cream and caramel sauce.

The Black Bear Pub at the inn welcomes guests with a cozy atmosphere. It's a lovely oak room done in the style of a European pub. A true haven for beer lovers, it also serves good food from its own menu at affordable prices. You can sip some real Gluh Wein or espresso made from freshly ground beans.

A Taste of the Mountains, a cooking school hosted by well-known area chefs, is designed for lovers of fine food. If you want to know more, do call or write for a brochure.

HOW TO GET THERE: From North Conway take Route 16 north. At Glen, turn left onto Route 302. The inn is on your right.

The Hancock Inn
Hancock, New Hampshire 03449

INNKEEPER: Robert Short

ADDRESS/TELEPHONE: 33 Main Street; (603) 525-3318 or (800) 525-1789 (outside New Hampshire); fax (603) 525-9301

WEB SITE: www.hancockinn.com

ROOMS: 15, all with private bath, air-conditioning, cable TV, and phone; 8 with fireplace or gas woodstove; 3 with whirlpool baths; 1 room with wheelchair accessibility.

RATES: $105 to $250 BP.

OPEN: All year.

FACILITIES AND ACTIVITIES: Dinner, lounge. Wheelchair ramp into the inn. Parking. Nearby: Swimming, hiking, antiquing, summer theater, skiing, tennis.

*R*eceiving guests since 1789, this is the oldest inn in New Hampshire, and it is a charmer. The governor of New Hampshire has given it a commendation for its long years of hospitality. It is now in the competent hands of Robert Short, who is working on restoring the inn and its furnishings to reflect its Federal heritage.

The name of the inn stems from the fact that John Hancock, the founding father, once owned most of the land that composes the present town of Hancock. Set among scenic hills and featuring a weathered clapboard facade, graceful white pillars, and a warm red door, the inn represents all that is good about old inns.

Guest rooms are well furnished with four-posters and Early American decor. The Rufus Porter Room is very special, with a well-preserved wall mural painted in the 1820s by primitive artists. The Moses Eaton room has a full wall stencil, and the Ball Room still has a domed ceiling from the days when it was part of the home's original ballroom. The Norway Plain room, one of the luxury accommodations with a fireplace and whirlpool tub, is another room with a delightful old New England mural on the walls. From the Bell Tower room, you have a fine view of the town church steeple, boasting an original Paul Revere bell.

The comfortable living room invites relaxing, with books and an antique chessboard set up in front of the fireplace. The cozy tavern is the place for libations or a game of checkers or Scrabble.

The Hancock Inn's highly rated dining room serves New England classics with a modern touch. *Bon Appétit* magazine requested and published the recipe for the famous Shaker cranberry pot roast, a perennial favorite. Other choices may be rack of lamb, shrimp scampi, breast of duckling, or a seafood casserole. The beef tenderloin is grilled over a wood fire. Save room for dessert. It's hard to resist choices like crème brûlée napoleon, a chocolate bourbon pecan torte, or Southern peach pie.

The surrounding Monadnock region is filled with activities, from hiking to antiquing to concerts. A walk around the hamlet of Hancock is a must. Founded in 1779, the entire village is on the National Register of Historic Places. Then you can return to the comfort of a four-poster with a serenade from the Paul Revere bell to lull you to sleep.

HOW TO GET THERE: From Boston take Interstate 93 north to Interstate 293, then Route 101 to Peterborough. Take a right onto Route 202, then a left onto Route 123. Turn left at the stop sign.

Colby Hill Inn
Henniker, New Hampshire 03242

INNKEEPERS: Cyndi and Mason Cobb

ADDRESS/TELEPHONE: P.O. Box 779; (603) 428–3281 or (800) 531–0330; fax (603) 428–9218

WEB SITE: www.colbyhillinn.com

ROOMS: 14, all with private bath and phone; 6 with working fireplace and whirlpool tub. Entire inn is air-conditioned. No-smoking inn.

RATES: $129 to $269 BP.

OPEN: All year.

FACILITIES AND ACTIVITIES: Breakfast, dinner. Swimming pool, badminton. Nearby: Tennis, canoeing, kayaking, fishing.

BUSINESS TRAVEL: Phone in rooms; fax available; meeting space; Wi-Fi access.

I just love this inn. Built more than 200 years ago as a farmhouse, it leans and dips here and there, but that only adds to its charm. The wide floorboards are authentic. They have seen a lot of history. The building has been a stagecoach stop and a meetinghouse for the antislavery and temperance movements.

The formal parlor with a fireplace is an inviting spot to enjoy afternoon tea and freshly baked cookies. The library overlooking the garden is a nice place to read a book, play a game of backgammon, or just enjoy the view. The sixteen guest rooms are furnished with period antiques and cozy down comforters. Some have fireplaces and two-person whirlpools.

Now to the good stuff: dinner. Candlelight dinners are served in a romantic dining room overlooking the inn's perennial gardens and a gazebo. During a recent visit, the appetizers included sautéed escargot in puff pastry and a savory Grafton cheddar cheese cake. Entrees ranged from a rack of lamb to a crispy duck breast and a caramelized Chatham cod. For those like me who

The Fiber Studio

One of the most charming aspects of journeying through New England is finding artists' studios and crafters' workshops tucked in the small towns we visit. A restored barn overlooking Henniker's Pat's Peak mountain is the home of the Fiber Studio (603–428–7830; www .fiberstudio.com), a glorious riot of color and texture hidden in the hills. Workshops are offered year-round in weaving, dyeing, spinning, basketry, and knitting. Hand-dyed woolens, mohairs, alpacas, cottons, linens, and silks for weaving and knitting are for sale here, as are beads from around the world, buttons galore of every description, handcrafted jewelry and jewelry-making supplies, and much more. Looms, spinning wheels, and books—you name it.

The shop is open year-round Tuesday through Saturday from 10:00 A.M. to 4:00 P.M. and on Sunday by chance. It's located at 9 Foster Hill Road in Henniker off Route 202/9.

can't wait for dessert, there was a chocolate caramel tart and a classic maple crème brûlée.

Breakfast is also great, with fresh fruit and juicies, homemade pastries and granola, and specials such as orange thyme pancakes or Colby eggs Benedict.

The inn has an in-ground pool overlooking Liberty Hill, and tennis, canoeing, kayaking, and fishing can be found nearby. Come winter, Pat's Peak Ski Area is just five minutes away, and Mt. Sunapee is a twenty-minute drive.

HOW TO GET THERE: Take Interstate 91 to Brattleboro, then Route 9 east to Henniker.

The Manor on Golden Pond
Holderness, New Hampshire 03245

INNKEEPERS: Brian and Mary Ellen Shields

ADDRESS/TELEPHONE: Route 3, Box T; (603) 968–3348 or (800) 545–2141; fax (603) 968–2116

WEB SITE: www.manorongoldenpond.com

ROOMS: 24, plus 1 cottage; all with private bath. No-smoking inn.

RATES: $225 to $475 BP.

OPEN: All year.

FACILITIES AND ACTIVITIES: Afternoon tea. Bar, lounge, swimming pool, tennis, canoeing, sandy beach. Nearby: Downhill and cross-country skiing.

*T*saac Van Horne, an Englishman, built this grand manor at the turn of the twentieth century overlooking Squam Lake and the White Mountains. It still retains the warmth of a country home, albeit a grand one.

The richly paneled living room has elegant carved wood trim and its original lead windows. Many of the bedrooms have wood-burning fireplaces and a view to take your breath away. Some have the added modern luxury of a Jacuzzi.

Breakfast is exceptional, with treats such as Belgian waffles with fresh fruit and whipped cream. What a way to start the day! And dinner is a regal experience, with choices such as quail with soy and ginger sauce, potato-encrusted salmon fillet with hazelnut butter, or maple-glazed venison chops. Afterward, you can linger over a drink in the cozy Three Cocks Pub.

The estate includes thirteen acres and 300 feet of sandy beach frontage on the lake. Among the activities on the property are a swimming pool, tennis, croquet, and canoeing. If it rains, all is not lost; tea is served every afternoon, and any time of day, it's a pleasure to be inside this beautiful mansion.

HOW TO GET THERE: Take Route 3 into Holderness. Cross the bridge, and on the right you will see the signs for the Manor on Golden Pond.

Christmas Farm Inn
Jackson, New Hampshire 03846

INNKEEPER: Tom Spaulding

ADDRESS/TELEPHONE: P.O. Box CC; (603) 383–4313 or (800) HI–ELVES; fax (603) 383-6495

WEB SITE: www.christmasfarminn.com

ROOMS: 42 rooms and suites in main inn and other buildings, several cottages; all rooms with private bath, air-conditioning, phone; some with whirlpool, fireplace, TV; all cottages with deck, TV, fireplace, refrigerator, and coffeemaker.

RATES: $80 to $298 BP. MAP available.

OPEN: All year.

FACILITIES AND ACTIVITIES: Dining room, pub, full-service spa. Indoor and outdoor swimming pools, fitness center. Eighty kilometers of cross-country trails. Nearby: Golf, tennis, downhill skiing, alpine slide, canoeing on Saco River.

*Y*es, Virginia, there is a Christmas Farm Inn, and it has the Mistletoe Pub and the Sugar Plum Dining Room to prove it. The food is fit for any Santa and his helpers, from the hearty, full country breakfast, which includes homemade breads, muffins, and sticky buns, to gracious dinners featuring a full menu of entrees, homemade soups, and desserts made by an on-site baker. Children age twelve and under have their own special menu.

Main courses include grilled pork tenderloin, braised lamb shank, and Parmesan-herb-breaded chicken breast. The crispy eggplant napolean layered with mushrooms is good enough to make me turn vegetarian. Entrees from the sea, such as grilled scallops, are real treats. The desserts do indeed make visions of sugarplums dance in your head. How about apple pie, crème brûlée, or the Christmas Farm special sundae? From here take a quick trip to the Mistletoe Pub for a nightcap.

The rooms, situated around the grounds, vary. Nine rooms in the main building have Christmas names: Holly, and Dasher, Prancer, Vixen, and the rest of the Santa's crew. They are simply done in old-fashioned colonial style. The adjacent Saltbox has larger rooms, some with canopy beds and whirlpool tubs. The loft suites on the second level of the barn behind the inn are good choices for families; they come with TV and lots of space. More luxurious suites are in the Carriage House, with king-size beds, whirlpool tubs, gas fireplaces, wet bars with refrigerators, and private decks with mountain views.

Downstairs is the fitness center and a Great Room with a massive fieldstone fireplace. For romance you may want to choose the Sugar House honeymoon suite in an authentic maple sugaring house, with a fireplace and a two-person Jacuzzi. Several two-bedroom cottages set on the hillside above the inn offer extra privacy and mountain views.

The Carriage House on the property is a perfect spot for small or medium meetings or for a wedding. An on-site wedding consultant will help ensure that the day is perfect. The newest addition to the Carriage House should please everyone who enjoys a little pampering: a full-service spa with a wide range of treatments available.

Christmas Farm offers plenty to do year-round. In summer, splash in the outdoor pool, go for a hike, or stroll through the gardens. In winter, you can cross-country ski right from the inn property onto the town's 150 kilometers of trails or take advantage of the many downhill ski areas in the region. The indoor pool and fitness center area are available year-round. Or you can do nothing at all. The inn is in the heart of the White Mountains, an area full of beauty, and it is a pleasure just to sit back and savor the view.

HOW TO GET THERE: Go north on Route 16 from North Conway. A few miles after Route 302 branches off to your left, you will see a covered bridge on your right. Take the bridge through the village and up the hill ¼ mile, and there is the inn.

Jackson Ski Touring Foundation

One of the best such operations in the entire Northeast, the Jackson Ski Touring Foundation maintains nearly 160 kilometers of cross-country ski trails over 60 square miles of this region. Skiers can use the trail system to ski from inn to inn; some trails are easy, and others are suited to experienced skiers. Races and workshops are held on these trails every winter weekend. Trail fees help to maintain the trails, and they were recently used to build a covered bridge to provide access to the Ellis River Trail, a 10-kilometer route from the village of Jackson to one of the inns in the area. Call (603) 383-9355 or log on to www .jacksonxc.org for more information.

Inn at Ellis River 💟
Jackson, New Hampshire 03846

INNKEEPERS: Frank Baker and Lyn Norris-Baker

ADDRESS/TELEPHONE: 17 Harriman Road (Route 16) (mailing address: P.O. Box 656); (603) 383–9339 or (800) 233–8309; fax (603) 383–4142

WEB SITE: www.innatellisriver.com

ROOMS: 17, plus 3 suites and 1 cottage for two; all with private bath, air-conditioning, phone, TV, hair dryer, iron; 16 with fireplace; 8 with two-person Jacuzzi.

RATES: $110 to $295 BP.

OPEN: All year.

FACILITIES AND ACTIVITIES: Game room/pub, hot tub and sauna, free Wi-Fi, weddings and other functions. Cross-country skiing, fishing, vineyard, swimming pool. Nearby: Shopping, golf, hiking, downhill skiing, and much more.

Calling all snow people: Have I found an inn for you! The inn's atrium is a glass-enclosed 24-by-24-foot room with a six-person hot tub in the center. Imagine relaxing in the warm tub and watching the snow coming down and cross-country skiers going by. That's the way for this inn creeper to go.

New owners have added a touch of elegance and romance to the inn. All the rooms are furnished with antiques and period furnishings, feather beds, and lots of amenities. Many have balconies, eight come with Jacuzzis, and most have a gas or wood-burning fireplace. Many rooms also have DVD/ VCRs, so you can take advantage of the inn's library of videos and DVDs.

For extra romance, many special packages are available for small intimate weddings, honeymoons, anniversaries, and special occasions.

Breakfast in the sunny dining room is delicious, with fresh baked muffins, and a changing choice of both sweet or savory entrees that may include a cinnamon crepe stuffed with apples; orange croissant French toast with fresh strawberries; a tomato, basil, and mozzarella omelet; or a roasted pepper and vegetable frittata. In the afternoon, home-baked sweets and cider or lemonade are served. The pub offers drinks, coffee and dessert and doubles as a game room with billiards, darts, and chess. If you don't feel like going out for dinner, you can order a Tête à Tête dinner, casual cuisine for two (by advance reservation only).

This is an inn that is always in season. In summer, head for the outdoor pool. In winter, you can connect to more than 200 kilometers of cross-country ski trails, try snowshoeing, visit one of the area's five downhill-ski mountains, or snuggle by the fireplace. That wonderful indoor hot tub is always a delight, and there's an outdoor sauna as well.

The surrounding White Mountains add more year-round pleasures. Walks, hiking trails, and waterfalls abound, along with scenic drives. Sportspeople will find golf and river sports, and shoppers will find plenty of bargains at the outlet stores nearby in North Conway. You may have to stay an extra day or two to fit it all in.

HOW TO GET THERE: Take Interstate 95 north to Route 16 north to Jackson. The inn is on the left, ¼ mile past the historic covered bridge.

The Whitney 🏠
Jackson, New Hampshire 03846

INNKEEPERS: The Levine Family

ADDRESS/TELEPHONE: Route 16B (mailing address: P.O. Box 822); (603) 383-8916 or (800) 677-5737

WEB SITE: www.whitneysinn.com

ROOMS: 30 rooms and suites, plus 2-bedroom cottages; all with private bath and air-conditioning; cottages with living room, fireplace, and TV/VCR.

RATES: $125 to $225 BP.

OPEN: All year.

FACILITIES AND ACTIVITIES: Bar, lounge, outdoor heated pool, outdoor Jacuzzi, skiing, tennis, pond, paddleboat.

This is an authentic mountain hideaway, a tradition since 1936, nestled at the base of Black Mountain ski area. You can't get much closer than this. It's pretty nice to be able to crawl out of bed, have a sumptuous breakfast, and walk across to the lifts, trails, ski shop, or ski school, all just a snowball's throw away.

There's lots to do in warm weather, as well. Play a set of tennis, do a couple of laps in the swimming pool, relax in the outdoor Jacuzzi, or take a paddleboat out on the pond.

The owners have upgraded the dining room, now known as the Grill Room. The prix-fixe three-course dinner begins with a soup of the day or the Whitney house salad, a delicious mix of apples, blue cheese, dried cranberries, brown-sugar walnuts, and fresh greens tossed with the inn's own raspberry vinaigrette dressing. Entrees range from grilled tenderloin of beef with molasses-bacon-scallion butter to shrimp scampi to roasted duckling with a cranberry-blueberry sauce. All the desserts are homemade by the chef.

The chef also shows off with a scrumptious breakfast featuring dishes such as double-thick French toast or blueberry pancakes made with the inn's own secret batter. It's just what you need before a busy day of skiing or playing in the great outdoors.

HOW TO GET THERE: Go north from Conway 22 miles on Route 16. Take a right on Route 16A through a covered bridge into Jackson Village. Take Route 16B to the top of the hill to the inn.

The Wildcat Inn

Jackson, New Hampshire 03846

INNKEEPERS: Pam and Marty Sweeney

ADDRESS/TELEPHONE: Route 16A; (603) 383–4245 or (800) 228–4245

WEB SITE: www.wildcattavern.com

ROOMS: 14; 12 with private bath and air-conditioning, TV, VCR, and phone. 1 cottage.

RATES: $129 to $149 BP. Cottage, $350 BP.

OPEN: All year.

FACILITIES AND ACTIVITIES: Lunch daily in-season, weekends off-season; no lunch served in April or May. Dinner, bar. Wheelchair access to dining room and tavern. Music in lounge. Nearby: Downhill and cross-country skiing, golf, hiking, tennis, horseback riding, outlet shopping.

*Y*ou'll feel like family at this casual and comfortable family-run inn, long a favorite in Jackson. The Sweeneys do everything, from checking you in to overseeing your delicious dinner, and they do it with welcoming warmth.

The Tavern, with two big fireplaces and comfy couches, is one of the most popular places in Jackson, especially après ski. It is a great spot whether you want a cappuccino, an informal meal, or one of the many microbrews on tap. The "supper" menu offers anything from burgers to pot roast or chicken pot-pie, spinach pie to ribs. Live music is on the menu on weekends and holidays.

The dining room is formal without being fussy, and in summer dinner moves outside to the lovely inn garden. The menu is aptly described as "country gourmet," with enough variety to please everyone. Shellfish risotto, duck breast with Grand Marnier glaze, rack of lamb, pan roasted halibut, the Tavern steak with a choice of sauces, and a hearty lasagna may be some of the choices in the changing lineup of entrees. One perennial specialty is the Extravaganza, shrimp, lobster, and scallops sautéed with garlic, peppers, onions, mushrooms, and fresh tomatoes and served with linguine or a rice pilaf—extravagant indeed! The breads and desserts are all homemade and not to be missed.

While it is best known for the Tavern and restaurant, the Wildcat is a fine place to stay. The location is convenient and the rooms are fine, simply but pleasantly decorated in old-fashioned country style, and with good beds and private baths. In the morning, you'll wake to the aroma of fresh baked rolls and muffins and enjoy a big breakfast. Summer afternoons, you can relax in the Tavern gardens, and in winter, you can curl up with a hot drink in front of one of the wood-burning fireplaces in the Tavern. After a fine dinner or an evening in the Tavern, it's so nice to just head upstairs to bed.

HOW TO GET THERE: Take Route 16 north from North Conway. Take Route 16A to your right, through a covered bridge, and into Jackson. The inn is in the center of town.

The Ammonoosuc Inn
Lisbon, New Hampshire 03585

INNKEEPERS: Peter Whitelaw and Karen LaRocco

ADDRESS/TELEPHONE: 641 Bishop Road; (603) 838–6118 or (866) 496–8148; fax (603) 369–3006

WEB SITE: www.ammonoosucinn.com

ROOMS: 9, all with private bath.

RATES: Rooms, $125 to $160 BP; suites, $175 to $300 BP.

OPEN: All year.

FACILITIES AND ACTIVITIES: Dinner, tavern, full license; Wi-Fi. Nearby: Fishing, canoeing, downhill skiing, hiking; inn adjoins a golf course.

Tucked away on a hillside overlooking the Ammonoosuc River, this peaceful inn surrounded by the green golf course of the Lisbon Country Club was originally a farmhouse built in 1888. It is a perfect retreat, whether you choose to play a round of golf, fish or tube the river, or just ensconce yourself in a rocker on the front porch to watch the golf

action and soak in the beauty of the surrounding mountains. In winter, you are fifteen minutes from skiing at Cannon Mountain.

Indoors at the inn, you can have a seat next to the woodstove in the tavern or settle into one of the sitting rooms, which are stocked with books, games, and videos.

Guest rooms are country fresh and simply furnished, most with flowered bedspreads and sheer pull-back curtains at the windows.

Karen, who studied at the French Culinary Institute, has brought her expertise to the White Mountains at the inn's Melanie's Bistro. Wait until you taste appetizers such as the French onion and bacon tart with flaky pastry, caramelized onions, and bacon, or entrees such as New Zealand baby lamb chops, housemade ravioli, or salmon. Don't forget dessert; they are homemade and delicious. Some of the choices: pumpkin crème caramel, banana-walnut cheesecake, or Karen's famous profiteroles.

The cozy tavern is a perfect spot to catch the news and scores on three TV screens. The menu here goes from comfort foods such as meat loaf to steak, and there is a nice selection of beer and wine.

When the hectic world gets to you, the peaceful Ammonoosuc is just the place to refresh and recharge.

HOW TO GET THERE: From Interstate 91 take exit 17 (Woodsville–Wells River). Go east on Route 302 to Lisbon. Two miles past Lisbon take a left on Lyman Road for about ½ mile, then left onto Bishop Road for about ¾ mile. The inn is on the right.

The Inns at Mill Falls
Meredith, New Hampshire 03253

INNKEEPER: Gail Batstone

ADDRESS/TELEPHONE: 312 Daniel Webster Highway; (603) 279–7006 or (800) 622–6455

WEB SITE: www.millfalls.com

ROOMS: Mill Falls: 54; some with fireplace; 1 equipped for the physically disabled. Chase House: 23, all with fireplace, lake view; some with whirlpool, balcony. Bay Point: 24, all with lake view; many with balcony, fireplace, whirlpool. Church Landing: 58 lakeview rooms, all with fireplace; most with balcony. All rooms have private bath, phone, and TV.

RATES: Mill Falls: $99 to $269 CP; Chase House: $159 to $319 CP; Bay Point: $139 to $329 BP; Church Landing: $199 to $409 BP.

OPEN: All year.

FACILITIES AND ACTIVITIES: Breakfast, lunch, dinner, Sunday brunch; bar and lounge. Indoor pool, sauna, spa, shops, conference centers, and a choice of restaurants. Boating, swimming, and fishing in Lake Winnipesaukee. Docking facilities for boats. Nearby: Golf, jogging, hiking, tennis, skiing in winter.

The Inns at Mill Falls comprise a mini-village of four inns, all adjacent to Lake Winnipesaukee, America's sixth largest natural lake, a sparkling beauty 28 miles long and 9 miles wide.

It all began with a single inn, Mill Falls, a restored nineteenth-century linen mill, set beside a covered bridge and a dramatic 40-foot waterfall. The inn is connected by a glass-enclosed, heated covered bridge to the Mill Falls

Marketplace, with lots of tempting shops and dining. Among the nice features of this inn are an indoor pool, whirlpool, sauna, and full-service spa.

The complex offers four settings for dining. The Waterfall Cafe has great breakfasts and a selection of good homemade soups, salads, and sandwiches for lunch. Giuseppe's, an Italian-style bistro, is open for both lunch and dinner and features live entertainment each evening. The menu includes delicious pastas and all the Italian favorites. During the summer months you can dine alfresco by the waterfall. The third option is Mame's, a small restaurant with many interesting dishes on the menu. At Sunday brunch, the eggs Benedict is perfection.

Next came the Bay Point at Mills Falls, a new inn built in a style to blend with the old. It is adjacent to the Marketplace and surrounded by more than 2,000 feet of manicured lakefront park. Bay Point directly faces Lake Winnipesaukee; in fact, part of the inn's restaurant, the Lago Trattoria, actually hangs over the water's edge. Many of the guest rooms offer balconies, cozy fireplaces, and personal whirlpool spas. All offer spectacular views of the lake and Gunstock Mountain beyond.

Chase House is another new building with the look of a classic resort hotel, with more lake view rooms, each with a fireplace, and again, many whirlpools and balconies. The Camp restaurant here is part of the Common Man chain. Chase House also includes a 150-seat conference center.

The newest inn, Church Landing, has the most dramatic site of all: three and a half acres of land forming a majestic point surrounded by almost 1,000 feet of Lake Winnipesaukee, with views in every direction. This, coupled with two natural sandy beaches shaded by 90-foot, one-hundred-year-old oak trees, is a fabulous setting. Similar to its neighbors, it is in the great shingled camp style of the 1880s. It includes the 200-seat Adirondack-style Lakehouse Grille. Facilities include an indoor/outdoor pool, a health club with a massage area, Jacuzzi and sauna, and a 300-seat conference center.

All the inns feature comfortable, well-furnished rooms, and all four properties serve a complimentary continental breakfast each morning in the lobby.

Whichever inn you choose, don't miss an excursion on the M/S *Mount Washington,* an excursion ship offering both day and evening dinner-dance cruises around Lake Winnipesaukee. It goes out of Meredith several times each week and is the best way to fully appreciate the beauty of the lake.

HOW TO GET THERE: From Interstate 93 take exit 23. Go east on Route 104 to its end. Turn left on Route 3 north. The inns are 1 mile farther, down the hill.

The Inn at Pleasant Lake
New London, New Hampshire 03257

INNKEEPERS: Linda and Brian Mackenzie

ADDRESS/TELEPHONE: 853 Pleasant Street (mailing address: P.O. Box 1030); (603) 526-6271 or (800) 626-4907; fax (603) 526-4111

WEB SITE: www.innatpleasantlake.com

ROOMS: 10 rooms and suites; all with private bath, air-conditioning; 1 with whirlpool; wireless Internet available.

RATES: $120 to $185 BP.

OPEN: All year, except early April and early November.

FACILITIES AND ACTIVITIES: Dinner Wednesday through Saturday, also Sunday May to October. Bar. Swimming, hiking, fitness equipment, private beach on the lake, 2 canoes, 1 rowboat. Nearby: Kayaking, golf, hiking, cross-country and downhill skiing, barn playhouse in summer.

The Inn at Pleasant Lake, the oldest operating inn in the area, has taken on new life since owner/chef Brian Mackenzie arrived in 1997. A graduate of the Culinary Institute of America, Brian has turned the inn into a gourmet's destination. His five-course dinners offer a choice of a fish or meat entree, but the rest is up to the chef, varying with the seasons, and his choices are sublime.

Guests are welcomed at a predinner reception where they get to meet the chef and hear about the night's menu, before being escorted into the candlelit dining room. It's worth the tab for this exceptional cuisine, classical French with an Asian influence.

The inn began its life as a farm in 1790 and still has the feel of the country, with antique furnishings and warming fireplaces. Guest rooms are country comfortable. The location couldn't be better, looking out on Pleasant Lake and Mount Kearsarge beyond, a vista that is simply spectacular in the fall. Many guest rooms have splendid views.

In winter you can cross-country ski nearby. Skiers will find Mount Sunapee and Ragged Mountain, each about fifteen minutes away.

One of the nicest activities here is simply gazing out of the window at those wonderful lake vistas.

HOW TO GET THERE: From Interstate 89 take either New London exit. Halfway through New London, turn at the Lake Sunapee Bank. This is Pleasant Street. Go about 2 miles, and the inn is on your left.

New London Inn
New London, New Hampshire 03257

INNKEEPERS: Bridget LeRoy and Eric Johnson

ADDRESS/TELEPHONE: 140 Main Street (mailing address: P.O. Box 8); (603) 526-2791 or (800) 526-2791; fax (603) 526-2749

WEB SITE: www.newlondoninn.net

ROOMS: 23 rooms and suites; all with private bath, TV, phone, Wi-Fi and dataports; many with DVD/VCR; some with whirlpool.

RATES: $115 to $205 BP.

OPEN: All year.

FACILITIES AND ACTIVITIES: Dinner Tuesday to Sunday, bar. Wheelchair access to dining room and bar. Nearby: Lakes, 2 public beaches, water sports, golf, summer theater, downhill and cross-country skiing, shopping.

*E*xciting things are happening at this venerable inn. Since new owners Bridget LeRoy and her husband, Eric Johnson, arrived in late 2004, a transformation has taken place. While taking into account the history of a building dating from 1792, they have brought everything up-to-date and created the best-reviewed restaurant in the area. Bridget, after all, is the daughter of the late Warner LeRoy, creator of New York's well-known Tavern on the Green, so she knows what it takes to create a memorable establishment. She is still a half-partner in the restaurant.

The couple faced quite a challenge in New London. The inn has been a landmark, receiving guests on Main Street since the late 1800s, but it had suffered badly from neglect in recent years and required structural work as well as redecorating. Now the lobby has been comfortably refurbished, and the bedrooms redone with antiques, beds with thick foam mattresses, and modern amenities such as TVs and DVD players and Wi-Fi connections. Some of the rooms have rainfall showerheads, providing a wonderful wide spray of water. Everything is fresh and stylish, but not overdone. You still have the feel of a classic New England inn.

The main parlor beckons with sunny yellow walls, big comfy sofas and chairs around the fireplace, and a library of books and games.

The dining room has a new look with deep red wall panels, translucent wooden lampshades handmade by a local artisan, and displays of Venetian glass. The 200-year-old fireplace remains.

The big change is the newly sophisticated cuisine, best described as American with a French accent. The menu stresses fresh ingredients and changes with the seasons. On a recent winter visit the menu included appetizers such as braised red onion and melted leek tart and butternut bisque, and entrees such as Hawaiian swordfish with citrus jasmine rice and osso bucco with a Parmesan polenta and smoked tomatoes. The dessert list has many tempting choices, but one not to be missed is the inn's homemade apple strudel served with cinnamon ice cream with rum raisin sauce.

The town of New London, home of Colby-Sawyer College, still conveys the feeling of a nineteenth-century village. From the wide main streets and gracious homes to the beautiful mountain backdrop, it is a wonderfully peaceful and unspoiled setting. The location in the Mount Sunapee region means that

New London Barn Playhouse

In the summer months the stage of the New London Barn Playhouse is lit for a full season of dramatic and musical entertainment suitable for the whole family. Well known on the summer-stock circuit, the theater is one of the oldest in New England. Special events and children's shows are also staged here from June through August. Regular performances are at 8:00 P.M. during the week, at 5:00 P.M. on Sunday, and at 2:00 P.M. on Wednesday. Call for information on the full schedule. Tickets are reasonably priced; call the box office at (603) 526-4631 or (800) 633-2276, or log on to www.nlbarn.com.

there are three lakes nearby offering public beaches, swimming, and water sports, as well as delightfully uncrowded golf courses and good skiing in the winter. If you go in summer, don't miss the wonderful League of New Hampshire Craftsmen Fair held at Mount Sunapee State Park in early August, a big event that shows the work of the state's artisans at its very best.

HOW TO GET THERE: Take exit 8 at Ascutney, Vermont, from Interstate 91. Follow signs to Claremont, New Hampshire. Take Route 11 east to Newport, Sunapee, Georges Mills, and New London. There is bus service via Vermont Transit from Boston and from White River Junction, Vermont.

The 1785 Inn
North Conway, New Hampshire 03860

INNKEEPERS: Charles and Rebecca Mallar

ADDRESS/TELEPHONE: Route 16 (mailing address: P.O. Box 1785); (603) 356-9025 or (800) 421-1785; fax (603) 356-6081

WEB SITE: www.the1785inn.com

ROOMS: 16, plus 1 suite; 12 with private bath.

RATES: $69 to $259 BP.

OPEN: All year.

FACILITIES AND ACTIVITIES: Dinner, bar, lounge. Wheelchair access to dining room. Swimming pool, cross-country skiing. Nearby: Golf, tennis, canoeing, fishing, skiing, outlet shopping.

The 1785 Inn is one of the oldest houses in all of Mount Washington Valley. It was built in 1785 by Capt. Elijah Dinsmore. Records indicate that Captain Dinsmore received a license to "keep a Publik House" in 1795. The lovely old inn also served as a stagecoach stop. The chimney and dining room fireplace with brick oven are original to the house. They form a beehive structure the size of an entire room in the center of the inn.

Guest accommodations are ample. The Mallars have completely refurbished the inn and done such a fine job. I find the in-room sinks a very nice feature in rooms with shared baths.

There are two living areas with their original working fireplaces; one has a television set and VCR. They are furnished with attractive chairs and couches for your comfort. The handsome old oak icebox is a conversation piece and a beautiful piece of furniture. The tavern has a large bar, a wood-burning stove, and good sitting areas.

This is an inn long known for fine dining. One favorite dinner dish is raspberry duckling: duck roasted with a brandy-laced raspberry sauce and served on wild rice. There are several veal selections, and, of course, seafood and chicken. More adventurous diners can try rabbit, venison, or elk. The desserts are wild. Chocolate strawberry shortcake. Coffee butter-crunch pie, as featured in *Bon Appétit*. Becky's wondrous raspberry desserts.

Candlelight casts a romantic glow throughout the evening, so take your time and enjoy your meal and fine wines. The wine list has been called "one of the finest in the world" by *Wine Spectator* magazine.

HOW TO GET THERE: Take Route 16 north. The inn is on the left just before you come to Route 16A.

Follansbee Inn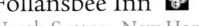
North Sutton, New Hampshire 03260

INNKEEPERS: Dave and Cathy Beard

ADDRESS/TELEPHONE: P.O. Box 92; (603) 927–4221 or (800) 626–4221

WEB SITE: www.follansbeeinn.com

ROOMS: 18, all with private bath; some with whirlpool.

RATES: $120 to $190 BP.

OPEN: All year.

FACILITIES AND ACTIVITIES: Beer and wine license, for inn guests only. Cross-country skiing from the inn, swimming, boating, bicycles, snow-shoes for guests. Nearby: Downhill skiing, golf, antiquing.

The Follansbee Inn is an 1840 New England farmhouse with a won-derful location on Kezar Lake. It has its own pier and private beach with lots of room for sunbathing and canoes, rowboats, kayaks, and a paddleboat provided for fun on the water.

You can easily spend a day at the lake. Take a swim to the float, bring your fishing pole, or settle into a hammock under the pines. For privacy, row out to a secluded island for a picnic.

The inn itself has old-fashioned appeal. Two comfortable sitting rooms offer a choice of moods. You can be rustic-cozy with barnboard walls and a wood-burning stove or choose a larger room facing the lake, with a wood-

Muster Field Farm Museum

The Muster Field Farm Museum in North Sutton was established to educate visitors about the history of New Hampshire agriculture, farm life, and early architecture. The farm consists of 250 acres of fields and woods with wonderful views of Mount Kearsarge and King Ridge. On the grounds are a collection of historic barns and other buildings; a working farm producing vegetables, flowers, hay, cord wood, and maple syrup; and the Matthew Harvey Homestead, a handsome eighteenth-century farmhouse listed on the National Register of Historic Places.

The farm is open daily for self-guided tours that include the original Harvey barn and flower and vegetable gardens. A number of buildings were moved to this site to be preserved, including several barns, an 1881 springhouse, a blacksmith shop, and an 1810 schoolhouse.

Sunday-afternoon open houses in July and August include tours of the Harvey homestead, an elegant example of rural Georgian architecture, circa 1787. It is little altered except for certain remodeling in the Federal style around 1800. It was built by one of New Hampshire's leading early citizens, the largest landowner in Sutton and a member of the state legislature. His sons followed their father's example of public service, and the house remained in the family until 1859.

Special events include Farm Days in late August, and demonstrations include farm tasks such as haying, threshing, and cider making and crafts including spinning, weaving, dyeing, and lace making. There's also Harvest Day in September, featuring old-time fiddling and demonstrations of corn and bean shelling, rope making, and canning on the old cookstove.

The farm stand is always stocked with fresh produce of the season and farm-fresh eggs.

For more information log on to www.musterfieldfarm.com or call (603) 927-4276.

burning fireplace; a goodly supply of books, games, and puzzles; and a bar stocked with beers and wines.

Off the wide corridors upstairs are cozy bedrooms, named for ancestors of the town, like Hannah or Ichabod. Recently redone, each room is unique, but all have cozy quilts and comfy pillows. Lucinda room is done in Country French decor, while Ichabod has soft blue floral paper and three windows facing the lake. Two third-floor suites are special: The Rebecca suite offers a queen-size four-poster bed and a whirlpool in the bath, while the Sarah suite provides four windows with views of the lake.

The dining room also has lake views and a choice of taking a table for two or four or joining other guests at the long center table. Breakfasts here are hearty, featuring homemade granola and tasty dishes such as crème brûlée French toast or the inn's special eggs Benedict. You can take your coffee out on the porch facing the town green and a 1790s meetinghouse framed by wooded hills. North Sutton's old church is right next door, and you can set your watch by the chimes.

The 3-mile walk around the lake is the most pleasant kind of exercise, and bikes are available for guests who want to explore the area. The Musterfield Farm Museum is just a mile up the road, and New London is 4 miles away. The innkeepers can guide you to a host of sports and attractions year-round. In winter, you can borrow snowshoes and take a hike right from the door of the inn. Guests who come in the winter receive a bonus—homemade soups, breads, and dessert, served in the evening from 5:00 to 7:00 P.M.

HOW TO GET THERE: Take Interstate 91 north to Route 9 in Brattleboro, Vermont. Continue to Henniker, New Hampshire, and go north on Route 114 for 18 miles to North Sutton. The inn is behind the church. From Boston take Interstate 93 north to Interstate 89 at Concord. Follow I–89 to exit 10 and turn left off the exit; continue 2 miles to North Sutton.

Home Hill Inn
Plainfield, New Hampshire 03781

INNKEEPERS: Victoria and Stephane du Roure, owners

ADDRESS/TELEPHONE: River Road; (603) 675-6165; fax (603) 675-5220

WEB SITE: www.homehillinn.com

ROOMS: 10 rooms, 1 suite in 2 buildings, 1 cottage; all with private, tile-and-marble baths; some with working fireplaces, private terraces; 1 room wheelchair accessible.

RATES: $295 to $495 CP.

OPEN: All year.

FACILITIES AND ACTIVITIES: Dinner Wednesday through Sunday. 25 acres with swimming pool, tennis, putting green, complimentary bikes, cross-country trails, complimentary snowshoes; spa treatments. Nearby: Dartmouth College, Saint-Gaudens National Historic Site, canoeing, fishing, golf, skiing.

Take a classic New England home, circa 1818, and add innkeepers who provide a luxurious touch of France, and you have one of the most elegant retreats in New Hampshire.

Stephane du Roure, a native of Provence, and his American wife, Victoria, who was classically trained at the renowned Ritz-Escoffier Culinary School at the Ritz Hotel in Paris, have transformed this country home overlooking the Connecticut River, adding luxurious rooms in the rich colors of Provence, with American antiques as accents. Victoria's menus have turned the dining room into a destination for gourmets. The inn has been chosen as a member of the highly selective Relais & Chateaux group.

Four rooms in the main house are named for famous local artists or residents. Augustus Saint-Gaudens, the famous sculptor, lived and worked in Cornish for the last thirty-six years of his life; his home is a major attraction in the area. The Saint-Gaudens room is decorated in French toile and furnished with a queen-size canopied bed, early French and American antiques, and a working fireplace. The luxurious Maxfield Parrish two-room suite, named for the noted illustrator who also lived and worked in Plainfield, has two fireplaces. One guest room was recently converted into a space for spa treatments.

Six additional rooms are in the Carriage House. Rooms here are named for towns in the south of France. Moustier and Cassis are both elegant and cozy, decorated in traditional French country toiles, with queen beds, fireplaces, private entries, and stone terraces. Fontvielle, beautifully decorated with French fabrics and antiques, also has a private terrace and is wheelchair accessible. La Piscine, a private cottage located near the pool and available seasonally, is a romantic retreat with a brass queen bed and a sitting room furnished in wicker.

The new vaulted dining room is charming, done in Provençal yellow and reds with rooster prints, a working fireplace, and dramatic floor-to-ceiling French doors. In warm weather, there is seating on an outdoor terrace with views of a reflecting pond and water garden. The old dining room now serves as a reception area and lounge and includes a boutique.

Victoria's menus are a modern twist on traditional Provençal cuisine. Guests can choose from an a la carte menu, a prix fixe dinner, or a tasting menu. Stephane is on hand to suggest proper wines to complement the meal.

Among Victoria's signature dishes are *daurade,* a fish roasted in a salt crust with herbed olive oil and chickpea "Panisses"; and braised osso bucco with baby fennel, roasted garlic, and saffron gnocchi. Her seasonal menus take advantage of New England and local products, such as an appetizer of Hudson Valley foie gras, served with fresh fig and port compote and brioche toast, and a main course of Vermont lamb with roasted shallots and thyme. Desserts? Well, how can anyone resist a Manjari chocolate cream martini or lemon-mascarpone shortcake? The menu changes often, so you will no doubt find other delicious choices.

If you are in the mood for somethig lighter, the inn recently added a bistro menu with traditional dishes such as skate, hangar steak, and coq au vin. Sunday brunch is another welcome addition.

Home Hill's twenty-five sylvan acres offer a pool and tennis court, and in winter, trails for cross-country skiing, and snowshoeing. Bikes are available to guests for local exploring. A short drive will take you to the many attractions of Dartmouth College in Hanover or to Saint-Gaudens's home. And when you come back, you can enjoy an inn that gives you a beautiful blend of New England hospitality and Gallic charm.

HOW TO GET THERE: Take Interstate 89 to exit 20 south onto Route 12A. Continue for 3 miles to River Road and turn right. Home Hill is 3½ miles farther on the left.

Philbrook Farm Inn
Shelburne, New Hampshire 03581

INNKEEPERS: Connie Leger and Nancy Philbrook

ADDRESS/TELEPHONE: 881 North Road; (603) 466–3831

WEB SITE: www.philbrookfarminn.com

ROOMS: 19, plus 6 cottages with fireplaces; 10 rooms and all cottages with private bath. 4 cottages have housekeeping arrangements. Pets welcome in cottages. Cottages open mid-May to Columbus Day.

RATES: $125 to $150 MAP (private bath); $115 MAP (shared bath); $800 per week, housekeeping cottages; $150 per night, MAP, one-room cottages. No credit cards.

OPEN: All year except April and October 31 to December 26.

FACILITIES AND ACTIVITIES: BYOB. Wheelchair access to dining room and first floor but not to restrooms. Library, pool table, Ping-Pong, swimming pool, cross-country skiing, snowshoeing, hiking. Nearby: Downhill skiing.

Philbrook Farm started as an inn in 1861. Now listed on the National Register of Historic Places, it is still an inn and still owned by the Philbrooks, who run it in fine New England tradition.

Everything you eat here is prepared from scratch in their kitchens. The baked goods are made daily. One entree is served each night. Roasts of everything you can want—pork, beef, turkey—and on and on. The New England

boiled dinner is a favorite, as is baked bean supper on Saturday night and roast chicken dinner on Sunday.

The downstairs playroom has Ping-Pong, a pool table, a piano, and fun. Fireplaces and a lot of reading material can be found all over the inn. Look for the wonderful selection of Philbrook Farm puzzles made by Connie's grandfather. They have large, ¼-inch-thick pieces and are just beautiful. A player piano, an old pump organ—where else can you find such unique things except in an inn?

Rooms are furnished with a lot of old family treasures. There are some nice four-posters and a wonderful collection of old bowl and pitcher sets. All the cottages are different. They are nice choices if you want to linger here a while. Some have dining rooms, most have fireplaces, and all have porches. If you are staying in a cottage, you can bring along your pet.

With more than 1,000 acres, the inn has plenty of room for you to roam any season of the year. Walking trails begin in the meadow in front of the inn, taking you to the river, through a white birch grove, and on three meandering trails back home. Look across their fields to the Carter-Moriah and Presidential mountain ranges. Behind the inn rises the Mahoosuc Range. This is the Androscoggin Valley. The inn cats are Felix and Spice, and the inn dog, Valkerie, is a German shorthair pointer.

HOW TO GET THERE: The inn is 1½ miles off Route 2. From Route 2 take Meadow Road. Cross the railroad tracks and then a bridge. Turn right at the crossroads and go ½ mile to the inn, which is on North Road.

Snowvillage Inn 💝
Snowville, New Hampshire 03832

INNKEEPERS: Karen and Bern Galat

ADDRESS/TELEPHONE: P.O. Box 68; (603) 447–2818 or (800) 447–4345

WEB SITE: www.snowvillageinn.com

ROOMS: 18, all with private bath; 4 with fireplace.

RATES: $129 to $249 BP, per person, double occupancy; MAP available.

OPEN: All year.

FACILITIES AND ACTIVITIES: Bar, lounge, sauna, cross-country skiing, showshoeing, nature trails. Nearby: Swimming, fishing, canoeing, hiking, downhill skiing.

In the winter Snowville lives up to its name. It snows a lot, and it is pristine and beautiful. The view from the inn is breathtaking, with Mount Washington and the whole Presidential Range in view wherever you look. In summer at the top of Foss Mountain, right at the inn, you can eat your fill of wild blueberries.

The guest rooms are comfortable and spacious, with tons of towels in luscious colors. The rooms are named after writers (funny, I did not find an Elizabeth Squier room), some have fireplaces, and all have private baths.

The living room, with its huge fireplace and nice couches, makes this an inn for rest and relaxation. The room includes a service bar, a lounge area, and books everywhere. A huge porch surrounds part of the inn. I could sit here all day and enjoy the incredible views.

Dinner is a delight in the very nice dining room. I could hardly decide between the home-baked sour cream rolls and rolls with sun-dried tomato and basil. Soups such as fresh tomato and corn chowder or wild mushroom, apple, and pistachio bisque are delicious and lead the way to wonderful entrees such as roasted duck with a blueberry green-peppercorn sauce, or medallions of veal sautéed with apples and calvados brandy cream sauce. The menu changes often, but rack of lamb, pork tenderloin, and roasted duck are almost always available, with different sauces and accompaniments.

Can you still find room for dessert? Who can resist when you have wonderful things like chocolate carrot cake or frozen lemon mousse with raspberry sauce.

You can work it off on nearby hiking trails, or by swimming or canoeing on Crystal Lake, not far from the inn. In winter, you can ski the 13 kilometers of cross-country trails on the inn property; ski rentals are available. Sledding is also fun.

Whatever the season, the discount shopping in North Conway beckons, just a short drive away.

HOW TO GET THERE: Outside of Conway on Route 153, go 5 miles to Crystal Lake. Turn left, follow the sign to Snowville, and go about 1½ miles. Turn right at the inn's sign, and go up the hill ¾ mile to the inn.

Sunset Hill House
Sugar Hill, New Hampshire 03585

INNKEEPERS: The Henderson family: Lon, Nancy, Mary Pearl, and Adeline

ADDRESS/TELEPHONE: Sunset Hill Road; (603) 823–5522 or (800) 786–4455; fax (603) 823–5738

WEB SITE: www.sunsethillhouse.com

ROOMS: 26, plus 2 suites; all with private bath, air-conditioning, mountain views; 7 with Jacuzzi; 7 with fireplace; 5 with porches; 1 equipped for the physically disabled.

RATES: $100 to $399 BP. MAP rates available.

OPEN: All year.

FACILITIES AND ACTIVITIES: Dinner daily from mid-June to November 1 and Thursday through Sunday the rest of the year. Full license. Meeting room, art gallery, heated swimming pool, cross-country skiing, hiking, golf. Nearby: Almost anything you might want to do.

The Sunset Hill House is perched on a 1,700-foot ridge with unparalleled views of New Hampshire's Presidential Mountain Range to the east and Vermont's Green Mountains to the west.

The inn was built in 1880, in an era of grand hotels and resorts, and is Second Empire Victorian in style.

In the past several years, the Hendersons have done a lot of upgrading, making this appealing property even better. Among the changes are redecorating most of the public rooms and overhauling the Hill House annex. Rooms are now air-conditioned, many have king beds, many more have whirlpools and fireplaces, and one has been equipped for the physically disabled. One thing needed no improvement: Every single room has a mountain view.

The dining room has also benefited from new attention, with a more sophisticated contemporary menu. You might start with sautéed wild mushrooms or the inn's own smoked seafood platter, featuring salmon, scallops, and trout with a horseradish lemon dressing. Main courses include roasted game hen, cod Provençal, and the very special duckling Bombay, with a sauce of almonds, chutney, and brandy. Choosing a dessert is no easy matter, as the menu offers such temptations as white chocolate cheesecake, a tartlet of mixed fruits with a fresh apricot glaze, and a cappuccino mousse.

From the big window in the main dining room you can look east instead of west to see the sunset ablaze on the White Mountains. The reason is a phenomenon known as "Alpen Glow." It is this unusual sight that inspired the name of the inn.

When you are in the mood for lighter fare, the tavern can oblige with pub fare from burgers to blackened tuna. Breakfast is always a treat at Sunset Hill. Fresh fruits and home-baked pastries are set on a buffet, plus a full menu of cooked-to-order dishes such as the inn's special maple–cream cheese French toast.

This is an inn with many special spots. I especially liked the art gallery in a wide hall. All the works are by local artists and are for sale. On the terrace level is a huge room for business meetings, weddings, and receptions. On the grounds is a lovely heated swimming pool. And just down the road a few miles is all the majesty of Franconia Notch State Park, one of the most scenic oases in New England.

This inn fully embodies what Lon and Nancy call the three Ms—the Majesty of the Mountains, the Magic of a Country Inn, and the Management of Every Detail.

HOW TO GET THERE: From Interstate 93 take exit 38 to Route 117 to the top of Sugar Hill. Turn left on Sunset Hill Road. From Interstate 91 take exit 17 to Route 302 east. Proceed approximately 18 miles to Route 117. Drive to the top of Sugar Hill and turn right on Sunset Hill Road.

Dexter's
Sunapee, New Hampshire 03782

INNKEEPERS: John Augustine and Penny Berrier

ADDRESS/TELEPHONE: 258 Stagecoach Road; (603) 763–5571 or (800) 232–5571

WEB SITE: www.dextersnh.com

ROOMS: 17, plus 1 cottage and 1 condo; all with private bath. Wheelchair access to specially equipped room and bath for the physically disabled.

RATES: $130 to $175 BP; cottage sleeping up to 8, $300 to $400, breakfast optional; 2-bedroom condo, sleeping up to 6, $200 to $300, breakfast optional.

OPEN: June 15 to October 15.

League of New Hampshire Craftsmen's Fair

The oldest continual crafts fair in the nation, dating from the 1930s, is held annually at the base of Mount Sunapee in early August. For nine splendid days, the fair features craft demonstrations; artists' workshops; displays and sales of hand-crafted clothing, furnishings, jewelry, weaving, basketry, and metalsmithing; and much more. A fabulous collection of the region's finest juried craftspeople are an inspiration to the thousands of visitors who come to the fair. The talent—well, let me just say, wow. Live theater and musical performances are a part of the excitement here.

The fair runs from 10:00 A.M. to 5:00 P.M. daily. Call for this year's exact dates. Admission (about $8.00 per adult, $6.00 for seniors, and free to children under twelve) includes all the exhibits and performances—and a return trip the next day so you can see anything you missed the first time. For information call (603) 224-3375 or log on to www.nhcrafts.org.

FACILITIES AND ACTIVITIES: Tennis, swimming pool, recreation barn, horseshoes, shuffleboard. Nearby: Skiing, golf, fishing, boating.

The main house was built in 1801 by an artisan, Adam Reddington. He earned his living by carving, from the huge knurls of the many fine maples on the grounds, the bowls in which sailing ships carried their compasses. In 1948 the house became a small country inn.

Dexter's owners make it a warm, informal place that welcomes children. Ten rooms in the main house are decorated in old-fashioned colonial style. Seven rooms in the Annex across the road are larger and a bit more rustic, with more room to accommodate families. You can even bring the family pet with you (with advance permission from the innkeepers). Other options include a two-bedroom, two-bath cottage with a full kitchen and an efficiency condo. Rates for larger accommodations vary depending on season and whether guests want to include the inn breakfast.

There is plenty to keep everyone occupied outdoors: three tennis courts, a swimming pool, volleyball, badminton, basketball, horseshoes, shuffleboard, and croquet, plus twenty acres with paths for walking. In winter cross-country skiing, showshoeing, and sledding are close at hand.

No sunshine? Not to worry. Inside the inn, a kids' play room offers videos, games, puzzles, books, coloring books, and stuffed animals, and a barn recreation room is equipped with billiards, Ping-Pong, Foosball, and darts. The comfortable living room has a fireplace and a library of books and magazines, and a home entertainment room features a big-screen TV.

Breakfast is a generous buffet, and while no other meals are presently served, guests are welcome to bring their own food to be enjoyed in the dining room, courtyard, or picnic area, another way that the innkeepers help everyone feel at home.

HOW TO GET THERE: Take Interstate 89 out of Concord and follow exit 12 to Route 11 west for 5½ miles. Turn left on Winn Hill Road for 1½ miles to the inn. Or take Interstate 91 out of Springfield and follow exit 8 to Claremont, New Hampshire, to Route 103/11 east for 18 miles to Newport. Follow Route 103 left onto Young Hill Road for 1²/₁₀ miles to the inn.

The Inn at Sunapee

Sunapee, New Hampshire 03782

INNKEEPERS: Ted and Susan Harriman

ADDRESS/TELEPHONE: Burkehaven Hill Road (mailing address: P.O. Box 336); (603) 763-4444 or (800) 327-2466

WEB SITE: www.innatsunapee.com

ROOMS: 16, plus 5 suites; all with private bath.

RATES: $120 to $175 BP.

OPEN: All year.

FACILITIES AND ACTIVITIES: Dinner (seasonal). Bar, lounge, full license. Pool, hiking. Nearby: Downhill skiing, cross-country skiing, hiking.

he Inn at Sunapee, an 1800s farmhouse with a classic wraparound porch, is nicely situated on a hilltop that overlooks beautiful Mount Sunapee. Nearby, Lake Sunapee is the second largest in New Hampshire, and it's a great spot for sailing, fishing, and waterskiing.

Attached to the house is a barn that has been turned into a lounge with a fieldstone fireplace and good couches. The views from the windows in here and in the dining room are spectacular any season of the year.

Dinner is now seasonal, and the days it is available vary; you'll have to ask when you reserve. But when it is served, you can be sure to find tasty choices

such as chicken marsala, steak, or salmon. During the summer, Thursday nights usually mean luscious lobster, served with all the trimmings.

Ted and Susan lived in the Far East and Southeast Asia for more than twenty-five years, and their wonderful collection of furnishings is used throughout the inn. Rooms are decorated with oak and iron furniture. Some rooms have wide-board pine floors. There is a cute and small, separate cottage. Five accommodations are family suites and children are welcome here.

HOW TO GET THERE: From Boston take Interstate 93 north to Concord, New Hampshire. Then take Interstate 89 north to exit 12 and follow Route 11 west to Sunapee. At the blinking light turn toward Sunapee Harbor. At the harbor you will see a park with a bandstand. Take the first right after the bandstand and go ½ mile up the hill to the inn.

The Tamworth Inn
Tamworth Village, New Hampshire 03886

INNKEEPERS: Virginia and Bob Schrader

ADDRESS/TELEPHONE: Main Street; (603) 323–7721 or (800) 642–7352; fax (253) 550–3204

WEB SITE: www.tamworth.com

ROOMS: 16, including 7 suites; all with private bath.

RATES: $115 to $300 BP.

OPEN: All year except April and two weeks in November.

FACILITIES AND ACTIVITIES: Dinner Tuesday through Sunday summer and fall, Thursday through Saturday mid-October to mid-June; Sunday brunch. Pub, swimming pool, hiking, fishing, snowshoeing and cross-country skiing. Nearby: Downhill skiing, Barnstormer's Theater, antiquing, biking.

Built in 1833, the Tamworth Inn is a rambling building in a lovely New England town. The inn sits across from the Congregational church and a thoroughbred horse pasture.

The Swift River, true to its name, flows swiftly behind the inn. If you're looking for a memorable spot for your wedding, the riverside gazebo is great; if you're inclined toward fly fishing, this is also the place for you. The hale and hearty might want to walk about a ¼ mile to the swimming hole. Anyone less adventuresome will find the inn's swimming pool just right.

The main attraction in town in the summer is the Barnstormer's Theater down the street, the oldest summer theater in New England. An "equity house," the theater offers eight different professional performances each summer. It certainly is nice to stay at the inn, have a tasty dinner, and walk to good theater.

There are lots of hiking trails in this area, and they are maintained by the Appalachian Mountain Club, the Tamworth Outing Club, and the Wonalancet Outing Club. They are within walking distance of the inn. In winter these trails become cross-country ski and snowshoe trails.

Back at the inn, guests enjoy sitting by the fireplace; tea is served here in the afternoon. The Library is a quieter spot for reading, having a go at the games or puzzles, or watching a movie from the inn's selection of videos. There's a fireplace here, as well.

A big country breakfast is served in the breakfast room, or in good weather, on the patio overlooking the Swift River. The dining room is drawing food lovers from the city who enjoy having gourmet fare in a rural village setting. Lighter fare is served in the pub, known for its antique sled collection. When the bartender is off duty, guests do the honors and pay on the honor system.

Virginia and Bob have considerably upgraded the inn decor since they arrived. Rooms are decorated with antiques and original art; beds have firm orthopedic mattresses and down comforters. "We are in the sleep business, after all," says Bob. The full-size family suite, with four beds, is ideal for larger families or groups of friends traveling together.

It's lovely here in summer, with the pool set amid landscaped gardens, and nearly two acres of lawns and gardens to enjoy. The gazebo on the banks of the Swift River has a hammock for two, plus several gliders and Adirondack chairs, the perfect spot to relax and be lulled to the sound of the gently rippling water. The cares of real life seem very far away.

HOW TO GET THERE: Tamworth is on Route 113, 3 miles northwest of the intersection of Routes 25 and 16.

The Birchwood Inn
Temple, New Hampshire 03084

INNKEEPERS: Andrew Cook, Nick Finnis, and Trish Bender

ADDRESS/TELEPHONE: Route 45 (mailing address: P.O. Box 23); (603) 878–3285; fax (603) 878–2179

WEB SITE: www.thebirchwoodinn.com

ROOMS: 7; 5 with private bath.

RATES: $79 to $99 BP.

OPEN: All year except two weeks in spring and one week in November.

FACILITIES AND ACTIVITIES: Dinner served Friday and Saturday, tavern fare Wednesday through Sunday. Wheelchair access to dining room. Nearby: Antiquing, cross-country skiing, hiking, golf, summer theater, lakes.

*L*isted on the National Register of Historic Places and part of the historic district of a charming colonial-era village, this inn is a classic. The building dates from 1800, the barns were added in 1848, and not much has changed since. The dining room boasts a mural painted in 1825 by Rufus Porter, one of the most famous mural painters in early America.

No doubt it was the history that lured two Englishmen to take over the inn in 2004. They came to the area for a friend's wedding, fell in love with the countryside, and with an American partner, Trish, were soon embarked on a new mission, providing a touch of Britain in America. Rooms have been given properly evocative names such as Oxford, Royal Bath, and Canterbury. They've also established a pub at the inn known as London Tavern where you can order dishes such as bangers and mash, shepherd's pie, and steak and ale pie. Desserts are equally traditional, with choices such as bread and butter pudding and "spotted dick," a suet pudding made with dried fruits. Candlelit dinners in the dining room are more formal and will reflect the recent culinary prowess of English chefs.

The inn is in the Mount Monadnock region of New Hampshire, so there is plenty to do here. From the top of the mountain you can see four states, a nice reward for you hikers. The trout are waiting for the angler, plus golf, summer theater and music, horseback riding, and skiing in winter. It's a wonderful, unspoiled corner of New England, now with the added lore of Old England hospitality.

HOW TO GET THERE: Take Route 3 out of Boston to Nashua, New Hampshire, exit 8. Follow Route 101 to Milford to Route 45 to Temple.

The Chesterfield Inn
West Chesterfield, New Hampshire 03466

INNKEEPERS: Judy and Phil Hueber

ADDRESS/TELEPHONE: Route 9; (603) 256–3211 or (800) 365–5515; fax (603) 256–6131

WEB SITE: www.chesterfieldinn.com

ROOMS: 13, plus 2 suites; all with private bath, air-conditioning, refrigerator, phone. Many rooms have a fireplace and/or a garden terrace; 2 with whirlpool; 1 has wheelchair access. Pets are welcome.

RATES: $150 to $320 BP.

OPEN: All year.

FACILITIES AND ACTIVITIES: Dinner Monday through Saturday. Wheelchair access to dining room. Full license. Gardens, pond, ice skating. Nearby: Fishing, boating, skiing, swimming.

A tavern from 1798 to 1811, and then a farm, the inn opened in 1984 after extensive renovations by talented architect Rod Williams of the Inn at Sawmill Farms. Exposed beams, many of them part of the original structure, and walls paneled with boards that came from an old barn make for a warm and friendly atmosphere.

The guest rooms are spacious. Some rooms have balconies or garden patios, others have a fireplace or whirlpool, and all are lovely, done in soft shades of blues, greens, and pinks. They have nice amenities such as televisions and telephones, including one in the bathroom. Good fluffy towels and an assortment of toiletries are here. To top it all off, each room has a refrigerator with juice, bottled spring water, beers, and wine.

The foyer has a large fireplace holding a bright red woodstove, and nice couches. It's a good place for cocktails. Off the foyer is the parlor, with a fireplace and good couches. A window seat overlooks an outdoor patio.

The chef here rates three diamonds, and you'll see why when you taste his creations. What about starting with pumpkin risotto or an apple, smoked Gouda cheese, and proscuitto turnover? Main courses may include house-smoked duck breast fanned over a sweet potato and soy bean succotash or a boneless pork loin with chestnut stuffing. Or maybe halibut fillet wrapped in bok choy over a leek, pearl onion, and turnip ratatouille, or twin quails braised in a Moroccan stew accompanied by a spiced polenta.

The menu changes often, but whatever the choices, you'll dine well, right through to the tempting desserts. Not the least of the pleasures of the two dining rooms are the outside views.

The inn's grounds are full of perennial, herb, and vegetable gardens. The beautiful Connecticut River is a short walk from the inn, so bring along your canoe or fishing pole. Lake Spofford has boats for rent. Pisgah Park has hiking trails and two spring-fed ponds for swimming. In winter, skiing is close at hand, and the inn's pond is lighted for night skating under the stars. And all year you'll find good antiques shops and arts and crafts shops in the appealing Monadnock region.

HOW TO GET THERE: Take exit 3 off Interstate 91. Take Route 9 east, going over the border from Vermont to New Hampshire. The inn is 2 miles on your left. Turn left on Cross Road, then right into the driveway.

Spalding Country Inn

Whitefield, New Hampshire 03598

INNKEEPERS: Walter and Dona Loope

ADDRESS/TELEPHONE: 199 Mountain View Road; (603) 837-2572 or (800) 368-8439; fax (603) 837-3062

WEB SITE: www.spaldinginn.com

ROOMS: 24 rooms and suites in lodge west wing; all with private bath; 12 in carriage house, some with whirlpools and ceiling fans; plus 6 guest houses, 1 to 4 bedrooms, with kitchen or kitchenette.

RATES: Rooms, $125 to $145 BP; suites, $168 to $285 BP; guest houses with 1 to 4 bedrooms, $199 to $598 BP. MAP available.

OPEN: May 1 through November 30.

FACILITIES AND ACTIVITIES: Dinner, tearoom, country store, heated swimming pool, four clay tennis courts, croquet, shuffleboard, basketball, volleyball, separate adult and kids' game rooms, exercise room, perennial gardens. Nearby: Weathervane Theater, golf, hiking, fishing, amusement parks, Franconia Notch, covered bridges, waterfalls.

*I*f you care to see how our parents and grandparents may have spent their summers years ago, come to the Spalding Country Inn. It's been welcoming people since the early 1800s.

It's easy to see the attraction. The inn is located on more than 210 acres with glorious White Mountain views. Families are welcome; suites and guest houses have plenty of room. For adults in search of a quiet getaway, the carriage house offers large, romantically furnished rooms. All the rooms and guest houses are nicely appointed.

Since the Loopes arrived, there have been nice changes at the inn, including amenities such as the tearoom and in-room libraries. Separate game rooms provide adults with a pool table, darts, chess, backgammon, and cards, while the kids' game room offers Ping-Pong tables, Foosball, board games, cards, and puzzles.

A full breakfast includes fresh juice, fruits, granola and yogurt, French toast, pancakes, and eggs any way you like them, including eggs Benedict, plus home fries, bacon, ham, or sausage.

Dinner menus change nightly, except on Friday, when you can always count on lobster. The menu is varied enough to please, with both simple home-style cooking and more sophisticated international dishes.

There is no dress requirement at the inn other than to be comfortable. And that's easy to do here. This is a glorious spot, inside and out, a delicious taste of yesteryear.

HOW TO GET THERE: Take Interstate 93 north to exit 41, Littleton/Whitefield. Follow Route 116 to Whitefield, and at the blinking yellow light in town, turn right (still Route 116) and continue for 3 miles. Make a left onto Mountain View Road. The Spalding Inn is 6/10 mile farther on the right.

Select List of
Other New Hampshire Inns

Three Chimneys Inn/ffrost Sawyer Tavern

17 Newmarket Road
Durham, NH 03824
(603) 868–7800 or (888) 399–9777; fax (603) 868–2964
Web site: www.threechimneysinn.com
26 rooms, all with private bath; some with four-poster bed, Jacuzzi, or two-person tub. Original home built in 1649 on the Oyster River.

Maple Hill Farm Country Inn B&B

200 Newport Road
New London, NH 03257
(603) 526–2248 or (800) 231–8637
Web site: www.maplehillfarm.com
10 rooms, all air-conditioned; 6 with private bath; 2-bedroom lake house. Bed-and-breakfast in 1824 farmhouse. Six-person hot tub spa, indoor basketball court, sand box, playground. Specializes in group and family package deals with meals.

Nereledge Inn

River Road
P.O. Box 547
North Conway, NH 03860
(603) 356–2831
Web site: www.nereledgeinn.com
11 rooms, most with private bath; full breakfast; game room, fireplace in sitting room; bed-and-breakfast in 1787 farmhouse.

Rhode Island

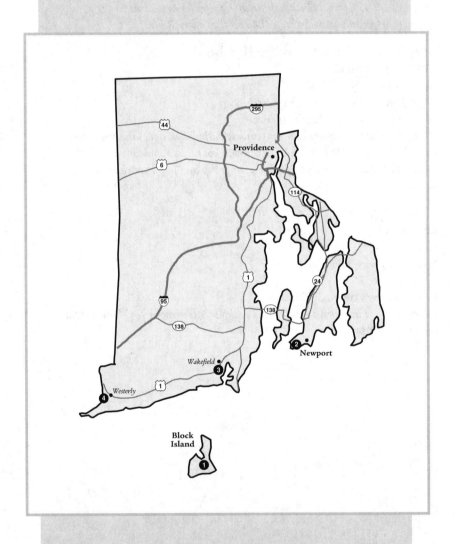

Rhode Island

Numbers on map refer to towns numbered below.

Atlantic Inn
Block Island, Rhode Island 02807

INNKEEPERS: Brad and Anne Marthens

ADDRESS/TELEPHONE: P.O. Box 1788; (401) 466–5883 or (800) 224–7422

WEB SITE: www.atlanticinn.com

ROOMS: 21, all with private bath, phone; 1 cottage suite with kitchen, TV.

RATES: $159 to $299 CP; cottage suite, $425 (seasonal).

OPEN: Late April through October.

FACILITIES AND ACTIVITIES: Dinner nightly in season, Thursday through Sunday from mid-September; gardens, lawns, croquet. Nearby: Beaches, boating, biking.

*B*lock Island is a trip to yesterday, an island of wild beauty with the look and serenity of long ago. Around every bend, flower-splashed meadows and pond-dotted moors come into view, open and inviting.

Island inns are the old-fashioned kind, white wooden structures cooled by the breezes. And one of the island queens is the Atlantic Inn, a Victorian beauty perched on its hilltop since 1879, surrounded by gardens and with a wraparound porch to take in the stunning views.

The inn is known for its fine dining room. The appetizers give a good idea of the creativity of the chef. How about starting with sautéed quail with an almond couscous strudel and tahini sauce, a ceviche salad roll, or crab, tuna, salmon, and calamari, with sprouts and a peach chutney. As you might expect for an isle surrounded by the sea, entrees stress seafood such as grilled striped bass or sautéed halibut, but choices such as grilled chicken and roasted duck fill out the menu. What's for dessert? Irresistible treats such as triple chocolate marquee or strawberry shortcake or a cooling iced lemon mousse.

The evening might start with cocktails and tapas on the porch or in an Adirondack chair on the lawn, facing the sunset. After dinner, you can enjoy an Atlantic Inn coffee, a delicious concoction made with Hennessey VS, Kahlua, and a splash of Frangelico, topped with Chantilly cream.

Guest rooms on the second and third floors are comfortable, simple, and summery, with some nice antiques as accents. But it isn't likely you'll be spending a lot of time in your room on an island rimmed with beaches and ideal for biking or walking. All of Block Island is only 7 miles long and 3 miles wide, so leave your car on shore; it's easy to explore on your own. And if you are feeling lazy, a dozen island taxis will gladly take you around.

HOW TO GET THERE: Ferry service to Block Island is two hours from New London, Connecticut, and forty-five minutes from Point Judith, Rhode Island. For information on the ferry, call (401) 783-4613 or log on to www.block islandferry.com. The inn is a short taxi ride from the ferry dock. Bus service (715-601-4707; www.adventurenortheast.com) is available from New York to the ferry docks, and commuter plane service (800-243-2460) is available from Westerly, Rhode Island, a fifteen-minute ride.

Castle Hill Inn
Newport, Rhode Island 02840

INNKEEPER: Natalie Ward, manager

ADDRESS/TELEPHONE: 590 Ocean Drive; (401) 849-3800 or (888) 466-1355; fax (401) 849-3838

WEB SITE: www.castlehillinn.com

ROOMS: 25 rooms, including 2 suites; all with private bath, air-conditioning, TV, phone with dataports, voice mail, radios, CD players; most with fireplaces; many with whirlpools. 10 beach cottages available in summer only.

RATES: $209 to $799 BP. Beach house suites open late June through August, $5,052 (weekly rentals only).

OPEN: All year except some weeks in January.

FACILITIES AND ACTIVITIES: Breakfast, lunch, Sunday jazz brunch, dinner. Decks with ocean views, Victorian garden and reflecting pool, private beach, walking trails. Nearby: Newport mansions, shops, sightseeing, dining.

*I*f you can't have your own shingled summer home overlooking the ocean, here's the next best thing. The very Victorian mansion on a forty-acre peninsula was built in 1874 by Alexander Agassiz, a renowned scientist and explorer, whose photo hangs in the lobby. Near the house was his summer laboratory, where he pioneered in the study of marine life and oceanography.

Step into the wood-paneled sitting room of the inn and admire the intricate marquetry over the fireplace, an Oriental symbol for good fortune. The William Morris wallpaper in the halls and throughout the house set a proper Victorian mood. The main floor includes four dining rooms, including the Agassiz room, with its own fireplace, and the striking round Sunset Room, with a draped ceiling and windows all around to bring in the view.

Rhode Island Monthly magazine called Castle Hill the best all-around dining experience in the state, an evaluation you may second when you taste the chef's appetizers, such as yellowfin tuna prepared three ways: sesame crusted with scallion and radish, orange-chile glazed with sea salad, and sashimi with soba noodles. Main courses include roasted free-range squab, roasted rack of monkfish with shrimp and Maine lobster, grilled beef fillet, and Colorado rack of lamb, all with inventive sauces and side accompaniments. In good weather, you can have a drink and dine outside on the terraces, watching the yachts sail into Newport harbor.

Because the dining rooms are so popular, the first floor tends to be busy at mealtimes, so a more private small sitting room has been built on the second floor just for inn guests, who also enjoy a formal tea service here every afternoon.

Some of the nine bedrooms in the main house are paneled, and some have wallpaper. All have been sumptuously decorated with fine fabrics and antique accents. No two are alike. Second-floor rooms tend to be larger, but the top

floor is cozy, with eaves, and many rooms have wonderful views. The turret suite is extraordinary, with a 360-degree view of the water, and a soaking tub positioned at one of the windows. Six rooms in the recently remodeled Harbor House have the bonus of private terraces with water views. The Chalet, Agassiz's former studio, has been transformed for functions, such as the many weddings held on the property, and the rooms upstairs include a bridal suite. The remodeled beach houses near the entry to the estate are directly on the water, luxurious lairs that are available in summer by the week.

Wherever you stay, you'll enjoy the best in service and amenities, and just outside is a view a millionaire might envy.

HOW TO GET THERE: From Boston take Interstate 93 south to Route 24 south to Route 114 south, which becomes Broadway in Newport. Continue down Broadway to Washington Square. Take a left onto Thames Street, pass the Brick Marketplace, and then bear right to the traffic light. At the light take a left (south) onto America's Cup Avenue and stay in the right-hand lane. Take a right onto Thames Street (just past the "Wave" statue and in front of the Red Parrot Restaurant). Continue down Thames to Wellington Avenue. Go right onto Wellington (across from the Shell station), and from this point on take every available right. This will take you past Fort Adams, Hammersmith Farm, Oceancliff, and the Coast Guard station. After going past the Coast Guard station, the road turns sharply to the right and then to the left. Castle Hill Inn is the first driveway on the right.

From Interstate 95 north take exit 3A (in Rhode Island) to Route 138 east. Follow Route 138 over the Jamestown and Newport Bridges. Take first exit (Scenic Newport) off bridge. Take a right at the end of the exit ramp. At the second light take a right onto America's Cup Avenue. Stay in the right lane and go right onto Thames Street at the "Wave" statue. Follow the directions from above.

Vanderbilt Hall 💟
Newport, Rhode Island 02840

INNKEEPER: Kristen Ward, manager

ADDRESS/TELEPHONE: 41 Mary Street; (401) 846–6200 or (888) VAN–HALL; fax (401) 846–0701

WEB SITE: www.vanderbilthall.com

ROOMS: 51 rooms and suites, all with private bath, TV, telephone with dataport, hair dryers, turndown service; many with whirlpool baths and heated towel bars.

RATES: Rooms, $129 to $609 EP. Many packages available.

OPEN: All year.

FACILITIES AND ACTIVITIES: Breakfast, lunch, dinner, afternoon tea. 24-hour room service, bar, roof deck, sitting rooms, billiards room, indoor pool, fitness room, sauna, steam room, whirlpool, patio. Nearby: Shops, beach, mansions, historic sites, scenic walks.

*T*he Vanderbilt family never lived in this fine hall; they gave it to the town of Newport, their longtime summer home, to serve as a rather opulent YMCA. But they would no doubt feel at home now that the 1909 building has been grandly renovated as a lodging, allowing visitors a taste of life as it was in Newport's gilded age. There will be some changes, things may be even grander when the inn reopens in spring 2006 after several months of additional renovations.

You know you've arrived somewhere special when you enter the chandeliered entry, facing a lovely curved double stairway. But while the setting is grand, it is not pretentious. The sitting room is enormous, but the seating has been arranged into comfortable settings conducive to conversation, and there are books and magazines inviting you to settle in. And there are several intimate side rooms for more privacy.

Beyond is the music room, where afternoon tea is set out; a bar area; and the Orangery, with plants, a greenhouse roof, ceiling fans, and latticework along the brick wall. Breakfast is served here along with light meals available from 11:00 A.M. to 11:00 P.M. Outside is a patio, and across the street, visible through the glass walls of the Orangery, is Newport's landmark Trinity Church, circa 1726.

The original restoration was no mean task. The placement of the old rooms made for unusual spaces. When you ascend the graceful stair you'll find that rooms vary tremendously in size and shape, some long and narrow, others square, depending on how the configurations worked best. The result is five room categories, making it possible for almost everyone to afford some type of lodging. Furnishings are equally eclectic, with some canopy beds, some iron beds, and some Victorian wooden headboards, and there is a different magnificent armoire in every room. The former ballroom and theater became suites, and the third-floor quarters under the eaves were turned into skylit accommodations. Many rooms have themes, from tennis or polo to art deco or Victorian. All the rooms have high ceilings and well-appointed bathrooms, many with whirlpool baths and heated towel warmers. Don't miss going up to the fourth floor roof deck for a fabulous view of the harbor.

On the lower level is a very masculine billiards room with an antique-style table and leather furnishings, as well as the restored swimming pool, with a delightful sailing mural on the wall. You can work out in the adjacent small fitness room, equipped with a treadmill, bicycle, and rowing machine, then enjoy a sauna, whirlpool, or steam room, or maybe arrange for a massage.

The dining room, with fireplace, paneling, and electrified pewter gaslights, is a fitting setting for true gourmet fare. The seasonal menu may begin with such pleasures as oysters Vanderbilt, oven roasted with a creamy arugula sauce, Parmesano-Reggiano cheese, and crispy bacon; or roasted pumpkin and potato ravioli. Crispy Lobster Tower, lobster wrapped in kataifi and nestled atop caramelized leeks, chive-whipped Yukon Gold potatoes, and baby vegetables, is an unusual main course, or there are classics such as roast duckling or cedar-roasted salmon. What to have for dessert? What a delicious dilemma. You won't go wrong with choices such as the white chocolate and strawberry torte served with fruit compote—or the Key lime, pecan, chocolate, and bourbon pie, not to mention the cinnamon bread-and-butter pudding with ice cream.

When you step out the door of Vanderbilt Hall, you are in the midst of Newport's large historic district, a prize colonial neighborhood, as well as 1 block from shops and the waterfront, and not far from the fabled mansions where the Vanderbilts did reside.

HOW TO GET THERE: From the north take Route 24 south and follow it until it becomes Route 114 south. Follow Route 114 south into downtown Newport until you can go no farther. At the traffic light turn left onto Thames Street and continue straight for approximately 50 yards. Take the first left onto Mary Street, and Vanderbilt Hall will be on your right, 1 block up.

From the south take Interstate 95 north to Rhode Island exit 3, Route 138 east. Follow this for approximately 35 miles, follow the signs for the Jamestown and Newport Bridges, and cross over the two bridges. Take the first exit off the Newport Bridge, marked "Scenic Newport," and turn right at the bottom of the ramp. Proceed straight to the second light and bear left onto Thames Street. Continue straight through the next set of lights for approximately 150 yards and take the first left onto Mary Street. Vanderbilt Hall will be on your right, 1 block up.

Larchwood Inn

Wakefield, Rhode Island 02879

INNKEEPERS: Francis and Diann Browning

ADDRESS/TELEPHONE: 521 Main Street; (401) 783–5454 or (800) 275–5450; fax (401) 783–1800

WEB SITE: www.larchwoodinn.com

ROOMS: 18, in 2 buildings; 11 with private bath; some with phone.

RATES: $65 to $150 EP.

OPEN: All year.

FACILITIES AND ACTIVITIES: Breakfast, lunch, dinner. Bar, tavern. Nearby: Swimming, fishing, skiing.

akefield is a charming and historic hamlet, and this stately inn has been an important part of the scene since 1831. Best known for its restaurant, it is also a good home base for exploring "South County," the sunny beach-rimmed lower part of Rhode Island, or for visiting the state university nearby in Kingstown. The presence of the ocean just a short drive away can be seen in the inn's decor, with model ships in the living room and a mural of the port of Galilee in one of the four dining rooms.

Dinner ideas are rack of lamb for one or two, lots of fresh fish, and a beefeater's special: a thick slice of prime rib Angus. Breakfast is very ample. I really like the special French toast topped with either sour cream or whipped cream and warmed strawberries. Perhaps you'd enjoy croissants or poached eggs with hollandaise and mushrooms and artichoke hearts. Come summer, the meals are served on the covered patio in the garden.

A bit of Scotch influence can be seen in the Tam O'Shanter Lounge, where a quote from Robert Burns's "Fast by an Ingle Bleezing Finely," is over the fireplace. The lounge offers cocktails and often live entertainment and dancing.

Twelve rooms are in the main inn, six in the equally nice Holly House across the street. Diann has a real decorator's touch, and the rooms are handsome, done in traditional style with brass and four-poster beds and attractive wallpapers.

While beaches are the big draw in South County, this is also prime antiquing country. Ask your innkeepers to direct you to some of the shops in

South County Museum

Not far from Wakefield is the town of Narragansett, on the western side of beautiful Narragansett Bay. Take Route 1A to the Narragansett Town Beach and Pier. A bit north of the pier, opposite the beach pavilion, you'll find Canonchet Farm and the South County Museum (401-783-5400; www.southcountymuseum.org). It holds a collection of more than 10,000 artifacts that demonstrate the history and culture of this area and its varied settlers. From farm tools and domestic implements to a gentleman's study and children's dolls, dollhouses, and trains, the museum imaginatively presents a real sense of the passage of time through three centuries. Next to the main museum building is a barn with displays of carriages and wagons; on the property are hiking trails, a fitness course, and lots of pretty places to picnic. The museum is open from May through October. A small admission fee is charged; parking is free. The farm and museum host frequent festivals throughout the summer; call for a schedule of family events, crafts workshops, and story hours for children.

Wakefield and to Wickford Village in North Kingstown. You may just go home with some special souvenirs to go with your seashells.

HOW TO GET THERE: Take Interstate 95 to Route 1. Exit from Route 1 at Pond Street, follow it to the end, and the inn will be immediately in front of you.

Shelter Harbor Inn
Westerly, Rhode Island 02891

INNKEEPER: Jim Dey

ADDRESS/TELEPHONE: 10 Wagner Road; (401) 322-8883; fax (401) 322-7907

WEB SITE: www.shelterharborinn.com

ROOMS: 24, all with private bath, TV, and phone; some with fireplace and private deck.

RATES: $96 to $228 BP.

OPEN: All year.

FACILITIES AND ACTIVITIES: Breakfast, lunch, dinner, Sunday brunch; bar. Private ocean beach, two paddle tennis courts with night lighting, rooftop hot tub, croquet court. Nearby: Golf, boat-launching area, tennis, summer theater, Block Island ferry, Newport, Mystic Seaport, Mystic Marinelife Aquarium, casinos.

BUSINESS TRAVEL: Desk and phone in all rooms; conference room; fax available; corporate rates.

Colonial Theatre

Theater lovers may want to make plans to see an Actor's Equity professional performance at Westerly's Colonial Theatre (401-596-0810), in the Greek Revival former First Congregational Church on Granite Street. Contemporary musicals, dramas, and comedies are on the bill from late April through Labor Day, and a special annual performance of Charles Dickens's *A Christmas Carol* or a similar holiday show suitable for the whole family is the traditional fare between Thanksgiving and Christmas. Tickets are reasonably priced.

Also popular is the theater's Shakespeare in the Park summer festival for three weeks each July. These outdoor performances at nearby Wilcox Park are free; bring a picnic and enjoy.

*I*f you would like guest passes and a shuttle ride to a 3-mile stretch of uncluttered ocean beach located just a mile from a lovely old country inn, find your way to Rhode Island and the Shelter Harbor Inn. Bring the children. When they're not playing in the ocean surf, there's a salt pond near the inn for them to explore.

Ten of the guest rooms are in the restored farmhouse, and ten more are located in the barn. The rest of the rooms are in the carriage house, which is a lovely addition to the inn. There is a large central living room in the barn that opens onto a spacious deck—how ideal for families! Or, if your business group is small, have a meeting right here. There is also a library with comfortable leather chairs where you can relax with a book.

The menu reflects the location of the inn, and at least half the items offered are from the sea. The finnan haddie is specially smoked in Narragansett. You can choose your place to eat—the formal dining room, the small private dining room with a fireplace, or the glassed-in terrace room. The sunporch has been turned into a pub bar, and plants are everywhere. If weather permits, take a drink out to the secluded terrace. On a clear day you can see Block Island from the rooftop deck, a private world complete with a hot tub, barbecue grill, and picnic tables.

If you can tear yourself from the beach, there is much to see around here. You are about halfway between Mystic and Newport. The ferry to Block Island leaves from Point Judith. It is an hour-long ride, and when you arrive on Block Island, you will find it a super spot for bicycling. You can charter boats for fishing or stand at the edge of the surf and cast your line into the sea. In the evenings you'll find Theater by the Sea in nearby Matunuck and the Colonial Theatre in Westerly.

HOW TO GET THERE: From the south take Interstate 95 to exit 92. Turn right onto Route 2 for 1 mile to Route 78. Continue to a stoplight and turn left onto Route 1. The inn can be seen 4 miles farther on the right. From the north take exit 1 and turn left. Follow Route 3 to Route 78 and proceed as above.

Select List of
Other Rhode Island Inns

The Blue Dory Inn

P.O. Box 488
Dodge Street
Block Island, RI 02807
(401) 466-5891 or (800) 992-7290; fax (401) 466-9910
Web site: www.blockislandinns.com
11 rooms, 3 suites in additional buildings, and 5 cottages; 100-year-old Victorian inn.

The 1661 Inn and Hotel Manisses

P.O. Box 1
Block Island, RI 02807
(401) 466-2421 or (800) 626-4773; fax (401) 466-2858
Web site: www.blockislandresorts.com
9 rooms at the inn, 17 at the hotel, plus several cottages; most with private bath, some Jacuzzis; breakfast and dinner; conference area.

Spring House Hotel

Spring Street, Old Harbor
Block Island, RI 02807
(401) 466-5844 or (800) 234-9263
Web site: www.springhousehotel.com
49 rooms, studios, and suites in 2 buildings; all with private bath; 1862 hotel.

Vermont

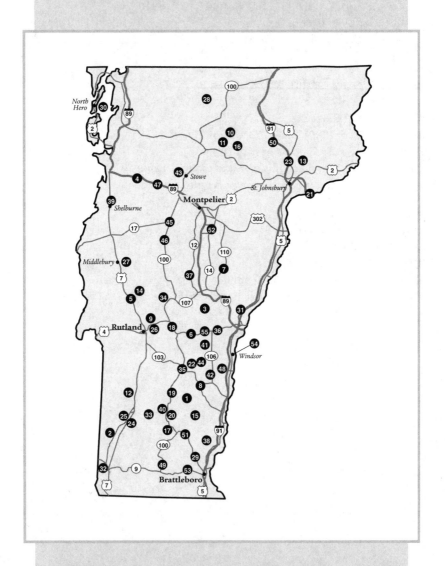

Vermont

Numbers on map refer to towns numbered below.

The Inn at High View

Andover, Vermont 05143

INNKEEPERS: Chuck Atwater and Darlene Doan

ADDRESS/TELEPHONE: 753 East Hill Road; (802) 875-2724; fax (802) 875-4021

WEB SITE: www.innathighview.com

ROOMS: 7, all with private bath, air-conditioning.

RATES: $135 to $265 BP.

OPEN: All year except the first two weeks in April and November.

FACILITIES AND ACTIVITIES: Dinner on selected Saturdays, BYOB. Conference room, swimming pool, hot tub, dry sauna. Nearby: Skiing, theater, antiquing, golf.

I felt like a mountain goat getting up to the Inn at High View, but once up there I was overwhelmed with the breathtaking views from the big porch. On a clear day, you can see for 50 miles. I would love to see it in the winter, surrounded by snow. It must be truly beautiful.

This is a cozy and comfortable inn, with a big curved sofa in the living room around a huge fireplace. The paneled dining room also has a fireplace and wide windows with a view. A full breakfast is served here each morning, and on Saturday nights when the inn is full, the innkeepers prepare an intimate dinner for guests.

The inn is set on seventy-two acres, glorious year-round, whether you don cross-country skis in winter or gather around the secluded rock-rimmed

swimming pool on warm summer days. There's an outdoor hydrotherapy Jacuzzi as well, great for achy muscles. The inn also offers lots of spa services, including massages, wraps, scrubs, and reiki treatments, all designed to make you even more relaxed.

The rooms are beautifully done, no two alike. Some have canopy beds, some have beamed ceilings, others have private decks. Many are furnished with handsome quilts and antiques, and all come with down comforters and cozy robes for guests. Names such as Grizabella and Pyewacket were inspired by T. S. Eliot's *Old Possum's Book of Practical Cats.*

There's lots to do in this beautiful part of Vermont, but you may find it hard to leave your hilltop aerie. I could be content all day with a seat on the porch gazing at that mesmerizing view.

HOW TO GET THERE: Take Interstate 91 north to exit 6 (Route 103 north) to Chester. Follow Route 11W to Andover-Weston Road. Watch for signs to the inn; turn right. It is the second farmhouse, ½ mile up the hill on the left.

Rowell's Inn
Andover, Vermont 05143

INNKEEPERS: Michael Brengolini and Susan McNulty

ADDRESS/TELEPHONE: 1834 Simonsville Road; (802) 875–3658 or (800) 728–0842; fax (802) 875–3680

WEB SITE: www.rowellsinn.com

ROOMS: 7, including 2 suites; all with private bath; 2 with fireplace.

RATES: $90 to $175 BP.

OPEN: All year except April and November.

FACILITIES AND ACTIVITIES: Dinner on weekend; full-service bar. Nearby: Skiing, fishing, biking, summer theater, and more.

uilt in 1820 as a stagecoach stop, this inn has served many purposes over the years. It was once a post office and general store, and then in 1910 F. A. Rowell came along and purchased it, and it became Rowell's Inn. He added the elegant tin ceilings, cherry and maple planked dining-room floors, central heating, and indoor plumbing. The brochure says that during the mid-1900s the inn was a preferred luncheon stop on the "Ideal Tour" between Manchester, Vermont, and the White Mountains for a hearty fare of trout and chicken. Today the inn is on the National Register of Historic Places.

All the rooms are full of atmosphere. The parlor is very Victorian, with a choice of some 800 books to read in front of the fire. The Sun Room has its own fireplace, and wooden booths to enjoy your choice of games and a chessboard. The tavern room is where folks gather for refreshments at 5:00 P.M. A jigsaw puzzle is usually in progress on the table, and there's an antique fortune-telling machine if you want to look into the future.

One entree is offered each night at the four-course dinner that is served on weekends and occasionally on weekdays in peak season. Some examples are beef tenderloin, cognac-glazed Cornish hens, smoked pork chops, or beef bourguignonne. This course is preceded by homemade soups and appetizers and a garden salad topped with the inn's own dressing. Dessert may be caramel fudge pecan pie, cheesecake, or another dreamy thing. All this good eating is served in the dining room lit by candlelight. Breakfast is a good, full one.

The innkeepers are also now offering take-out dinners on Friday and Sunday nights. Ask Michael to tell you about them.

All the rooms have cozy feather beds and down comforters, and two of the lovely rooms have working fireplaces. Some brass and canopy beds and hooked rugs add to the tasteful decor.

Close at hand you'll find hiking, golf, tennis, biking, trail riding, and fishing in trout streams. The area provides summer theater, great shopping, and antiquing. All this plus—as you'd expect in a good Vermont country inn—alpine and cross-country skiing nearby.

HOW TO GET THERE: The inn is on Route 11, 7 miles west of Chester.

The Arlington Inn 🎔
Arlington, Vermont 05250

INNKEEPERS: Eric and Elizabeth Berger

ADDRESS/TELEPHONE: 3904 Route 7A (mailing address: P.O. Box 369); (802) 375–6532 or (800) 443–9442; fax (802) 375–6534

WEB SITE: www.arlingtoninn.com

ROOMS: 18, in 3 buildings; all with private bath, TV, phone, wireless Internet access, and air-conditioning; 12 with fireplace; 4 with whirlpool tub.

RATES: $100 to $325 BP.

OPEN: All year.

FACILITIES AND ACTIVITIES: Restaurant and tavern. Gardens. Nearby: Fishing, hiking, skiing, shopping, and much more.

*Y*ou can recapture the gracious living of the Victorian period in this historic Greek Revival mansion. It was built in 1848 by Martin Chester Deming. The lovely rooms in the inn are named after Deming's family members. There are Sylvester's Study, Pamela's Suite, Martin Chester's Room, Sophie's Room, Mary's Room, and (I love this name) Chloe's Room.

They are all beautifully furnished and very comfortable. Rooms are located in three buildings, with six in the main house. Many rooms have fireplaces, a few offer Jacuzzis, and six provide private porches.

It matters not what season you are here; there is much to do year-round. The famous Battenkill River nearby is loaded with fish, and you can find opportunities for hiking, biking, golf, swimming, and canoeing. Winter brings sleigh rides, cross-country skiing and downhill skiing just a short drive away. If you'd prefer to go shopping, it's very close by.

Dining at the Arlington is very gracious. Start your dinner right with Maine crab crakes, pancetta-wrapped shrimp, or a selection of other first courses. Move on to entrees such as veal scallopini, the Arlington mixed grill (filet mignon, duck breast, and loin lamb chop), or porcini mushroom ravioli. The house salad is a winner. The inn uses authentic Vermont products whenever possible.

Breakfasts, served in the cheerful solarium, are ample. You'll find omelets, eggs any style, blueberry pancakes, French toast, and huge blueberry muffins.

When looking for the ideal spot to host your management retreat or workshop, look no farther. Weddings, rehearsal dinners, anniversaries, and parties are done very well here at the Arlington. The Victorian garden gazebo is a favorite spot.

HOW TO GET THERE: The inn is located on Historic Route 7A between Bennington and Manchester in the center of Arlington.

West Mountain Inn 👪
Arlington, Vermont 05250

INNKEEPERS: The Carlson family

ADDRESS/TELEPHONE: 144 West Mountain Road; (802) 375–6516; fax (802) 375–6553

WEB SITE: www.westmountaininn.com

ROOMS: 17 rooms and suites in 3 buildings; all with private bath; some with fireplaces, some with porches; 1 specially equipped for the physically disabled.

RATES: $149 to $304 BP; MAP available.

OPEN: All year.

FACILITIES AND ACTIVITIES: Wheelchair access to all common rooms. Bar. Hiking, cross-country skiing, fishing, tubing, canoeing, swimming. Nearby: Antiquing.

*T*he Carlsons are really the ideal innkeepers. From the minute you arrive, you feel at home. The inn is always being updated. Recent additions include a lovely suite of rooms with a gas fireplace and a room and bath with complete facilities for people with physical disabilities.

There are too few people who care enough to spend a bit more for other people's comfort.

The family's love of nature is evident in the busy bird-feeding station, pond with a collection of exotic goldfish, and the llamas. Each guest takes home a homegrown African violet.

The rooms, all named for famous people, are quite different. Grandma Moses, Robert Frost, and Booker T. Washington are among them. I have stayed in the Norman Rockwell Room, which is up in the treetops. Down comforters are provided to keep you toasty warm.

In the lounge area are tables set with games, rockers, and a view of the bird feeders and beyond to Red Mountain.

There are three suites at the historic mill located close to the river. Each has two bedrooms and a bath upstairs and a living room and kitchen downstairs. Two of the suites have private decks, and two have open-hearth fireplaces. The Cottage in the Pines has lovely rooms, some with housekeeping facilities.

The inn prepares great dinners and has some excellent wines in an extensive wine cellar. They are the perfect complement to the meal. The crab cakes are delicious, and the pan-seared salmon is excellent. Desserts, well, I gained a pound—but it was worth it.

This inn is truly in the country, with 150 acres of trees, trails, pastures, and ponds, all on the mountainside overlooking the village of Arlington. Cross the trout-filled Battenkill; wind your way over the bridge, which is flower-laden in summer; go by the millhouse, up past the main cottage and spring-fed rock quarry, to the seven-gabled inn. The grounds around the inn are reputed to have more species of evergreens than any other place in New England. There

are lovely trails for hiking, jogging, or cross-country skiing, depending on the season, and the inn provides a trail map for your pleasure.

HOW TO GET THERE: Midway between Bennington and Manchester, the inn is ½ mile west of Arlington on Route 313. Turn onto River Road, cross the river, turn left, and go up the hill until you come to the inn.

Twin Farms 💚
Barnard, Vermont 05031

INNKEEPERS: Twin Farms Management Company

ADDRESS/TELEPHONE: Barnard; (802) 234-9999 or (800) 894-6327; fax (802) 234-9990

WEB SITE: www.twinfarms.com

ROOMS: 10 cottages, 10 suites; all with private bath, phone, TV, air-conditioning, minirefrigerator, and CD player.

RATES: $1,050 to $2,700; all inclusive. $35,000 per day for the whole property.

OPEN: All year except April.

FACILITIES AND ACTIVITIES: Full license. Spa, fitness center. All winter sports, mountain bikes, tennis, croquet, swimming, canoeing.

As you can see from the rates, this may be the ultimate in inn luxury. Twin Farms is a 300-acre hideaway estate that was owned by novelist Sinclair Lewis and given to his wife, Dorothy Thompson, as a wedding present. During the 1930s and '40s, they came here to rest and entertain many literary figures of the time.

You arrive at the entry gate and dial a number. After being buzzed in, you enter an unbelievably unique and luxurious property. Drive down the lane and along a circular drive to the main house.

The game room, with a beautiful fireplace, has many games and Stave wood puzzles. Off this is the Washington Suite, where my friend Audrey and I stayed. It has beautiful quilts and down-filled beds, two televisions, a CD player, and a bathroom with a large skirted antique tub and a huge shower. The sitting room has a bay window with a nice view, good couches, and a beautiful fireplace. There's a fireplace in the bedroom, too.

Red's Room, the original master suite, is glorious, with a view of Mount Ascutney. Red was Sinclair's nickname.

The Guest Room walls and curtains are covered in toile de Jouy, a green and ivory French linen that tells a story. It's just beautiful.

The cottages have fireplaces, sumptuous baths, very private screened porches, and lots of comfort. They all have names. The Studio is splendid and has a huge copper soaking tub and front and back porches. The Treehouse is beautiful, with Chinese fretwork in the bedroom. Orchard Cottage is set amid the old apple orchard and features two handcarved granite fireplaces. The two-story Barn Cottage offers grand views, and the Meadow, with its Moroccan interior reminiscent of a desert king's traveling palace, is stunning; the tent ceiling is something you'll just have to see. Wood Cottage has an Italian oak writing table and much charm. And the Log Cabin is an authentic old Tennessee log cabin refurbished the Twin Farms way. It's very hard to choose but wherever you stay, you won't be disappointed.

A covered bridge takes you to the pub. Here are a bar, pool table, fireplace, and television. Below this is a fully equipped fitness center. In-room massages are available. Up the road is a Japanese Furo. There are separate tubs for men and women, separated by fragrant pine walls, and one larger one for both men and women.

The main dining room is rustic; however, you can dine wherever you choose. We were in the original dining room, and both the food and the service were incredible. Cocktails are at 7:00 P.M. Lunch may take any form, and you can have it anywhere. Tea is glorious.

There is much to do here, whatever the season. Tennis and croquet; a lake for swimming, canoeing, or fishing; walking; biking. You can use the inn's mountain bikes. The inn also has its own ski slopes, ski trails, snowshoes, toboggans, and ice skating.

This is an experience few may be able to afford, but what a wonderful trip. The inn was awarded five stars by the *Mobil Travel Guide*.

HOW TO GET THERE: The inn is 10 miles north of Woodstock, Vermont. Driving directions are supplied when you make reservations.

The Black Bear Inn
Bolton Valley, Vermont 05477

INNKEEPERS: Brian and Jill Drinkwater

ADDRESS/TELEPHONE: 4010 Bolton Valley Road; (802) 434–2126 or (800) 395–6335; fax (802) 434–5161

WEB SITE: www.blkbearinn.com

ROOMS: 24, all with private bath and color TV; 15 with Vermont firestove or a fireplace; 9 with private hot tubs.

RATES: $104 to $300 BP; MAP available. Many ski packages.

OPEN: All year.

FACILITIES AND ACTIVITIES: Breakfast, dinner, lounge. Swimming pool, tennis, hot tubs, Jacuzzis, sauna, cross-country skiing, downhill skiing, hiking. Nearby: Fishing, golf.

Five miles up twisting, curving Bolton Valley Road, you come across this contemporary country inn, nestled in the mountainside as if it had been here forever. Once inside, you are greeted by the warmth of a big stone fireplace and the aroma of freshly baked breads and muffins that fills the air.

Everything is homemade. You could stay here for two weeks and not be served the same thing twice, and that even includes the breads and muffins. You can begin your dinner with some good soups, like Vermont cheddar cheese, chilled gazpacho, or corn chowder. Yum. There are always several entrees offered, one of which is seafood. You might find salmon, tenderloin of beef, or chicken medallions with Hungarian cream sauce as some of the choices on the menu one evening. For a happy ending, try the Swedish apple pie.

The rooms are simply and pleasantly decorated, with patchwork quilts, color televisions, good beds, and lovely balconies, where in summer you may sit and smell the good clean air and enjoy the views of the grounds, covered

with wildflowers. The pool beckons you, comfortable lawn furniture is all around, and the beautiful blue skies are yours to enjoy. They are spectacular this far up in the mountains.

Some of the rooms have a fireplace and some a Vermont firestove. The inn's 54 miles of cross-country ski trails make good paths for a hike. When you return to the inn, there are outdoor hot tubs or a nice cozy bar with four bar stools and a sign behind the bar that says TEDDY BEAR CROSSING.

The inn comes alive in winter. You can ski out the door on a trail that connects to the main mountain for downhill skiing at Bolton Valley. Cross-country enthusiasts can also strap on their skis right outside the door and enjoy a 120-kilometer network of trails.

Bolton Valley's nearby indoor sports center, with swimming, exercise rooms, saunas, and tennis, is the place to be when you're not skiing. There is so much to see and do in the area in all seasons, you'll find it a great place to bring your children.

HOW TO GET THERE: Coming north on Interstate 89, take exit 10 at Stowe-Waterbury. Turn left, then turn right onto Route 2 and follow it 7 miles. Turn right onto Bolton Valley Road in Bolton where Interstate 89 passes over Route 2. The inn is 5 miles up the mountain.

The Churchill House Inn
Brandon, Vermont 05733

INNKEEPERS: Seth and Olya Hopkins

ADDRESS/TELEPHONE: 3128 Forestdale Road (Route 73 east); (802) 247–3078 or (877) 248–7444; fax (802) 247–0113

WEB SITE: www.churchillhouseinn.com

ROOMS: 9, all with private bath; 4 with whirlpool tub.

RATES: $125 to $160 BP; MAP available.

OPEN: All year except April.

FACILITIES AND ACTIVITIES: Swimming pool, hiking, biking; cross-country skiing from the inn door. Nearby: Green Mountain National Forest, antiquing, art galleries, Middlebury College.

*T*he Churchill House has been welcoming guests since 1872 with warm hospitality and good food. The setting couldn't be much better—a lovely town and 22,000 acres of the Green Mountain National Forest right outside the door.

Four inviting common rooms are great for relaxing, and the inn's guest rooms are country cozy, with handmade quilts and antique accents.

Innkeepers Seth and Olya Hopkins arrived in 2005 and have already made welcome changes, such as a new central heating system with thermostats in each guest room. They've also introduced a complimentary twenty-four-hour

Walking around Brandon

Established 200 years ago between the Neshobe River and Otter Creek, Brandon has one of the most unusual town layouts in New England. Distinguished by its two greens, one on each bank of the Neshobe, the town also boasts a collection of nearly 250 nineteenth-century homes, ranging in styles from late Georgian through Federals, Greek Revivals, and Queen Anne Victorians. Almost every one of these homes is on the National Register of Historic Places. The Brandon Chamber of Commerce (802-247-6401; www.brandon.org) has published a walking tour around the village. You might see the birthplace of Stephen A. Douglas, a U.S. senator famed for his debates against Abraham Lincoln.

Brandon also borders the Green Mountain National Forest, which has miles and miles of hiking and cross-country ski trails. Ask at the inns for the best access routes to these trails or pick up a copy of the Green Mountain Club's *Day Hiker's Guide to Vermont*.

beverage bar and a changing plate of "goodies" on the front desk, and they installed a guest computer with Internet access.

The Hopkins have also joined the Vermont Fresh Network, emphasizing locally produced foods. For example, your breakfast eggs will be organic, produced locally by free-range chickens. How good are the breakfasts? The house specialty, cottage-cheese pancakes, was recently featured in *Gourmet* magazine.

At dinner, the signature dish is chicken Vermont, a herbed breast of chicken wrapped in bacon and roasted. Some other favorites are orange-curried beef, mustard loin of pork, tenderloin of beef, and a choice for vegetarians, such as asparagus lasagna. All the breads and desserts are homemade, and many of the vegetables and herbs are grown in the inn's own garden. The menu has been livened up by a few select Russian dishes such as borscht, prepared by Olya, who is a native of western Siberia. Her breakfast crepes, known as blinis, are also popular with guests.

This is a perfect inn for outdoors enthusiasts, with biking, hiking, and skiing trails beginning just yards away in the national forest. Ask the night before, and the innkeepers will prepare a picnic lunch for you.

Churchill House is also a longtime participant in an inn-to-inn program, with participants hiking, biking, or cross-country skiing to a different inn each night, a great way to experience some of New England's best scenery.

If you want a more peaceful getaway, you've still come to the right place. The inn's own pool is a refreshing spot to relax in summer, and Brandon is a wonderful town for strolling, with lots of galleries and antiques shops. You're only about 15 miles from Middlebury or Rutland, both with many more attractions to offer. Just ask the innkeepers; they'll be glad to fill you in on the best of the region.

HOW TO GET THERE: Go up Route 7 to Brandon and turn right on Route 73 east; the inn is about 4 miles ahead on the left.

The Lilac Inn 💙 📱
Brandon, Vermont 05733

INNKEEPERS: Doug and Shelly Sawyer

ADDRESS/TELEPHONE: 53 Park Street; (802) 247-5463 or (800) 221-0720; fax (802) 247-5499

WEB SITE: www.lilacinn.com

ROOMS: 9, all with private bath, TV, and air-conditioning; 1 with whirlpool tub; 3 with fireplace. Phone available.

RATES: $145 to $295 BP.

OPEN: All year. Restaurant closed to public between Easter and Mother's Day.

FACILITIES AND ACTIVITIES: Sunday brunch, dinner Wednesday through Saturday. Catering and room service, wedding planning.

BUSINESS TRAVEL: Ballroom for meetings. Function planning, secretarial services, telephone, computer, fax, and modem available.

Wow! This is a beauty. It's a 10,000-square-foot Georgian Revival mansion that was built in 1909 as a summer "cottage." Adorned with yellow and white paint, it has become a lovely country inn that has recaptured the charm of the era in which it was built.

To the left of the coach entrance is the library, which has a nice fireplace, books galore, chess, and a ton of comfort and charm. On the right is a stupendous butler's pantry hall leading to the tavern. Here is a beautiful copper-topped bar with six leather chairs with backs.

The tavern has its own menu, full of glorious food. How about a Loaf of Soup—a freshly baked mini-boule, filled with the soup of the day?

The dining room menu changes weekly. Usually there are several appetizers and soup du jour. A couple of the recent entree choices were macadamia-crusted double-thick pork chops with maple glaze and blackened red snapper.

The staircase is grand. In 1991 a time capsule was inserted into its newel post. At the top of the stairs is an ornate Chinese chest from the 1850s.

The rooms are spacious and well appointed. The bridal suite has a two-person whirlpool tub and wedding dolls on the fireplace mantel. It is used frequently, as the inn specializes in weddings.

HOW TO GET THERE: Follow Route 7 to Brandon. Turn right on Route 73 east (Park Street). The inn is the seventh building on the right.

The October Country Inn
Bridgewater Corners, Vermont 05035

INNKEEPERS: Chuck and Edie Janisse

ADDRESS/TELEPHONE: 362 Upper Road (mailing address: P.O. Box 66); (802) 672-3412 or (800) 648-8421

WEB SITE: www.octobercountryinn.com

ROOMS: 10; 8 with private bath.

RATES: $100 to $165 BP; MAP available.

OPEN: All year except April and two weeks in November.

FACILITIES AND ACTIVITIES: Pool. Nearby: Downhill and cross-country skiing at Killington and Okemo, antiquing, horse shows.

*T*here are a lot of comfortable things about this inn. It has a very cozy living room, with overstuffed furniture and a fireplace at one end and an old, old woodstove at the other. The fire is usually blazing, and the library offers an extensive supply of books as well as a great selection of games and puzzles.

Rooms are country comfortable, with the original farmhouse wide-plank pine floors, braided rugs, quilts or down comforters, wing chairs, and rockers.

On a summer day you can sit by the pool and enjoy a glass of lemonade. The pool is in a peaceful meadow, and the view is great. If you want to stay out of the sun, relax under an apple tree or on the secluded deck.

Of course, if you can tear yourself away from all the comfort and relaxation, there are lots of things to do in this area. The Quechee Hot Air Balloon Festival is in June, and the Scottish Festival is in August; there are horse

Bridgewater Mill Mall

Built in 1825 as a cotton mill, the Bridgewater Mill Mall on Route 4 also had a long history as a woolen textile mill. For many years it processed the fine wool from the 9,000-plus sheep that lived in Bridgewater in the 1840s, and during World War I and World War II, uniforms and blankets for soldiers were made here. In 1925 the owners of the Bridgewater Mill changed its name to Vermont Native Industries.

The mill was closed in 1973 because flood waters from the Ottauquechee River destroyed the dye room, but in 1978 the mill building was reopened for a new life as the Bridgewater Mill Mall, also known as the Old Mill Marketplace. Home again to Vermont native crafters and artists, it also houses the Sun of the Heart Bookstore, a furniture workshop, and a ski/sports outlet. Visit such artists as David Crandall, born in Springfield, Vermont, and a jewelry maker since the age of fourteen! His beautiful work in gold, platinum, diamonds, and gemstones is glorious. The mall is open seven days a week, but some artists have hours by chance or by appointment only. See what's open on the day you visit or call (802) 672-3049 or log on to www.thebridgewatermill.com for more information.

shows, antiquing, and Calvin Coolidge's birthplace. Winter brings a winter carnival, and downhill and cross-country skiing are nearby.

Dinner is served family style. The French menu has onion soup, French baguette, sole au gratin, vegetable strudel, oven-roasted potatoes, salad, and apple cheese torte. The Italian menu offers summer-garden minestrone soup (the inn has its own vegetable and herb gardens), Italian bread, garlic-baked chicken, eggplant parmigiana, homemade pasta with garlic and olive oil, salad, and chocolate cake with raspberry cassis sauce. Other nights bring African, Greek, Scandinavian, Mexican, and good old American menus. I'm impressed that the innkeepers are so inventive. Breakfast includes fresh fruit, homemade granola, freshly baked small muffins, breads, and something hot, such as pancakes with Vermont maple syrup.

HOW TO GET THERE: From Interstate 91 north take exit 9 to Route 12, then go west on Route 4. From Interstate 89 north take Vermont exit 1 to Route 4. The inn is at the junction of Routes 4 and 100A, across from the Long Trail Brewery, halfway between Killington and Woodstock.

Shire Inn 🖤
Chelsea, Vermont 05038

INNKEEPERS: Jay and Karen Keller

ADDRESS/TELEPHONE: Box 37; (802) 685–3031 or (800) 441–6908; fax (802) 685–3871

WEB SITE: www.shireinn.com

ROOMS: 6, all with private bath; 4 with working fireplace.

RATES: $144 to $195 BP; MAP available.

OPEN: All year.

FACILITIES AND ACTIVITIES: Dinner for inn guests. Bicycles and cross-country skis available. Meeting facilities for small parties and social events; fishing, biking, snowmobiling. Nearby: Downhill and cross-country skiing, swimming, boating, theaters.

Constructed in 1832 of Vermont brick, this inn was truly built to last. It is situated in a lovely part of the state. The White River is close by—actually, it's in the backyard. It's a paradise for fisherfolk. Lake Fairlee is the place to be for swimming and boating in the summer and ice skating in the winter, and cross-country and downhill skiing are within an easy drive. The shops and restaurants of Woodstock are nearby, and only a little farther is Hanover, New Hampshire, the home of Dartmouth College, offering theaters, art, and more.

The living room/library with its neat fireplace beckons all who pass through the door. Lots of books and a good collection of *National Geographic* magazines make this room very enticing on a cold or rainy day. Be sure to ask about the history of the antique French buffet in the living room. A circular stairway goes up to some of the rooms, and they are lovely, with high ceilings, tall windows, and wood-plank floors. Four rooms have working fireplaces. They are furnished with period antiques. A canopy bed is in one room; a king-size bed is in another. Good feather or foam pillows assure you of a good night's sleep.

Climb the hill to the Adirondack chairs under the apple tree and just sit and enjoy the view of the town. If you want to take a walk, there's a bridge over the river leading to an open field. In the wintertime this is a great spot for sledding or skiing—or take a ride on the skimobile trail. There is also a nature trail about 1 mile above the inn.

Breakfast is not to be missed. There are six different muffins and all sorts of fresh fruits, Maine blueberry or apple pancakes, waffles, French toast, omelets, and quiche. I hope you like to start your day with a stupendous breakfast.

Dinner, available to inn guests only, is a six-course affair served by candlelight. There is a choice of three entrees, such as rainbow trout, chicken boursin, or eggplant ravioli. The inn keeps a fine cellar of more than 1,000 wines to complement your meal.

After dinner, lots of guests return to the parlor to read, play backgammon, or chat with newfound friends at this sociable inn.

HOW TO GET THERE: From Interstate 89 take the Sharon exit via Route 14 to South Royalton, then Route 110 north to Chelsea.

Chester House Inn
Chester, Vermont 05143

INNKEEPERS: Paul Lantieri and Bill Lundy

ADDRESS/TELEPHONE: 266 Main Street; (802) 875-2205 or (888) 875-2205; fax (802) 875-6602

WEB SITE: www.chesterhouseinn.com

ROOMS: 7, all with private bath, phone, Wi-Fi, and dataport; 5 with gas fireplace; 2 with Jacuzzi; 1 with steam shower.

RATES: $99 to $195 BP.

OPEN: All year.

FACILITIES AND ACTIVITIES: Full breakfast, dinner by reservation for house guests only, wine and beer license. TV in the bar area.

*T*he inn was built in 1780, and the rooms are named for King George IV and his wife and children. There's a booklet in each room with a short biography of the person for whom that room is named. I was in the room named for Prince Octavius; he was the thirteenth child of King George and Queen Charlotte-Sophia, born on February 23, 1779—my birthday, but not the year. Ho ho. He died only four years later. The rooms are all very different. One has a table made from English stovepipes, and a sleigh bed; all are very comfortable.

The inn is on the village green, where there are good shops and restaurants also. Dinner at the inn is served in the keeping room by a colonial fireplace, and I enjoyed the spring menu. Antipasto and bread sticks, garden salad, a choice of shredded pork tenderloin with lime sauce (it was excellent), Gorgonzola ravioli with butter herb sauce, or chicken Wellington, plus vegetable du jour. Tea or coffee and ice cream or rhubarb ice finished that wonderful meal.

For winter activities, the inn is close to the major ski mountains, cross-country-skiing touring center, ice skating, and sleigh rides.

HOW TO GET THERE: From Interstate 91 take exit 6 and watch for Chester signs; the inn is on the green.

Fox Creek Inn ♥
Chittenden, Vermont 05737

INNKEEPERS: Alex and Ann Volz

ADDRESS/TELEPHONE: Chittenden Dam Road; (802) 483–6213 or (800) 707–0017

WEB SITE: www.foxcreekinn.com

ROOMS: 9, all with private bath; 7 with Jacuzzi; 3 with fireplace.

RATES: $190 to $409 MAP.

OPEN: All year except April, early May, and part of November.

FACILITIES AND ACTIVITIES: Full license. Fishing. Nearby: Swimming, hiking, golf, tennis, canoeing, bicycling, horseback riding, downhill and cross-country skiing.

This inn was once selected as one of the top ten country inns in the nation. You can't beat that! You arrive, and a lovely front porch with wicker chairs beckons you at once. Beautiful woods surround you. You hear a brook babbling, and a feeling of sheer peace comes over you. Inside you find a nice living room with a fireplace, a small bar and library, a den with a fireplace, and a great assortment of chairs, love seats, and couches throughout.

The rooms are the sort you never want to leave. Puffy comforters on the beds are inviting to curl up under, and the Jacuzzi tubs in seven of the rooms feel so great after a long day. There are nice antiques, including a huge pine bed with pineapple finials.

Dining is very special at the inn. Pretty, too, with yellow and white napery in the summer and red, white, and blue in the winter. Breakfasts are full Vermont style. That means you'll find cereals; yogurt; juices; sweet breads; and apple, cheese, or blueberry pancakes, waffles, or French toast, all with pure Vermont maple syrup.

If you think that's good, come back at dinnertime, when Ann really shines. There are homemade breads and soups such as Vermont cheddar or mushroom chive bisque. A fresh salad begins the meal, and then it might be grilled pork tenderloin, veal marsala, the fish of the day, or fillet of beef with port wine sauce. Oh my, and her desserts! . . . Well, just save some room, because they are so good.

The inn is only a mile from the Chittenden Reservoir, where the fishing and swimming are superb. Fox Creek runs right by the house. Trout anyone?

There's a saying up here that a traffic jam in Chittenden is one farmer with one tractor towing two wagons.

HOW TO GET THERE: From Rutland drive north on Route 7. Just outside Chittenden you will see a redbrick power station on the left. Just beyond it is a Y in the road, with a red country store in the middle. Keep right of the store and follow the road approximately 6 miles. Just past the fire station, go straight ahead ½ mile to the inn, which will be on your left.

Mountain Top Inn and Resort
Chittenden, Vermont 05737

INNKEEPERS: Steve and Lauren Bryant

ADDRESS/TELEPHONE: 195 Mountain Top Road; (802) 483-2311; (800) 445-2100 from out of state

WEB SITE: www.mountaintopinn.com

ROOMS: 33, plus 5 cabins and a variety of chalets; all with private bath.

RATES: $135 to $485 BP.

OPEN: All year.

FACILITIES AND ACTIVITIES: Breakfast, lunch, dinner. Wheelchair access to dining rooms. Heated pool; sauna; tennis; lawn games; private lake beach with canoes, kayaks, rowboats; pontoon boat rides; fly-fishing lessons; claybird shooting; horseback riding and lessons; horse-drawn sleigh rides; cross-country skiing; ice skating; sledding; dog sledding; snowshoeing. Nearby: Downhill skiing.

In the 1870s the Mountain Top property was part of the Long family's turnip farm. In 1940 William Barstow, an engineer and philanthropist from New York, purchased the farm and converted the barn into a wayside tavern as a hobby for his wife.

Today, the inn is just beautiful, recently refurbished by the owners and with views that no money can buy. At a 2,000-foot elevation, the inn overlooks Mountain Top Lake, which is surrounded by fantastic mountains. When you enter the inn, you are in a very inviting living area with a large fireplace. Ahead of you are the view and a spectacular two-story glass-enclosed staircase that leads to the Highlands dining room and tavern. The chef's specials range from pepper-crusted grouper to veal medallions. Don't miss the signature appetizer, buttermilk calamari with spicy chipotle aioli.

The rooms, most overlooking the lake and mountains, are large and luxuriously furnished. All have spacious baths. An in-room coffeemaker for your early morning coffee is a nice convenience.

The resort's Nordic Ski and Snowshoe Center has an excellent ski touring program, as well as instructors and all the latest equipment. There are 80 kilometers of trails over 350 acres, and the views are awesome. Snow making and careful grooming ensure good conditions. Ice skating and dog sledding are also fun, and downhill skiing is nearby at Pico and Killington.

Summer brings horseback riding, walking, or hiking through the lovely countryside, and in fall the color show of the trees is breathtaking. And in winter, riding in sleighs drawn by draft horses is a wonderful yesteryear experience.

HOW TO GET THERE: From Rutland head north on Route 7. Pass the power station, turn right on East Pittsford Road, and follow it into Chittenden. Follow the signs up to the inn.

The Craftsbury Inn ¢¢¢
Craftsbury, Vermont 05826

INNKEEPERS: Bill and Kathy Maire

ADDRESS/TELEPHONE: Main Street; (802) 586–2848 or (800) 336–2848; fax (802) 586–8060

WEB SITE: www.craftsburyinn.com

ROOMS: 10; 6 with private bath. Pets accepted with prior approval.

RATES: $90 to $125 BP; MAP available.

OPEN: All year except April and November.

FACILITIES AND ACTIVITIES: Dinner for public, by reservation, Tuesday through Saturday. Bar, cross-country skiing. Nearby: Canoeing, swimming, fishing, horseback riding, tennis, golf.

*T*he inn is a lovingly restored Greek Revival house that was built circa 1850. The little town of Craftsbury, said by the *Boston Globe* to be Vermont's most remarkable hill-town, was founded in 1788 by Col. Ebenezer Crafts and lies in what is called the Northeast Kingdom. The population today is something less than 900, and that includes Craftsbury, East Craftsbury, and Craftsbury Common.

One year I arrived at the inn on a chilly day in the middle of June and was greeted by a lovely fire in the fireplace. Speaking of fireplaces, the one in the living room is the original that warmed the first post office in Montpelier, Vermont's capital.

The rooms here are filled with antiques, and the beds have handsome heirloom quilts. Fresh paint and paper have made this lovely old inn even nicer.

Innkeeper Bill Maire is your talented chef. He was trained in France and before coming to Vermont was at the prestigious Arizona Biltmore Resort, so you know good things are ahead. The menu changes with the season to take advantage of fresh ingredients. Hostess Kathy sees that the ambience and service match the food, and though the table settings are formal, there is no dress code, and the mood is comfortably casual.

There is much to do in this area. Cross-country ski trails connect the inn to the Craftsbury Sports Center and the Highland Lodge trail systems. In the summer you can rent a canoe, swim, or fish in the center's lake. You can also ride horseback, play tennis, or play golf at Vermont's oldest course, in Greensboro, where the greens are fenced to prevent intrusion of the grazing cattle. Throughout July and August the Craftsbury Chamber Players perform every Thursday evening. Come and enjoy.

HOW TO GET THERE: Take Interstate 91 to St. Johnsbury, pick up Route 2 west, and at West Danville take Route 15 to Hardwick. Follow Route 14 north to Craftsbury. Take a right off Route 14 onto South Craftsbury Road. The inn is 2 miles down on the right, across from the general store.

The Inn on the Common
Craftsbury Common, Vermont 05827

INNKEEPERS: Jim and Judi Lamberti

ADDRESS/TELEPHONE: Main Street; (802) 586–9619 or (800) 521–2233; fax (802) 586–2249

WEB SITE: www.innonthecommon.com

ROOMS: 16, in 3 buildings; all with private bath; some with fireplace or woodstove.

RATES: $135 to $279 BP. Pets okay by prior arrangement.

OPEN: All year.

FACILITIES AND ACTIVITIES: Dinner, food and drinks to the public by reservation. Solar-heated swimming pool. Nearby: Boating, hiking, biking, cross-country skiing.

he innkeepers have brought new life to this fine old inn. After fourteen years managing the busy Inn at Essex near Burlington, the Lambertis decided it was time for a place of their own, and what better location than this classic village, a rural hamlet with a green surrounded by dazzling white clapboard buildings and a church. The Inn on the Common occupies three of these lovely white Federal houses in the center, surrounded by lawns and gardens. The innkeepers are at home here, always on hand to see that things are just right.

Everything has been freshened and improved since they arrived. Rooms are furnished with hand-stitched quilts, original art, and lots of antiques. Some have canopy beds, some fireplaces, and all have comfortable chairs for reading and relaxing.

In the main house, dinner tables are set with fine china and crystal and lit by candles. The elegant menu changes daily, so you never know for sure what treats are in store. You might start with mussels steamed in white wine or baked spanakopita triangles, followed by sautéed tenderloin of beef topped with béarnaise sauce, baked chicken Elizabeth, or the fish dish of the day. The chef makes full use of the fresh produce from Vermont farms. When it comes to dessert, you can't go wrong with profiteroles with Ben & Jerry's ice cream

and chocolate sauce, but the daily specials are just as tempting. The inn has long been known for its fine wine cellar.

Breakfast is equally generous. You can help yourself to fruit and pastries and enjoy one of the house-specialty omelets.

Craftsbury Common is truly a town for all seasons, picture-perfect in the greens of spring and summer, and the pool is refreshing on a warm summer day. The scenery is dazzling in fall colors, and the town becomes a haven for cross-country skiers in winter.

The nearby Craftsbury Nordic Center offers more than a hundred miles of beautifully groomed trails, and they run right past the inn.

It's a long drive to this placid corner of Vermont's Northeast Kingdom, but you'll be glad you came.

HOW TO GET THERE: From Interstate 91 take exit 26, Orleans, and follow Route 58 west 4 miles to Route 14 (Irasburg). Follow Route 14 south for 12 miles to North Craftsbury Road. Turn left and proceed 2 miles through Craftsbury Common, past Sterling College. The reception office is on the left just past the college.

Barrows House

Dorset, Vermont 05251

INNKEEPERS: Jim and Linda McGinnis

ADDRESS/TELEPHONE: Route 30; (802) 867–4455 or (800) 639–1620; fax (802) 867–0132

WEB SITE: www.barrowshouse.com

ROOMS: 28 rooms and suites in 8 houses; all with private bath and air-conditioning; 2 with fireplace; some with whirlpool, porch, or terrace; 1 room specially equipped for the physically disabled. Pets welcome.

RATES: $205 to $300 MAP.

OPEN: All year.

FACILITIES AND ACTIVITIES: Dinner nightly, tavern; wheelchair access to dining room. Cross-country ski shop, rentals, heated swimming pool, 2 tennis courts, bicycles, sauna. Nearby: Golf, skiing, shopping, hiking, horseback riding.

BUSINESS TRAVEL: Meeting facilities; fax available; corporate rates.

The Barrows House is an inn for all seasons and all reasons. The unique facilities and extensive grounds make the inn a special place for a family gathering, honeymoon, small business meeting, or spur-of-the-moment vacation.

Sitting on twelve acres, the Barrows House is a 200-year-old estate. The house was built for the pastor of the Dorset Congregational Church (you can walk there from the inn), and in 1888 it became an inn. The first innkeepers were Theresa and Experience Barrow. Don't you love his name? The front living rooms and entryways have some of the original stenciling, which was found after removing thirteen layers of wallpaper.

There is a story to every Barrows House room or cottage. Each is a furnished unit with its own restful style, antiques, old family pieces, and modern bedding. Each of the eight houses has its own sitting room and porch or terrace, as well as its own fire control system.

There are three delightful dining settings at the inn: the rustic tavern, bright greenhouse, or the Dorset Room, with a wonderful mural of town landmarks on the walls. The menu changes with the seasons.

Two of the appetizers are pumpkin ravioli and duck spring roll. In winter there are entrees such as medallions of pork, pan-seared salmon, grilled lamb loin, sautéed calf's liver with caramelized shallots and bacon, and grilled eggplant napoleon. The Maine crab cakes Chesapeake-style are a house specialty. For "finishers," well, come on up and taste.

There's so much to do in this area. The skiing is superb, antiques shopping is near, and the Dorset Playhouse is here. Horseback riding and hiking or golf are available in nearby Manchester. And when you're tired of all the activity, come back to the inn to enjoy the cozy tavern, the glowing fire in the main living room, or the grounds. Bring the whole family—children of all ages are welcome.

HOW TO GET THERE: The inn is 6 miles northwest of Manchester, Vermont, on Route 30.

Dorset Inn
Dorset, Vermont 05251

INNKEEPER: Sissy Hicks

ADDRESS/TELEPHONE: 8 Church Street, Route 30; (802) 867–5500 or (877) 367–7389; fax (802) 867–5542

WEB SITE: www.dorsetinn.com

ROOMS: 29, including 2 suites; all with private bath and air-conditioning.

RATES: $92 to $225 BP.

OPEN: All year.

FACILITIES AND ACTIVITIES: Breakfast, lunch, dinner; bar. Wheelchair access to dining room. Nearby: Golf, theater, hiking, bicycling, skiing.

Built in 1796, this is the oldest continuously operating inn in Vermont. Today the inn has been completely restored and is listed on the National Register of Historic Places. There are wide-board floors, and beautiful Vermont pine is around the fireplace in the living room.

While the inn has retained the feeling of the eighteenth century and is decidedly old-fashioned, it is modern in its conveniences. It has been completely insulated. The bathrooms have been redone, rooms have been air-conditioned, and firm mattresses have been purchased. There is no crowding in this large and rambling inn.

Sissy Hicks, who presides over the kitchen, is a very well-known lady. So many people requested recipes, she has put them into two books, *Flavors from the Heart* and *Elegant Comfort Food from the Dorset Inn*. At dinner the appetizers

are numerous, from steamed mussels to raclette. Sissy's entrees are delicious, whether you order the inn "burger" with a mushroom red wine sauce, or duck confit with red cabbage and plum chutney. The most requested dish? Her calf's liver with bacon and onions. The breakfast menu is pure ambrosia.

A fine golf course is nearby for anyone who likes to play. Swimming is a lot of fun in a huge marble quarry up the road. If culture turns you on, the Southern Vermont Arts Center and the Dorset Playhouse will provide the comedy and drama of good theater. There are two inn dogs—a Lab and a bassett hound. Christmas is special up here, and the inn is glorious with lights.

HOW TO GET THERE: Leave Interstate 91 at Brattleboro and go left on Route 30 to Dorset. Or take Route 7 to Manchester Center and go north on Route 30.

Inn at West View Farm
Dorset, Vermont 05251

INNKEEPER: Christal Siewertsen

ADDRESS/TELEPHONE: 2928 Route 30; (802) 867–5715 or (800) 769–4903; fax (802) 867–0468

WEB SITE: www.innatwestviewfarm.com

ROOMS: 10, all with private bath; 1 with wheelchair access.

RATES: $110 to $200 BP.

OPEN: May through October and mid-November through March.

FACILITIES AND ACTIVITIES: Breakfast, dinner, tavern. Dining room closed on Tuesday and Wednesday. Nearby: Tennis, golf, swimming, skiing.

This is an authentic Vermont country inn, informal and relaxed. The living rooms, with their glowing fireplaces and good couches and chairs, are restful after a day of skiing or shopping. The guest rooms are warmly furnished with four-poster beds and antique dressers.

The dining room is highlighted by a tin ceiling and a broad bay window. The stunning place plates are a floral pattern from Villeroy and Boch, and Botanica made in Luxembourg. Needless to say, with such magnificent surroundings, the food served here is excellent. The menu changes often, but you can expect appetizers such as Maine crab cakes or wild mushroom and mascarpone ravioli, and interesting main courses that may include braised Niman Ranch beef short ribs, roasted wild king salmon, coriander-crusted venison, or pan-roasted free-range chicken. There is always a nice selection of wines by the glass.

What's for dessert? The warm chocolate cake is delicious, not to mention the pear tart with vanilla Swiss almond ice cream. What a way to go!

A lovely stained-glass window separates the dining room from the tavern. The bar is done in rich, warm wood and is a real beauty.

The inn is only 5 miles north of Manchester, where there are shops for your every wish. Three downhill ski areas and cross-country skiing are all nearby, and the Dorset Playhouse is less than a walk around the block from the inn.

To see this beautiful inn in the snow is a picture to remember. And in warm weather, the porch with its wooden rocking chairs beckons. What a great view from here!

HOW TO GET THERE: Take Interstate 91 north to Brattleboro, then take Route 30 to Manchester. At the blinking lights, take a right and an immediate left, which brings you back on Route 30 north. Go about 5½ miles north of Manchester. Look for the inn on your right.

Inn at Mountain View Farm
East Burke, Vermont 05832

INNKEEPERS: Marilyn and John Pastore

ADDRESS/TELEPHONE: Darling Hill Road, Box 355; (802) 626–9924 or (800) 572–4509

WEB SITE: www.innmtnview.com

ROOMS: 14 rooms and suites, some with Jacuzzi or fireplace.

RATES: $155 to $275 BP; Westmore Wing sleeping six, $430.

OPEN: All year except April and November.

FACILITIES AND ACTIVITIES: Breakfast and dinner; dining room open daily except Tuesday in season, Wednesday to Sunday in winter; 440 acres; farm animals; trails for walking, mountain biking, or cross-country skiing; wagon and sleigh rides; sauna, massage by appointment. Nearby: Skiing, biking, golf, fly fishing, canoeing, kayaking, swimming.

his is an exceptional inn in every way, from the extraordinary restored farm architecture to the endless views from 440 hilltop acres.

The property was built in 1883 as a gentleman's farm by Elmer A. Darling, a Vermonter who trained in architecture at M.I.T. The impressive cow barn is one of the largest ever built in Vermont, a landmark for students of barn design and history. It was home to one hundred Jersey cows who provided the 1890 Creamery with milk needed to produce butter and cheese. The farm supplied both dairy products and meat for Darling's elegant hotel in New York City.

When the Pastores arrived in 1989, the original buildings remained but were in need of major restoration. They have accomplished the transformation into a country inn so beautifully that the inn has won two awards for preservation from the governor of Vermont and has been chosen as an Editor's Pick in *Yankee* magazine and the Inn of the Month in *Country Living* magazine.

olivemetcalf

The redbrick Creamery, a Georgian colonial with a butter-churn cupola, has become the main inn, with a gracious parlor downstairs done in English country style and casually elegant rooms and suites above, decorated in chintzes and checks and furnished with country antiques, handmade quilts, and botanical prints. The Westmore Wing of the inn offers sleeping space for six. Almost all provide wonderful views of Burke Mountain.

The yellow farmhouse next door now holds suites, each with a sitting area, whirlpool, or fireplace.

The room that was the heart of butter and cheese production is now a warm dining room with brick walls and hand-painted stenciling. Organic herbs and vegetables from the bountiful inn gardens enhance the menu. The chef's specialties include grilled filet mignon with a wild mushroom demi-glaze, and a Tuscan chicken stew served with polenta. Dinner is preceded most Friday and Saturday nights by a horse-drawn wagon or sleigh ride across the inn's 440 acres.

Those acres include many activities, from admiring the flower and vegetable gardens to visiting the resident farm animals to miles of trails for walking, mountain biking, or cross-country skiing in winter. Burke Mountain offers downhill skiing just five minutes away. Should you want a little pampering, the inn offers a sauna and massages, by appointment.

This is a particularly beautiful part of Vermont's Northeast Kingdom, with scenic drives in all directions, and you'll have the very best of the views from your very special hilltop aerie at Mountain View Farm.

HOW TO GET THERE: Follow Interstate 93 north to Interstate 91 north. Take exit 23 at Lyndonville. Follow Route 5 north through the town of Lyndonville to Route 114. Bear right onto Route 114 and continue for 4⁹⁄₁₀ miles. Turn left at Burke Hollow sign, bearing left to go straight up hill. At top of hill, turn left onto Darling Hill Road. Entrance to the inn is inside the brick Creamery, 100 yards on the right.

Blueberry Hill ♥
Goshen, Vermont 05733

INNKEEPERS: Tony Clark and Shari Brown

ADDRESS/TELEPHONE: Blueberry Hill, RD 3; (802) 247–6735, (802) 247–6535, or (800) 448–0707; fax (802) 247–3983

WEB SITE: www.blueberryhillinn.com

ROOMS: 11, plus 1 cottage; all with private bath; 1 specially equipped for the physically disabled. No-smoking inn.

RATES: $260 to $340 MAP.

OPEN: All year, except for mid-November to early December.

FACILITIES AND ACTIVITIES: Packed lunch available, BYOB. Sauna across the pond. Cross-country skiing, swimming, fishing.

*S*tart with the location, a nature lover's dream, 120 secluded acres of forest, woodlands, lakes, ponds, and alpine terrain. The pristine environment includes miles of marked hiking and walking trails and more

than 75 kilometers of groomed cross-country ski trails. The property has a spring-fed freshwater pond for swimming. The Cross Country Skiing Center, a barn-style building offering rentals and lessons, also houses cycling equipment and the building containing a sauna. To add to the peace and privacy, the property is surrounded by 22,000 acres of Moosalamoo, a lush nature preserve with well-maintained trails.

The inn itself, an 1813 farmhouse, was to be the owners' dream house, restored to its early-nineteenth-century appearance. Instead, in 1971, the Clarks hung out the Blueberry Hill shingle and began new careers as innkeepers. They seem to have been made for the job. Guests are immediately at home here. The common rooms invite company, with comfortable seating and a warming fire in the hearth. An open kitchen is the focal point of the inn, enticing with its aromas. And everyone loves the plant-filled greenhouse, cheerful even on the dreariest day. Complimentary hors d'oeuvres are served here before dinner.

Guests also tend to linger over their candlelit dinners in the congenial dining room, hung with herbs and with a crackling fire to warm chilly nights. Tony Clark, a Welshman, was raised in Bordeaux, and good food is among his passions. Entrees include such dishes as Truite Antoine, lobster and crab ravioli with roasted garlic cream sauce, beef tenderloin with Irish whiskey sauce, and soufflé roll with chicken béchamel filling and roasted red pepper coulis. So many people ask for recipes that he has published *Tony Clark's New Blueberry Hill Cookbook.*

One recipe Tony won't give out is for the inn's famous oversize chocolate-chip cookies. The inn does a brisk mail-order business with guests who long for them.

Rooms are in the original inn or in an added wing overlooking the pond. Each has antiques, a handmade quilt, and amenities including inn-made herbal bath salts and body lotion.

The herbs used for these products and also instrumental in the kitchen are from the inn's own gardens, where more than fifty culinary and twenty-five medicinal herbal varieties are grown. Shari, who has done extensive study on herbs, looks after the gardens, which also include lovely flowers that adorn the rooms and your dinner plate.

Glorious in summer, a skier's haven when the snow falls, Blueberry Hill is truly an escapist's inn for all seasons.

HOW TO GET THERE: From Rutland take Route 7 north to Brandon, then Route 73 east for 6 miles. Turn left at the inn's sign, and follow the signs up the mountain on a dirt road to the inn.

The Old Tavern 🌿
Grafton, Vermont 05146

INNKEEPER: Kevin O'Donnell

ADDRESS/TELEPHONE: Route 121 (mailing address: P.O. Box 9); (802) 843–2231 or (800) 843–1801; fax (802) 843–2245

WEB SITE: www.old-tavern.com

ROOMS: 30 rooms and suites in 2 buildings; 4 guest houses (sleeping 6 to 12) with kitchens; all with private bath, air-conditioning, phone.

RATES: Rooms, $175 to $245 BP; suites, $260 to $350 BP; guest houses, $650 to $850 BP.

OPEN: All year except April, Christmas Eve, and Christmas Day.

FACILITIES AND ACTIVITIES: Breakfast, lunch, dinner; bar, cafe; retail store. Wheelchair access to inn, bar, lounge, and dining room. Television in lounge, parking, elevator, swimming. Nearby: Tennis, nature walks, cross-country skiing, bicycle rentals.

*I*f you're looking for perfection in a country inn, go to a charming Vermont village called Grafton, where you'll find the Old Tavern. It has been operated as an inn since 1801. Since the inn was purchased by the Windham Foundation in 1965, it has been restored and is now one of those superb New England inns we are all seeking.

Grafton's Renaissance

In the early nineteenth century, Grafton's 1,400 or so citizens managed pretty tidily from the profits derived from the 75,000 yards of wool produced annually from the 10,000 sheep that grazed in Grafton pastures. Thirteen soapstone quarries produced sinks, stoves, and other household goods. The Phelps Tavern—now known as the Old Tavern—was upgraded with innkeeper Marlan Phelps's gold rush profits and entertained illustrious guests from poets to presidents.

Unfortunately, Grafton lost scores of its citizens in the Civil War, sheep farmers went looking for bigger pastures out West, and floods and new highways changed the look and the lure of this once-prosperous village. By 1940, the town's economy had trickled down to nearly nothing. Along came the Windham Foundation in 1963, and suddenly Grafton had new life in its center. Find out the history of the remarkable transformation of Grafton in its "new" Old Tavern Inn and in its three museums dedicated to the human and natural history of the town. Call the Grafton Historical Society (802-843-2564), the Grafton Museum of Natural History (802-843-2111), and the Windham Foundation (802-843-2211) for information about historical exhibits and tours. You can also visit the Grafton Village Cheese Co. (802-843-2348) for a look at its cheese-making operation, and you can see "demonstration" flocks of sheep at the village's sheep barn viewing area. Horse-drawn sleigh rides are offered in the village in the winter, and the village's many walking paths, also popular in summer, are opened to cross-country skiers. Inquire at the Old Tavern about bicycle rentals and the Windham Foundation's horse stable.

When you turn your car off pounding interstate highways to the tree-shaded route that winds to this quaint village, you step back in time. The loveliest of the old combined with the comfort of the new makes this an unbeatable inn. No grinding motors can disturb your slumber when you are in what are possibly the best beds in all New England. The sheets and towels are the finest money can buy, and there are extra pillows and blankets in each room. The spacious rooms are filled with antiques, all in mint condition. The guest houses across the street that are also part of the inn are enchanting.

There is no "organized activity" at the Old Tavern. The swimming pool is a natural pond, cool and refreshing. There are tennis courts nearby and marked trails in the woods for walkers. This is the place to calm your spirits and recharge your batteries.

The cocktail barn is charming, connected to the inn by a covered walk. There are flowers everywhere, in hanging baskets, in flower boxes, and on various tables in the gracious public rooms. The cuisine is excellent, with unusual soups and varied entrees, all cooked well and served by pleasant waitresses.

Up the street a bit, there is a six box-stall stable that will accommodate guest horses, plus a four-bay carriage shed, if you care to bring your own carriage. All this is for the exclusive use of Old Tavern guests.

The Old Tavern has a heritage that goes back almost as far as our country's. It first opened twelve years after America's independence. It still looks very much as it did in former days, when, over time, it accommodated the likes of Daniel Webster, Oliver Wendell Holmes, Ulysses S. Grant, Rudyard Kipling, Ralph Waldo Emerson, and Henry David Thoreau.

HOW TO GET THERE: From Interstate 91 take exit 5 at Bellows Falls. Take Route 5 north to Route 121, on which you will get to Bellows Falls (12 miles from Interstate 91) and the inn. As you come down the exit ramp, watch for Route 121, which you'll take to the inn.

Highland Lodge 🖼️
Greensboro, Vermont 05841

INNKEEPERS: Wilhelmina and David Smith

ADDRESS/TELEPHONE: 1608 Craftsbury Road; (802) 533–2647; fax (802) 533–7494

WEB SITE: www.highlandlodge.com

ROOMS: 11 rooms, plus 11 cottages; all with private bath; 1 cottage equipped for the physically disabled.

RATES: $220 to $310 MAP.

OPEN: All year except March 15 to Memorial Day and October 15 to December 20 (or nearest weekend thereto).

FACILITIES AND ACTIVITIES: Lunch, dinner, and Sunday brunch; beer and wine license. Wheelchair access to dining room. Tennis, bicycle rentals, lawn games, hiking trails, swimming, boating, fishing, nature trail, cross-country ski touring center. Nearby: Working dairy farm, golf, horseback riding, shopping, antiquing.

*W*hen the snow starts falling up here, it has to be one of the most beautiful places in the world. And you can bet that it's popular with cross-country skiers. There is a complete ski touring center with daily instruction, ski shop (sales, rentals, and repairs), guided tours, marked trails, and skier's lunch. All this is at an altitude of 1,800 feet, a mini-snowbelt where there are miles of ski touring through the wonderful scenery.

Winter isn't the only fun time of year to be here. Caspian Lake, with the lodge's own beach house, is just across the road for swimming, canoeing, kayaking, and sailing. Fishing is good in June and from September to mid-October for salmon, lake trout, rainbow trout, and perch. Tennis is on the premises, and golf and horseback riding are nearby for those so inclined.

Any inn that sends its chef to Italy to train for the kitchen surely gets my nod. The food has always been outstanding here, and now it is even better. The menu is inventive, and there are great grilled Black Angus sirloin steaks to prove it. The innkeepers grow all their own herbs in a lovely herb garden.

I love the desserts. They have great names and taste equally great. Ishka-bibble is a brownie topped with ice cream and homemade hot fudge. Forgotten Dessert is a meringue with ice cream and strawberries. It's nice to find these old favorites on a menu.

Children of all ages are welcome at the Highland Lodge. Babysitters are available. In July and August a play lady comes in for the three-to-nine set. The playroom offers amusement for kids of all ages, and the playhouse has a supervised play program for youngsters. With the children happily occupied, the living room and library remain free and quiet for you.

This is the place to get away from it all. The views and utter peace are so wonderful, they are hard to describe. Come and enjoy.

HOW TO GET THERE: Greensboro is in the Northeast Kingdom of Vermont, 35 miles northeast of Montpelier. From the south take Interstate 91 to St. Johnsbury and follow US Highway 2 west to West Danville. Continue west on Vermont Highway 15 to the intersection with Vermont Highway 16, about 2 miles east of Hardwick. Turn north on VT 16 to East Hardwick and follow signs west to Greensboro, at the south end of Caspian Lake. Highland Lodge is at the north end of the lake, on the road to East Craftsbury.

Three Mountain Inn
Jamaica, Vermont 05343

INNKEEPERS: Jennifer and Ed Dorta-Duque

ADDRESS/TELEPHONE: Route 30; (802) 874–4140 or (800) 532–9399; fax (802) 874–4745

WEB SITE: www.threemountaininn.com

ROOMS: 14 in 2 buildings, 1 cottage; 11 with fireplace or cast-iron stove.

RATES: $165 to $325 BP; cottage, $325 to $345 BP.

OPEN: All year except for occasional weeks in November, April, and May.

FACILITIES AND ACTIVITIES: Dinner; pub, lounge; outdoor swimming pool. Nearby: Downhill and cross-country skiing, ice skating, Jamaica State Park, tennis, golf, fishing, horseback riding, summer theater.

The inn is well named, since it is within a few minutes of Stratton, Bromley, and Magic Mountains. Mount Snow is also within easy range. Skiers should love this location. Cross-country buffs will find a multitude of trails in nearby Jamaica State Park, including a dramatic trail along the long-defunct West River Railroad bed, and in summer there are lovely walks along the West River. Tennis is available both indoors and out at nearby Stratton. Horseback riding is superb on lovely trails in the area, or go swimming in the inn's own beautifully landscaped pool.

This small, authentic country inn was built in the 1780s. The living room has a large, roaring fireplace, complete with an original Dutch oven. The floors and walls are of wide, planked pine, and there are plenty of comfortable chairs. A picture window offers views of the Green Mountains to complete the scene.

A cozy lounge and bar area make you feel very comfortable for sitting back to enjoy good conversation and a before- or after-dinner drink. A good wine selection is at hand.

The rooms are tastefully decorated. No two are alike; depending on the room, amenities include four-poster king-size beds, wood-burning fireplaces, private balconies, and Jacuzzis. A charming Hansel and Gretel cottage is also available. Perfect for honeymooners, especially since the inn can host small weddings.

Everything has been upgraded since Jennifer and Ed arrived in 2004, and amenities such as gas-burning stoves are being added to the guest rooms all the time.

Dining is set in two intimate rooms with original wood-burning fireplaces. The ground-level Library, entered from the living room through French doors, can seat thirty and is a popular spot for private functions, but when it is not in use, it is another nice place to relax by the fire or play a game of cards or Scrabble. The eclectic menus offer something for almost everyone, from traditional French cuisine to regional Indian or Southeastern specialties. Homemade soups and breads baked in the beehive oven are longtime inn favorites, as are the chef's breakfast scones and famous Three Mountain Inn cookies.

HOW TO GET THERE: Follow Interstate 91 to Brattleboro and take the second exit to Route 30, to Jamaica.

Mountain Meadows Lodge
Killington, Vermont 05751

INNKEEPER: Michelle Werle

ADDRESS/TELEPHONE: 285 Thundering Brook Road; (802) 775–1010
or (800) 370–4567; fax (802) 773–4459

WEB SITE: www.mtmeadowslodge.com

ROOMS: 18 rooms, including 2 family suites; all with private bath; some
with phones and television; 1 wheelchair-accessible room. No-smoking
inn.

RATES: $114 to $240 MAP; $85 to $200 BP.

OPEN: All year except April 20 to May 20.

FACILITIES AND ACTIVITIES: Wheelchair-accessible dining room; full-
license bar; lake frontage with fishing, boating, swimming; outdoor pool
and hot tub, sauna; hiking trails; farm-animal feeding; volleyball, croquet,
bocce ball, yard games; Nordic skating, snowshoeing, sledding; shuttle bus
to ski areas. Nearby: Full-service cross-country ski center next door, golf,
tennis, alpine slide, horseback riding, downhill skiing.

*F*amilies with children feel right at home at this casual and relaxed
lodge, a Vermont classic built in the 1850s. The location couldn't
be better, directly on a lake and the Appalachian Trail.

Rowboats, canoes, and kayaks are waiting by the lake, and the water is
stocked with rainbow trout and largemouth bass. If you don't have your own

fishing pole, the inn has poles you can borrow. You can swim in the lake, too, or in the lodge pool.

Lots of activities are planned for the kids, from crafts projects to barn visits. In winter, snowshoe walks are available. Right next door to the lodge is the largest cross-country ski-touring center in the area, with 57 kilometers of groomed trails. Snowmaking begins as early as November. Alpine skiing at Killington and Pico is just five minutes away, accessible by shuttle bus from the lodge.

Meals are served in the post-and-beam dining room. Breakfast buffets offer homemade granola, mixed-berry pancakes, eggs, and fresh fruits. Homey dinner choices include country meat loaf, roast turkey, homemade chili, and lasagna. During the winter months, dinner buffets on weekends include all-you-can-eat prime rib, chicken, and vegetarian offerings, and children's choices are always available. Hearty picnic lunches are available year-round, featuring oversized sandwiches, fruits, and baked goodies. Afternoon refreshments are served in the sunken living room.

Rooms at the lodge vary from spacious quarters just right for families to rooms with balconies overlooking the lake. Seems like this is a place with something to please just about everyone.

HOW TO GET THERE: The inn is 10 miles east of Rutland, just off Route 4. Follow Route 4 from Rutland for 12 miles, and at Thundering Brook Road you will come to the inn's sign. Turn left. The inn is ¼ mile beyond.

The Vermont Inn
Killington, Vermont 05751

INNKEEPERS: Megan and Greg Smith

ADDRESS/TELEPHONE: Route 4, H.C. 34, Box 37K; (802) 775–5810 or (800) 541–7795 (outside Vermont); fax (802) 773–2440

WEB SITE: www.vermontinn.com

ROOMS: 18, most with private bath; some with fireplaces and whirlpools; 1 specially equipped for the physically disabled.

RATES: $60 to $215 MAP.

OPEN: All year except mid-April to Memorial Day.

FACILITIES AND ACTIVITIES: Dinner every day, bar. Wheelchair access to dining room. TV, game room, sauna, hot tub, pool, tennis, lawn games. Nearby: Gondola ride, alpine slide, summer theater, Norman Rockwell Museum, farmers' market, skiing.

*Y*ou may be greeted at the door of this friendly red house by the inn cats, Sunshine and Tails. Innkeepers Megan and Greg are always here, and a nicer couple you'd have to travel a long way to find.

The Vermont Inn is well known locally for the fine food it serves in its lovely dining room. As a matter of fact, three years in a row the restaurant was awarded the Killington Champagne Award for fine dining. To give you an idea of what awaits you: There are six appetizers, including mussels Dijon. Excellent entrees include rack of lamb persillé, Delmonico steak au poivre, and Vermont Inn chicken sautéed in brown sauce with Madeira wine being some of the best known. There is a fine wine cellar to enhance the good food, and a special children's menu.

The inn's guests are a mixed bag and include many Canadian visitors. You'll run into young professional people from Boston or New York, a grandparent or two, families—anyone from honeymooners to golden oldies.

The room for handicapped guests has a ramp, a queen-size bed, a beautiful daybed, a specially equipped bathroom, and air-conditioning.

This old house has sturdy underpinnings. Some of the original beams still have the bark on them, and how the rocks of the foundation were ever put in place I cannot imagine. Everything was changed around—the old dining room became a lounge to make the inn cozier—so take advantage of the glorious view of Killington, Pico, and Little Killington, straight ahead across the valley. The bar was handmade locally of Vermont cherrywood, and it's a beauty. Couches and a woodstove make this room a great spot for relaxing. There is also a room that houses a hot tub, exercise machines, and lots of plants and offers a wonderful view. It's handsome and is ideal for anyone who wants to unwind after a day on the slopes.

HOW TO GET THERE: The inn is 6 miles east of Rutland, on Route 4. It is also 4 miles west of the intersection of Route 4 and Route 100 north (Killington Access Road).

The Landgrove Inn

Landgrove, Vermont 05148

INNKEEPERS: Tom and Maureen Checchia

ADDRESS/TELEPHONE: 132 Landgrove Road; (802) 824–6673 or (800) 669–8466

WEB SITE: www.landgroveinn.com

ROOMS: 18; 16 with private bath; some with fireplace, jet tubs.

RATES: $80 to $225 BP.

OPEN: All year except April 1 to May 22 and October 20 to Thanksgiving.

FACILITIES AND ACTIVITIES: Dinner, except Monday and Tuesday. Pool, tennis, pond. Hiking trails, hay and sleigh rides, bumper pool, Ping-Pong, bocce, croquet, cross-country skiing, ice skating. Nearby: Downhill skiing, alpine slide, summer theaters, golf, shopping.

This is a family-run inn that especially welcomes families. Your children will be well entertained, and so will you. Indoors is a fun game room, and outside are playthings, a heated swimming pool, two Plexipave tennis courts, and a bocce court. A hike through the national forest is unbelievably scenic, and summer theater is nearby.

Winter means snow, and there is plenty of it. It's only a short hop by car to Bromley, Stratton, Magic Mountain, or Okemo. Cross-country skiing begins at the inn's door, or try your skills at snowshoeing or ice skating. After a long day, revive yourself in a deluxe room with jet tub and fireplace, and then enjoy the fireside warmth in the Rafter Room lounge. A room near the lounge holds a big-screen television with a VCR.

The architectural style of the inn is peculiar to Vermont, with one building added onto another building. It turns out to be charming. The first part was built in 1810. It has been an inn since 1939. The rooms are spick-and-span, spacious, and very comfortable. The common rooms, dining room, and just everything about this quiet spot are relaxing. And the Checchias, who are cordial and welcoming innkeepers, make you want to return year after year.

The food is excellent. Just a few choices are pork tenderloin with apple-pear chutney; garlic linguine with chicken, broccoli, and roasted red peppers; roast duckling with blueberry sauce; and grilled Atlantic salmon with yogurt dill sauce. Desserts? Well, do save room.

The inn hosts many workshops and seminars in the arts, including writing and painting, for all levels of ability. Phone for the current schedule.

HOW TO GET THERE: From Interstate 91 take exit 2 and go left onto Route 30 to Bondville. Take a right onto Route 100 to Londonderry, then go left on Route 11 and right on Landgrove Road. Go 4 miles to the inn, on your right.

From Manchester take Route 11 past Bromley Ski Area, and turn left into Peru Village. At the fork in Peru, bear left and continue 4 miles through the national forest to the crossroads in Landgrove. Turn left toward Weston, and the inn will be on your right.

Frog's Leap Inn
Londonderry, Vermont 05148

INNKEEPERS: Kraig and Dorenna Hart

ADDRESS/TELEPHONE: RR 1, Box 107, Route 100; (802) 824–3019 or (877) 376–4753; fax (802) 824–3657

WEB SITE: www.frogsleapinn.com

ROOMS: 12 in main inn, 8 in Lily's House, 1 two-bedroom apartment with kitchen; all with private bath, hair dryers, iron and ironing board, alarm clocks, coffeemakers.

RATES: $89 to $215 BP. Many MAP packages available. Children age 16 and under free in parent's room; added rollaway, $10.

OPEN: All year.

FACILITIES AND ACTIVITIES: Dinner Tuesday through Sunday July 1 to mid-October, Thursday through Sunday rest of year. Pub; full liquor license. Pool, all-weather tennis court, 32 acres of field and forest, hiking/biking/cross-country ski trails, Ping-Pong, croquet, volleyball, golf-driving cage, gardens. Nearby: Skiing, fishing, golf, horseback riding.

*H*igh on a hill with wonderful views, this is a quiet retreat on thirty-two acres. Sammy, the resident cat, and Charlie and Angel, the inn dogs, will welcome you to the handsome rambling inn, built in 1842. If there is a chill in the air, you can gather round the toasty Franklin stove in the comfortable living room. A second seating area is fine for readers, with a love seat and chair and bookshelves. A recent 3,600-square-foot addition includes a dining/pub area, and more couches and chairs in front of a Rumford-style fireplace. An original Natalee Everett mural is painted above the fireplace.

Rooms are in pleasant country decor, each one different, with many prints and accessories by Vermont artists. There are many nice furnishings, such as sleigh beds. All beds are queen size and have hand-crafted quilts or down comforters. Six rooms are in the main house, while Lily's House houses eight more accommodations, four of them suites. On the second floor of the Tad Pool House is a spacious set-up with two bedrooms, a kitchen, living room with TV, bathroom, and kitchen. One of the living room couches is a sleeper, making this a grand place for families.

You'll not lack for activity here. On the expansive property are a hilltop heated pool with more of those heavenly views, an all-weather tennis court, and trails for hiking or cross-country skiing. Trout fishing, golf, and horseback riding are nearby. Go picnicking and hiking in the Green Mountain National Forest. Weston is close by, and its summer playhouse is fun. Fall foliage is spectacular throughout the area, or you can sit right here and watch the inn's 200-year-old maples turn color. Winter brings downhill skiing at Bromley, Stratton, or Okemo. All are within twenty minutes of the inn. In addition to cross-country skiing on-site, three ski touring centers are nearby.

The dining room is charming, especially when the weather is brisk and you can dine by the fireside. Menus take advantage of each season's bounty. A sample menu may start with baked sweet onion soup with Vermont cheddar cheese or harvest ravioli with Alfredo sauce and pesto. Typical entrees are baked Arctic char; boneless duck breast with honey and thyme; chicken cutlet with Vermont honey and maple; or veal marsala. What to have for dessert? You simply can't go wrong.

HOW TO GET THERE: Take exit 2 from Interstate 91 at Brattleboro. Take Route 30 north to Route 100, and the inn is just north of town on Route 100.

Rabbit Hill Inn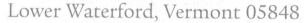
Lower Waterford, Vermont 05848

INNKEEPERS: Brian and Leslie Mulcahy

ADDRESS/TELEPHONE: Lower Waterford Road; (802) 748–5168 or (800) 76–BUNNY; fax (802) 748–8342

WEB SITE: www.rabbithillinn.com

ROOMS: 19 rooms: 9 luxury (fireplace and whirlpool tub for two), 6 rooms with fireplaces, and 4 classic rooms; all with private bath, CD player, hair dryer, robes, coffeemaker. 1 room specially equipped for the physically disabled (wheelchair access to dining rooms). No-smoking inn.

RATES: $195 to $350 BP.

OPEN: All year except first two weeks of April and first two weeks of November.

FACILITIES AND ACTIVITIES: Breakfast and dinner served. Bar, game room, library, video den; in-room massage available. Access to fax machine and copying services; two guest phone rooms; wireless Internet available.Snowshoeing, sledding, cross-country and downhill skiing, hiking, biking, swimming, and canoeing. Nearby: Ice skating, golf. Shopping, antiquing, museums, art galleries.

Rabbit Hill Inn is one of the lovingly restored crisp white buildings that make up Vermont's tiny "White Village." This historic district is one of the state's prettiest and most photographed places.

The inn was built by Samuel Hodby in 1795 as a tavern, general store, and lodging for those traveling between Canada and the ports of Boston and Portland. In 1825 Jonathan Cummings built his home and workshop here (it is now part of the foyer and front dining room). The two properties have operated as one since the 1830s. In the 1930s the inn was renamed the Rabbit Hill Inn for the many rabbit warrens then found on the property. The inn's present owners have preserved the charm of this lovely old inn. And what a job they've done!

Accommodations are grand. Every room has its own enchanting theme. Some of them are the Hampshire (designed to resemble an English study), the Music Chamber (with a 1857 pump organ and antique Victrola), and Cedar Glen (like stepping into a Vermont country cabin, with a glorious mountain view from the king-size log bed). I was in Victoria's Chamber, a lovely room with a king-size 1850s reproduction bed, empire sofa, and glorious mountain view. A diary is in each room for people to write in during their stay. What fun they are to read! In every room you'll find pretty things, wonderful touches, and a stuffed rabbit sitting on the bed.

The first- and second-floor porches face the Presidential Range. It is a special place to just sit and rock.

Do spend some time in the inviting common rooms. Afternoon tea and pastries are served in the Federal Parlor. The old crane in the fireplace here is still used in the winter for hearth cooking on Saturday afternoons. The Snooty Fox Pub is modeled after Irish pubs of the eighteenth century. Oh boy, what a place! There's also a comfortable library full of books and games to enjoy.

Everything is very nice indeed at the award-winning restaurant. The intimate, candlelit dining rooms feature good Thumb chairs and polished tables set with crystal and fine china.

Five-course gourmet dinners here are a true joy. It takes two hours to dine; it is all done right. The menu changes seasonally and frequently, each time bringing new delights. Everything is prepared from scratch. Try the house-cured salmon carpaccio or smoked breast of duck to start. Then sample the roast tenderloin of beef, coffee-marinated free-range chicken breast, or grilled mahimahi with basmati rice. There are always vegetarian options available. Be sure to savor the homemade sauces, mustards, and salsas prepared with herbs and edible flowers from the inn's garden. Save room for dessert. Cinnamon cheesecake and pumpkin flan are a sampling of the goodies you might find.

In the evening while you're dining, your bed is turned down, soft music is turned on, and oil lamps and candles are lit. A hand-crafted fabric heart is placed on your doorknob. You are invited to use it as your do-not-disturb sign and then to keep it as a memento of your visit.

You'll wake in the morning to a full candlelit breakfast of homemade granola (not to be missed), fruits, yogurts, juices, and hot entrees such as apple cheddar crepes or roasted red pepper egg Napoleon. Delicious!

The inn is splendid. So is the pretty little village. You will not be disappointed.

HOW TO GET THERE: From Interstate 91 (north or south): exit 19 to Interstate 93 south. Take exit 1 onto Route 18 south and go 7 miles to inn. From I–93 north: Take exit 44 onto Route 18 north and go 2 miles to inn.

The Andrie Rose Inn
Ludlow, Vermont 05149

INNKEEPERS: Michael and Irene Maston

ADDRESS/TELEPHONE: 13 Pleasant Street; (802) 228–4846 or (800) 223–4846; fax (802) 228–7910

WEB SITE: www.andrieroseinn.com

ROOMS: 9, plus guest house with 13 suites; all with private bath; all suites and 5 rooms with whirlpool tub; steam showers in 2 suites; 2-, 3-, and 4-bedroom family units. No-smoking inn.

RATES: $90 to $325 BP.

OPEN: All year.

FACILITIES AND ACTIVITIES: Dinner Friday and Saturday, full liquor license. Meeting facilities. Nearby: Skiing, golf, hiking, fishing, theater, antiquing.

Andrie Rose was the former owner of this lovely inn, built in 1829. She would no doubt be pleased to have her name connected with this very gracious inn.

When you arrive, a personalized welcome card is in your room, highlighting area activities and events. If you are celebrating a special event, you may receive chilled champagne, flowers, or a Vermont specialty product. You can help yourself at any time to the cookies and candies found throughout the inn. In the fall and winter, guests enjoy hot chocolate, cider, tea, or coffee; in the summer lemonade and iced tea are served. All of these are very nice, thoughtful touches.

The front porch is a great place to just relax, have a cocktail, or read a book. A fireplace is in the living room, and games are in the front room. Bombay paddle fans are in all of the common rooms and guest rooms. These are lovely at any time of the year. The innkeepers are always thinking about what will make your stay memorable.

The rooms are decorated beautifully. Some are done in Laura Ashley prints. Caswell-Massey almond-scented bath accessories are in all the bathrooms. Soft pastel colors are used on the walls, towels, and linens. I found them very restful. Most of the rooms have whirlpool tubs, so nice after a day of skiing. The beds are turned down in the evening, and soft music plays through the stereo system in each room.

On Friday and Saturday nights a four-course dinner is served, with a choice of four entrees. The menu changes seasonally. On a recent fall menu, interesting appetizers included grilled duck and mango sausage with Asian spiced red cabbage slaw or curried butternut squash soup. Medallions of pork tenderloin with cider sauce, herb grilled lamb chops, confit of duck with glazed apples and green peppercorn sauce, and dill-and-pepper-crusted salmon were some of the divine dinner entrees. This is also a great place to be a vegetarian, with choices such as wild mushroom risotto with black truffle oil and roast tomatoes, and roast artichoke tart with caramelized onions, roast tomatoes, wilted spinach, and Vermont chèvre.

My last trip was made during the week, when dinner is not available, so the innkeepers sent me to a nearby restaurant called Cappuccino's at 41 Depot Street. The food was so good. It was a wonderful recommendation.

Breakfast comes in a basket by your door, ordered the night before. One highlight is the inn's "cuckoo's nest," a small soufflé.

Ludlow is a wonderful town. It is home to Okemo, a very popular down-hill ski area. During the rest of the year, the inn has bicycles for your use, so go and have a Vermont adventure. Be sure to take along a picnic lunch.

The entire inn is available for a small business retreat or other function, including weddings. What great surroundings you'd have!

HOW TO GET THERE: From Interstate 91 or Route 131, follow Route 103 west to Ludlow.

The Governor's Inn
Ludlow, Vermont 05149

INNKEEPERS: Cathy and Jim Kubec

ADDRESS/TELEPHONE: 86 Main Street; (802) 228-8830 or (800) GOV-ERNO (468-3766)

WEB SITE: www.thegovernorsinn.com

ROOMS: 8, plus 1 suite; all with private bath; many with gas fireplace, TV and DVD player, whirlpool.

RATES: Rooms, $149 to $269 BP; suite, $249 to $319 BP. Saturday dinner by advance reservation only, from $55 per person.

OPEN: All year except two weeks in April, two weeks in November, and December 23 to December 26.

FACILITIES AND ACTIVITIES: Afternoon tea, picnic hampers available for lunch. Bar. Cooking seminars (send for brochure). Nearby: Skiing, boating, fishing, golf, historical attractions, antiquing.

Cathy is the chef, and she really does justice to the title. She is not only an honors graduate of the Connecticut Culinary Institute but has a certificate from the Cesar Ritz Course at the Ritz Escolier École de Gastronomie Française in Paris. Needless to say, this is an inn known for fine food!

The treats begin at breakfast. Have you ever tasted ice-cream-dipped French toast? It's special. So is the inn's "cuckoo's nest," a small soufflé. To make things even nicer, the table is set with crystal, silver, and antique china.

Saturday dinner in the formal lantern-lit dining room is different every week. Here's one sample: eastern crab cake appetizer, wine broth soup, pepper-crusted beef tenderloin or stuffed game hens, and Apricot Victorian for dessert.

Cathy regularly offers Culinary Magic Cooking Seminars for those who want to learn her secrets.

The inn itself is very Victorian. It was built in 1890 by William Wallace Stickney for his bride, Lizzie. Eight years later, Stickney became governor of Vermont, hence the inn's name. The parlor has a magnificent 1890s corner slate fireplace where guests tend to congregate, and lots of period antiques.

Cozy rooms have lovely printed wallpapers. I'm partial to the third-floor rooms under the eaves, each with a gas-lit Vermont firestove and whirlpool tubs for two.

The Governor William Wallace Stickney Suite is the grandest. It has a living room, a large bedroom with queen-size four-poster bed, a sitting room with a chaise longue, a whirlpool bath, and a walk-in closet. The rooms have windows overlooking the village church steeples and Okemo Mountain 1 mile away.

There's much to see and do in this area, and the innkeepers will gladly fill you in on the best places. Ask for one of Cathy's gourmet picnic lunches and enjoy the sights.

HOW TO GET THERE: Take exit 6 north from Interstate 91 and follow Route 103 northwest to Ludlow and the inn.

The Wildflower Inn
Lyndonville, Vermont 05851

INNKEEPERS: Mary and Jim O'Reilly

ADDRESS/TELEPHONE: Darling Hill Road; (802) 626–8310 or (800) 627–8310

WEB SITE: www.wildflowerinn.com

ROOMS: 10, plus 14 suites; all with private bath; many with kitchenette; 1 specially equipped for the physically disabled; 1 cottage with fireplace and Jacuzzi.

RATES: $99 to $289 BP; cottage, $159 to $319 BP.

OPEN: All year except April, the last week in October, and the first three weeks in November.

FACILITIES AND ACTIVITIES: Dinner, lunch in season. Gift shop, meeting room, heated pool, children's pool, sauna, spa, ice-skating rink, cross-country skiing, petting barn and farm animals, summer children's theater, art gallery.

This is a beautiful place to be—with children or without. Tired of traveling for Jim's job as a civil engineer, the O'Reillys came to this beautiful spot in 1984, opening a bed-and-breakfast inn as a way for the growing family to settle down and be together. Since then, the rooms have grown from four to twenty-four, the children have multiplied from three to eight, and the inn has established itself as one of New England's best places for a family vacation. The spectacular location on 570 panoramic ridgetop acres means this is a great romantic escape for couples as well, and the inn is also popular for weddings.

But it is probably families who most appreciate the rarity of an inn that goes out of its way to make them welcome. During the summer, a daily two-hour activity program keeps kids ages four to eleven busy and happy with games, crafts, and nature walks while the adults have a bit of private time. And it is included in the rates!

Daisy's Diner offers a special extra kids' dinner three nights each week with themed activities and a movie, giving grown-ups an evening to themselves. In June and September, families with infants and preschoolers get a break with the Butterflies, Tots, and Forget-Me-Nots program, based on a successful Danish outdoor preschool model that allows young children to explore nature, use their imaginations, and have fun with other children. Again, the adults get a little time off. Kids also have two outdoor play areas, a splash area, and a playroom to themselves.

There's plenty for all ages to do together, as well. The outdoor pool is great in summer, there are lovely trails and walks in all directions, and everyone enjoys a wagon ride to visit the animals in the barn. Badminton, volleyball, shuffleboard, and a batting cage make for family fun, and in winter ice skating, sledding, and snowshoeing are available on the property, along with downhill skiing at nearby Burke Mountain.

Accommodations are comfortable, and rooms can be set up with bunk beds to accommodate families. Larger suites come in studio, two-, and three-bedroom sizes, most with convenient kitchenettes. Couples who want privacy can opt for the Schoolhouse Cottage, with a fireplace and Jacuzzi as well as a kitchen.

The day begins with a big breakfast, starting with a buffet of homemade muffins or coffee cakes, fresh fruit, yogurt, cereals, and homemade maple pecan granola. Then comes a hot dish, eggs or maybe pancakes with bacon or sausage. Kids just love the teddy bear pancakes served in summer and the snowmen in winter.

The inn's Juniper Restaurant stresses healthy eating: lots of farm-fresh produce, and no meats or other foods containing antibiotics, hormones, preservatives, or artificial ingredients on the menu. They offer several organic wines and a big selection of Vermont microbrews to go with your dinner.

In summer, a cafe bar is set up on the terrace, not far from the pool, serving sandwiches and salads. And year-round, afternoons mean the inn's famous chocolate chip cookies. It's hard to say who is most impatient for the cookies to appear, the kids or their parents!

HOW TO GET THERE: Take exit 23 off Interstate 91 in Lyndonville. Go north through town on Route 5 to Route 114. Follow Route 114 for ½ mile. Darling Hill Road is a left turn immediately after the second bridge you cross. The inn is in 2 miles.

The Inn at Ormsby Hill 💚
Manchester Center, Vermont 05255

INNKEEPERS: Chris and Ted Sprague

ADDRESS/TELEPHONE: Historic Route 7A (mailing address: 1842 Main Street); (802) 362–1163 or (800) 670–2841; fax (802) 362–5176

WEB SITE: www.ormsbyhill.com

ROOMS: 10, all with private bath, air-conditioning, double whirlpool tub, fireplace, phones, and robes; some with 2-person steam showers.

RATES: $170 to $370 BP.

OPEN: All year.

FACILITIES AND ACTIVITIES: Hammock, porch. Nearby: Golf, bicycling, antiquing, fishing, tennis, hiking, downhill and cross-country skiing.

What a beautiful inn this is! When you enter, the first room on the left is a beautifully furnished formal living room. Go on into the gathering room, which has a huge fireplace, games, and books. Continue into the conservatory–dining room. It's great. When the inn is full, three tables are in use. There's a really different-looking fireplace in here. The mantel came from either Europe or Newport. It's a beauty. The glass windows at the end of the room remind me of a ship, and Chris has nice plants all around and an apple checkerboard at the ready. The view of the mountains is awesome.

The Jelly Mill . . . & Friends

On Historic Route 7A in Manchester, you can visit the restored four-story dairy barn called the Jelly Mill Marketplace (802–362–3494; www.jellymill.com). This barn, the brick home next door, and the surrounding acreage were once home to Loveland Munson, former Chief Justice of the Vermont Supreme Court. The barn now houses a wonderful country store that had its beginnings in an old cider jelly mill and later moved here. The proprietors still sell cider jelly plus eighty-eight other flavors of jellies, jams, and preserves. Along with these goodies you'll find jelly beans, chocolates, and Vermont maple sugar products and cheeses. Also here are "the Friends"—other businesses that sell country furnishings and accessories, jewelry, Christmas collectibles, handblown glass, pottery, handcrafted teddy bears, toys, doll furniture, and much more. The Buttery Restaurant serves breakfast and lunch daily from 10:00 A.M. to 3:00 P.M. The rest of the Jelly Mill is open from 10:00 A.M. to 6:00 P.M. daily, except for New Year's Day, Easter, Thanksgiving, and Christmas Day.

The inn was built around 1760 and added onto in the 1800s. The new wing was renovated in 1996, and improvments are made every year. You cannot tell where the old and new meet. All rooms have two-person whirlpool baths and fireplaces, either gas or wood. The latest amenity is state-of-the-art flat-screen TVs in five of the rooms. The beds are canopied kings and queens and so comfortable. The colors are muted and restful, the towels are big and fluffy. The inn reminds me of a gracious manor house in the English countryside.

The tower room is a dream. Up seven steps from the second floor to a queen-size canopy bed, a gas fireplace, and lots of windows. Up a few more to an unbelievable bathroom with a Jacuzzi for two as well as a two-person shower/steam shower (making a total of four in the inn) and more windows.

Chris Sprague is an exceptional chef, winner of many awards, and breakfast at Ormsby Hill is an extravaganza; you may not need to eat again until dinnertime. After juice and fresh-fruit starters, you get delicious treats such as lemon almond bread fresh from the oven, then unusual main courses such as breakfast bacon-and-egg risotto, raisin bread-and-butter pudding, or Chris's famous baked pancakes. Then she serves dessert! Honest. Things such as blueberry and peach crisp with vanilla ice cream or warm gingerbread with vanilla ice cream. Delicious.

Ask Chris or Ted to tell you about the inn's unusual past. The original portion of the house still contains Manchester's first jail cell in the basement, complete with marble floor. It was part of the Underground Railroad used by runaway slaves. In the late 1800s it was bought and expanded by Edward Isham, a law partner of Robert Todd Lincoln, son of Abraham Lincoln. As you might expect with all that history, the house is listed on the National Register of Historic Places.

HOW TO GET THERE: From Route 30 go north to Historic Route 7A in Manchester. Turn left. Go south about 3 miles to the inn.

The Inn at Manchester
Manchester Village, Vermont 05254

INNKEEPERS: Frank and Julie Hanes

ADDRESS/TELEPHONE: Route 7A, Box 41; (802) 362–1793 or (800) 273–1793; fax (802) 362–3218

WEB SITE: www.innatmanchester.com

ROOMS: 13, plus 5 suites; all with private bath and air-conditioning; 4 suites with fireplace.

RATES: $145 to $295 BP.

OPEN: All year.

FACILITIES AND ACTIVITIES: Swimming pool; 4 acres of lawn and gardens. Free Internet station and wireless access. Nearby: Skiing, golf, tennis, hiking, theater, shopping outlets.

This is a charmer, an old-fashioned village beauty with a wraparound porch that has graced the covers of a pair of inn books. The grounds and gardens are exceptional, and when you step through the double doors into the living room, perfectly done in soothing colors with a fireplace and big bay window, you know you've found a special inn.

Rooms are individually decorated with a mix of interesting furnishings. Blue Phlox, one of three first-floor rooms, has a handsome antique brass bed. Upstairs, you might choose the Primrose Suite, with a king-size four-poster, or the Garden Suite, with a king-size canopy bed; both have comfortable sitting areas and fireplaces. The recently redone Sage Suite is prime; it comes with a vaulted ceiling, fireplace, whirlpool tub, and private balcony.

Breakfast is a highlight of the day. Cottage cakes with warm apricot sauce is an inn trademark, so special it has been featured in *Gourmet* magazine.

The inn is conveniently located in the heart of just about everything, with skiing, downhill and cross-country, only minutes away. Summer brings great antiquing, summer theater, specialty craft shops, and boutiques. Golf and tennis are within walking distance of the front door, and the swimming pool is in a lovely meadow between the carriage house and the creek.

HOW TO GET THERE: The inn is approximately 22 miles north of Bennington, Vermont, on Route 7A.

The Reluctant Panther
Manchester Village, Vermont 05254

INNKEEPERS: Liz and Jerry Lavalley

ADDRESS/TELEPHONE: 17–39 West Road (mailing address: P.O. Box 678); (802) 362–2568 or (800) 822–2331; fax (802) 362–2586

WEB SITE: www.reluctantpanther.com

ROOMS: 20 rooms and suites; all with private bath, TV, air-conditioning, phone, Internet access, hair dryers; most with fireplace; some with Jacuzzi; 1 specially equipped for the physically disabled.

RATES: $249 to $599 BP. Inquire about packages.

OPEN: All year.

FACILITIES AND ACTIVITIES: Dinner, tavern. Nearby: Golf, tennis, hiking, skiing, museums, outlet shopping, fishing.

Phones, wireless Internet access in all rooms; desks in some; conference room; midweek corporate rates.

*L*ocated right in the heart of Manchester Village at the foot of Equinox Mountain, the Reluctant Panther is a longtime favorite for upscale lodgings and dining, and new owners are continuing that tradition. The inn should be better than ever by the fall of 2006, completely rebuilt after a fire in October 2005 that destroyed the 150-year-old main building and its restaurant. Fortunately, eight luxury suites in the inn's cottages were untouched and continued to operate during reconstruction, with guests taking breakfast at the Colonade restaurant in the nearby Equinox Hotel. These nineteenth-century cottages will continue to be available to guests, connected to the main inn by marble sidewalks.

The innkeepers promise finely appointed rooms in the newly built inn, with king-size beds, fireplaces, a mix of period and contemporary furnishings, and whirlpools in the bath. The new dining room takes full advantage of a dramatic view of Equinox Mountain. The menu features New England regional cuisine, using local food products whenever possible.

The landscaped grounds include a quiet pond behind the inn, a nice spot for relaxing and, in fall, a prime place for viewing the brilliant foliage across the mountains.

HOW TO GET THERE: As you approach Manchester Village from the south on Route 7A, keep an eye on the left. Soon the Reluctant Panther will pop into view, 1 block north of the Equinox Hotel.

The Village Country Inn 💚
Manchester Village, Vermont 05254

INNKEEPERS: Jay and Anne Degen

ADDRESS/TELEPHONE: 3835 Main Street (Route 7A); (802) 362–1792 or (800) 370–0300; fax (802) 362–7238

WEB SITE: www.villagecountryinn.com

ROOMS: 11 standard rooms, plus 21 luxury rooms and suites; all with private bath, phone, TV, and air-conditioning; 5 with fireplace.

RATES: $129 to $345 BP.

OPEN: All year.

FACILITIES AND ACTIVITIES: Restaurant, bar-lounge, boutique, swimming pool, tennis. Nearby: Golf, shopping, skiing, ice skating.

*M*anchester's favorite front porch beckons you as you arrive at the Village Country Inn, located in the heart of town. The porch is 100 feet long, with wicker furniture and rockers covered with rose chintz.

This is a beautiful country inn reflecting the expertise of innkeeper Anne, who is also a professional interior decorator. Three sitting rooms are done with lots of antiques and in one of my favorite colors, mauve, along with celery and ecru. One is especially inviting, with sofas and chairs around a big fieldstone fireplace.

The rooms are magnificent, and each one is different. Pastel colors, canopied beds, lace, plush carpets, down pillows, and nice things on dressers and tables give the rooms an elegant atmosphere. They haven't forgotten important little touches, such as good towels.

I was in a suite called Chantel's Boudoir, done in soft greens and pinks. The king-size wrought-iron bed is a beauty. There's also a fireplace, television, phone, chaise longue, and couch. I could live in here.

Victoria's Room, overlooking the pool area, has similar amenities, a queen-size bed with a lovely floral spread, a gas fireplace, a chaise longue, air-conditioning, a television, phone, and a two-person Jacuzzi in a lovely large bathroom.

Dining is a joy in Angel's restaurant. Lace curtains and trellis alcoves create a cozy and romantic atmosphere. The eclectic New England menu uses as many locally produced ingredients as possible. The four-course prix fixe dinner includes entrees such as Scallops Nantucket, fresh sea scallops pan

sautéed, then deglazed with sherry and topped with Grafton cheddar cheese; or hazelnut-encrusted breast of duck with a Frangelico orange sauce.

Tavern in the Green, the bar and lounge, has an upright piano. One night when I stayed here, a playwright guest entertained us with a marvelous selection of music and songs. What an unexpected treat! A door from here leads out to the swimming pool and gardens. In the summertime breakfast and dinner may be served out on the patio.

The interesting breakfast menu has choices such as cheese blintzes with spiced apple compote or a farmer's quiche made with fresh vegetables and Grafton cheddar.

The inn has many attractive theme packages. Rekindle the romance by having a romantic getaway, what the innkeepers call "Affairs of the heart" for the "too busy" and "too stressed." Also offered is the "Shop 'Til You Drop," featuring champagne and a coupon book for the Manchester Designer Outlets. Christmas, as you can imagine, is very special up here.

Be sure to stop in at the inn's boutique, the French Rabbit. The wares are another example of Anne's wonderful taste.

HOW TO GET THERE: Coming north on historic Route 7A, you will find the inn on your left in Manchester Village.

Wilburton Inn
Manchester Village, Vermont 05254

INNKEEPERS: Georgette and Albert Levis

ADDRESS/TELEPHONE: River Road (mailing address: P.O. Box 468); (802) 362–2500 or (800) 648–4944

WEB SITE: www.wilburton.com

ROOMS: 11 in main house, 19 in other 5 houses; all with private bath.

RATES: $115 to $315 BP. MAP rates available.

OPEN: All year.

FACILITIES AND ACTIVITIES: Breakfast, dinner. Tennis, heated pool, sculpture garden. Nearby: Skiing, shopping, art gallery, theater, music festivals, hiking, swimming, canoeing, trout fishing, golf.

This inn was built in 1902 for a friend of Robert Todd Lincoln. In 1906 James Wilbur purchased the estate and lived here until his death in 1929. Later, during World War II, it was a boarding school for daughters of European diplomats. In 1946 the estate became a very elegant

inn, and in 1987 Georgette and Albert became the new owners. The inn is set on a twenty-acre knoll that rises above the lush Battenkill River Valley.

When you enter the inn, you are in a large living room with couches and chairs, a huge table for serving tea, and a wonderful fireplace with a set of huge carved brass andirons. A library and a porch where breakfast is served are also on the ground floor, along with the dining rooms.

The food here is glorious. For starters I was able to try the vegetarian ravioli with a tomato-sage cream sauce. On another night the gravlax was ambrosia, as were the rack of lamb and the salmon, sweet potato crusted with raspberry gastrique. Very different. Salads are excellent, and the desserts—well, you'd better come up here and see for yourself. Breakfast? Usually I could turn it down, but not when it's this grand. Fresh blueberry muffins and, of course, much, much more. The menus change monthly, and specials abound. The pink and white napery add to the pretty ambience.

Accommodations in the main inn are luxurious. Most beds are queen or king size, with lovely bedspreads. Wonderful large windows provide a view of the surrounding mountains. Five other houses on the estate are just as well appointed and so nice for families, wedding parties, or corporate meetings.

After a day of whatever you do, return to the inn for tea or cocktails in the living room by the fireplace. This is truly a grand setting.

HOW TO GET THERE: From the blinking light in Manchester, go 1½ miles south on Route 7A to River Road. Go left for 1 mile—the driveway is on the left.

Red Clover Inn
Mendon, Vermont 05701

INNKEEPERS: Tricia Treen Pederson and Bill Pederson

ADDRESS/TELEPHONE: 7 Woodward Road; (802) 775-2290 or (800) 752-0571; fax (802) 773-0594

WEB SITE: www.redcloverinn.com

ROOMS: 14 in farm house and carriage house, all with private bath and air-conditioning; 6 with fireplace; 5 with whirlpool tub. TV in some rooms. No-smoking inn.

RATES: $135 to $290 BP. Packages available.

OPEN: All year.

FACILITIES AND ACTIVITIES: Dinner Thursday through Sunday, daily during foliage and holidays. Pub, Wi-Fi. Nearby: Skiing at Killington and Pico, shopping, lakes, hiking, golf.

uilt as a summer estate for Gen. John Woodward of Washington, D.C., the inn is nicely tucked off the main road, about 5 miles east of Rutland. All you hear are the sounds of nature.

The inn is very comfortable. The living room has cozy chairs and couches. This is also the library. Curl up in front of the fire with a good book or a friend. Adjacent to the living room is the pub, to provide you with your favorite drink. The guest rooms are nicely appointed and restful—just what you expect in a good inn.

The dining rooms are lovely, and the food is just glorious. The chef's menu changes daily. There are fine soups and appetizers such as broccoli and

Gorgonzola cream soup. Roasted tomato, garlic, and garden basil soup is a real winner. Medallions of beef, fettucine, vegetarian pasta, sautéed duck breast, pork tenderloin, and venison are among the entrees. Save room, everyone; the desserts are all homemade. They have won the *Wine Spectator*'s award of excellence since 1995 under three different owners, and they have a grand wine cellar.

There are several assistant innkeepers here. They include not only permanent residents like the barn and office cats, but also occasional visitors such as the mallard ducks who visit the inn's pond every year. Four-footed inn guests are also accepted in some rooms, but only with prior notice.

The area offers a lot to do. Killington and Pico are nearby for skiing, or you can go hiking, golfing, swimming or fishing in nearby lakes, and shopping. Do go and have a great time.

HOW TO GET THERE: Take Route 4 east from Rutland. The inn is on the right, down narrow Woodward Road.

Middlebury Inn
Middlebury, Vermont 05753

INNKEEPERS: Frank and Jane Emanuels

ADDRESS/TELEPHONE: Court House Square, Route 7; (802) 388-4961 or (800) 842-4666; fax (802) 388-4563

WEB SITE: www.middleburyinn.com

ROOMS: 75, including 6 suites in 4 buildings; all with private bath, air-conditioning, TV, and phone with dataports; some with whirlpool; suites with refrigerator; 3 specially equipped for the physically disabled.

RATES: $98 to $395 CP.

OPEN: All year.

FACILITIES AND ACTIVITIES: Breakfast, lunch, afternoon tea, dinner, bar. Privileges at nearby fitness center. Business center with two computer stations, wireless high-speed Internet. Wheelchair access to dining rooms and all public areas. Parking, elevator, gift shop. Nearby: Skiing, swimming, golf, fishing, boating, museums.

Founded in 1761, Middlebury is a classic Vermont college town with the requisite white church steeples and a bandstand on the village green. The inn has presided from its central spot since 1827, its porches overlooking the green.

olive Metcalf

The venerable three-story redbrick inn is adorned with white shutters and cheerful yellow and white canopies. Rooms in the main inn are in traditional colonial decor and vary from snug to spacious. Two-room suites with pull-out sofas are ideal for families.

Ten additional rooms are in the adjacent Porter Mansion, an elegant home in Second Empire style, known for its beautiful curved stairway. Many rooms here have fireplaces (nonworking) of Vermont marble.

Those who prefer more modern accommodations can opt for one of the twenty motel-style rooms in a contemporary wing, which have the added convenience of coffeemakers. Pets are accepted for motel guests.

Guests can come down to the lobby for early-morning coffee or tea or even have it delivered to the room on a silver tray. Continental breakfast and lunch are served in the Rose Room, or, in fine weather, on the spacious front porch. Almost everyone comes back for the generous afternoon tea in the Morgan Tavern each day from 2:30 to 4:30 P.M., featuring scones, cakes, and cookies. A traditional Old English Carvery is the main attraction at dinner in the handsome Founders Room.

If you want to work off some of the calories, you can take advantage of complimentary membership for inn guests in the nearby Vermont Sun Fitness Center.

By all means, save time for a stroll around lovely Middlebury, a town filled with historic buildings, and have a look into the Frog Hollow Vermont State

Craft Center, housed in an old mill on Otter Creek. The center shows both traditional and contemporary crafts by some 250 talented state artisans.

HOW TO GET THERE: Go up Route 7, and you will run right into Middlebury. The inn is in the middle of town, overlooking the town green.

Swift House Inn
Middlebury, Vermont 05753

INNKEEPER: Donna Lee Phillips; John K. Nelson, owner

ADDRESS/TELEPHONE: 25 Stewart Lane; (802) 388–9925; fax (802) 388–9927

WEB SITE: www.swifthouseinn.com

ROOMS: 21, all with private bath, air-conditioning, and phone; some with cable TV, working fireplace, double whirlpool baths, patios. One room specially equipped for the physically disabled.

RATES: $110 to $295 CP.

OPEN: All year.

FACILITIES AND ACTIVITIES: Breakfast, dinner. Wheelchair access to dining room. Sauna, steam room. Nearby: Downhill and cross-country skiing, hiking, fishing, golf.

Three historic buildings make up this lovely inn. The handsome Federal-style main house was built in 1814, the Carriage House added in 1886, and the very Victorian Gate House was constructed in 1906 near the entrance to the house on Stewart Road. I stayed in a glorious room with a patio in the Carriage House, which has been renovated to hold six luxurious rooms, all with fireplaces and double whirlpool tubs.

The main house also has many lovely accommodations, especially the Garden Room, which has a whirlpool tub and its own entrance from a private patio, and the Swift Room, which has a fireplace and canopy bed as well as a private terrace. Rooms in the Gate House are more modest, but still inviting; the round turret room is especially appealing. The inn living rooms have fireplaces and comfortable chairs and couches, nice places to relax.

The complimentary continental breakfast is grand, a buffet spread that includes juices, yogurt with fresh and dried fruits, granola, cereals, bagels with cream cheese and smoked salmon, homemade quiche, and all sorts of delicious muffins, breads, and pastries.

This inn has an interesting history. The original portion was built by Samuel Swift, who had a long career of public service in Vermont as a lawyer, judge, legislator, and local historian. After his death in 1875, the home was purchased by John W. Stewart, another attorney, whose political career included eight years in Congress and one term as governor of Vermont. By romantic coincidence, his daughter Jessica married Charles M. Swift, grandson of the original owner of the house. Ask the innkeepers to tell you more about the many accomplishments of the Swift and Stewart families, who continued to live in this home until 1941.

HOW TO GET THERE: Take Route 7 to Middlebury. The inn is 2 blocks north of the center of town on the corner of Route 7 and Stewart Lane.

Black Lantern Inn
Montgomery Village, Vermont 05470

INNKEEPERS: Deb and Bob Winders

ADDRESS/TELEPHONE: 205 North Main Street, Route 118; (mailing address: P.O. Box 128); (802) 326-4507 or (800) 255-8661; fax (802) 326-2024

WEB SITE: www.blacklantern.com

ROOMS: 8, plus 7 suites; all with private bath, TV; suites with wood-burning fireplace; some with whirlpool tub or steam shower.

RATES: $109 to $202 BP.

OPEN: All year except mid-April to mid-June.

FACILITIES AND ACTIVITIES: Breakfast and dinner. Bar, outdoor hot tub, cross-country skiing. Nearby: Downhill skiing, fishing, swimming, golf, tennis, bicycle rentals.

When you get to Montgomery Village, you are nearly in Canada, perhaps 6 or 7 miles from the border. This is a quaint and quiet Vermont village, and the Black Lantern, which is on the National Register of Historic Places, has been nicely restored. The double-peaked roof on the old, 1803 farmhouse covers a typical north-country inn: small, friendly, just a little bit different. Whether you come in the snow for a skiing vacation or on a green summer day, there is a warm welcome. It is a pleasant surprise to encounter a rather sophisticated menu in this out-of-the-way corner of the world—French onion soup, stuffed mushrooms, and entrees such as duck with dried cherry and bourbon sauce, salmon with spicy maple glaze, and much more.

You can ski at Jay Peak, where there are 50 miles of trails for every kind of skier, outright novice to expert. Four Canadian mountains are not too far away, over the border, and ski-week tickets are available. Cross-country skiing starts at the inn door and is undoubtedly the best way to see beautiful Vermont in the winter.

Summer brings the joy of outdoor life. Fishing, swimming, golf, tennis, and hiking are all very near. You've heard about those country auctions, haven't you? Or would you rather spend the day browsing through antiques shops? Whatever you choose to do, there will be a superbly quiet night to catch up on your sleep. The inn's guest accommodations are very comfortable, all furnished with interesting Vermont antiques. The suites come with a

Jay Country Store

Just north of Montgomery Village on Route 242 in Jay is the Jay Country Store (802–988–4040), the perfect place to go for a taste of the real Vermont. "Sustenance for both body and spirit" is what they say you'll find here—and they are right. It's just fabulous, a destination in itself, filled to the brim with everything Vermont—handmade quilts, hand-forged lamps, gallery-quality primitives, trunks and boxes, cookbooks by Vermont authors, wonderful hand-painted pottery, lead-free ceramics, and tons more. Two levels of art galleries include lots of American folk art, including the largest selection anywhere of limited-edition lithographs by Will Moses, great-grandson of Grandma Moses. Also here are limited-edition prints by a famed New York naturalist and lithographer—come spend the afternoon and see for yourself.

Don't be afraid to come in hungry. The store also has a terrific deli counter and lunch room where you can feast on an old-fashioned country-style sandwich, a steaming bowl of homemade chili or soup, crispy pickles, and Green Mountain coffee. Fine wines, Vermont cheeses, honey, maple syrup, and a full line of groceries and baked goods are also here. The Christmas World shop includes decorations and ornaments from around the world as well as some handcrafted by local artisans. I've probably left out a whole other list of the things the shop carries—come to discover whatever I left out. Hours are 8:30 A.M. to 7:00 P.M. (and until 9:00 P.M. on Friday) every day of the year except Christmas and Thanksgiving.

fireplace and a whirlpool tub or steam shower. Some of these suites have a balcony. There is also a nice and bright lounge area with a woodstove and a TV.

HOW TO GET THERE: Go north from Stowe on Route 100 and turn left on Route 118 at Eden. This will take you into Montgomery Center. Continue down the main street and out of town, and before too long you will reach Montgomery Village and the inn. From Interstate 89 in Burlington turn right at St. Albans onto Route 105, toward Enosburg Falls. Pick up Route 118 at East Berkshire and follow it to Montgomery Village and the inn.

The Four Columns Inn
Newfane, Vermont 05345

INNKEEPERS: Bruce and Debbie Pfander

ADDRESS/TELEPHONE: West Street (mailing address: P.O. Box 278); 802) 365–7713 or (800) 787–6633; fax (802) 365–0022

WEB SITE: www.fourcolumnsinn.com

ROOMS: 15 rooms and suites; all with private bath and air-conditioning; most with gas log fireplaces; some with whirlpool and/or deck.

RATES: Rooms, $160 to $225 BP; suites, $265 to $385 BP. MAP packages available.

OPEN: All year.

FACILITIES AND ACTIVITIES: Restaurant closed Tuesday. Wheelchair access to dining room and bar. Bar, swimming pool. Nearby: Hiking, ice skating, skiing.

This stately Greek Revival Inn, circa 1832, is located on the most photographed town common in Vermont. The area is beautiful, and so is the inn. The Pfanders are continually upgrading the rooms and adding luxury touches. Many now have fireplaces, and suites may feature whirlpools, vaulted ceilings, skylights, and decks. I'm partial to Suite

12, with French doors opening to a deck with mountain views, and also like Suite 18, occupying the entire second floor of the garden wing, for its cheerful yellow print wallpaper and king-size sleigh bed.

The inn has an attractive living room with a fireplace where you can gather to visit with other guests. The beamed dining room with a fireplace has elegantly appointed tables.

The inn has long rated raves from food critics. Chef Greg Parks is the reason. With the inn for more than twenty years, he is nationally known and has attracted many celebrities to the dining room. He loves to use local suppliers. I've tasted the Vermont-raised, milk-fed veal he insists on, and it is heavenly. His menus always have a delicious soup of the day, as well as appetizers such as spicy Vermont quail with greens, goat cheese, and smoked bacon, or smoked salmon mousse. A salad with balsamic vinaigrette and a slice of Pecorino cheese comes before the main course.

Deciding on an entree is not an easy matter, when you have choices such as grilled salmon fillet and shrimp with coconut milk, lime, lemongrass, and green curry; seared venison loin with a spiced zinfandel glaze; or a veal T-bone with a sauce of five peppercorns, roasted garlic, and mushrooms. The desserts are outstanding. Guests are served a hearty country breakfast each morning.

The lounge has a pewter bar, which is very unusual, lots of plants, and country charm galore.

The inn's 150 acres include gardens, a stream, and two ponds. Ready to relax? There are rockers on the porch, lounges at the pool, and wooden Adirondack chairs by the stream, all just waiting for you.

HOW TO GET THERE: The inn is 220 miles from New York and 100 miles from Boston. Take exit 2 from Interstate 91 at Brattleboro to Route 30 north. The inn is in Newfane, 100 yards off Route 30, on your left.

Old Newfane Inn
Newfane, Vermont 05345

INNKEEPERS: Eric and Gundy Weindl

ADDRESS/TELEPHONE: Route 30 and Village Common; (802) 365-4427 or (800) 784-4427

WEB SITE: www.oldnewfaneinn.com

ROOMS: 10, all with private bath.

RATES: $135 to $165 CP. No credit cards.

OPEN: All year except April to mid-May, late October to mid-December, and Monday.

FACILITIES AND ACTIVITIES: Dinner, bar. Parking. Nearby: Skiing, swimming, hiking.

he inn is well named, for old it is—1787, to be exact. It has been carefully kept, however, and the weary traveler will find great comfort and fabulous food.

Almost all the rooms have twin beds and are large and tastefully furnished. Gundy is a very good decorator. There is an informal bar and lounge, and the dining room has beams and a brick wall with a fireplace, giving it a wonderful feeling of colonial warmth and good cheer. The floors here are polished to a turn. And not just run-of-the-mill glassware for the inn. The drinks I had before lunch were served in crystal.

Like his counterpart at the Four Columns Inn, Eric Weindl has been here for a long time, more than thirty years, and he has built a notable reputation for his prowess in the kitchen. It is unusual for one small hamlet to have two such talented chefs, and Newfane has become a popular destination with gourmets. Eric trained in Switzerland, and his menu remains European, with dishes such as veal goulash with spaetzle; snails, Burgundian style; and game in season.

His soups are a bit different and very good. I have tried both the cold strawberry and the creamed watercress. Loved them both. By the way, I hate calf's liver, but Eric asked me to try his. What magic he performed I do not know, but I ate every bite. Veal is king here. Eric butchers his own, so he gets the exact cuts he wants. Of course, the menu also has seafood, lamb, fowl, pheasant, venison, and fine steaks. The dessert menu reads like poetry, from the flaming suzette and jubilee to a fabulous omelet surprise. There are also some cream pies demanding that you do not even think of calories.

HOW TO GET THERE: Take exit 2 from Interstate 91 in Brattleboro, and follow Route 30 north. The inn is on the corner of Court Street and Route 30, on the left in Newfane.

North Hero House
North Hero, Vermont 05474

INNKEEPER: John Martinez

ADDRESS/TELEPHONE: Route 2 (mailing address: P.O. Box 207); (802) 372-4732 or (888) 525-3644; fax (802) 372-3218

WEB SITE: www.northherohouse.com

ROOMS: 26 in 4 buildings; all with private bath; most with screened porch overlooking the lake; some with fireplaces and Jacuzzis.

RATES: $95 to $295 BP (CP November to April).

OPEN: Daily May to November, weekends Thanksgiving to April 30.

FACILITIES AND ACTIVITIES: Dinner (Friday and Saturday only out of season), full license, TV in living room, outdoor hot tub, games, swimming, boating, tennis, shuffleboard, fishing, ice skating, cross-country skiing, ice fishing.

*G*etting here is a treat for the eyes. North Hero is the county seat of Grand Isle, one of the Champlain Islands. It's so scenic and offers so much to do. And as you look across Lake Champlain, you can see Mount Mansfield.

North Hero House was founded in 1891. Most of the rooms, located in four buildings, have screened porches overlooking the lake. There are spacious lakeside rooms in Homestead, which is done in barn siding; Southwind, made out of pine; and Cove House, in brick.

There is outdoor dining on the patio overlooking the lake. Inside are a colonial-style dining room and a very bright greenhouse–dining room behind it.

Dinner is a real treat. There are several different appetizers, often including delicious house-cured gravlox. Entrees include steak, chicken, and lamb, all done in many interesting ways, as well as seafood—salmon, fresh walleye, scallops, and shrimp. The inn's famous lobster buffet is a favorite Friday-night feature in July and August. If you don't feel like a formal meal, Oscar's Oasis offers a casual menu of salads, burgers, ribs, and snacks such as buffalo wings.

In the morning, breakfast offerings are fresh fruit, coffee, tea, cold cereal, and freshly baked muffins (blueberry, cinnamon apple, and carrot are some of

the favorites). During the warm-weather season, May to October, guests may order from the full menu as well.

The inn offers boat rentals—canoes, kayaks, fishing boats—or come in your own boat. Fishing is good for bass, walleye, and Northern pike. Looking for another kind of adventure? Try a guided kayak tour of the islands. Need to relax? The sandy beach and lawn chairs are inviting.

In winter, there's still plenty to do, what with ice skating, cross-country skiing, ice-fishing, excursions, and special events such as murder-mystery weekends and wine-tasting dinners.

The outdoor hot tub is a perfect ending to the day whatever the season.

Champ is a cousin of Scotland's famous Nessie and lives in the lake. Come up and see if you can spot her.

HOW TO GET THERE: Take exit 17 from Interstate 89 onto Route 2 west about 17 miles to North Hero. The inn is in the center of the village.

The Norwich Inn
Norwich, Vermont 05055

INNKEEPERS: Sally and Tim Wilson

ADDRESS/TELEPHONE: 325 Main Street (mailing address: P.O. Box 908); (802) 649-1143

WEB SITE: www.norwichinn.com

ROOMS: 27, including 4 two-bedroom suites; all with private bath, TV, and phone.

RATES: $79 to $149 EP.

OPEN: All year.

FACILITIES AND ACTIVITIES: Breakfast, lunch, dinner, Sunday brunch; bar; dining room closed Monday. Nearby: Swimming, canoeing, golf, skiing, tennis, biking, hiking.

*R*ight on the sign for the inn it says SINCE 1797, and it is truly said, because travelers up the beautiful Connecticut River Valley have been finding a warm welcome at this grand old house for well over 200 years. It is just a mile away from Dartmouth College, and alumni, skiers, tourists, and commercial travelers all find a special homelike atmosphere here that is dignified but a lot of fun.

The friendly bar and lounge area is named the Jasper Murdock Ale House after the inn's first owner. All the draft beers are brewed on the premises, just as they were in colonial "public houses" before the advent of commercial breweries. Some of them are Whistling Pig Red Ale, Jasper Murdock's Old Ale, Pompanoosuc Wheat Beer, and Fuggle & Barley Corn, and there are more. Go and have fun.

The food is glorious. The Sunday champagne brunch offers you a glass of bubbly or a mimosa, along with eggs Benedict, a crepe or quiche of the day, or chicken duffina (sautéed with artichoke hearts in Madeira and cream). Dinner is always good here. Blackened carpaccio is an appetizer done with thinly sliced sirloin, capers, and garlic rounds. For entrees there are poached North Atlantic salmon, crisp roasted boneless duckling with raspberry glaze, and

escallops of veal with julienne prosciutto, among others. The desserts are wonderful, and the wine list is one of the most extensive I have seen.

Breakfasts are ample, with fruit, cereals, toast, muffins, eggs any way, crepes, French toast, pancakes, and a deep-dish quiche of the day. There is a very full lunch menu; if you can't find something to eat, then you must not be very hungry.

The rooms have a mix of furnishings, some canopied beds and some iron and brass beds. All have pretty print wallpapers and a warm, old-fashioned appeal. Guest pets are welcome in the carriage house rooms.

Make sure you ask for a copy of the history of the inn—it's fascinating.

HOW TO GET THERE: Take exit 13 from Interstate 91. Go west a bit less than 1 mile to the center of town. The inn is on your left.

The Four Chimneys
Old Bennington, Vermont 05201

INNKEEPERS: Lynn and Pete Green

ADDRESS/TELEPHONE: 21 West Road; (802) 447-3500; fax (802) 447-3692

WEB SITE: www.fourchimneys.com

ROOMS: 11, all with private bath, air-conditioning, phone, TV and wireless Internet; 8 with fireplace; 1 specially equipped for the physically disabled.

RATES: $115 to $230 BP.

OPEN: All year.

FACILITIES AND ACTIVITIES: Dinner, bar and lounge. Full license. Nearby: Facilities at Mount Anthony Country Club.

This stately white home is on an eleven-acre estate in historic Old Bennington and boasts a highly regarded dining room. When you come into the inn, straight ahead is the bar and lounge. The lounge is so comfortable, with a fireplace and light-colored couches and chairs. If you turn right down the hall, you'll find the dining room, and the food is grand. For dinner, appetizers might include sautéed escargots or Brie en croute with poached pears and walnuts. Main courses could be duck breast, lamb, fillet mignon, free-range quail, or lots more really good choices. Desserts? Oh boy—one is French pecan torte too good to resist. In summer the porch overlooking the gardens is ambrosia.

There are eleven guest rooms, and they are beauties. They have queen- or king-size beds, quilts and comforters, and luxurious linens and towels. Cut-glass lamps in the bedrooms are pretty and give good light for reading. On the third floor the bathroom has a huge Jacuzzi for two, with seats. The icehouse has a wonderful suite; so does the carriage house.

This inn is a wonderful setting for weddings or family reunions.

HOW TO GET THERE: From Route 7 north or south, take Route 9 west in Bennington to the inn.

Johnny Seesaw's
Peru, Vermont 05152

INNKEEPER: Gary Okun

ADDRESS/TELEPHONE: Route 11; (802) 824–5533 or (800) 424–2729

WEB SITE: www.jseesaw.com

ROOMS: 18, plus 4 cottages with fireplaces; all with private bath, TV, phone.

RATES: $60 to $230 BP. Pets welcome.

OPEN: All year except end of skiing season to Memorial Day.

FACILITIES AND ACTIVITIES: Dinner, liquor license. Wheelchair access to dining room. Game room, swimming pool, tennis. Nearby: Skiing, hunting, golf, horseback riding, fishing, hiking, biking, outlet shopping.

Skiing Magazine once said that this inn has the best Yankee cuisine in New England. The food is good, tasty country food prepared with imagination, featuring home-baked bread and homemade soup.

The inn has a unique character, mostly because of the guests who keep coming back. It is set 2,000 feet up, on Bromley Mountain. The 65-by-25-foot marble-rimmed pool is a great summer gathering place, and the tennis court is always ready. There are six nearby golf courses, and riding horses can be hired in Peru.

For the many skiers who come to Vermont, Bromley's chairlifts and GLM Ski School are right next door. Stratton Mountain, the Viking Ski Touring Center, and Wild Wings X-C are but a few minutes away.

For fishers and hunters, or those who wish to take up the sport, the Orvis Fly-Fishing and Wing Shooting schools in nearby Manchester have excellent instruction. Classes are held regularly, and participants can stay at the inn. The nearby towns boast many attractive and interesting shops.

The circular fireplace in the lounge really attracts me at the end of a long day, to say nothing of the cushioned platform along one side of the library. Merlin, the inn dog, will keep you company here. Wood-paneled guest rooms are cozy and cheerful.

There is a lot of history here. The back of the extensive menu details the legend of the inn and is well worth reading.

HOW TO GET THERE: The inn is 220 miles from New York, 150 miles from Boston. From Route 7 take Route 11 right at Manchester Depot. The inn is 6 miles east, on Vermont Route 11. From Interstate 91 follow exit 6 to Route 103 to Chester. The inn is 20 miles west, on Vermont Route 11.

Wiley Inn
Peru, Vermont 05152

INNKEEPERS: Judy and Jerry Goodman

ADDRESS/TELEPHONE: Route 11 (mailing address: P.O. Box 37); (802) 824-6600 or (888) 843-6600; fax (802) 824-4195

WEB SITE: www.wileyinn.com

ROOMS: 16, all with private bath; some with Jacuzzi, fireplace.

RATES: $115 to $250 BP.

OPEN: All year except two weeks in May.

FACILITIES AND ACTIVITIES: Breakfast, picnic lunch available, dinner for inn guests, by reservation. Swimming pool. Large Jacuzzi outside. Gift shop. Nearby: Hiking, skiing, horseback riding, fishing, golf, canoeing, antiquing, skiing, sleigh rides, ice skating, snowmobiling.

The Wiley Inn has been greeting guests for more than half a century. The main house was built in 1835 and was turned into an inn in 1943. Over the years it has been a farmhouse, stagecoach stop, and tearoom. It has changed a lot since it was built, having had at least ten additions, which is typical of Vermont's continuous architecture.

Jerry and Judy are friendly and pleasant innkeepers who do a good job of making guests feel right at home. The lower living room has a fireplace, a bar, a huge couch, and tons of things to do, such as a player piano with a lot of rolls, a television and VCR with a library of films (including a lot of Disney films for the kids), and games.

The library is a good place for a glass of wine, a quiet read, or good conversation. There's free Internet access if you want to check your e-mail.

Guest rooms range from rustic, wood-paneled country decor to canopy beds in Victorian rooms with clawfoot tubs. Some romantic rooms come with whirlpool.

You will always find something to do at the inn. The swimming pool is heated and has a deck; there's an outdoor children's play set for climbing, sliding, and swinging; and the Long and Appalachian Trails are nearby. So are several golf courses, horseback riding, fishing, and the alpine slide and other amusements at Bromley. During fall the foliage is king, and in winter Bromley, Stratton, Magic, and Okemo Mountains beckon downhill skiers. Cross-country ski touring centers are within minutes. Go and enjoy.

Dinner is offered by reservation for guests of the inn in season; families are most welcome. The fireside bar in the living room offers après-ski refreshments and year-round evening bar service, with a nice selection of wines and both local and imported beers.

HOW TO GET THERE: From Interstate 91 take exit 6 to Route 103 to Chester. Go left on Route 11. The inn is 20 miles west, in Peru.

Casa Bella
Pittsfield, Vermont 05762

INNKEEPERS: Franco and Susan Cacozza

ADDRESS/TELEPHONE: P.O. Box 685; (802) 746–8943 or (877) 746–8943

WEB SITE: www.casabellainn.com

ROOMS: 8, all with private bath.

RATES: $100 to $145 BP.

OPEN: All year.

FACILITIES AND ACTIVITIES: Breakfast and dinner, 7 days. Beer and wine license.

This 1835 inn, formerly the Pittsfield Inn, has Italian owners and a new personality, a bit of Tuscany in the Green Mountains, with authentic Northern Italian cuisine. The menu features calamari, lots of pasta choices, and main dishes such as gamberoni, jumbo shrimps sautéed with diced tomato, lemon, and white wine; veal marsala; and saltimbocca alla Romana, veal scallopini topped with ham, cheese, and sage.

Redecorated guest rooms vary in decor, but all are country comfortable, with colorful print wallpapers, antiques, and cozy quilts on the beds.

The inn is nestled in the tiny village of Pittsfield, surrounded by the mountains and just 8 miles north of Killington and minutes from two PGA golf courses. The area is great for outdoor fun year-round. Biking, hiking, and fly

fishing are prime in season, and when the snow falls, skiing, snowshoeing, and snowmobiling are on the agenda.

If shopping and antiquing are your favorite sports, it's nice to know that Manchester and Woodstock are close enough for a day's outing.

HOW TO GET THERE: The inn is 20 miles northeast of Rutland. Take Route 4 east and Route 100 north to the village of Pittsfield. The inn is on the green.

The Golden Stage Inn
Proctorsville, Vermont 05153

INNKEEPERS: Sandy and Peter Gregg

ADDRESS/TELEPHONE: 399 Depot Street; (802) 226–7744 or (800) 253–8226

WEB SITE: www.goldenstageinn.com

ROOMS: 10, most with private bath; 1 suite.

RATES: $79 to $300 BP.

OPEN: All year.

FACILITIES AND ACTIVITIES: Swimming pool, bike tours. Nearby: Hiking, skiing, alpine slide, gondola rides, antiquing, golf, biking, fishing, summer theater.

The Golden Stage Inn still is known locally as the Skinner place, for Otis, the actor, and his daughter Cornelia Otis Skinner, the author. The house was built more than 200 years ago, shortly before Vermont's founding in 1791. It was once a stagecoach stop and is reputed to have been a stop on the Underground Railroad.

When you drive in, you immediately notice the rockers on the porch and the abundance of flowers that surround the inn. It's very pretty in the summertime. Sit and rock on the porch and enjoy the breathtaking views of the Black River Valley and Okemo Mountain.

One of the rooms has its own little porch. There are lovely quilts, many antiques, and lots of books. The living room, with its cozy fireplace, is very comfortable after a day of doing your own thing. There are all sorts of games and puzzles, too, but maybe all you want to do is sit and knit or read.

The food is delicious. Tomato bisque is my favorite appetizer. Roast duck with a mango wine sauce and pork tenderloin in an orange-ginger sauce are just two of the good entrees. A chocolate walnut torte makes any chocolate lover swoon. Scones on Sunday morning are a heav-

olive Metcalf

enly way to start the day. The inn also has a huge vegetable and herb garden, so necessary to the good cooking here.

Ten acres of rolling lawns, beautiful gardens, and trees are just what you need for a picnic, a long walk, or simply being alone. Surrounding this haven of loveliness are thousands of acres of forests to hike in and four mountains noted for their good skiing. They are Okemo Mountain, Mount Ascutney, Bromley (fun in summer, too, with its exciting alpine slide down the mountain), and Killington Peak, which has year-round gondola rides, the longest in the United States. Killington often has one of the longest ski seasons in the East.

For nonskiers the inn has many workshops in conjunction with Fletcher Farm School for Arts and Crafts, located just 1 mile away.

Biking from inn to inn is another way to see this wonderful country. While you bike to the next inn, a support van transfers your luggage. This is my idea of neat.

The whole first floor is handicapped accessible. A nice touch for deaf guests are rooms specially equipped for the deaf; they have Strobe lights for the fire alarm. The Otis room has a print of Otis Skinner as Romeo—this room has a double hideaway bed, an iron queen-size bed, and books.

Also in residence are the inn's two sheep, 'Lil April and Shayla.

The inn has a cookie jar that is never empty. Nice.

HOW TO GET THERE: From Interstate 91 take exit 6 to Route 103 north toward Chester/Ludlow, then take a right off Route 103 at the Proctorsville sign. The inn is the first driveway immediately on the right.

Arts and Crafts in Quechee

Downer's Mill in Quechee is now the site of Simon Pearce's beautiful glassworks, operated in part through the harnessing of the Ottauquechee River's hydropower. In the center of Quechee overlooking the waterfall of the dam and the covered bridge, you will find the mill and its glassworks. Visitors can watch the glass-blowing process and view the hydroelectric turbine that fuels Simon's glass furnace. You may also see a potter throwing a piece of pottery on the wheel. You can admire or shop for the finished products; both first-quality pieces and seconds are sold in the lovely retail shop. Along with the glassware are Simon Pearce pottery, plus quilts, sweaters, baskets, linens, jewelry, and other Vermont-made handcrafts. The Simon Pearce Restaurant at the mill serves lunch and dinner daily. For information on the glassworks and shop, call (802) 295-2711. For restaurant information or reservations, call (802) 295-1470.

Parker House
Quechee, Vermont 05059

INNKEEPERS: Adam and Alexandra LaNoue-Adler

ADDRESS/TELEPHONE: 1792 Quechee Main Street (mailing address: P.O. Box 780); (802) 295-6077

WEB SITE: www.theparkerhouseinn.com

ROOMS: 7, all with private bath; some with air-conditioning, Jacuzzi or spa shower.

RATES: $110 to $195 BP.

OPEN: All year.

FACILITIES AND ACTIVITIES: Dinner. Nearby: Woodstock shops, Dartmouth College, Quechee Gorge.

Parker House Inn, a registered National Historic Site, is a brick Victorian beauty built in 1857 by a Vermont state senator, Joseph C. Parker. The Ottauquechee River flows along the rear of the property.

All the rooms were refurbished in 2005 by the new innkeepers, who are actually old hands, coming here from L'auberge Country Inn in Maine. Walls are painted in decorator colors, and cozy floral comforters are at the foot of the beds. My friend Audrey and I had Emily, the former master bedroom. At the top of the steps is another beauty, Rebecca; down the hall are Joseph and Walter, which look over the river. The third floor has cozy rooms under the eaves.

Chef-owned inns are often special, and this one is no exception. Dinner is by candlelight with soft music in the background in a dining room decorated with vintage mirrors, and with antique china and garden flowers on each table. On warm evenings, you may dine on the porch overlooking the river.

The menu is French and changes with the seasons. You might start with wonderful homemade country-style pâté or baked Brie, followed by pork medallions, grilled salmon, stuffed chicken breast, sea bass Provençal, or bouillabaisse. Save room for dessert; they are too good to miss.

There's much to do here, with Woodstock and Hanover, New Hampshire, each a short drive away, but tiny Quechee has a couple of attractions of its own. It is worth a trip in mid-June to see the annual balloon festival, with colorful balloons taking off and soaring over the village green. And be sure to have a look at Quechee Gorge, approximately 200 feet deep and truly an amazing sight.

HOW TO GET THERE: Take exit 1 off Interstate 89 north. Turn left on Route 4 for 4 miles, crossing the Quechee Gorge. Turn right at the flashing traffic light. Cross the covered bridge and turn left. The inn is on the left.

The Quechee Inn at Marshland Farm
Quechee, Vermont 05059

INNKEEPER: Michael Maderia

ADDRESS/TELEPHONE: Quechee Main Street; (802) 295–3133 or (800) 235–3133; fax (802) 295–6587

WEB SITE: www.quecheeinn.com

ROOMS: 24, all with private bath, phone, and TV.

RATES: $90 to $245 BP.

OPEN: All year.

FACILITIES AND ACTIVITIES: Dinner nightly; lounge, full license. Wheelchair access to dining room. Cross-country ski learning center, fly-fishing school, bicycles and canoes to rent, fishing, hiking. Nearby: Downhill skiing. Privileges at Quechee Club, including two eighteen-hole golf courses, tennis, indoor and outdoor pools, sauna, skiing.

The first time that I saw and heard Quechee Gorge, I was standing on the bridge that spans it. Now I know another way to approach this remarkable quirk of nature. The inn is but a half mile from it, an easy and beautiful walk on a well-marked footpath.

The inn was a private home from 1793 until 1976 and has been beautifully converted to an inn. Rooms in the inn have a variety of beds, doubles to king size, and some lovely queen canopy beds. Seven more guest rooms, in the wing off the original building, have windows overlooking the meadow and lake. All rooms are equipped with private bath and color cable television, and the whole inn is air-conditioned.

There are paintings by local artists in the dining room and a beautiful awning over the porch. Adjoining the dining room is a small library used for meetings or private dining. It's a real treat to be able to have a business meeting at a place like this. The living room has an abundance of comfortable chairs and couches, a piano, color television, books, and a fireplace. One feels at home here any season of the year.

The food here is also excellent. Appetizers include lamb sausage crepe and gingered crab salad. Among the varied entrees may be crispy Long Island duckling, poached Maine salmon, black Angus sirloin, or a cassoulet of lamb. The inn recently introduced a popular new alternate supper menu featuring lighter dishes such as chicken potpie, crab cakes, or vegetarian pasta.

The inn guests have club privileges at the nearby private Quechee Club. The two championship golf courses are breathtakingly scenic and are challenging. You can also play tennis and squash here for a fee.

HOW TO GET THERE: From Interstate 91 take Interstate 89 north to exit 1. Go west on Route 4 for 1²/₁₀ miles, then right on Quechee Main Street for 1 mile to the inn.

Three Stallion Inn
Randolph, Vermont 05060

INNKEEPER: Martina E. L. Rutkovsky; Sam and Jinny Sammis, owners

ADDRESS/TELEPHONE: Lower Stock Farm Road; (802) 728–5575 or (800) 424–5575; fax (802) 728–4036

WEB SITE: www.3stallioninn.com

ROOMS: 15; 13 with private bath, air-conditioning, phone, Internet access.

RATES: $105 to $190 CP.

OPEN: All year.

FACILITIES AND ACTIVITIES: Dinner. Two all-weather tennis courts, pool. 1,300 acres with 35 kilometers of trails for mountain biking or cross-country skiing, two stocked trout ponds. Nearby: Downhill skiing, golf, swimming and fishing in White River, Chandler Music Hall.

The full name of the inn is Three Stallion Inn at the Green Mountain Stock Farm, a sign that this valley is the original birthplace of the Morgan horse. The emphasis used to be on riding, but today this is an inn with all kinds of recreation. The 1,300-acre property includes a swimming pool, two tennis courts, two stocked trout ponds, and 35 kilometers of trails for mountain biking or cross-country skiing. You can rent equipment right on the property. The Montague Golf Club, one of the oldest in the state, adjoins the inn's property along the White River. Swimming and fishing in the river is also fun, and at the end of the day, you can relax in the inn's whirlpool and sauna or take advantage of the well-equipped fitness center.

Guest rooms and suites are spacious. Two-bedroom suites are perfect for families. Guests wake up to a bountiful continental breakfast of fresh fruit, juices and cereals, homemade breads, and freshly made granola from a local farm.

Dinner at Lippitt's Restaurant and Morgan's Pub changes monthly and emphasizes foods of the season. The summer menu might begin with steamed mussels or crepes stuffed with diced shrimp, spinach, boursin cheese, and gratineed tomato sauce. Entrees include Paella Valencia, with clams, mussels, shrimp, chicken, and chorizo nestled in saffron rice; roasted pork tenderloin stuffed with spiced peaches and sweet onions; or veal scallopini, with ham, mushrooms, and tomato and white vermouth sauce over sweet corn–studded sage grits. Lighter choices such as burgers, sandwiches, and salads are always on the menu. In summer, you can enjoy a cocktail before dinner on the covered deck overlooking the lawns, trout pond, and lovely gardens.

With all these attractions, part of the inn property is being devoted to lots for private homes.

An added bonus in the town of Randolph is the Chandler Music Hall, featuring chamber music, jazz, and popular concerts. If you want more amusement, the town also offers a movie theater, bowling alley, and ice-skating rink.

HOW TO GET THERE: Take exit 4 off Interstate 89. Go 1⁸/₁₀ miles toward Randolph. Turn left on Stock Farm Road and go ⁷/₁₀ mile to the inn.

The Inn at Saxtons River
Saxtons River, Vermont 05154

INNKEEPER: B. Stuart Pease

ADDRESS/TELEPHONE: 27 Main Street; (802) 869–2110; fax (802) 869–3033

WEB SITE: www.innsaxtonsriver.com

ROOMS: 15, all with private bath; 2 with porch.

RATES: $130 to $160 CP.

OPEN: All year.

FACILITIES AND ACTIVITIES: Dinner nightly except Monday; Sunday brunch. Pub open nightly. Nearby: Downhill and cross-country skiing, horse-drawn sleigh rides, country fairs.

This wonderful Victorian inn started life in 1903 as a hotel and then became an inn several years later. It's a rare gem. When you see it, you'll see what I mean.

The guest rooms are well decorated, and two have private porches, so you can sit and listen to the quiet. There's a Victorian pub, and the porches have rockers. What a comfortable way to spend a summer evening. Winter is glorious. Take a sleigh ride through the pristine white snow or just enjoy the warmth of the inn and the fireplace.

When you enter the inn, the parlor is on the left. It has a baby grand piano, fireplace, and good couches and chairs. On the right is the pub, and ahead is the dining room.

The menus are enticing. One really excellent appetizer is the baked cheese; it's a blend of three cheeses, sun-dried tomatoes, tarragon, and Dijon mustard, all wrapped in puff pastry. Go on to delicious soups, salads, and entrees such as roast Vermont turkey, sautéed pork medallions, boneless roast duck, and pasta of the day. Espresso and cappuccino and lovely desserts cap off the meal, especially nice when they are served in the living room in front of the fire. A lighter menu is always available in the pub and also in the dining room.

The brochure says a lot: Service is the key word, and the service is the same that has been practiced in small New England hotels and inns for more than a century. It is "above and beyond."

HOW TO GET THERE: Take Interstate 91 to exit 5. Proceed on Route 5 north to Route 121 to Saxtons River and the inn.

Inn at Shelburne Farms
Shelburne, Vermont 05482

INNKEEPER: Karen Polihronakis

ADDRESS/TELEPHONE: 1611 Harbor Road; (802) 985–8498; fax (802) 985–8123

WEB SITE: www.shelburnefarms.org

ROOMS: 24; 17 with private bath; 2 cottages.

RATES: $135 to $395 CP.

OPEN: Mid-May to mid-October.

FACILITIES AND ACTIVITIES: Breakfast, dinner, Sunday brunch. Bar, library; tennis court, lake beach and swimming, boating, billiards, 8 miles of trails. Nearby: Hiking, fishing, biking, sailing, golf.

*I*f you want to live like a turn-of-the-twentieth-century millionaire, here is your chance. The Queen Anne–style, sixty-room mansion on a point overlooking Lake Champlain was the home of William Seward and Lila Vanderbilt Webb on what is still a model 1,400-acre working farm. The Webbs had their mansion designed in shingle, slate, and limestone to blend with the landscape.

The house retains the feel of a family residence, and many rooms still have the original furnishings. They vary in size and decor, but even some of the more modest chambers, such as the Oak Room, with a shared bath, may offer peerless lake views. Others overlook the grounds (designed by Frederick Law Olmsted) and the gardens.

One of the most lavish choices is Overlook, Lila Webb's bedroom, with outstanding views of the lake, meadows, and gardens of the estate. Her dressing room is now the South Room, an example of several rooms where the tiles surrounding the fireplace inspired the color scheme.

The Webb Room, originally used as a nursery, became Dr. Webb's bedroom after his children grew up. The spiral staircase was added to connect his quarters with a dressing room and valet's bedroom above, now a separate guest room called White. The Renaissance Revival–style bedroom furniture in the Webb Room originally belonged to Lila's father, William Henry Vanderbilt.

The Brown Room, belonging to Vanderbilt Webb, the youngest son in the family, has a fine set of marquetry furniture that features sycamore and holly inlaid in mahogany. The painted furniture in the Louis XVI Room was purchased for this room in 1899, and the use of pastel colors, floral patterns, and elaborate applied decorations was the style popular at that time.

Keeping up such a huge old property is difficult, and you may find signs of genteel shabbiness here and there, but the total experience is first-rate.

For privacy, opt for the Treehouse, an 1890 bungalow nestled among the trees overlooking the lake, with a porch and a small kitchenette. The Pottery, built around 1945 as a pottery shed for Aileen Webb, wife of Vanderbilt Webb, also has a kitchenette and a patio.

Meals are served in the stately Marble Dining Room or on the terrace. The menu features food grown in the market garden on the estate and on local Vermont farms. A typical dinner may begin with asparagus soup, beef carpaccio, or pan-seared scallops. Among a long list of entrees you may find seared Alaskan halibut cheeks, free-range duck, crusted tenderloin of beef, pan-braised rabbit with asparagus risotto, or rack of lamb with rosemary polenta cakes. The inn does not serve lunch, but picnic lunches are available for

Down on the Farm

The Webb family created Shelburne Farms as an experimental agricultural showplace in 1886, and Webb descendants have continued it as a model of progressive cattle and dairy farming, as well as a demonstration cheese-making operation. Many educational programs are held for children and adults. A herd of 125 purebred Brown Swiss cows produces milk for the farm. The tour includes the manor house, the great barns and the dairy building, flower and vegetable gardens, and exhibits of Vermont agriculture. Farm activities focus on caring for animals, a personal connection that many visitors have never had a chance to experience. Farm animals in residence include cows and calves, goats and kids, sheep and lambs, pigs and piglets, rabbits, bantam hens, ducks, turkeys, miniature donkeys, Clydesdale and Belgian draft horses, and honeybees. The farm store features Vermont crafts and farm products, including the very tasty Shelburne farmhouse cheddar cheese. The $6.00 admission includes the chance to enjoy the farm's 8 miles of scenic walking trails. For a calendar of events, call (802) 985-8686 or log on to www.shelburne farms.org.

guests. Coffee and muffins are complimentary for guests, and a full breakfast is available in the dining room.

The lavish grounds of the estate offer many diversions. Stroll the 8 miles of walking trails, play a set of tennis, or take a swim in the lake. Guests of the inn are considered guests of the farm, with complimentary tours of this exceptional property during your stay and the chance to enjoy many special events, including family programs, bird walks, campfires, and several concerts of the Vermont Mozart Festival.

Children can watch and take part in farm activities such as milking a cow, collecting eggs, brushing the horses and donkeys, butter making, and carding and spinning wool.

Proceeds from the inn help support the farm's environmental programs. HOW TO GET THERE: Shelburne is just south of Burlington. From Boston: Take Interstate 93 north to Interstate 89. Follow I-89 north to Vermont exit 13 (Interstate 189). At the first traffic light, turn left onto Route 7S. Follow for 5 miles to traffic light in the center of Shelburne. Turn right at this light onto Harbor Road. Follow to the first stop sign and turn left into Shelburne

Farms. From New York: Take the New York Thruway north to Interstate 87 north. Take exit 20 for Route 149 to Route 4 north. Take exit 2 (in Vermont) for Route 22A and follow it to Vergennes, Vermont. Turn north on Route 7. In the center of Shelburne, turn left at the light onto Harbor Road. At first stop sign, turn left into Shelburne Farms.

The Londonderry Inn
South Londonderry, Vermont 05155

INNKEEPERS: Chrisman and Maya Kearn

ADDRESS/TELEPHONE: 8 Melendy Hill Road, Route 100; (802) 824–5226 or (800) 644–5226

WEB SITE: www.londonderryinn.com

ROOMS: 21 rooms and family suites; all with private bath, TV.

RATES: $99 to $246 BP.

OPEN: Summer, fall, and ski season.

FACILITIES AND ACTIVITIES: Dinner. Swimming pool, nature trail, indoor aviary, sledding hill, playground, game room, gallery, and gift shop. Nearby: Skiing, horseback riding, hiking, canoeing, summer theater.

The location is lovely, high on a hill overlooking the West River. Once a dairy farm, circa 1826, the house has grown into a comfortable rambling inn with many common areas, a great place for families as well as grown-ups. You can relax in the living room in front of the big stone fireplace or head for the movie room. Three major ski areas are within a ten-minute drive, and there's sledding on the expansive property. A spring-fed swimming pool and nearby hiking trails call in summer. With so much to do for all ages, and dormitory rooms available, this is an ideal inn for family reunions.

The old woodshed is now the dining room, where you'll have a hearty vegetarian buffet breakfast. Choices include multi-whole-grain pancakes or sourdough French toast with Londonderry-made maple syrup; local free-range eggs scrambled with green onions, tomatoes, and Londonderry's Taylor Farm smoked gouda cheese; plus home-fried potatoes and onions. Only organic foods are served. In the afternoon, fresh baked cookies are served with hot apple cider, cocoa, and tea.

In your room, you'll find fresh country decor, hand-hooked rugs, teddy bears, quilts, and folk art. Several rooms can be combined to form a family suite. Room 29 is special, with a king-size bed and fireplace.

Chrisman and Maya enjoy the natural world and are committed to conservation and to natural organic foods. Many of their guests go home inspired, as well.

HOW TO GET THERE: Take exit 2 from Interstate 91 at Brattleboro, and follow Route 30 north to Rawsonville. Then take Route 100 north (right turn) for 4 miles. The inn is on your left before the bridge.

Kedron Valley Inn ♥ 👪
South Woodstock, Vermont 05071

INNKEEPERS: Nicole and Jack Maiden

ADDRESS/TELEPHONE: Route 106 (mailing address: P.O. Box 145); (802) 457–1473 or (800) 836–1193; fax (802) 457–4469

WEB SITE: www.kedronvalleyinn.com

ROOMS: 23 rooms and 5 suites, in 3 buildings; all with private bath, TV; many with fireplace or Franklin stove; 5 with Jacuzzi.

RATES: $133 to $299 BP.

OPEN: All year except April and a few days before Thanksgiving.

FACILITIES AND ACTIVITIES: Dinner daily in season; closed Tuesday and Wednesday November through July. Tavern, lounge, meeting facilities;

private beach on swimming pond, hiking. Nearby: Golf, horseback riding, tennis, skiing.

In the peaceful countryside south of Woodstock, in a hamlet with more horses than cars, this rambling inn with rockers on the front porch has been welcoming visitors since the 1820s. It is the picture of tranquillity, set on fifteen acres with tall trees, a babbling brook, and a spring-fed pond. There's lots of colorful history, especially in the 1860s, when fugitive slaves traveling the Underground Railroad to freedom were harbored here in a secret attic passageway. You may even recognize the inn; it was the backdrop for a Budweiser Christmas commercial featuring the Clydesdale horses pulling a sleigh.

The Maidens have maintained the comfortable country ambience that has made Kedron Valley a longtime favorite. Rooms are furnished with canopy beds, hooked rugs, rockers, needlepoint, and family memorabilia. Most have a fireplace or a woodstove.

The dining room has wide windows to bring in the scenery, two cozy fireplaces, and an excellent contemporary American menu, changing with the seasons to take advantage of local produce and products. The goat cheese is made nearby, the wild mushrooms come from a nearby forest, and local lamb and game birds are featured.

You might start with the soup of the day, barbecue baby-back ribs, or pierogies filled with potato and cheese. Entrees include rack of lamb, smoked duck breast, oven-roasted pork tenderloin, and sautéed scallops. You won't want to miss desserts such as maple walnut cake, orange caramel cream puffs, or crème brûlée.

When you aren't feeling quite so hungry, a lighter menu is always available in the tavern. Nor are kids forgotten at this family-friendly inn. The children's menu features favorites such as hot dogs, spaghetti, and chicken fingers.

This is a fine choice in summer, with a private lake for swimming and two white-sand beaches, one for adults, one for families. Within walking distance is a thirty-horse stable with mounts for all levels of riders. And while you may feel a million miles from everywhere, Woodstock's shops and winter skiing are only 6 miles away.

HOW TO GET THERE: Take Route 4 to Woodstock. Turn south on Route 106 and go 5 miles to South Woodstock and the inn.

The Hartness House
Springfield, Vermont 05156

INNKEEPERS: Alex and Alla Leonenko

ADDRESS/TELEPHONE: 30 Orchard Street; (802) 885-2115 or (800) 732-4789; fax (802) 885-2207

WEB SITE: www.hartnesshouse.com

ROOMS: 45, all with private bath, air-conditioning, and TV.

The Hartness House Observatory

Unique among all the inns in this book, the Hartness House is the only one with a historic observatory. James Hartness was an aviator, the builder of Vermont's first airport, an inventor who patented more than 120 different machines, as well as the governor of the state from 1920 to 1922. As if that were not enough, he was also an astronomer. When he completed his stone-and-shingle mansion, he added an observatory and a 600-power Turret Equatorial Telescope. Built in 1910, it was one of the first tracking telescopes in the nation. You can see this telescope and others at the James Hartness–Russell Porter Amateur Astronomy Museum at the inn, which also features important amateur-astronomy works. In addition, the Hartness House offers a unique underground museum and an antique 1910 Brashear telescope and observatory. The Hartness House Observatory is reached from the inn by way of a secret 240-foot underground tunnel. Museum tours can be arranged by appointment.

Also, located nearby, the Miller Art Center and Museum provides a historical look at James Hartness and the Hartness House.

RATES: $99 to $215 EP.

OPEN: All year.

FACILITIES AND ACTIVITIES: Breakfast, lunch on weekdays, dinner. Free wireless Internet in main house and restaurant. Lounge and bar, swimming pool. 35 wooded acres, nature trails. Nearby: Cross-country and downhill skiing.

The Victorian mansion on a thirty-five acre estate was built in 1903 for James Hartness, inventor, astronomer, and one-time governor of Vermont. The rooms are all different in size and decor. There are period wallpapers, some antiques, and twins, doubles, and queens—even some canopies. The Charles Lindbergh Room, in a corner, has a wonderful window seat.

For relaxation try the swimming pool and nature trails. For winter exercise a snowshoe trail, ice skating, and skiing are nearby.

The dining-room chandeliers set an elegant tone for meals at the inn. The lunch offerings include soups; salads; quiche; a variety of sandwiches, hot and cold; and platters such as a tuna melt, fish 'n' chips, or breaded chicken cutlets topped with marinara sauce and melted mozzarella, served on a roll or over pasta. The special Hartness House Grill is turkey and ham with barbecue sauce, cheddar cheese, and tomato on grilled Texas toast. For dinner, a good start is the inn's terrific onion soup or maybe grilled tuna skewer with garlic butter. The entrees are equally enticing. How about filet mignon with béarnaise sauce? Or maybe a roast half-duckling with a pomegranate molasses. Many tasty dishes come from the grill, everything from pork chops to sirloin steak.

The telescope lounge overlooks the pool, a lovely spot, and drinks and food are available on the deck. The inn will also prepare a picnic lunch if you want to explore the area or head off on the nature trails on the property, many along a mountain stream crossed by stone bridges.

HOW TO GET THERE: From the police booth in downtown Springfield, go up Summer Hill, starting at the light. Keep going up the hill as it curves around the left until it levels off (a cemetery is on the right) at the five-street intersection. Bear left on Orchard Street. The inn is 300 yards ahead of you.

Edson Hill Manor
Stowe, Vermont 05672

INNKEEPERS: William and Juliet O'Neill

ADDRESS/TELEPHONE: 1500 Edson Hill Road; (802) 253-7371, (802) 253-9797, or (800) 621-0284

WEB SITE: www.edsonhillmanor.com

ROOMS: 9, all with private bath, in the manor; 16, all with private bath and fireplace, in the carriage houses. Smoking in carriage houses only. Bathroom equipped for the physically disabled in 1 carriage house.

RATES: $159 to $219 BP; MAP and package rates available.

OPEN: All year.

FACILITIES AND ACTIVITIES: Dinner, fully licensed bar, après-ski lounge. Wheelchair access to dining room. Pool, fishing, horseback riding, cross-country skiing with rentals and instruction, ice skating. Nearby: Ice skating and golf at Stowe Country Club.

*H*ere you are, halfway between Stowe and Mount Mansfield, 1,500 feet above the hubble-bubble of that lively village of Stowe, living the good life in a handsome home that was built in 1939 for a family that loved to ski and ride.

The swimming pool here is so lovely, it won an award from Paddock Pools of California. The stocked trout pond is a must for anglers, and you can use the inn's boat. How nice to go catch a fish and have it for your breakfast! When the snow comes, the stables turn into a cross-country ski center, so there you are, taking off practically from the inn door.

This attractive house has been run as an inn since 1953, and there are still homelike touches. The old delft tiles around many of the fireplaces are so appealing. The pine-paneled living room has an aura of quiet elegance that reflects the feeling of gracious living all too often missing from our busy lives.

Downstairs are a bar and lounge where a skier's lunch is served in season. The dining room is splendid, and the food is grand. The menu changes quite often, but to give you an idea, here are some of the summertime offerings: chilled melon soup with honey and lime; summer beefsteak tomato with grilled eggplant; warm fresh mozzarella crostini with balsamic vinegar; grilled Vermont rabbit; barbecued shrimp; swordfish, salmon, steak. . . .

One wintertime favorite is the homemade butternut squash ravioli. There are also sweetbreads, calf's liver, and pork tenderloin; this is really good food. Choose a wine from the wonderful wine cellar, or complete your meal with one of the great hot beverages.

The inn has very nice guest accommodations. The rooms in the carriage houses have beamed ceilings, brick fireplaces, and private baths.

This is a beautiful inn with a view that is spectacular.

A note of particular interest to all you moviegoers: Edson Hill Manor was the winter filming location for Alan Alda's *The Four Seasons.*

HOW TO GET THERE: Take Route 108 north from Stowe 4⁹/₁₀ miles, turn right on Edson Hill Road, and follow the signs uphill to the manor.

Foxfire Inn
Stowe, Vermont 05672

INNKEEPERS: Bob and Kate Neilson

ADDRESS/TELEPHONE: 1606 Pucker Street (Route 100); (802) 253–4887; fax (802) 253-7016

WEB SITE: www.foxfireinn.com

ROOMS: 5, all with private bath.

RATES: $85 to $130 BP.

OPEN: All year.

FACILITIES AND ACTIVITIES: Dinner, bar, full license. Wheelchair access to dining room. Parking. Nearby: Downhill and cross-country skiing, fishing, skating, hiking.

*L*ots of people know the Foxfire best as a great Italian restaurant, but it actually began as a bed-and-breakfast more than two decades ago. It still offers five cozy guest rooms furnished with antiques and inviting living rooms where you can sit and talk or maybe play a few rounds of checkers in front of a crackling fire. The owners like to say that the inn glows with warmth, like the iridescent moss it is named for.

When the Neilsons arrived in 1975, they began serving family-style dinners to guests, and that grew into the restaurant that is now a local tradition. For starters, wait until you taste the home-baked bread sticks, still warm from the oven and drizzled with olive oil and fresh garlic. Besides the usual Italian dishes like veal parmigiana or lasagna, there are not-to-be-missed house specialties such as chicken Ripieno and their own special eggplant parmigiana. Desserts? Taste the Killer Mousse, so thick they call it "a slice of chocolate."

And when you can push yourself away from the table, you have the charming town of Stowe at your door, with some of New England's best skiing, plus ice skating, antiques, shops, summer hiking, fishing, and more.

Pass me another tortoni, please. I am settled in for the season.

HOW TO GET THERE: Take Interstate 89 to Route 100 north into Stowe. The inn is on the right, 1½ miles north of town.

Green Mountain Inn
Stowe, Vermont 05672

INNKEEPER: Patti Clark

ADDRESS/TELEPHONE: 18 Main Street (mailing address: P.O. Box 60); (802) 253-7301 or (800) 253-7302; fax (802) 253-5096

WEB SITE: www.greenmountaininn.com

ROOMS: 105 rooms, suites, and village town houses in 7 buildings; all with private bath, TV, air-conditioning, and phone; many with canopy beds, Jacuzzis, fireplaces, and DVD/CD players.

RATES: Rooms, $119 to $269 EP; suites, $139 to $409 EP. Higher rates in fall and during Christmas week.

OPEN: All year.

FACILITIES AND ACTIVITIES: Breakfast, lunch, dinner, afternoon tea. Lounge; health club with sauna, whirlpool, massage, exercise machines year-round; heated outdoor swimming pool, game room, 120 private acres with trails. Nearby: Skiing, hiking, biking, golf, fishing, shopping.

This venerable inn, built as a private residence in 1833, has been receiving visitors since the mid-1800s, but never in such style as you'll find here today. In the past few years, it has expanded to 105 rooms, suites, and town houses, in several buildings in the center of the village. The original inn and annex rooms still offer antiques, stenciling, Early American–design draperies, and country quilts to give you that warm, old-fashioned feel, but the inn also has updated with many added luxuries.

Fifty of the rooms and suites offer canopy beds, large Jacuzzis, and fireplaces. Rooms in the Mill House, Club House, and Depot have added DVD and CD players. Sanborn House suites have full kitchens. The newest addition, the Mansfield House, opened in 2000 with twenty-two rooms and additional amenities such as marble baths, fireside Jacuzzis, large-screen TVs, and DVD/CD players.

A bountiful breakfast for all guests is available in the colonial-style Main Street Dining Room looking out on the village. Dinner is also served here in season. Year-round, the downstairs Whip Bar and Grill, named for its collection of antique buggy whips, serves lunch, dinner, and Sunday brunch. The dinner entrees include seafood, steaks, pasta, and vegetarian choices, along with homemade soups, breads, and desserts. Guests are treated to afternoon cookies and hot cider or lemonade, depending on the weather.

You can work off dessert at the inn's health club. It offers state-of-the-art exercise equipment, plus Jacuzzi, sauna, and massage services, and the heated outdoor pool is open year-round.

When you step out the door, you are in the heart of Stowe, surrounded by shops and scenery. What more could you wish for?

HOW TO GET THERE: Take Interstate 89 to Route 100 north into Stowe. The inn is at the intersection of Routes 100 and 108.

Ten Acres Lodge
Stowe, Vermont 05672

INNKEEPERS: Robin and Frank Wilson

ADDRESS/TELEPHONE: 14 Barrows Road; (802) 253-7638 or (800) 327-7357; fax (802) 253-6589

WEB SITE: www.tenacreslodge.com

ROOMS: 15, plus guest cottage; all with private bath, phone; some with fireplace, TV, Wi-Fi connections; 1 room equipped for the physically disabled. Pets welcome in cottage.

RATES: $79 to $325 BP.

OPEN: All year.

FACILITIES AND ACTIVITIES: Dinner nightly in season, Thursday to Sunday off season. Liquor license. Outdoor pool, hot tub, sauna, Hill House cinema. Nearby: Skiing (downhill and cross-country), skating, Stowe recreation path, shopping.

The living rooms at Ten Acres Lodge are inviting, with soft couches and large chairs, fireplaces, books, and windows looking out on sheer beauty year-round. In summer, dairy cows graze in the rolling fields across the road, and in winter, cross-country ski trails crisscross the hillside. Around the inn, maples more than a century old provide lazy New England shade.

The dining rooms are beautifully appointed, from the artwork to the napery. The menus use the freshest local ingredients, changing with the seasons. Starters could include skillet-roasted shrimp or stuffed portobello mushrooms, and the main course might be honey-soy-glazed quail, grilled fillet of beef, or forest mushroom ravioli.

Eight comfortable main lodge guest rooms have pine walls or wallpaper with pine trim. Beds are all king or queen size, with down comforters. Each room has been individually decorated and has its own New England country charm. All of the rooms have nice sitting areas with a sofa or two chairs and are air-conditioned in summer.

The Hill House suites are more deluxe, with wood-burning fireplaces, cable television, and private balconies with views. The four upstairs rooms have an

airy cathedral ceiling. The guest cottage has two bedrooms, a kitchen, fireplace, and TV/VCR.

The inn has a sociable bar area with a large selection of fine wines, as well as liquors. A special feature is the private Hill House cinema for guests, featuring a 9-foot screen. Outside in winter, you are in the ski capital of the East. But the mountains are simply beautiful anytime, whether covered in snow or painted in blazing autumn colors. Ten Acres thoughtfully provides an outdoor hot tub where you can soak away your cares while savoring the views.

HOW TO GET THERE: From Route 100 north in Stowe, turn left at the three-way stop onto Route 108. Proceed about 2 miles, then bear left onto Luce Hill Road. Ten Acres is located about ½ mile up, around the sharp left, then on your right.

Echo Lake Inn
Tyson, Vermont 05149

INNKEEPERS: Lawrence and Beth Jeffrey

ADDRESS/TELEPHONE: Route 100 (mailing address: P.O. Box 154, Ludlow 05149); (802) 228-8602 or (800) 356-6844; fax (802) 228-3075

WEB SITE: www.echolakeinn.com

ROOMS: 23, all with private bath and free high-speed wireless Internet; 7 condos, some with fireplace, 2-person Jacuzzi, TV, air-conditioning.

RATES: $99 to $299 BP.

OPEN: Closed first three weeks in April and November.

FACILITIES AND ACTIVITIES: Breakfast, dinner, full license. Swimming pool, volleyball, badminton, fly fishing, lighted tennis court, dock with canoes and boats.

Built in 1840 as a summer hotel, the Echo Lake Inn is one of the few inns remaining in Vermont that was originally constructed to operate as an inn. There have been many illustrious guests over the years, including Thomas Edison, Henry Ford, and President Calvin Coolidge.

The living room is country comfortable, with two sofas at the big fireplace, a grandfather's clock, and lots of books. The pub is also furnished like a sitting room, a nice place to relax and with a well-stocked bar.

Many of the guest rooms have been recently refurbished. They range from small and simple like Room 21 to lavish layouts like Rooms 10 and 11, with king-size beds, gas fireplaces, and Jacuzzis. All have country antiques and pleasant furnishings. Some of the suites are ideal for families.

Now for my favorite pastime—food—which I certainly enjoyed in the cozy dining room. The menu changes twice a year, and there are always specials. The daily soup selections are really good. I have some of the recipes so I can make them at home. Among the entrees are grilled sirloin, sautéed fresh rainbow trout, and roast country duckling. I had veal, which was yummy. The inn also serves a full and tasty breakfast.

On a warm day you're sure to enjoy the lighted tennis courts, the pool, and the canoes and rowboats waiting at the inn's own dock on the lake. Some of Vermont's best trout fishing awaits on the Black River, which runs just a few feet away from the inn. Secluded waterfalls, golf, and much more are

nearby, and in winter, Okemo Mountain is just five minutes away. If you decide to stay in, you can head for the six-person Jacuzzi or the Stoned Tavern, which has a pool table, Ping-Pong, darts, and video games.

Echo is the middle lake of the three-stream, spring-fed Plymouth Lakes. Any season here is beautiful, but the lakes mirror the brilliant colors of fall like nowhere else in New England. Spectacular!

HOW TO GET THERE: From Interstate 91 take exit 6 to Route 103 to Ludlow. One and a half miles north of Ludlow, turn right on Route 100. The inn is in 3½ miles on the left.

Tucker Hill Inn
Waitsfield, Vermont 05673

INNKEEPERS: Phil and Alison Truckle

ADDRESS/TELEPHONE: 65 Marble Hill Road (off Route 17); (802) 496–3983 or (800) 543–7841; fax (802) 496–3203

WEB SITE: www.tuckerhill.com

ROOMS: 18 rooms and suites; all with private bath, TV/VCRs, telephone with dataports; 1 suite with fireplace, Jacuzzi.

RATES: Rooms, $89 to $209 BP; suites, $149 to $279 BP.

OPEN: All year.

FACILITIES AND ACTIVITIES: Dinner nightly in season, Friday through Monday rest of year except closed mid-April to end of May. Full-service

pub. Outdoor pool, two red-clay tennis courts, 14 acres of property with hiking trails. Nearby: Skiing, golf, canoeing, fishing, biking, shopping.

*I*f you knew the venerable 1940s vintage Tucker Hill Lodge in the past, you'll hardly recognize the place. Everything has been renovated and refurbished—rooms, restaurant, pub—and more rooms and suites have been added. Rooms have been furnished with antiques and Ethan Allen furnishings and updated with telephones, TV/VCRs, and computer dataports.

How well did things work out? Well, *Ski* magazine named Tucker Hill its "Inn of the Month" a few years back. Even the name has been changed from *lodge* to *inn* to tell you things are less rustic now.

The welcoming living room has pine floors and a big fieldstone fireplace, and there is another fireplace in the restaurant. Some of the favorites here include rack of lamb, osso bucco, and veal tenderloin. There is always a fresh fish of the day, plus seafood specialties such as saffron marinated scallops. Before or after dinner, you can relax in the fireside pub.

The Mad River Valley is a beautiful, peaceful area of Vermont, with the quaint villages of Waitsfield and Warren waiting to be explored. In winter, you are in prime ski country, with Sugarbush and Mad River Glen nearby. In summer, the inn offers an outdoor pool, two clay tennis courts, and lots of walking trails on its fourteen acres.

Try to come up sometime for the famous Fourth of July parade in Warren, a wonderful bit of small-town Americana come to life.

HOW TO GET THERE: Turn west off Route 100 onto Route 17 in Waitsfield in the Mad River Valley. Go 1½ miles west; the sign for the inn will be on your left.

The Pitcher Inn ♥
Warren, Vermont 05674

INNKEEPER: Ari Sadri

ADDRESS/TELEPHONE: 275 Main Street; (802) 496–6350 or (888) 867–4824; fax (802) 496–6354

WEB SITE: www.pitcherinn.com

ROOMS: 9 rooms and 2 suites; all with private bath, phone with dataport, TV, VCR, stereo system; most with wood-burning fireplaces, whirlpools, or steam showers.

RATES: $350 to $700 BP.

OPEN: All year.

Breakfast, dinner. Game room, library, spa treatments by appointment, ski and hiking storage room with ski boot and glove warmer. Nearby: Skiing, hiking, golf, tennis, polo, shopping.

When the Pitcher Inn was lost to fire in 1993, the town of Warren mourned the loss of a beloved landmark that had been on Main Street since the 1800s. But when the new inn opened in 1997, there was a collective sigh of relief. It was a remarkable likeness of the old inn—at least on the outside. Within, the town had gained one of the most luxurious and unique lodgings in Vermont, a member of the prestigious Relais and Chateaux group.

The guest rooms in this inn are originals, each with original art and antiques, and a theme carried out with imagination and charm. The School Room, for example, in addition to its king-size bed and Jacuzzi tub, features a period school desk and an original slate blackboard with chalk and erasers. On the walls are dioramas of the Vermont seasons, and a mural that combines Greek Revival art and popular storybook characters. The Mountain Room reminds me of a ranger's cabin, with a fireplace and a hand-painted mural of the nearby mountains. Decorations include authentic artifacts from the 10th Mountain Division, including classic skis, snowshoes, and pitons for climbing. The Calvin Coolidge Room boasts a portrait of this president hailing from Vermont, and murals showing life in the state during the 1920s when he was in office. The Hayloft, one of two luxury suites in the barn, is appropriately decorated with antique barn supplies.

The forty-seat dining room has a menu as elegant as the setting. Dinner might begin with lobster and corn chowder, steamed mussels in a saffron broth, or a foie gras terrine. A wide choice of main courses includes grilled

olive Metcalf

wahoo with lemon mint risotto, corn, and blueberry salsa; jalapeño roasted duckling with cabbage salad; almond-crusted venison loin with poblano red rice; or grilled beef tenderloin on brioche with a fricassee of escargots and wild mushrooms. A "don't-miss" among the tempting desserts is the special Pitcher Inn "ice cream sandwich," made with Grand Marnier frozen crème brûlée with chocolate wafers, citrus crème anglaise, and chocolate sauce. Wine with your meal? You may choose from a notable wine cellar boasting some 6,500 bottles.

Guests can enjoy a game room with an eighteenth-century billiards table, find a book in the Robert Frost library, or pick a video from a large selection for both children and adults. Just across the street, the Warren General Store is filled with temptations, and all the year-round facilities of the Sugarbush ski area are just down the road. It's hard to imagine a better location—or a finer inn.

HOW TO GET THERE: From Interstate 87 north take exit 20. Go northeast on NY 149 to Route 4. Follow Route 4 through Rutland, Vermont, to Route 100. Go north on Route 100 to Warren Village. The entrance to the village will be on your right. Take the main street through town (½ mile), and you will find the inn right in the center of town. From Interstate 89 take exit 10 (Waterbury). Take Route 2 east to Route 100 south. Follow Route 100 south to Warren Village. The entrance to the village will be on your left. Take the main street through town (⅛ mile), and you will find the inn right in the center of town.

Thatcher Brook Inn
Waterbury, Vermont 05676

INNKEEPERS: Lisa and John Fischer

ADDRESS/TELEPHONE: Route 100 North (mailing address: P.O. Box 490); (802) 244-5911 or (800) 292-5911

WEB SITE: www.thatcherbrook.com

ROOMS: 24, all with private bath, phone, clock radio; some with whirlpool tub, fireplace; 1 specially equipped for the physically disabled; 3 with wheelchair access.

RATES: Rooms, $80 to $225 BP; suites, $305 to $399 BP.

OPEN: All year.

FACILITIES AND ACTIVITIES: Dinner, choice of restaurants. Wheelchair access to dining room. Nearby: Canoeing, biking, hiking, cross-country and downhill skiing, golf, horseback riding, Ben and Jerry's Ice Cream Factory.

*T*hatcher Brook, named after Col. Partridge Thatcher, was quite a powerful stream in the late 1800s. It had two sets of beautiful waterfalls, and during the nineteenth century two mills were constructed at these falls. In 1894 Stedman Wheeler purchased the upper sawmill and a small house. He became so prosperous in his business that he decided to construct a larger house on land directly across from the mill. Today that house is Thatcher Brook Inn.

It is obvious from the fine attention to detail and workmanship in the inn that old Stedman spared no expense. The house took two years to construct. Several types of lumber were used in the inn, including oak, bird's-eye maple, spruce, cherry, and birch. The hand-carved fireplace and stairway are original to the house, as are the pocket doors between the two front dining rooms and the window seat in the "romantic room," a cozy room with fireplace reserved just for couples. Especially attractive is the gazebo-type front porch.

Rooms in the main inn vary from simple to luxurious. Some of the most romantic have queen-size four-poster or Shaker-style beds, beams, and a brick fireplace. Some rooms also offer whirlpools. Most luxurious of all is the suite, with a canopy bed, an oversize whirlpool, and a fireplace set into a wood-paneled wall.

There is a dining room for every mood. For fine dining, Michael's on the Hill offers European cuisine plus a beautiful Green Mountain view. Live piano music in the lounge adds to the atmosphere on weekends. Marsala Salsa is a change of pace, with Caribbean, Mexican, and Cajun dishes such as Baja rellenos, curried chicken, and island shrimp. A comfortable place for families, it offers a special children's menu. Tanglewoods, with casual and cozy quarters in a renovated barn, has both a regular American menu and a lighter cafe menu, and Arvad's is a pub and grill serving everything from prime rib to pasta. And don't forget Waterbury Wings, serving the inn's famous chicken wings, plus ribs, salads, sandwiches, and burgers.

The inn is nicely situated for skiers, about midway between Stowe and Sugarbush, and don't miss a visit to the Ben & Jerry's Ice Cream Factory just down the road. Don't forget to wander across the street to look at the two sets of beautiful waterfalls.

HOW TO GET THERE: The inn is ¼ mile north of exit 10 off Interstate 89, on Route 100, the road to Stowe.

The Inn at Weathersfield
Weathersfield, Vermont 05151

INNKEEPERS: Jane and David Sandelman

ADDRESS/TELEPHONE: 1342 Route 106; (802) 263-9217; fax (802) 263-9219

WEB SITE: www.weathersfieldinn.com

ROOMS: 12 rooms and suites; all with private bath, robes, phone; 9 with fireplace; some with TV, DVD and CD players; 2 suites with whirlpool.

RATES: $140 to $285 BP.

OPEN: All year, except April.

FACILITIES AND ACTIVITIES: Dinner served Thursday through Sunday. Tavern, wine cellar, TV and VCR with movies, large library, gift shop. Outside amphitheater, gardens, and recreation area suitable for weddings or small conference groups.

This beautiful old inn was built circa 1792 and has a wonderful history. Prior to the Civil War, it was an important stop on the Underground Railroad, sheltering slaves en route to Canada. The inn is set well back from the road on twenty-one acres of property. Your rest is assured.

All the renovations to the inn have been done with care to preserve its vintage flavor. In the reconstructed barn attached to the inn are five beamed-ceiling guest rooms with sensational old bathtubs. These are honest-to-goodness Victorian bathrooms. There are fourteen fireplaces in the inn, and each of these rooms has one. Three of the suites have a bedroom and sitting room—the innkeepers say that these are ideal for honeymooners; the other sleeps four and is good for families. All the rooms come with feather beds, luxury linens, and plush robes and slippers.

Stencils copied from those used in the early 1800s decorate many of the rooms. The tavern is modeled after eighteenth-century Massachusetts taverns. The greenhouse–dining room is a handsome complement to the other rooms.

Excellent, four-diamond-rated food is served here by candlelight. In 2006 the chef was honored with an invitation to cook at New York's prestigious James Beard House as part of a "Great Country Getaways" series. The menu changes weekly, taking advantage of what is in season. They grow their own herbs in a special space in the garden. Expect elegant appetizers such as sea scallops with tomato tartare. Main courses might be roasted half duckling with a homemade fresh raspberry glaze or seared tuna with lemongrass and coconut sushi rice. Be sure to save room for desserts. They are prepared fresh daily and are irresistible!

The newest addition at the inn is the wine cellar, with a "chef's table," a special location for dinner that can also accommodate a private dinner for six or more. Bring some friends and the chef will design a menu just for your party.

HOW TO GET THERE: Take Interstate 91 north to exit 7 (Springfield, Vermont). Take Route 11 to Springfield, and then take Route 106 in town to the inn, which is on your left, set well back from the road.

Deerhill Inn ♥
West Dover, Vermont 05356

INNKEEPERS: Michael Allen and Stan Gresens

ADDRESS/TELEPHONE: 14 Valley View Road (mailing address: Box 136); (802) 464-3100 or (800) 993-3379; fax (802) 464-5474

WEB SITE: www.deerhillinn.com

ROOMS: 13 rooms, 1 suite; all with private bath, robes, wireless Internet access; many with fireplace; 2 with decks; 2 with porches; 3 with balconies.

RATES: $140 to $295 BP. MAP available.

OPEN: All year, except selected weeks in spring and fall.

FACILITIES AND ACTIVITIES: Bar, full license. Wheelchair access to dining room. Swimming pool. Nearby: Golf, fishing, cross-country and downhill skiing, tennis court, hiking, mountain biking, theater, and music hall.

The setting for the Deerhill Inn is perfect. Surrounded by lovely maple and fruit trees, it is perched on a hill with views of the countryside's beautiful mountains and lush meadows. Everything is nice and quiet up here.

The inn dogs, Fergie and Sophie, may greet you when you arrive. The downstairs parlor has a beautiful copper-topped table, couches, and good chairs for settling in front of the fireplace. As you wander on, you arrive in the dining rooms, with wonderful views and a magnificent mural done by a local artist. The artwork on the other walls is for sale.

Michael is the innkeeper/chef responsible for the excellent dining room. The menu changes often to take advantage of fresh local ingredients. The first course may include a blue cheese custard or a selection of homemade pâtés. Entrees range from fillet of beef to Long Island duckling or a fresh fish selection. What's for dessert? Wonderful things such as chocolate molten cake, a seasonal fruit crisp, or homemade ice creams and sorbets.

Upstairs is a well-stocked library with a fireplace, TV, and that wonderful view. Eleven rooms have direct access to a balcony or deck with spectacular mountain or garden views. The rooms are beautifully furnished. I'm partial to Apple Blossom, with a lacy canopy bed and a fireplace, and Dahlia, done in cheerful red and white, with a woodstove and a private balcony. All the rooms come with fine linens and robes, and in winter you'll find cozy flannel sheets on the beds. One of the rooms won the Room of the Year award from Waverly fabrics for its lovely prints.

If ever I had wanted to own an inn, this would have been the one.

There's much to do in the area. For skiing Mount Snow and Haystack are nearby, along with cross-country areas. In the summertime cast for trout on the Battenkill River, go play a game of golf, or use the inn's pool. It's beautiful up here.

A flash for all anglers: The inn is a short drive to Lake Whitingham, the second largest lake in Vermont, and just 20 miles from the Connecticut River and New Hampshire lakes, so come on up! This is some of the most productive fishing in the Northeast.

For something different at the end of summer, there's the wicked wild mountain bike race.

HOW TO GET THERE: Take Route 9 to Wilmington; turn north onto Route 100 at the traffic light and continue to West Dover village. Pass the church and post office; at the antiques store turn right onto Valley View Road. The inn is 300 yards up the road, on the right-hand side.

Doveberry Inn
West Dover, Vermont 05356

INNKEEPERS: Michael and Christine Fayette

ADDRESS/TELEPHONE: Box 1736, Route 100; (802) 464-5652 or (800) 722-3204; fax (802) 464-6229

WEB SITE: www.doveberryinn.com

ROOMS: 11, all with private bath and TV; some with fireplaces, whirlpools, balconies.

RATES: $95 to $225 BP. MAP rates available.

OPEN: All year except last two weeks of April and first two in May.

FACILITIES AND ACTIVITIES: Breakfast and dinner (no dinner on Tuesday night); sugar house nearby has swimming pool, sauna, basketball, exercise room. Nearby: Skiing, cross-country trails, biking, fishing, golf, music and art festivals, shopping, antiquing.

*T*his sweet country inn looks a little like a cross between a country cottage and a Swiss chalet. The Fayettes have done a lot to upgrade things since they arrived in 1994. Room sizes vary, but all have country touches such as rocking chairs, antiques, quilted comforters, and hardwood floors. Many now include Jacuzzi tubs and fireplaces. My favorites are those with private balconies overlooking the surrounding hills.

Dinner is served in an intimate dining room seating just thirty-two. Both Michael and Christine are trained chefs who learned their trade well in restaurants from California to Nantucket before settling here in Vermont. Their sophisticated Northern Italian cuisine has won kudos from many publications.

A typical dinner might begin with a shrimp and radicchio risotto, followed by a veal chop over apple and mesquite wood, ending with an orange-

cinnamon crème brûlée. One very special dish is the rare grilled tuna over risotto, with wilted Italian greens, roasted garlic cloves, and sun-dried tomatoes, drizzled with white truffle oil. The accompanying wine list features offerings from around the world.

This inn is just 1¾ miles from Mount Snow on Route 100 in a lovely area with much to do. The Marlboro Music Festival is but a short drive away.

Nicholas is the innkeepers' young son, and I'm so glad I got to meet him. What a future he has!

HOW TO GET THERE: Take exit 2 from Interstate 91 in Brattleboro, then take Route 9 west to Wilmington and Route 100 north about 7½ miles to West Dover. The inn is on the right.

The Hermitage
West Dover, Vermont 05356

INNKEEPER: Winter Knight

ADDRESS/TELEPHONE: 21 Handle Road; (802) 464–3511; fax (802) 464–2688

WEB SITE: www.hermitageinn.com

ROOMS: 15, all with private bath, wheelchair accessibility, phone, TV, VCR, and wood-burning fireplace. Brook Bound B&B, 14 rooms, 10 with private bath.

RATES: $125 to $185 BP.

OPEN: All year.

FACILITIES AND ACTIVITIES: Brunch every Sunday. Wheelchair access to dining room. Restaurant is air-conditioned. Sauna, wine cellar, trout pond, hiking, cross-country skiing from the door.

High on a hill facing Haystack Mountain is this secluded and welcoming country inn. The original home was an eighteenth-century farmhouse; later the property was the summer estate of one Bertha Eastman Berry, an editor of the exclusive *Social Register*. Today this is an inn that manages to be both elegant and informal.

Since innkeeper Winter Knight arrived, she has upgraded the menu with varied and sophisticated dishes such as honey Dijon scallop and shrimp, sweet cherry and fennel pork, pear pecan boneless duck breast, lamb chops, Delmonico steak, venison, and Weiner schnitzel. The baked French onion soup is a great way to start the meal.

Guest rooms are attractively decorated with antiques; each has a welcome wood-burning fireplace. The artwork of native wildlife and rural scenes is by

well-known New England artists. If you want to bring your favorite four-footed friend along, the Carriage House is pet-friendly. In fact, two Portuguese water dogs, Pasha and Leo, are part of the inn family.

The property is a big part of the attraction of the Hermitage. This is a lovely place to stroll, with gardens and an orchard, woodland trails, a trout pond, and a rippling brook. In season, the trees are tapped to make maple syrup. For skiers, Mount Snow and Haystack are both just a few miles away, and the region abounds with opportunities for outdoor sports.

On a snowy day, of course, you might be happy just settling in front of your own private wood-burning fireplace.

HOW TO GET THERE: Take Route 9 to Wilmington; follow Route 100 north. In about 3 miles on your left you'll see signs for Haystack Mountain and the inn. Turn left onto Coldbrook Road and pass the entrance to Haystack Mountain. The Hermitage is just around the next corner, on the left.

The Inn at Sawmill Farm
West Dover, Vermont 05356

INNKEEPERS: Rodney, Ione, and Brill Williams and Bobbie Dee Molitor

ADDRESS/TELEPHONE: Cross Town Road (mailing address: P.O. Box 367); (802) 464–8131

WEB SITE: www.theinnatsawmillfarm.com

ROOMS: 10, plus 11 in cottages; all with private bath and air-conditioning; some with fireplace.

RATES: Rooms, $175 to $325 EP; cottages, $350 to $750 EP.

OPEN: All year, except April and May.

FACILITIES AND ACTIVITIES: Bar, lounge. Swimming pool, tennis court, 2 trout ponds, fitness room. Nearby: Skiing at Mount Snow, biking, fishing, golf, music festivals, shopping, antiquing.

The Williamses have transformed an old Vermont barn into the warmest, most attractive inn that I have seen in a long time. Ione is a professional decorator and Rod is a noted architect, which makes for a wonderful marriage of talents and an almost perfect inn. The Williamses' son, Brill, runs the kitchen, and he does a superb job as well.

The inn's copper collection is extensive. The oversize fireplace in the living room is surrounded with it, and there's a huge copper-topped coffee table that's a beauty. They also have a most incredible bar made of solid copper and a handsome brass telescope on a tripod for your viewing of Mount Snow.

Accommodations vary, with some rooms done in Victorian motif, some in Chippendale, and all with the flavor of New England at its best. The cottage rooms have fireplaces. I was in Farm House, and my room was done in the softest pastels, with a king-size bed and a lovely dressing room and bath. All the rooms are color coordinated and come with thick towels and extra pillows. Little boxes of chocolates are in each room. A very nice touch. The inn's facilities are not well suited to children under ten.

Dinner is beyond exceptional. Coquille of crabmeat imperial under glass was my choice among many tempting appetizers. Delicious entrees include medallions of pork tenderloin with Robert sauce and baked stuffed apple, rack of lamb, potato-crusted grouper, and game dishes such as squab, pheasant, rabbit, quail, or grilled loin of venison. They are perfectly complemented by wines from Brill's impressive wine cellar, winner of *Wine Spectator*'s "Grand

Award." The 28,000-bottle wine cellar has a selection of some 1,240 wines. Desserts are all homemade. Breakfast is also special. Fresh orange juice and homemade tomato juice are just starters.

The inn makes a specialty of special occasions. Do try to get up here for Christmas. It's something you will never forget.

HOW TO GET THERE: Take Interstate 91 to exit 2 in Brattleboro. Take Route 9 west to Wilmington, and then follow Route 100 north for 6 miles to West Dover.

West Dover Inn
West Dover, Vermont 05356

INNKEEPERS: Kathy and Phil Gilpin

ADDRESS/TELEPHONE: Route 100 (mailing address: P.O. Box 1208); (802) 464–5207; fax (802) 464–2173

WEB SITE: www.westdoverinn.com

ROOMS: 8, plus 4 suites; all with private bath and TV; suites have whirlpools and fireplaces.

RATES: $100 to $288 BP.

OPEN: All year except mid-April through Memorial Day weekend and first and second weeks in November.

FACILITIES AND ACTIVITIES: Dinner Thursday through Sunday, live jazz band Friday and Saturday; tavern. Nearby: Mountain biking, golf, swimming, hiking, skiing (all types).

*I*t's a lovely old place, an inn since 1846. Originally built as a stage-coach stop, it has been lovingly restored with the addition of modern amenities.

When you come in the door, to the left is the office and on the right is an inviting living room with a fireplace, good couches, and books. Comfortable accommodations offer many queen-size beds and a variety of antiques. For a family, a pair of twins and a double are nice. The suites are a joy; all have a fireplace and whirlpool tub.

In the handsome breakfast room, the offerings are bountiful. Anything you can put syrup on is served, along with eggs and fresh fruits.

The sophisticated dinner menu is tempting. Appetizers might include Asian spring rolls, Maine crab cakes, or almond-crusted duck tenders, and among the entrees are grilled salmon, New York sirloin, applewood-smoked pork tenderloin, roast duck with plum sauce, or lamb Noisette. In warm weather, dining moves outdoor to the patio. One very popular addition since the Gilpins arrived is a four-piece jazz band playing on Friday and Saturday nights.

The tavern has a menu in keeping with its more casual ambience. Guests like to mingle at the full-service bar, where ten stools invite socializing.

Skiers will like the proximity to Mount Snow, and everyone will enjoy the options for outdoor fun that abound year-round.

HOW TO GET THERE: From Brattleboro take exit 2 off Interstate 91 north to Route 9 west. Go 20 miles to Wilmington. Turn right at the traffic light onto Route 100 north. Proceed 6 miles to the inn. From Bennington take Route 9 east 21 miles to Wilmington. Turn left at the traffic light onto Route 100 north. Proceed 6 miles to the inn.

Willough Vale Inn 💟
Westmore, Vermont 05860

INNKEEPER: Patrick Haugwitz

ADDRESS/TELEPHONE: Route 5A South; (802) 525–4123 or (800) 594–9102; fax (802) 525–4514

WEB SITE: www.willoughvale.com

ROOMS: 11 rooms and 4 lakeside cottages; all with private bath; 1 specially equipped for the physically disabled. Fireplaces, porches, and kitchens in cottages; 1 with Jacuzzi.

RATES: Rooms, $85 to $245 CP; cottages, $155 to $265 CP.

OPEN: All year.

FACILITIES AND ACTIVITIES: Dinner for guests daily in season, Thursday through Saturday remainder of year. Bar and lounge. Wheelchair access to dining room and restrooms. Fishing, swimming, and boating at the lake. Nearby: Snowshoeing, snowmobile trails, hiking. Snowmobile trail from back door.

This is a scenic paradise with one of the most beautiful lakes I've seen in many a country mile. Do you like to fish? Lake trout, landlocked salmon, perch, and rainbow trout are just waiting for your line. Or try one of the inn's boats, kayaks, and canoes, or the row boat and sailfish.

A porch with a gazebo at one end overlooks the lake. Around it are beautiful flowers. Lupine and wildflowers are all over the place.

The inn is full of antique and Vermont-handcrafted furniture. The guest rooms are all furnished differently, but all have comfortable queen beds. There's even a whirlpool for two in one lovely bathroom. I liked the nice parlor and library. It's a quiet spot for cards, writing, reading, or just relaxing after an active day.

The taproom has an elegant bar and tables and is a pleasant gathering place. Dinner offers a nice variety of entrees to be enjoyed along with the lake view. You can choose light fare such as burgers or quesadillas, or main courses such as roast duckling, steak, or maple barbecued chicken.

You'll find plenty to do here year-round—climbing trails on Mount Hor and Mount Pisgah and skiing at nearby Burke Mountain. Snowmobiling across the frozen lake is invigorating in winter; in summer a canoe ride on a moonlit night would be wonderful.

The fully equipped cottages along the lake are special. They have a fireplace, screened porch, private dock, and a deck with a fabulous view. Pet lovers take note: pets less than fifty pounds are welcome here in certain rooms.

HOW TO GET THERE: From the south leave Interstate 91 at Lyndonville (exit 23) and proceed north on Routes 5 and 5A. From Canada get off Interstate 91 at Barton and follow Route 16 to Route 5A.

Windham Hill Inn
West Townshend, Vermont 05359

INNKEEPERS: Marina and Joe Coneeny

ADDRESS/TELEPHONE: 311 Lawrence Drive; (802) 874–4080 or (800) 944–4080; fax (802) 874–4702

WEB SITE: www.windhamhill.com

ROOMS: 21, all with private bath, phones, and air-conditioning; 16 with fireplace or porch; 1 equipped for the physically disabled; 11 with Jacuzzi or soaking tub.

RATES: $195 to $395 BP.

OPEN: All year except one week in late December and first two weeks in April.

FACILITIES AND ACTIVITIES: Dinner by reservation, full liquor license. Conference facilities. Heated pool, tennis, hiking, cross-country skiing, snowshoeing, ice skating. Nearby: Downhill and cross-country skiing, kayaking, horseback riding.

f you are a dreamer as I am, and you dream of a perfect country inn, this is as close as you will come. At Windham Hill you are sitting on top of the world. The West River valley stretches as far as the eye can see. The 160-acre site was a working dairy farm when the house was built about 1825, and in 1962 it was converted to an inn.

When you arrive at the inn, on the right is one of the living rooms with a fireplace. Keep on walking into the next room, where there is a nice bar with three bar stools. Take another right into a room with a porch and a fantastic view. Here's where you'll find a piano, books, chess, and games.

Straight ahead are the lovely dining rooms. The Frog Pond dining room has a view of Frog Pond, of course, and the great beyond, and it also has a cozy fireplace and private tables. The "Big Table" dining room is available for private parties or for guests to join together.

The menu changes nightly and offers a choice of a la carte selections or a sumptuous four-course dinner. When I was visiting, there were crab cakes, sautéed sea scallops with a tomato-corn relish, sun-dried tomato ravioli with a pesto beurre blanc, good soups, and salads. For entrees I had my choice of grilled veal medallions, fillet of salmon, and grilled medallions of beef tenderloin. The desserts were very tempting—fresh peach almond tart, chocolate mousse cake, spiced raspberry-rhubarb cobbler, and fresh seasonal fruit. All this, plus you have your pick of wines from an extensive wine cellar.

The accommodations are awesome. All have views that are enough to keep you in your room all day. Beds are queens and kings, and some rooms have a fireplace or porch. The White Barn has glorious rooms. I was in Meadowlook with a million-dollar view. Marion Goodfellow has its own cupola, and North Loft has an amazing sunken bathroom and a spacious seating area.

For those looking for a space for meetings, the conference room is 1,000 square feet of sheer beauty. Birch and cherry floors, a fieldstone fireplace, Oriental rugs, and all of the business equipment necessary for anything.

You'll never lack for things to do here. There's a heated pool and tennis courts, all with a view. Ten kilometers of groomed cross-country trails are available at the inn, as are snowshoes and skis for guests to use. Hiking on the inn's trails is breathtaking. Downhill skiing is close by, or you can ice skate on the inn's pond.

What in the world are you waiting for? At least come and say hello to Bart the Bear in the lounge area and the real live labradors, Rosalie, Maggie, and Pippa, the inn dogs.

HOW TO GET THERE: The inn is located just off Windham Hill Road, approximately 1½ miles from Route 30.

Autumn Harvest Inn ♥
Williamstown, Vermont 05679

INNKEEPER: Carolyn White

ADDRESS/TELEPHONE: Clark Road; (802) 422–1255; fax (802) 433–5501

WEB SITE: www.central-vt.com/web/autumn

ROOMS: 18, all with private bath, TV, VCR, phones, and air-conditioning.

RATES: $99 to $159 EP.

OPEN: All year except Christmas day.

FACILITIES AND ACTIVITIES: Breakfast, dinner served Wednesday to Saturday. Full liquor license. Nearby: Horseback riding, cross-country skiing.

What a heavenly location for an inn, high on a knoll overlooking 1,000 acres of mountains and rural Vermont countryside. The property was known as Autumn Crest Farm for more than a century before the name was changed to Fogged Inn. The original name has now been reinstated. It was a dairy farm for most of those years, and then a horse farm before being completely restored as a country inn. Five of the guest rooms and the breakfast area were part of the original farmhouse and still have their wide-board wooden floors. On chilly days, the large common room welcomes with a great brick fireplace, and the wraparound porch is wonderful on a summer day. In keeping with the rural setting, the bedrooms are simple country with Bates bedspreads and ruffled curtains.

The surroundings are part of the pleasure of this inn. You can dine with a view of the countryside and, in warm weather, be served outside on the veranda. Horseback riding is a favorite pastime, and abandoned town roads across the hillsides are ideal for walking or mountain biking. In winter these become snowmobile trails and connect with the expansive trail system of the Vermont Association of Snow Travelers.

Dinner is a highlight of the day. Typical appetizers are crab cakes with Dijon sauce or bacon-wrapped scallops. For your main course you can choose from dishes such as medallions of beef, prime rib, chicken Dijon, or baked salmon. Dinner always comes with a crisp house salad and homemade bread. Desserts are sinfully delicious.

After dinner you can relax in the lounge and compare stories of your day in the great outdoors.

HOW TO GET THERE: The inn is just two minutes from Interstate 89; take exit 5 onto Route 64 east.

Red Shutter Inn
Wilmington, Vermont 05363

INNKEEPERS: Lucylee and Gerard Gingras

ADDRESS/TELEPHONE: Route 9 West; (802) 464–3768 or (800) 845–7548; fax (802) 464–5123

WEB SITE: www.redshutterinn.com

ROOMS: 7 rooms, 2 suites; all with private bath; some with fireplace, TV, whirlpool, air-conditioning.

RATES: $110 to $280 BP.

OPEN: All year.

FACILITIES AND ACTIVITIES: Full license; breakfast; dinner every night except Monday in season, weekends year-round. Nearby: Shopping, skiing, fishing, boating, theater.

Nestled on five wooded acres, this handsome colonial-style inn, circa 1894, offers a country setting within walking distance to town. The comfortable living room beckons with a fireplace, and the inn also offers a small bar with its original tin ceiling and the Lincoln Library, comfortable places to relax with a cocktail or dessert. Chef Michael's Restaurant has a creative and eclectic menu, with specialties from risotto and game dishes to sushi-grade seafood. All the dishes use the finest natural and organic ingredients, and the delicious breads and desserts are baked right here. In warm weather, you can enjoy cocktails or dinner outside on the porch.

The main inn holds four guest rooms, plus a grand suite with a queen-size brass bed, fireplace, whirlpool bath, and a private porch overlooking the hillside. Three more rooms and a suite are in the renovated carriage house, also circa 1894. The suite here is for romantics, with a fireplace and a whirlpool bath for two with a skylight overhead. If you don't want to miss your favorite show, choose the carriage house, where all the rooms have a TV.

Just down the road a bit is the charming little village of Wilmington, with many appealing shops to explore. Haystack and Mount Snow skiing is a short drive away, and your innkeepers can lead you to many interesting places in this beautiful area of southern Vermont.

HOW TO GET THERE: The inn is located on Route 9, just west of the intersection of Route 100.

The White House 💙
Wilmington, Vermont 05363

INNKEEPER: Robert Grinold

ADDRESS/TELEPHONE: 178 Route 9 East; (802) 464–2135 or (800) 541–2135; fax (802) 464–5222

WEB SITE: www.whitehouseinn.com

ROOMS: 16 in main house, 7 in guest house, 2 in deluxe cottage; all with private bath; 10 with fireplace; 5 with whirlpool.

RATES: $98 to $285 BP. MAP available.

OPEN: All year.

FACILITIES AND ACTIVITIES: Sunday brunch, dinner served all year except Easter to Memorial Day. Wheelchair access to dining rooms and common room and two guest rooms on first floor. Bar, lounge. Swimming pool inside and out, health spa with sauna, steam room. Cross-country skiing. Nearby: Downhill skiing and tubing on the inn's own hill.

*Y*ou would expect an inn named the White House to be elegant, and, believe me, this one is. Built in 1914, the mansion has much to offer.

The gallery on the main floor has an extremely unusual wallpaper that was printed in Paris in 1912. There are high ceilings throughout the inn, and the living room is large, with a fireplace and beautifully covered couches and chairs. The Casablanca bar has wicker chairs, couches, pretty flowered pillows, and Bob's collection of angels all around. So nice to come back to after a day on the ski trails.

There are two dining rooms, both of which are very elegant, and a small private dining room. The food served in this three-star inn is superb, but would you expect anything else in the White House? Here's just a sampling of what is offered: There are several appetizers, including garlic bruschetta, pan-seared tuna, and a roasted portobello mushroom. Entrees are numerous and varied. One is semi-boneless stuffed duck. Of course, all the desserts are homemade. I get hungry just writing about Bob's inn.

The grounds are sumptuous, with a lovely rose garden and fountain, and below this is a beautiful 60-foot swimming pool. There's another small fountain outside the lounge, and from this delightful room you watch spectacular sunsets over the Green Mountains.

The guest rooms here are all sizes. The wing that faces west has rooms with, as Bob says, two-passenger whirlpool tubs.

The health spa is what you need after a day of fun: sauna, steam room, and showers. There's also an inside pool to relax in. Ah, what an inn!

Intrigue: Why did the original owner of the house put in a secret staircase? You will have to ask where it is.

HOW TO GET THERE: From Interstate 91 take Route 9 to Wilmington. The inn is on your right, just before you reach the town.

The Inn at Windsor
Windsor, Vermont 05089

INNKEEPERS: Larry Bowser and Holly Taylor

ADDRESS/TELEPHONE: 106 Apothecary Lane; (802) 236–3441

WEB SITE: www.bbonline.com/vt/innatwindsor

ROOMS: 2 rooms and 1 suite, all with private bath and fireplace or wood-stove.

RATES: $125 to $165 BP.

OPEN: All year.

FACILITIES AND ACTIVITIES: Breakfast only meal served. BYOB.

*T*he inn is perched on a hill overlooking the historic village and shaded by tall trees. There's a driveway up the hill, next to the town's old burying ground; you park at the top and proceed through the gate into a terraced garden. You may find shoes and slippers at the door because no one wears shoes inside—the innkeepers provide clean slippers for you.

There is so much history connected to this house it would take pages to tell it all, so come on up and ask because it's really a lovely story.

The bedrooms and suite are very pretty and comfortable. The suite has a TV and VCR, a library, a king-size bed, and the original Indian shutters. Bathrobes are provided along with natural Vermont soaps. The living room looks out at a 250-year-old sugar maple.

The homestead, begun in 1786, was the home of an early physician and apothecary named Green, who added the carriage house in 1804 as a distribution center for his patent medicines. It stayed in the Green family until 1963,

when it was sold to the Knights of Columbus. During restoration they discovered hand-hewn beams, hand-planed planks on the walls, spruce flooring, and even pencil inscriptions on the bedroom walls made by Green's daughter Ann Elizabeth in 1847.

Breakfast may include orange Julius, fruit salad with yogurt and nuts, apple-walnut or blueberry pancakes, hot glazed pears with cool yogurt topping, or eggs baked with garden herbs and Vermont cheese. Before breakfast, coffee, tea, or juice may be brought to your room, such a lovely way to start the day.

HOW TO GET THERE: From Interstate 91 take exit 9. Go down Apothecary Lane in Windsor to number 106; it's on the right.

Juniper Hill Inn 🖤
Windsor, Vermont 05090

INNKEEPERS: Art Nikki and Robert Dean

ADDRESS/TELEPHONE: 153 Pembroke Road; (802) 674–5273 or (800) 359–2541; fax (802) 674–2041

WEB SITE: www.juniperhillinn.com

ROOMS: 16, all with private bath; 11 with fireplace.

RATES: $105 to $215 BP.

OPEN: All year except two weeks in April and November.

FACILITIES AND ACTIVITIES: Dinner by advance reservation five days a week; open to the public by advance reservation Tuesday through Saturday. Full license, swimming pool. Nearby: Downhill and cross-country skiing, museums, antiquing, canoeing, hiking.

The upper valley of Vermont is lovely and full of history. Windsor is the birthplace of Vermont, and the longest covered bridge in America is here. The inn is a 1902 Colonial Revival mansion that is listed on the National Register of Historic Places. It was once known as a summer White House because former presidents Rutherford Hayes, Benjamin Harris, and Theodore Roosevelt were frequent guests of the original owners.

Large white columns lead into a 30-by-40-foot oak-paneled entry hall. You'll think it's big enough to be a ballroom, and it once was. Hunting trophies used to be displayed here. Today it is one of the parlors and called the Great Room. There are two smaller parlors for reading or quiet conversation.

There is a beautiful grand staircase centered under a large Palladian window in a very private library wing. There are two guest rooms at the top of the stairs, both with canopy beds. One has a porch and both are charming.

Some of the other rooms have marble sinks and canopy and four-poster beds, and two have their own private porch. Two rooms offer balconies with a view of Lake Runnemeade and Ascutney Mountain.

Please note the great table in the Great Room, where afternoon beverages and snacks are set out. Its top weighs more than 1,000 pounds.

Some of the goodies from the chef are maple-glazed salmon, beef with mushroom and spinach filling, prosciutto-stuffed pork tenderloin, and chicken with champagne sauce.

Windsor Attractions

Whether you are interested in history or arts and crafts, there are several good reasons to visit Windsor. The Vermont State Crafts Center at Windsor House (54 Main Street; 802-674-6729; www.vmga.org/windsor) has a fine inventory of handmade furniture, quilts, pottery, wood crafts, weavings, baskets, and sculpture by more than 150 Vermont artisans, as well as a stock of Vermont-made foods. It is open Monday through Saturday from 10:00 A.M. to 5:00 P.M. (to 6:00 P.M. June to December) and Sunday from 11:00 A.M. to 5:00 P.M. North of town off Route 5 is the workshop and showroom of Simon Pearce (802-674-6280; www.simonpearce.com), where you can watch glassblowers creating exquisite goblets and home accessories by hand and pick up seconds at good prices in the shop.

On the history side, Windsor is known as the birthplace of Vermont; the state constitution was adopted here in 1777 in a tavern that is now a museum of state history known as the Old Constitution House (17 North Main Street; 802-828-3051). It is open Wednesday through Sunday 11:00 A.M. to 5:00 P.M., Memorial Day to Columbus Day.

This small town also boasted one of the nation's first modern systems of industrial production. The American Precision Museum (196 Main Street; 802-674-5781; www.americanprecision.org), housed in an 1846 armory and machine shop, has the National Machine Tool Collection, a notable gun collection, and a scale model collection of actual working models of various manufacturing processes. See the products of Thomas Edison and Henry Ford; learn about the famed Sharps, Enfield, and Springfield rifles; and peruse the outstanding collection of photographs, drawings, catalogs, and other documents related to the history of industry in the United States. The museum is open daily from 10:00 A.M. to 5:00 P.M. Memorial Day through October.

Just outside of town, at 1747 Hunt Road, visit the beautiful gardens at Cider Hill (802-674-6825; www.ciderhillvt.com). Browse the footpaths through gardens and greenhouses, and visit the gallery for lithographs and prints. Plants and garden accessories are also for sale here. Cider Hill Gardens is open Thursday through Monday from 10:00 A.M. to 6:00 P.M. May through November.

HOW TO GET THERE: From Interstate 91 south take exit 9. Go about 3 miles on Route 5 south, then take a right onto Juniper Hill Road. At the first junction turn left and continue up the hill to the driveway on the right.

The Jackson House Inn
Woodstock, Vermont 05091

INNKEEPERS: Juan and Gloria Florin

ADDRESS/TELEPHONE: 114-3 Senior Lane; (802) 457-2065 or (800) 448-1890; fax (802) 457-9290

WEB SITE: www.jacksonhouse.com

ROOMS: 9, plus 6 one-room suites; all with private baths, Casablanca fans, and air-conditioning; phones in the suites.

RATES: $195 to $380 BP.

OPEN: All year.

FACILITIES AND ACTIVITIES: Full breakfast and dinner. Nearby: Glass blowing, art galleries, biking, hiking, horseback riding, canoeing, swimming, golf, tennis, theater, skiing, sleigh rides, and more.

What a beauty this is! The long porch with both rockers and chairs and beautiful hanging plants is the first thing you see. The Jackson House was built in 1890 by Wales Johnson, a local sawmill owner. He wanted to build the finest example of late Victorian architecture possible, with cherry and maple floors, fine furniture, walls, and moldings of

the finest workmanship. The many exterior eaves and twin chimneys reflect pure classical design. The building is listed on the National Register of Historic Places.

In 1940 the house was bought by the Jackson family and opened as the Seven Maples Tourist Home. In 1983 it was sold to the third owners in one hundred years. Later owners completely renovated the inn, and in 1996 four opulent suites and the restaurant were added. The most recent owners, the Florins, are continuing the long tradition of excellence.

The dining room is elegant, with white napery and a double fireplace. There's a chef's tasting menu—that's a grand idea—a spring vegetable menu, and a prix fixe menu. One appetizer that caught my eye was wild ramp soup.

Entrees include veal tenderloin, free-range chicken, lobster, beef, and fish. Desserts—well, as you can imagine, save room. Before the evening meal, complimentary wine or champagne and hors d'oeuvres are served. Breakfast the next morning is ample; almond-crusted French toast is just one idea.

Accommodations are grand. Four guest rooms are on the first floor, where there is wheelchair access. The rest are on the second and third floors. Two of the suites are on the third floor and are beauties. They open to a deck overlooking the landscaped gardens. One room has a Jacuzzi, and a few more have thermal massage tubs.

HOW TO GET THERE: Go through Woodstock, and from the town green it is 1⁶/10 miles to the inn, which is on the right on old Route 4.

The Lincoln Inn
at the Covered Bridge ¢¢¢
Woodstock, Vermont 05091

INNKEEPERS: Amy Martsolf and Teresa Tan

ADDRESS/TELEPHONE: Route 4 West; (802) 457–3312; fax (802) 457–5908

WEB SITE: www.lincolninn.com

ROOMS: 6, all with private bath.

RATES: $125 to $175 BP.

OPEN: All year except after Easter to May 1 and November 1 to Thanksgiving.

FACILITIES AND ACTIVITIES: Dinner Tuesday through Sunday. Bar, lounge, TV room, games, VCR for movies. Nearby: Golf, fishing, cross-country and downhill skiing.

The Lincoln Covered Bridge is the only remaining wooden bridge of its kind and design left in America. In 1844 T. Willis Pratt invented and patented the bridge plans. In 1869 storm waters pushed the bridge from Dewey's Mill in Woodstock Village to an island downstream. In 1877 Charles Lincoln (cousin of Abraham) had the bridge moved to its current location by floating it on "jack" skates. It was renovated in 1947. It spans the Ottauquechee River and is at one end of the inn's property.

The inn, a 200-year-old farmhouse, sits on about six acres of rolling lawn alongside the river. You can stroll along the banks to the bridge, cross over, and explore the country roads and trails, then come back and stop at the gazebo on the lawn to watch the river run by.

Back at the inn, relax in the library or the tavern, enjoying a glass of wine or hot cider, then proceed to dinner by candlelight in front of a warming fire in the inn's Mangowood Restaurant.

The American menu has an Asian accent. Favorite appetizers include crispy pork and shrimp dumplings with three dipping sauces and a pear and Vermont chèvre tart. Entrees include sesame seared yellowfin tuna served with noodle cake, wasabi, and pickled ginger, and the house specialty, Angus sirloin steak with an Asian garlic marinade, served with mashed potatoes and roasted root vegetables. Desserts include the aptly named "To Die For" English sticky toffee pudding with warm caramel sauce, or you can go traditional with a Vermont apple-cranberry crisp served with vanilla ice cream.

Guest rooms are country fresh and vary in mood. Room 6, the Federal Room, has pine furniture and local primitive art; Room 5 is the Floral Room, named for the decor; and Room 4 is the Victorian Room, with an appropriate white metal and brass headboard. Room 2, the Romantic Room, has a ruffled canopy bed. Rooms 2, 3, and 4 overlook the river. What could be nicer than waking to the sounds of the rippling water and the birds?

HOW TO GET THERE: From Interstate 91 take exit 9 and follow Route 12 north to Route 4. Take Route 4 to the inn; it is 3 miles west of the village green in Woodstock.

The Village Inn
Woodstock, Vermont 05091

INNKEEPERS: Evelyn and David Brey

ADDRESS/TELEPHONE: 41 Pleasant Street; (802) 457–1255 or (800) 722–4571

WEB SITE: www.villageinnofwoodstock.com

ROOMS: 8, all with private bath, TV, and air-conditioning; 4 with fireplace.

RATES: $125 to $300 BP.

OPEN: All year, except two weeks in late April.

FACILITIES AND ACTIVITIES: Dinner five nights, bar, lounge. Nearby: Golf, tennis, skiing, swimming, boating, shopping.

oodstock is a beautiful town with a classic village green. The inn was once part of a forty-acre estate on the Ottauquechee River. The old-fashioned Victorian mansion and carriage house, built in 1899, are all that remain of the estate. The location, within walking distance of the town's many shops and the green, couldn't be better.

Lots of charm and comfort are found in the bar. The very pretty ceilings are of pressed tin, and there is a beautiful stained-glass window. The room also has a nineteenth-century oak bar. Upstairs is a large common room with a porch, television, and games.

Evelyn and David Brey had been searching for just the right inn for years before finding this classic Victorian. The location on the edge of charming Woodstock village was ideal. It lured them from business careers in Pennsylvania to Vermont. Since they arrived in 2001, they have been busy making a good property even better.

Guest rooms vary in size, but all have been nicely refurbished with canopy, brass, and four-poster beds. I'm partial to Room 3, the former master bedroom, with a working firplace and a picture window with a panel of original stained glass. Room 6, done in a pretty blue and white print, has a whirlpool tub, and Room 9 will please fans of Victoriana with its tall, dark carved-wood headboard and period loveseat. Two rooms have the original marble sinks in the bathroom.

The day starts right with Evelyn's home-baked muffins or coffee cake, followed by David's special of the day, omelets, French toast, or pancakes or your choice of eggs cooked to order. The dinner menu, which changes with the seasons, features a nice variety of meats, poultry, and seafood.

When you step outside, Woodstock is waiting to be explored. Covered bridges, elegant shops, skiing, sleigh rides, golf, or tennis anyone? Go swimming or boating at one of the many lakes. Come on up and enjoy yourself. This whole area and this lovely refurbished inn get my applause.

HOW TO GET THERE: From Interstate 91 take Interstate 89 north to exit 1. Turn left into Woodstock. The inn is on the left.

The Woodstock Inn
Woodstock, Vermont 05091

INNKEEPER: Paul Ramsey

ADDRESS/TELEPHONE: Fourteen the Green; (802) 457–1100 or (800) 448–7900; fax (802) 457–6699

WEB SITE: www.woodstockinn.com

ROOMS: 144 rooms, 7 suites, 1 house; all with private bath, color TV, phones; 23 with fireplaces; some with VCR.

RATES: $149 to $664 EP. Special package rates and MAP are available.

OPEN: All year.

FACILITIES AND ACTIVITIES: Breakfast, lunch, dinner, Sunday brunch. Richardson Tavern, full license. Country club, golf, tennis, health and fitness center with spa treatments, pool, classes, tennis, ski touring center, and downhill ski area. Nearby: Horseback riding, hunting and fishing, bicycling.

BUSINESS TRAVEL: Located 260 miles from New York; 166 miles from Hartford; 148 miles from Boston; 180 miles from Providence; 206 miles from Montreal, Canada; 138 miles from Albany; and 89 miles from Burlington.

This is a classic, a grand hotel with resort facilities and hotel amenities but without losing the comfortable feel of a country inn. An inn has stood at this site since 1792, when the Richardson Tavern was built, presiding over the town as it grew from a stagecoach stop to a summer retreat for the wealthy. A fine new inn went up 1892, renamed the Woodstock Inn. Age had caught up with the inn by the 1960s, and modernization was badly needed when Laurance S. Rockefeller, a summer resident who had recently purchased Suicide Six and the Woodstock Country Club, was approached about the project. He found the old inn unsalvageable and replaced it with the current handsome structure, which opened in 1969, located just behind the original site.

The present inn is deliberately low-key. If there is any nip in the air, you'll be greeted with a welcoming fire in the huge fieldstone fireplace that dominates a whole wall of the lobby. The furnishings are country antique, the colors are subdued, and spacious guest rooms are decorated with hardwood furniture, handmade quilts, and original Vermont prints. Many rooms have wood-burning fireplaces and built-in bookshelves.

The main dining room is elegant, and so is the food. It has been awarded four diamonds and four stars. Seared Hudson Valley foie gras or New England lobster and crab cakes are wonderful starters, or you may want to try the wild mushroom bisque with chive crème fraiche. Char-grilled black Angus filet mignon with Green Mountain blue cheese butter was my choice for dinner, but there are wonderful alternatives such as Vermont organic chicken breast, pan-roasted Maine lobster, rack of lamb, or ahi tuna. Wines are suggested with each entree.

In the more casual Eagle Cafe, a chilled gazpacho is a nice start for lunch, followed by salads, sandwiches, or a delicious grilled salmon dish. For dinner,

Billings Farm and Museum

Frederick Billings was a Vermont native who went west long enough to make his fortune during the gold rush and have a town, Billings, Montana, named for him. The farm he established when he returned home became a model for dairy farmers and environmentalists throughout the state. Many of Vermont's green hills are the result of his reforestation efforts.

Billings Farm, in Woodstock, is still a working dairy. Come here to see its fine Jersey cows and learn about the concepts of responsible agriculture and land stewardship that distinguished this farm. Reforestation and selective breeding were among the practices of scientific farm management that led to the success of this dairy. Visit the fields, the barns, the 1890 farmhouse, the heirloom garden, the dairy barn, and the farm museum. Be sure to see the wonderful short film documenting farm life, the passage of the seasons, and the history of farming and logging in Vermont. You can watch the afternoon milking daily at 3:00 P.M. with an explanation of the process of milk production. In winter, come to enjoy such seasonal activities as wagon rides and sleigh rides. Admission is charged.

Billings's late granddaughter, Mary, married another noted conservationist, Laurance S. Rockefeller, and they were responsible for the preservation of the farm, which opened in 1983. Their nearby estate later was donated to the United States to become the Marsh-Billings-Rockefeller National Historic Park in 1998, the only national park to tell the story of conservation history and the evolving nature of land stewardship in America. Visits include tours of the Billings-Rockefeller home.

Billings farm (802–457–2355; www.billingsfarm.org) is open daily from April 30 through October 31, as well as holiday weekends in November, December, January, and February, and the week of December 24–31 (except Christmas Day). The Marsh-Billings Rockefeller National Historic Park (802–457–3368; www.nps.gov/mabi) is open Memorial Day through October 31; 20 miles of trails on the grounds are open year-round. The two properties have separate admission fees.

don't miss the inn's own clam chowder or the crusted tuna roll appetizers. Vermont turkey and oven-roasted Atlantic scrod are offered, along with a sirloin burger platter and some of the best barbecued baby-back ribs I've tasted.

Can't stop now, because it's on to Sunday brunch, and it's a beauty. The way the food is displayed boggles my mind. A display of domestic, imported, and Vermont cheeses with assorted crackers was awesome. Tri-colored pasta and vegetable salad, country pâtés, baked herb-encrusted chicken breast, lamb chop on lentil mushrooms, and couscous with sun-dried tomato madeira sauce is just a sample. There is much more. The Woodstock Inn's pastry display—well, it's just spectacular.

Richardson's Tavern, paneled and cozy, also has a lighter menu of salads, burgers, and such, and live music on Friday and Saturday nights.

Inn guests have privileges at the Woodstock Country Club, the Woodstock Ski Touring Center, and a state-of-the-art health and fitness center with an indoor pool; tennis, squash, and racquetball courts; a sauna; and a whirlpool.

There is a shuttle bus to the inn's sports center and country club. No need to use your car.

Woodstock is one of the most beautiful villages in New England, and the inn is worthy of its setting.

HOW TO GET THERE: From Boston take Interstate 93 north to Interstate 89 north to Route 4 west. From Connecticut, eastern New York, or New Jersey, take Interstate 95 or the Merritt Parkway to Interstate 91 north, to Interstate

89 north, to Route 4 west. Then travel 10 miles to the village green (traffic rotary). Keep the village green on your left, and the inn will come up on your right. From western New York and other points west, take Interstate 87 to Route 9 north to Route 149 east to Route 4 east. Travel 12 miles to Whitehall and bear right on Route 4 east near the Silver Diner, then travel 35–40 miles into Rutland. At the end of the four-lane road, turn left on Route 4 east/Route 7 north, travel about 3 miles, and take Route 4 east after the Grand Union on your right. Follow Route 4 for 31 miles to Woodstock. As you begin to circle the village green, the inn will be on your right.

Select List of
Other Vermont Inns

Alexandra B&B

Historic Route 7A
Bennington, VT 05201
(802) 442-5619 or (888) 207-9386; fax (802) 442-5592
Web site: www.alexandrainn.com
6 rooms, all with private bath; in 1859 Victorian house; 6 rooms in modern addition.

Willard Street Inn

349 South Willard Street
Burlington, VT 05401
(802) 651-8710 or (800) 577-8712
Web site: www.willardstreetinn.com
14 rooms, all with private bath; bed-and-breakfast in brick Victorian mansion.

Hugging Bear Inn and Shoppe

244 Main Street
Chester, VT 05143
(802) 875-2412 or (800) 325-0519
Web site: www.huggingbear.com
6 rooms, all with private bath; bed-and-breakfast in Victorian house.

The Sumner Mansion

4 Station Road
Hartland, VT 05048
(802) 436-3386 or (888) 529-8796
Web site: www.sumnermansioninn.com
4 rooms, 1 suite in mansion, all with private bath. Mansion on National Historic Preservation List.

1811 House

Route 7A
Manchester Village, VT 05254
(802) 362-1811 or (800) 432-1811
Web site: www.1811house.com
14 rooms (3 in cottage), all with private bath; full breakfast; bed-and-breakfast in 1770 home.

Basin Harbor Club

on Lake Champlain
Vergennes, VT 05491
(802) 475–2311 or (800) 622–4000
Web site: www.basinharbor.com
34 rooms, 77 cottages, all with private bath; two restaurants; 700 acres, private airstrip, 18-hole golf course, tennis courts, and pool. Open mid-May through mid-October.

West Hill House Bed and Breakfast Inn

1496 West Hill Road
RR 1, Box 292
Warren, VT 05674
(802) 496–7162 or (800) 898–1427
Web site: www.westhillhouse.com
6 rooms, 2 suites; all with private bath; some with fireplace, Jacuzzi; 1 with steam shower; bed-and-breakfast in 1850s farmhouse; sometimes serves dinner on Saturday nights.

Indexes

Alphabetical Index to Inns

Romantic Inns

Inns Serving Lunch

Inns Serving Sunday Brunch

Inns with Accommodations for Families

Lakeside Inns

Inns on or near Saltwater
(* denotes on beach)